B C L

DATE DUE

OCT 1 9 1993		
MAY 0 2 2005		
MAY 0 1 2007		

DEMCO NO. 38-298

PATERNALISM

PATERNALISM

John Kleinig

Rowman & Allanheld
PUBLISHERS

ROWMAN & ALLANHELD

Published in the United States of America in 1984
by Rowman & Allanheld, Publishers
(A division of Littlefield, Adams & Company)
81 Adams Drive, Totowa, New Jersey 07512

Copyright © 1983 by Rowman & Allanheld

Library of Congress Cataloging in Publication Data
Kleinig, John, 1942–
  Paternalism.

  (Philosophy and science)
  Bibliography: p.
  Includes index.
  1. Paternalism. 2. Paternalism—Social aspects—Case
Studies.

I. Title. II. Series.
HM73.K58 1983   303.3′6   83-13962
ISBN 0-8476-7207-7

83 84 85/ 10 9 8 7 6 5 4 3 2 1
Printed in the United States of America

To the memory of my father
C.N. Kleinig
1912–82

Contents

Acknowledgments   ix

Preface   xi

Part One   THEORY

1   *The Scope of Paternalism*   3
Paternalism and Coercion, 5; Paternalism and Liberty of
Action, 6; Paternalism and Moralism, 14

2   *Paternalism, Freedom, and Self-Regarding Conduct*   18
Freedom and Freedom(s), 19; Justifying Freedom(s), 24; Paternalism
and Freedom(s), 27; Self- and Other-Regarding Conduct, 32

3   *Approaches to Justification*   38
Arguments from Interconnectedness, 39; The Argument from
Future Selves, 45; Consequentialist Arguments for Paternalism,
48; Consent-based Arguments for Paternalism, 55; The Argument
from Personal Integrity, 67; Limits to Paternalism, 74

Part Two   APPLICATIONS

4   *Physical Protection*   81
Seat Belts and Safety Helmets, 82; Attempted Suicide, 96

5   *Health*   106
Regulating for Health, 107; Medical Paternalism, 115

6   *Long-Term Welfare*   143
Children and Paternalism, 144; Adult Welfare and
Paternalism, 156; Political Paternalism, 169

7   *Marketplace*   176
Detecting Paternalistic Rationales, 177; Regulations Relating to the
Purchase of Goods and Services, 180; Regulations Relating to the
Financing of Purchases, 192; Regulations Relating to Sales
Practices, 195; Labor Laws, 197

8 *Character* 200
Moral Harm, 201; Moral Harm and the Formation of
Character, 204; Paternalistic Punishment, 205; Religious
Paternalism, 213

References and Bibliography 218
Index 237

Acknowledgments

Most of the work for this study was done over a period of three years in four locations. That it was completed as expeditiously owes much to the hospitality and help I received from those with whom I worked in those places.

The initial collection of materials was undertaken toward the end of 1980, with the assistance of a Macquarie University Research Grant. Then in 1981 I was fortunate enough to be seconded to the Australian National University, Canberra, where, in the congenial surroundings of the Department of Philosophy, Research School of Social Sciences, I was able to do much of the basic reading and drafting. My debts there are very considerable. Stanley Benn and Gerald Gaus constantly pressed me to articulate my intuitions more clearly, and on more than one occasion forced me to revise not merely my arguments, but my opinions. They were not the only ones to contribute. Fred D'Agostino, Chris Mortensen, Bob Meyer, Bill Sparkes, and Bob Norman took more than a passing interest in the several work-in-progress papers I gave. Elizabeth Clancy provided valued research assistance and Hazel Gittins was always generous with her typing skills.

Following this secondment, I was able to spend six months at the University of Arizona. Joel and Betty Feinberg were endlessly hospitable, and I was as always provoked and stimulated by Joel's clear and comprehensive grasp of the issues. I owe much to him. I also should not forget Jules Coleman and Ron Milo. While in Tucson, I was privileged to conduct a graduate seminar in the philosophy of the law. This provided an incentive to write a first draft of the book and gave me the opportunity to receive some valuable feedback. Joan McGregor, William Archer, and James Hallmark deserve special mention.

The remainder of 1982 was spent at Macquarie University, where I commenced my revision of the text. This was completed during a two-month period at the Westminster Institute for Ethics and Human Values, London, Ontario, where I was a Visiting Scholar (under the auspices of the Social Sciences and Humanities Research Council of Canada). The up-to-date library and willing assistance of the Institute staff, especially Michael Bayles, made the task much easier. From Benjamin Freedman and Bruce Chapman I received a good deal of specialized philosophical help. While in Canada I was able to read parts of the material at various universities—Western Ontario, Waterloo, Guelph, Toronto, Queen's, and Wayne State (Detroit). The vigorous discussions were challenging and useful. Norman Brown's response at Queen's was particularly acute.

My debts do not end there. I owe continuing thanks to Robert Young. He is the patient recipient of almost all my half-baked drafts, and can always be relied upon for robust and penetrating criticism. Andrew von Hirsch also wrote me some encouraging and provocative comments. I doubt whether I have successfully accommodated the criticisms he made of an earlier version of the Argument from Personal Integrity. For typing up the final draft, I am grateful for the ever-willing help of Barbara Young.

A few small portions of the script have been or are being published elsewhere. An earlier version of the material on compulsory schooling in Chapter 6 appeared in the *Journal of Philosophy of Education* 15 (1981), and the discussion of slavery contracts is being published in *Politics* 18 (1983). An edited version of the seat belt and safety helmet discussion was published in the *Westminster Institute Review* 2, no. 3 (1983). I am appreciative of the permission to use this material here.

Preface

It is a mark of liberalism that when one person imposes on another, be it in a public or private capacity, a problem of moral justification is raised. There is an onus on the imposer to make good what appears to violate a norm governing interpersonal relations. The onus can be shouldered. If the person interfered with is acting or has acted to constrain the nonthreatening acts of another, we have the makings of a case for intervention. It is also a mark of much liberalism that *only* where the onus is shouldered in this way can there be a case for imposition. The point is not self-evidently true. Might not a reason for constraint exist where moral boundaries are transgressed or offense is caused or social benefits can be conferred? Or might not a reason for intervention exist when the person's own good can be secured or advanced? It is this last question that provides the focus for the present study. Though liberals have tended to answer it in the negative, it is not always clear why this is so, or, if clear, why the reasons are compelling. My thesis in this book is that the liberal rejection of paternalism, though grounded in considerations of deep moral significance, is not watertight, and that there is some room in liberalism for paternalistically motivated constraints.

Most discussions of paternalism have focused almost exclusively on legal paternalism—not surprising, given the liberal preoccupation with the relationship between the state and the individual. The preoccupation is in some respects obsessive, given the multiplicity of networks in which the individual is caught up and by which he or she is constrained. It may also exercise a distorting influence, since its purposes and limitations could introduce a bias of their own into the consideration of acceptable grounds for constraint. What is morally impermissible if incorporated into social policy, may be allowable in the context of friendship. Although my own discussion in some ways reflects the liberal concentration on legal paternalism, I have attempted to cast the terms of the discussion rather wider, taking into account less formal and less coercive relationships. In doing so, I am hopeful that some of the traditional legalistic bias will have been moderated.

Part One is oriented to general theoretical concerns, more or less abstracted from the finer nuances of particular instances of paternalistic interference. In Chapter 1, I attempt to provide some reference range for what is generally characterized as paternalism. This includes, on the one hand, an analytic study that distinguishes paternalism from similar and related phenomena, and, on the other, an attempt to locate the discussion of paternalism within an identifiable social tradition. Paternalism, I argue, involves an imposition, the exercise of freedom-diminishing control by one person over another. The nature and significance of this freedom are considered in Chapter 2, where I seek to lay bare the substance of liberal opposition to acting "on a person's behalf but not at that person's behest" (Childress 1980, p. 30). Here the Millian notion of individuality plays a key role. There is also a further refinement of the terms of the debate. It is in virtue of a distinction between self- and other-regarding conduct that the liberal case against paternalism stands, according to its supporters, and falls, according to its detractors. To the former, it marks off a domain that is private from a domain that may be invaded; to the latter, the distinction is at best a chimera, at worst question-begging. I argue that although the detractors have the best of the argument, the concern of the supporters can be reexpressed in a way that keeps the onus on those who would defend paternalism.

Various strategies for justification are explored in Chapter 3. In some cases, the very presuppositions of liberalism are questioned; in other cases, an attempt is made to assimilate the principle of paternalism to the harm principle; in yet other cases, one strand within liberalism (utilitarianism) is played off against another (individual sovereignty). I claim that in none of these cases are the arguments able to justify paternalism where voluntary conduct is involved. The dictates of individuality take precedence. To accommodate this, two further approaches are considered—one that exploits the notion of consent, and the other the notion of personal integrity. The former is rejected, but I maintain that the latter provides enough room for strong paternalism in just those cases where it has some intuitive plausibility.

Because the debate about paternalism does not go on in a vacuum, Part Two provides a more detailed discussion of the applicability of paternalistic considerations and limits of paternalistic concern. I commence with those areas in which the case for paternalism might seem strongest, concluding where it is likely to be most intrusive. Thus I move from the concern for physical protection to health, and thence to long-term welfare, economic well-being, and finally character. Of course, these are not totally dissociated areas of concern, and so any attempt to argue a general case would founder on the rocks of qualification. My strategy, therefore, has been to focus on concrete examples. I have attempted to determine whether and to what extent they reflect and depend on paternalistic concern, and, if they do, whether they can be justified. As it turns out, not everything that is dubbed "paternalistic" is so, and even where some paternalism is involved, it is not always the kind of paternalism charged by critics.

As I worked on this material, I became increasingly aware of and overwhelmed by its complexity, and of the need for case-by-case discussions if one is to speak with any sort of confidence. Yet one cannot profitably engage in case-by-case discussion without a sensitivity to wider and more general concerns, without a feel for the broader traditions within which the investigation is being conducted, and the moral commitments that inform it. What I hope to have provided here is some indication not merely of the relevance of theoretical reflection, but the beginnings of a contribution to its embodiment in ongoing practical debates.

A word concerning terminology may be in order. The term "paternalism" bespeaks a social order in which formal familial authority resides with the father. The sexism in this has worried some commentators. This is not merely because it locates *de jure* familial authority in the father, but also because it obscures the *de facto* (though unrecognized and unrewarded) childrearing authority that generally resides in the mother. Perhaps we should, as Alan Soble suggests, speak instead of "maternalism" (1976, p. 49; cf. T. H. Green's reference to "grandmotherly government"). But there is more to be said for talking of "parentalism," an option taken up by one or two writers, and one toward which I am attracted. I have chosen nevertheless to bow to convention, not through some desire to perpetuate the sexist environment from which it comes, but for reasons of convenience. The general sense of the traditional term remains clear, some of the confusion caused by a terminological switch is avoided, and, given the generally derogatory associations that the term has for most users, its continued use is not likely to advance the cause of sexism.

Part One

Theory

1

The Scope of Paternalism

Though talk of "paternal authority" has a long history, the term "paternalism" makes its appearance only in the latter part of the nineteenth century. Probably this reflects no more than the proliferation of "-isms" that marked that period (cf. Höpfl 1983), but it is also convenient to see it as embodying a conceptual shift, having its origins in the sixteenth century and term of maximum influence in the nineteenth. I shall mark this change by distinguishing between (an older) patriarchalism and its legacy in paternalism.

The movement I have in mind is from a social order and world-view in which communal and relational categories predominate to one in which "the discrete individual" holds center stage. The medieval world-order was one in which individuals saw themselves primarily as occupants of preexisting, determinate, and relatively fixed social roles. But with the emergence of liberal society there came into being the fundamentally asocial conception of Man as a rational rather than relational being. Sociality was viewed as contingent and optional and the civil order became morally problematic. The old idea of a natural hierarchy, presided over by the monarch as patriarch, was challenged in the name of an individual no longer under tutelage, but endowed with reason and natural rights, able to be accounted the overseer of his own life-plans (Locke 1690, ch. 6).

We may generally characterize patriarchalism as a social order in which the pattern of individual life is determined by considerations relating to the social whole, these being mediated and enforced by patriarchal authority. More specifically, and more appropriately to our present purposes, patriarchalism can be seen as a social order in which the patriarch's concern to secure individual good is subsumed under a general good that gives it definition and to which it contributes.

With the rise of liberal society we see the decline of patriarchalism. A sphere of conduct private to the individual is differentiated over which others have no legitimate jurisdiction, and a conception of individual good evolves that is rooted in the individual's own nature rather than in some social end. Though in some areas patriarchal perspectives and practices persist,[1] liberal reconceptualization articulated a new *bête noire*—paternalism. The latter represents an attempt to ensure the good of individuals, where, it contradistinction to patriarchalism, that good is conceived as sufficiently independent of the good of others or some social whole to constitute *on its own* a focus of attention.

Although the foregoing sketch does not yet give us the precision that our later inquiry will demand, it serves to locate the discussion of paternalism squarely within the liberal tradition. For that tradition not only renders paternalism problematic, but it also makes its conceptual differentiation possible. This will assume some importance when we come to consider the matter of justification, for some of the arguments we canvass presuppose, whereas others call into question, those elements of liberalism to which the concept of paternalism is indebted.

Use of the term "paternalism" to characterize relations between individuals, or between institutions and individuals or groups, is clearly intended to recall familial relationships, particularly those traditionally existing between parent (or father) and child. Yet not all relationships between parents and children can be dubbed paternalistic. There is nothing paternalistic about a mother who intervenes to protect her child from attack by a rabid dog, or about a father who offers advice to a child requesting it. So-called paternalistic relationships are those in which parents act on the presumption that they know better than the child what is best for the latter. It is for this reason that paternalism toward adults or older children is so frequently regarded as offensive or insulting. It is supposed that adults and older children have a reasonable idea of what is good for them, or, if not, are at least competent to take advice on the matter. And so to treat them as young children is to derogate from their capacities and standing.

Sometimes the use of "paternalism" is made to draw more specifically on its implicit sexism, to characterize circumstances in which women are singled out as the special object of enforced benevolence. The "protective" exclusion of women from certain forms of employment (in virtue of their status as "the weaker sex") is paternalistic in this narrower, sexist sense.[2] Although such sexist paternalism falls within the scope of the present study, our concern will be more generally with enforced benevolence than its sexist manifestations—with parentalism rather than paternalism in a restricted sense.

Within liberal circles, paternalism is frequently considered a distasteful and insulting practice, without any redeeming features. There are those who, while allowing a proper place to the exercise of paternal authority, see in paternal*ism* an excess of such authority (Kao 1976, pp. 182, 184); there are others who find outrageous the implication that parental attitudes should be thought appropriate in relationships between adults. If we accept these points at face value, seeing paternalism as a moral notion, then there is clearly little further to be said beyond spelling out at greater length those features that make it so condemnable to moral consciousness.[3] But I am not so sure that paternalism is a moral notion in this sense. It is not on a moral par with "murder," where condemnation is built into the concept, such that its removal would divest the term of its point. It is more like "killing," where, although no moral judgment is embodied, there is accorded sufficient importance to the life/death distinction to warrant our marking the circumstance of being moved from one condition to the other. This significance, moreover, is of a kind that, by virtue of the values associated with life, raises a *moral question* about killing. In like manner, the freedom-diminishing character of paternalism raises a moral question about it. Whether that question can be satisfactorily answered, and if so under what circumstances, is to be decided on the basis of an extended consideration of the factors involved rather than the expedient of name-calling.

Let us now attempt to delineate more precisely the subject of this study. Gerald Dworkin provides a useful starting point. In an influential discussion, he writes that paternalism may be roughly characterized as "the interference with a person's liberty of action justified by reasons referring exclusively to the welfare, good, happiness, needs, interests or values of the person being coerced" (Dworkin 1971, p. 108).[4] The roughness, we are told, is because "the class of persons whose good is involved is not always identical with the class of persons whose freedom is restricted" (p. 110).

The chief merit of this account lies in its juxtaposition of the two values that make the issue of paternalism a morally interesting one: freedom and benevolence. Individual freedom is abrogated in the name of benevolence. Yet there are several deficiencies in the account that render it less than fully satisfactory. Some of these will emerge in the following discussion.

Observe, first, that for Dworkin paternalism involves "interference with a person's liberty of action," in particular, "coercion." It is doubtful whether these claims can be sustained. Paternalism need not be either coercive or restrictive of liberty of action.

Paternalism and Coercion

This is probably not the place to add to the burgeoning literature on the nature of coercion (Nozick 1969; Pennock and Chapman 1972; Murphy 1981; Feinberg [forthcoming], ch. 18). A workable account for present purposes might go as follows: X coerces Y to do a if and only if X gets Y to do a as the result of a threat to interfere with Y (or one of Y's interests) or to withhold from Y something that Y has reason to expect. What is important is that something is elicited that would not have been given in the absence of *threat*. So understood, many standard examples of paternalism are properly seen to involve coercion. A paternalistic requirement that motorcycle riders wear protective helmets or that travelers in motor vehicles wear seat belts, on pain of a fine for neglect or refusal to do so, is undoubtedly coercive so far as some road users are concerned.

But there are other ways in which paternalistic limitations of liberty of action can be achieved, but where coercion need not be involved. If Ruritania restructures its aid program so that needy citizens are given food, clothing, and free medical treatment instead of cash, their liberty to spend is limited though no coercion takes place. Should the motivation behind such changes be a determination to minimize the squandering and waste of aid, there is good reason to consider the changes paternalistic. If the Outer Slobbovian Town Council seals off a dangerous track that is often used by motorists as a short cut, there is no coercion, though motorists' liberty of action is paternalistically limited. Suppose Adam is awarded $150,000 as compensation for injuries received at work, but cannot get it as a lump sum, unless he first satisfies a judge that his long-term welfare is not being sacrificed to short-term advantage. Adam's liberty of action is being noncoercively limited. Lusitanian law renders null and void finance agreements in which interest exceeds the equivalent of a flat rate of 15%. Alice is thus denied access to short-term finance that would otherwise have been forthcoming. In this, as in the other cases, there is some measure limiting liberty of action, but without the use of threat, and hence coercion.[5]

Paternalism and Liberty of Action

A less stringent restriction on the scope of paternalism is suggested by its characterization as an "interference with a person's liberty of action." This is broad enough to accommodate both *active* and *passive* restrictions. A person's liberty is actively interfered with in cases where he or she is positively required to do certain things. If, in order to ensure that its employees make some provision for their retirement in advance of the time when they can be expected more or less automatically to do so, Midas Inc. requires that every employee under the age of forty years at the commencement of employment join a superannuation fund, it acts in an actively paternalistic way. The same is likely where safety regulations require the use of certain equipment—safety belts or helmets, brightly colored jackets, etc. Passive interferences with liberty occur where there is a requirement to refrain from doing certain things. Examples with possibly paternalistic overtones would include a sign next to a cliff-edge lookout that prohibits passage beyond a certain point, a law making attempted suicide a criminal offense, and the refusal to allow people to volunteer for dangerous experiments or to consent to potentially therapeutic but risky operations (e.g., psychosurgery).

Not only these, but all of the examples we have so far considered might be said to involve some restriction on liberty of action. We should not be surprised at this, given its ideological centrality to liberalism. Nevertheless, there are cases of paternalism that do not fit neatly into this account. Bernard Gert and Charles Culver (1976, p. 46) draw attention to the situation in which a woman, in her dying moments, enquires after her son. The doctor tells her that he is doing well, though it is known that the son has just been killed trying to escape after being charged with multiple rape and murder. A somewhat similar case (Cryer and Kissane, 1978) is that of a seventy-four year old, happily married woman who is not told that tests associated with a herniorrhaphy she has just undergone have revealed that she is genetically male, despite her apparently female appearance. Both these cases involve paternalistic deception without there being any obvious limitation on liberty of action. It is true that they are somewhat unusual cases, and that the withholding or falsification of information generally does constitute a constraint on liberty of action. But the paternalism involved in these cases does not require that this be so. We need sufficient flexibility to accommodate paternalistic restrictions on freedom beyond those affecting liberty of action.[6]

If, as we have suggested, paternalism requires neither coercion nor interference with liberty of action, it is tempting to take the further step of arguing that not even freedom need be at issue. This is the position of Gert and Culver (1976, pp. 48–52). They contend that it is not constraint on freedom but only the violation of some moral rule that is demanded by paternalism. Unfortunately, their argument embodies a *non sequitur*, and its conclusion is false (cf. Dworkin 1983). Although they (sometimes) successfully show that paternalism may be practiced without any interference with *liberty of action*, this falls short of the conclusion that loss of *freedom* need not be involved. They neglect to consider that other freedoms, such as freedom of thought and expression, and the freedom to be let alone, may be abrogated by paternalistic behavior in just those cases where no interference with liberty of action takes place. Although there is an obvious enough connection between these other freedoms and liberty of action, they are not reducible or rigidly tied to it. Doctors who deceive their patients are not simply violating a moral rule, as Gert and Culver suggest. They are also imposing their will (however well-intentioned) upon their patients. Their patients are being made to believe certain things. Control over what they are to believe is taken out of their hands; they are denied access to information that, since it concerns their interests, they have a good (if not overriding) reason to possess.

I would suggest, then, that it is best to see in acts of paternalism a constraint on freedom, albeit not necessarily a coercive one or even an interference with liberty of action. We can speak of there being an *imposition*, for, whatever else we may want to say about paternalistic relationships, one party imposes upon another. The paternalist exercises some measure of control over some aspect of the life of another—be it a thwarting of the other's desires, a manipulation of the other's beliefs, or a channeling of the other's behavior.

In speaking of paternalism as being in some sense freedom-diminishing, we have allowed our net to be cast pretty wide so far as the possible objects of paternalism are concerned. Dworkin limits his account to "persons," but we might consider extending it to cover nonhuman animals (cf. Mill 1848, p. 952; Crocker 1980, p. 133). Do not the latter have a good that is susceptible to frustration and that may sometimes be more effectively preserved or furthered by means of some imposition? If Georgina confines her dog to the backyard in order to deny it access to a busy main road and Harry has his cat vaccinated against feline enteritis, do they not act paternalistically toward them? We may even find some such impositions morally problematic. It should cause us moral qualms if Georgina, in order to protect her dog, confines it to a small cage. There is a cruelty in certain kinds of confinement.

Nevertheless, we may have some hesitation about allowing the concept of paternalism so much elasticity. Restrictions on the liberty of nonhuman animals do not trouble us in the way that restrictions on the freedom of persons do. Generally it is only where suffering is caused that we experience difficulties with the confinement of animals, whereas even contented slaves pose a problem for moral consciousness.[7] We are not as bothered by "paternalism" in the case of animals as we are in the case of human beings. But these are not sufficient reasons for refusing to speak of paternalism in the former case. The killing of animals does not generate the same moral questions as the killing of persons, but this is not sufficient reason for refusing to speak of "killing" when the object is a nonhuman animal. Unless we are prepared to argue that paternalism is a moral notion, comparable to murder or lying, we can expect to find evidence of it in a variety of contexts, each context giving rise to its own moral questions. Just as "the morality of killing" is not to be determined exclusively by reference to persons, neither is "the morality of paternalism." This is not to deny that some of the most difficult and pressing moral questions about it are to be found where persons are the object of paternalistic impositions, as our subsequent discussion will amply demonstrate.

Our consideration of animal paternalism has been no mere diversion, for the conceptual questions raised here may sometimes be just as pressing in the case of some human beings. The reference to "person" in Dworkin's account may be interpreted broadly or narrowly. Interpreted broadly, it is equivalent to "human being," a member of the species *homo sapiens*. So understood, it would encompass not only "competent adults" but infants, the retarded, the insane, and comatose, among others. On the narrow interpretation, "person" refers to any being (whether or not human) possessing certain specified capacities, usually those that enable us to call it "competent" or to hold it accountable in some particular respects. Dworkin appears to favor a broad interpretation, but several writers opt for something narrower (e.g., Soble 1976, ch. 1; T. L. Beauchamp 1976b, p. 366; T. L. Beauchamp 1982; Arneson 1980, p. 471).

Alan Soble speaks for those who favor the narrower understanding when he writes that if "paternalism" is permitted to include impositions on those who are not competent or who have not competently expressed themselves on the matter at issue, there is an obscuring of "the interesting question," viz. "whether there are good moral reasons for the state to coerce reasonably mature and intelligent persons for their own benefit" (1976, pp. 1–2). But the assumption here, that paternalism generates only *one* interesting question, cannot be sustained, except as an exercise in definitional *fiat*. It is undoubtedly true that the question posed by Soble is (more or less) the most difficult and important one—and the one to which we will devote most attention—but it is hardly the only interesting or important one, and certainly not the only difficult one. Soble complains of an obscuring of his question if the scope of paternalism is permitted to include the noncompetent. This seems to amount to a fear of "innocence by association." If it is possible to justify paternalism in some cases, it might be tempting to think it possible to justify it in others. But innocence by association is to be handled in the same way as guilt by association—by attending to the particulars of cases and not being misled by overall associations. Otherwise we might as well argue that the separating off of cases where the noncompetent are imposed upon will tempt us to think that they escape all moral questioning.

We may, nevertheless, think it important to distinguish the sort of case Soble has in mind when he poses his "interesting question" from other cases of paternalistic imposition. This is usually done via a distinction between *strong* and *weak* (or, sometimes, *hard* and *soft*) paternalism (Feinberg 1971).[8] But Tom Beauchamp, whose views accord with Soble's, doubts the adequacy of this expedient. So-called "weak paternalism," he writes, is not paternalism "in any interesting sense, because it is not based on a liberty-limiting principle independent of the harm principle" (1976b, p. 366). So far as justificatory questions are concerned, weak paternalism is handled in terms of considerations more closely aligned to the harm principle, since such cases are defended as a "protection from harm *caused to* the individual by conditions beyond his control" (T. L. Beauchamp 1978, p. 1197). Mill's (1859, p. 294) example of a man about to cross a river via an unsafe bridge is enlisted: if there is no time to warn the man of danger, Mill allows, he may be forcibly prevented from crossing, at least until he is properly apprised of the bridge's condition. On this Beauchamp comments:

> It is not a question of protecting a man *against himself* or of interfering with his liberty of action. He is not *acting* at all in regard to his danger. He needs protection from something which is precisely *not himself*, not his intended action, not in any remote sense of his own making (1977a, p. 68).

It is not really open to us to argue that all we need to justify interference in a case such as this is the harm principle. The harm principle operates only where two parties are involved, and in this case (as in many other cases) there is only one party involved. This doesn't mean, of course, that there are no similarities in justificatory structure. In both one- and two-party cases, the person on whose behalf there is some intervention has not consented to the danger that threatens, and this lack of consent is a factor that enters into our justification of that intervention. But this similarity is not itself sufficient to make the distinction of cases otiose.

Likewise, the dissimilarities in justificatory structure required for strong and weak paternalism do not *ipso facto* make it pointless or misleading to see them both as forms of paternalism. Only if we were able to argue that paternalism is a moral notion would this be plausible. Nevertheless, it may still be thought inappropriate to treat weak paternalism as *paternalism*. In support of this, it can be contended that the concern in cases of so-called weak paternalism is not with the wisdom of whatever it is that has elicited the imposition, but with whether whatever that is genuinely represents the person's will. So, the focus of attention and ground for interference in the case of the man about to cross the unsafe bridge is not the danger involved, but the fact that it could not (in the first instance) be said to be *his* decision to undertake that risk. If we can subsequently assure ourselves that he is aware of and prepared to run that risk, then, despite our strong reservations about its wisdom, we must let him proceed. This, I believe, misconstrues the issue. While it is true that an important factor in the justification of weak paternalism is the failure of a person's conduct to express a genuine choice, it is not the only factor involved. There would be no question of intervening were the conduct not dangerous or were it likely to be highly beneficial. It begs the question, moreover, to assume that if the question of voluntariness is settled in the person's favor, the wisdom or otherwise of the conduct becomes (or remains) irrelevant to the justifiability of (continued) interference.

How are we to construe the distinction between strong and weak paternalism? Do they represent the two poles of a continuum, in which particular cases of paternalism are assessed by reference to the degree of voluntariness ascribable to the conduct that is imposed upon? Or is the distinction made by reference to a "voluntariness-threshold," above which paternalistic interferences are to be seen as strong and below which they are to be regarded as weak?[9] There is something to be said for each of these views. On the side of a "degrees" account, it might be claimed that there is a recognition that people's conduct does not come neatly categorized as "voluntary" and "nonvoluntary," but as more or less voluntary. Because of this, the responsibility to be borne by individuals for what they do is also to be seen as a matter of degree. Some circumstances may diminish responsibility, others may increase it. That being the case, it might be argued that the justification of paternalism will be made harder or easier, depending on the extent to which a person can be held responsible for the behavior that evokes it. *Ceteris paribus*, the stronger the paternalism, the heavier the burden on the interferer; the weaker the paternalism, the lighter the burden. On the side of a "threshold" account, it might be asserted that although voluntariness is a matter of degree, there is a point at which the question of a person's competence to accept responsibility for (some particular piece of) conduct is decisively determined. Above that point or threshold, paternalism will be strong and constitute an invasion of an individual's right to self-determination; below that point the issue of a right to self-determination (so far as that matter is concerned) does not arise.

Thus the problem posed by strong paternalism is substantially different to that presented by weak paternalism.

It probably does not matter too much which way we go, so far as these alternatives are concerned, for what is obviously at stake are the underlying claims and not the terminology used to express them. Most writers on the topic have implicitly adopted the "threshold" account, but what is there highlighted can also be expressed in terms of the "degrees" account. It may be claimed that there is some point where paternalism becomes so strong that the right to self-determination is invaded. Nevertheless, there may be some advantage in persisting with the threshold account, as it enables us to refer economically to classes of cases in which the moral issues are distinctively different. However, it ought not to be forgotten that the threshold is determined by reference to considerations that may be to varying degrees present or absent, and that this may have some bearing on whether, and if so how easily, the right to self-determination might be overridden.

To advance our discussion further, let us return to Dworkin's account. He contends that paternalism is "justified by reasons referring exclusively to the welfare," etc., of the person imposed upon. As it stands, this will not quite do. For one thing, there is a misleading ambiguity about the term "justified," which is frequently used as a "success-word," and, if understood in that way here, the term "paternalism" must be taken to apply to all and only those impositions for which welfare, etc., considerations are sufficent to justify. It is unlikely that Dworkin intends "justify" to be understood in this sense. More likely it is a "task" sense of the word that is in view. "Paternalism" refers to impositions *intended to be* or *purportedly* justified by reference to considerations of welfare, etc.

But there is an additional problem, which casts doubt on the appropriateness of the language of "justification." While it is true that where it is sought to justify paternalism, reference is made to welfare, etc., it is not essential that for some act to be regarded as paternalistic, what is presented as its rationale is intended as justification. The person who says: "I know I have no business interfering, but I can't stand by and let someone do that to himself," is acting paternalistically even though the welfare considerations involved are not being put forward as justification. There is therefore some reason for preferring the simpler account that Dworkin later gives, "roughly, interference with a person for his own good" (1971, p. 110). And it may be better to replace "justified" in the original characterization with "motivated" or the more encompassing "having as its rationale," with its explanation/justification ambivalence.

Seeing in the rationale behind conduct the ground for calling it paternalistic introduces certain complications. Suppose that a prime motivating factor of a law requiring the wearing of seat belts is the welfare of citizens. Harry is brought before a local magistrate, charged with having violated this law, and he complains that his own safety is none of the law's business. The magistrate's response is that Harry's behavior substantially increases the chances of his becoming dependent on the public purse, and that for this reason he is properly accountable at law. Harry is fined. Has he been treated paternalistically? Or, to take a different case, suppose a company is taken to court for entering into wage agreements with its employees that fall below the legal minimum wage. The law was brought in to protect workers against exploitation, to secure for them a wage that individually they were not capable of negotiating. The company claims that the wage contracts were freely entered into, and that it has therefore wronged no one. The judge, however, argues that even so, workers need to be protected against unwise agreements. The company is liable. Have the workers been treated paternalistically?

We can best approach these questions by distinguishing the rationales of laws from the rationales behind their applications. In Harry's case, the law requiring the wearing of seat belts is paternalistic in so far as it has been promulgated to counteract imprudence. But the magistrate to whom he complains does not act paternalistically in finding him guilty.[10] This of course does not mean that Harry has not been subject to paternalism, since the law under which he has been charged is paternalistically motivated. This would be true, even if the magistrate's reasons for rejecting Harry's complaint are believed sufficient to sustain a law of the kind under which he was convicted. In the second case, the judge has acted paternalistically toward workers in finding the company guilty of a wrong, though the law is not paternalistic in its intent. Though the workers have been treated paternalistically, they would not be justified in claiming that the law forbidding them from entering the particular wage contract was itself paternalistic.

Is it sufficient to refer to an imposition's rationale in order to characterize it as paternalistic? Some think not (Soble 1976, ch. 1). It might be argued that if an imposition is to be regarded as genuinely paternalistic it must have not only a particular motivation (the welfare, etc., of the person who is imposed upon) but also a particular means (an imposition on that person alone) and a particular result (benefit to that person alone).

One reason for thinking more is required than a particular rationale is that this allows *any* imposition to be construed as paternalistic, so long as the imposer is motivated by concern for the welfare, etc., of the person imposed upon. But this need not be seen as objectionable. Where it occurs, we are then entitled to question the sufficiency of the motive. To show its insufficiency would not be to show the unjustifiability of an imposition of that kind, since other, better reasons may be available.

But should we regard as paternalistic an imposition that does not have as its direct object the person whose good is being secured? If, in order to protect Iris (and those like her), Syldavian law proscribes the manufacture and sale of certain drugs, the direct object of interference is not Iris (and those like her) but manufacturers and sellers of drugs, who may not be personally at risk. Is such a law paternalistic? I believe so. Even though the direct object of interference is not the person whose good is being sought, the latter is also, albeit indirectly, being imposed upon. Access to these drugs is being made that much more difficult (cf. Mill 1859, p. 293). It is true that in cases of what we might call indirect paternalism an additional justificatory burden might be placed on the imposer in virtue of there being someone imposed upon for whom no paternalistic rationale can be provided (Dworkin 1971, p. 111; Soble 1976, p. 32), but this does not make it inappropriate to see the imposition as paternalistic. However, it may give some moral point to a distinction between *direct* and *indirect* paternalism.

What, then, about cases where the results of some imposition benefit not only the person imposed upon but others? Should this influence us to withhold characterizing the imposition as paternalistic? Suppose Janis is prohibited by court order from entering premises where gambling is taking place, the reason being Janis's compulsive gambling habit and the effect that this is having on her well-being and that of her children. Is she being treated paternalistically? Or suppose the Republic of Moravia requires all its citizens to be periodically

X-rayed, and, if necessary, treated for tuberculosis. Are the Moravians being treated paternalistically? Our inclination to treat these cases as other than paternalistic leads Soble to refuse that label to any impositions that benefit others besides those directly imposed upon (1976, p. 35f). And he clearly has a point. But it may be better, given that it is likely to be almost impossible to find impositions that satisfy Soble's stringent requirements, to make a distinction between *pure* and *impure* (or, as Feinberg suggests [forthcoming, ch. 12], betweeen "unmixed" and "mixed") paternalism. This allows us to mark and discuss the paternalistic elements at work in impositions without seeing them as exhaustive.

Some of the confusion surrounding discussions of paternalism can be removed if, instead of attempting to identify "instances of paternalism," we look for evidence of paternalistic rationales. Then we can say that impositions are paternalistic *to the extent that* they are motivated by consideration of the welfare, etc., of the person imposed upon (albeit only indirectly). It may, of course, be possible to advance other considerations in their favor. In some cases these other considerations will be sufficient to sustain the imposition, and where this is the case attention must be shifted from the conduct to the attitudes that inform it. But in other cases nonpaternalistic considerations, although perhaps relevant, will not be sufficient to justify the imposition, and an appeal to paternalistic considerations will be integral to the justificatory process. Where this is so, we may consider it appropriate to call the conduct paternalistic, albeit only impurely so. What is important so far as paternalism is concerned is not whether it is possible to isolate a class of "paternalistic" impositions, but whether a particular (e.g., paternalistic) rationale for imposing upon others has any moral standing, and if so, how much. Thus what we shall later discuss as cases of paternalism are better understood as impositions for which paternalistic reasons are often, and perhaps necessarily, advanced. Our concern will be not so much with whether those impositions are justified but with the extent to which their justification would be dependent on paternalistic considerations, and the weight that can reasonably be given to them.

We have not yet said much about the specifics of a paternalistic rationale. Dworkin refers variously to "welfare, good, happiness, needs, interests or values" when addressing this issue. His catalogue is reminiscent of Mill, who reinforces his exclusive commitment to the harm (to others) principle by asserting:

> His own good, either physical or moral, is not a sufficient warrant. He cannot rightfully be compelled to do or forbear because it will be better for him to do so, because it will make him happier, because, in the opinions of others, to do so would be wise, or even right (1859, pp. 223–24).

The only difference worth noting is that Mill here rejects not only paternalism but also moralism: that something is (believed to be) morally right is no reason for enforcing it any more than that it is (believed to be) wise. The distinction between paternalism and moralism is one to which we will presently need to attend more closely.

We need not take it that in cataloguing various paternalistic rationales, Dworkin and Mill are intending any hard and fast distinctions. The various reasons simply enumerate some general and more specific considerations that serve to constitute an imposition as paternalistic. For convenience we shall characterize all such reasons as having regard to the *good* of the person concerned.

Two complicating factors warrant our attention. The first is directly prompted by Dworkin's own discussion, for at one point he toys with the idea that paternalism "might be thought of as the use of coercion to achieve a good which is not recognized as such by those persons for whom the good is intended" (1971, p. 112). This is a more restrictive account than the one with which we commenced, for on that account, whether or not the person in question recognizes the (putative) good as such is immaterial. No doubt, if a person recognizes what another does as contributing to his or her good, there is a reasonable probability that it will be consented to and thus not be paternalistic. But there is nothing hard and fast about this. People sometimes wish to go their own way, even though they recognize the detriment involved. This is particularly common in the case of so-called "life-style" decisions, where work, recreational, or eating habits may be persisted in despite an acknowledgment of the serious danger involved. There does not seem to be any good reason for excluding impositions in such cases from the realm of paternalism. Perhaps there is a heavier burden of justification on the imposer where the supposed good is not acknowledged as such by the person on whom it is imposed, but that is another matter.

The second complication is generated by the fact that some writers tend to restrict their accounts and attention to cases in which it is not the securing of good in some general sense, but only protection from harm, that is in view (e.g., Hart 1963, p. 31). There does not seem to be any compelling reason for this restriction, only an expectation that if paternalism is ever likely to be justifiable it will most likely be so in cases where protection from harm constitutes its rationale. It may therefore be useful to distinguish *negative* from *positive* paternalism. An imposition will be negatively paternalistic to the extent that it has as its rationale the protection of its primary object from harm or some similar detriment; it will be positively paternalistic to the extent that it has as its rationale some positive benefit for its primary object. If Lower Slobbovian law prohibits participation in certain dangerous sports (say, hang-gliding and water-rafting), and tightly regulates participation in certain others (say, boxing and go-karting), it is probably negatively paternalistic. The same can be said if Lucille is given a blood transfusion without her consent because it is judged that she will not otherwise survive the effects of necessary surgery. On the other hand, if Upper Slobbovian law requires that all children attend school until age fifteen, in order to ensure that they are adequately prepared to enter the adult world, or if Karen requires her child Karl to continue at school until he is eighteen, in order to improve his job options, the impositions are positively paternalistic. It is of course possible for the one requirement to have both harm-preventing and benefit-promoting aspects. Compulsory schooling might be a good example of this.

At this stage it will be useful to bring together the various conclusions we have reached. In preference to Dworkin's account of paternalism, I would suggest the following:

> X acts paternalistically in regard to Y to the extent that X, in order to secure Y's good, as an end, imposes upon Y.

This account does not beg the question either for or against paternalism, though the fact that it involves an imposition on those whose good is sought indicates why, within the liberal tradition, paternalism generates a justificatory question. The precise nature of the freedom that is diminished is at this point left open. Further, my account is framed in a way that acknowledges that paternalism is better seen as a rationale for acting rather than as a form of behavior, thus obviating some of the difficulties encountered in seeking "cases" of paternalism. It is the moral standing of that rationale that constitutes the central (though by no means only) problem of paternalism.

There is some likelihood that the justificatory problems surrounding paternalism will be clarified if several sets of distinctions are taken into account. Of first importance is a distinction between *strong* and *weak* paternalism. We can say that an imposition is strongly paternalistic if, in order to secure *Y*'s good, *X* imposes upon *Y* without considering *Y*'s capacity to choose that good for him- or herself. It is weakly paternalistic, however, if *X*'s imposition is premised upon *Y*'s incapacity to make that choice. Also of considerable importance is a distinction between *positive* and *negative* paternalism. *X* acts toward *Y* in a positively paternalistic fashion to the extent that *X*, in order to secure some positive benefit for *Y*, imposes upon *Y*. If, however, *X*'s rationale for imposing upon *Y* is to protect *Y* from (further) harm or to restore *Y* from some harmful condition, then to that extent, *X* acts in a negatively paternalistic fashion. There are, further, distinctions to be drawn between *active* and *passive*, and *direct* and *indirect* paternalism. Where *X* requires *Y* to do certain things, in order to secure *Y*'s good, *X* acts toward *Y* in an actively paternalistic manner. An imposition is passively paternalistic if, instead of being required to do certain things, *Y* is required to refrain from doing certain things. A paternalistic imposition is direct to the extent that *X*, in order to secure *Y*'s good, imposes only upon *Y*; it is indirect where the imposition on *Y* is achieved via an imposition on *Z*.

Paternalism and Moralism

Earlier I adverted to a distinction between paternalism and moralism. It is important that we now explore this more thoroughly. Its importance resides in the fact that some writers (e.g., Hart 1963, pp. 30–34) believe a measure of paternalism though not moralism to be compatible with liberalism.

Mill does not seem to recognize such a distinction. He appears to speak interchangeably of interferences intended to secure a person's "moral good" and those originating in beliefs about what is morally "right" (Mill 1859, pp. 223–24). It is to Hart that we owe the distinction. In his debate with Lord Devlin over the limits of criminal law, Hart argued that "the rules excluding the victim's consent as a defense to charges of murder or assault" are not to be explained as a piece of moralism, as Devlin had claimed (Devlin 1965, pp. 6–7), but "as a piece of paternalism, designed to protect individuals against themselves" (Hart 1963, p. 31). It is not the enforcement of morality, but protection against self-harming behavior, that explains such rules, and, more importantly so far as Hart is concerned, gives to the latter an acceptability that the former lacks. Devlin was singularly unimpressed. Not only did the distinction subvert the intentions of the liberal tradition Hart believed he was defending, but it could not be sustained:

> Neither in principle nor in practice can a line be drawn between legislation controlling the individual's physical welfare and legislation controlling

his moral welfare. If paternalism be the principle, no father of a family would content himself with looking after his children's welfare and leaving their morals to themselves. If society has an interest which permits it to legislate in the one case, why not in the other? If, on the other hand, we are grown up enough to look after our own morals, why not after our own bodies (Devlin 1965, pp. 135–36).

There is a certain sense in which Hart is right in believing that a distinction can be drawn between moralism and paternalism, at least as he construes them. And even if we focus more narrowly (as he doesn't) on moral paternalism we can recognize a distinction. An imposition directed to securing someone's moral good may not be one designed to make that person conform to some particular precept. Quite the contrary. It may have as its end an increase in that person's moral autonomy. But the issue is more complex than this, for it concerns not merely formal but morally significant distinctions. It is possible that moralism and paternalism, though distinct, are related as genus and species, and that the problems that Hart believes fatal for moralism turn out to be equally deadly in the case of paternalism (whether physical or moral).

Before pursuing this possibility further, I want to look at a strategy for distinguishing them that I believe has only limited relevance. It is implicit in Hart's own discussion, where he notes Mill's failure to be aware of the "great range of factors which diminish the significance to be attached to an apparently free choice or to consent" (1963, p. 33). The detailed statement is provided by C. L. Ten (1971; cf. Ten 1969, pp. 659–61), who argues that confusion over the differences has arisen from an overly narrow focus on the "consequence-aspect" of acts, to the neglect of their "decision-aspect." He allows that attention to the consequences of acts will yield no clear-cut way of differentiating paternalism from moralism. Differentiation becomes possible only if we consider the conditions under which they are chosen. Here we find that, where acts have been proscribed for paternalistic reasons, there is a presumption that those choosing them do so under conditions of immature, defective or impaired decision-making capacity. This enables us to distinguish paternalism and moralism on three related counts (Ten 1971, pp. 63–64):

1. Paternalism is concerned with self-harming acts performed under conditions of impaired decision-making capacity. Moralism is not so restricted. No vitiating factors need be present.
2. Paternalistic impositions are not intended as punishment for moral blameworthiness. On the contrary. Blameworthiness, if any, is reduced by the factors that prompt paternalism.
3. The rationale for paternalism is to be found in the interests of the objects of its concern. The rationale for moralism, however, is to be found in more impersonal interests, such as preservation of the society's shared values and distinctive institutions.

It is 1. that makes the crucial moral difference, yet it is also that which limits the usefulness of Ten's account. As Ten himself acknowledges in a later work (1980, pp. 110–14), it serves at best to distinguish moralism from weak (negative) paternalism. But Hart wants to distinguish moralism from strong paternalism as well, for he argues that even where there is no doubt about consent, (some) paternalistic interferences can be explained and defended as part of a policy of harm-minimization (Hart 1963, p. 33).

Does this differentiate them sufficiently? That it may is suggested by 3. above. Whereas the interests sought to be protected by paternalism are those of the individual who is imposed upon, the interests that motivate moralistic interferences can be quite alien to that individual. The latter kind of motivation lends itself to quite illiberal impositions. The same point is probably implicit in Hart's own account. When he opposes "the enforcement of morals," it is only the enforcement of "positive morality" that he objects to. "Critical morality," is, on the other hand, properly a matter for enforcement. For Hart, positive morality comprises the moral traditions of a particular society, without regard to their defensibility. But critical morality, in contradistinction, is "enlightened," by which Hart appears to mean that it rests "on rational beliefs as to matters of fact, and accepts all human beings as entitled to equal consideration and respect" (1961, p. 201). The harm principle is a principle of critical morality, since harming others is, paradigmatically, to deny them equal consideration and respect. Can we say the same for a principle of strong negative paternalism? Hart appears to think so. So far as the harm is concerned, there may not seem to be any significant difference whether it is inflicted upon another or upon oneself. And in one sense this is so. A broken leg is a broken leg. But the harm principle is not concerned with harm merely in the sense of damage. It is concerned with harm as an injury, a wrong. It is because of this that it involves a denial of "equal consideration and respect." But the principle of strong negative paternalism that Hart espouses operates only with the first sense of "harm." The person who endangers him- or herself does no wrong, violates no rights.[11] Indeed, it might be charged that it is the paternalist who, in such cases, is guilty of denying "equal consideration and respect." For what the strong paternalist does is to intervene in the activities of another without regard for that other's will. The other's "interests" are given priority over the other's "autonomy." This is a difficulty that Hart does not appear to have faced, and suggests, on somewhat different grounds, that Devlin may have been right in thinking that his "modification" serves to "tear the heart out of [Mill's] doctrine" (Devlin 1965, p. 132).

We shall return to these questions in Chapter 3, but we have probably said enough to indicate that such distinctions as can be drawn between paternalism and moralism may not be decisive so far as the moral standing of each is concerned. Defenders of strong paternalism may also, *ipso facto*, need to be prepared to defend a limited measure of moralism.

Notes

1. Cf. descriptions of Japanese industry (Marsh and Mannari 1972; Azumi 1977) and various U.S. industrial towns—Pullman, Illinois; Kohler, Wisconsin; etc. (Alanen and Peltin 1978).

2. Cf., too, the preponderance of female status offenders in juvenile courts (Chesney-Lind, 1977).

3. This is, no doubt, too quick. Even in the case of moral notions, we may call into question the framework in terms of which the conceptualization takes place.

4. Dworkin has subsequently had "second thoughts" about this account (1983), and some of the criticisms I make here he has independently accepted.

5. It is not my present purpose to insist that such limitations can be justified, if at all, only as instances of paternalism (see Weale 1978). The point I am making is simply that they may be paternalistically motivated without being coercive. The initial disclaimer applies equally to other examples used in this chapter. See also Lee (1981, p. 194).

6. A somewhat different range of cases is suggested by Peter Gill's (1976) critique of "free schools": progressive teachers who leave children to "find out things for themselves," believing that "experience is the best teacher," may be depriving these children of information or advice to which their pupil status gives them entitlement by their very refusal to intervene. But it is possible to construe such apparent non-interference with liberty of action as just the opposite: an omission that diminishes the pupil's realistic options.

7. This is, I suspect, an oversimplification. If the confinement of a particular species of animal were to affect its mating habits and lead to its extinction, we might well consider that to have some moral significance.

8. In a later comment, Feinberg expresses serious doubts about the language of "weak paternalism" (1980, p. x).

9. In setting up this contrast, I have been helped by Wikler (1979), though he would probably dispute the use I have made of it.

10. I am of course assuming that what the magistrate says genuinely expresses his reasons. By the same token, I am assuming that the reasons that originally motivated the passing of the law continue to motivate its retention. If these assumptions are incorrect, then obviously different responses to the questions would be required.

11. Is the situation changed in two-party cases? There is some initial plausibility in thinking that less than equal consideration and respect is shown by a party who deliberately impairs another, albeit with that other's consent.

2

Paternalism, Freedom, and Self-Regarding Conduct

Central to understanding paternalism is the conjunction of two factors: an imposition and a particular rationale. X acts to diminish Y's freedom, to the end that Y's good may be secured. It is the *conjunction* that renders paternalism particularly problematic within liberalism. The liberal presumption that individuals ought to be left free to pursue their own ends in their own way may be overridden if the nature of the ends or the means of their attainment is such that their prosecution would be dangerous or harmful to others. This ground for interference does not accommodate paternalism, in which impositions are directed not to the protection of unwilling others but only to securing the good of the agent him- or herself. This much granted, however, why shouldn't a paternalistic rationale legitimate impositions? If the commitment to individual freedom can be overridden where there is some danger posed by others, why can't it also be overridden where the danger posed is to the individual him- or herself? Or where the individual might be benefited in some way by means of such imposition? In order to respond to these questions, we need first to understand the nature and value of this freedom, and then to consider the limitations to which it might legitimately be subject. Both of these tasks will claim our attention in this chapter, though attempts to create moral space for paternalism will be explored in detail only in Chapter 3.

There is one other general issue with which an examination of paternalism needs to come to terms: the assumed distinction between self- and other-regarding conduct. When liberals condemn paternalism, they do not usually consider their condemnation to be without practical force. They imagine that the good of the party interfered with on paternalistic grounds can be construed and pursued sufficiently independently of the good of others to constitute a distinct and sometimes separable ground for interference. Unless something like this is assumed, the whole issue of paternalism is rendered academic. Yet the liberal supposition is by no means uncontroversial, having attracted criticism in respect of both its intelligibility and plausibility. Since some of the arguments to be considered in Chapter 3 arise out of such criticism, I devote the latter part of this chapter to its clarification and problems.

Freedom and Freedoms

Paternalism is freedom-constricting. But what is the nature of the freedom that is constricted? Is it the liberty to pursue an occurrent desire? Is it some capacity for rational choice? Or is it a personality ideal such as automony? There is probably no general answer to this question. I have deliberately provided an account of paternalism that accommodates a plurality of understandings. This has had a dual purpose. It enables us to get a better perspective on the limits to benevolence as a motivation for action. It also recognizes that the moral questions associated with impositions are not confined to those in which "the deliberate decisions of rational adults" are interfered with, but also arise in cases where the formation of wants or the expression of occurrent desires is impeded. This is not to deny that the liberal critique of paternalism has been more concerned with some kinds of freedom than with others, though there is no unanimity over the character (or even value) of such freedom. If for no other reason than this, it is worth looking more generally at the question.

Liberals have traditionally operated with a conception of freedom in which it is understood as noninterference, an absence of coercion or constraint on the implementation of *desires*. Some writers, however, have preferred an account in terms of the nonrestriction of *options*. Each formulation has something to be said for it, though each is also problematic. The attractiveness of the "desires" account lies precisely in its linking of freedom with the concerns of the individual. Am I not free if what I want to do I can do? Is my freedom limited if all I can do is what I want to do? The tendency to see in these questions a rhetorical confirmation of the "desires" view is diminished when its consequences are reflected upon. If it is the nonfrustration of desires that is constitutive of freedom, then obstacles to it can be removed by the extinction of those desires. Hence the attractiveness of the "options" view. The contented slave, though not frustrated so far as the implementation of his or her desires is concerned, lacks freedom because of his or her constricted options. But the "options" view is also problematic. For how are options to be individuated? And if they can be, is it the number or the nature of the options that is important? Is the person who has only one option—a desired one—less free than the person with many options, but none that is desired? Neither view is satisfactory as it stands. But this need not delay us here.

Taken at face value, both the foregoing accounts treat the confining of a young child to a playpen as a restriction on freedom no less than the imprisonment of an adult. The liberty to give effect to desires or the nonrestriction of options is all that matters. A supposed virtue of these accounts is that they are "merely descriptive," though such a judgment is not shared by all writers in the tradition. Some argue that "all restraint, *quâ* restraint, is an evil" (Mill 1859, p. 293), and that an onus is placed on any who would constrain another. Perhaps that burden of justification can be discharged more easily in certain classes of cases than in others, but a burden there is, nevertheless.

Liberals who view the foregoing as "merely descriptive," but who yet wish to defend liberty, usually do so by appealing to a *principle of liberty*, which circumscribes a limited realm of noninterference. Children and others deemed noncompetent are excluded from its purview, and the protected desires or options are restricted to those of a self-regarding kind. In terms of this understanding, paternalism is said not only to diminish or abrogate liberty but also to violate it, by invading its rightful sphere.

There are some benefits in construing liberty broadly and in seeing the liberal principle as simply an attempt to mark out that sphere within which individual jurisdiction should be *absolute*. For it should not be concluded that if a case for absolute liberty can be established in one sphere, no claims may be asserted on its behalf outside that sphere. Thus Mill, who expends most of his energies in defending a *principle of liberty*, nevertheless recognizes that interferences falling outside its purview are not just on that account morally insignificant. Those not yet competent to engage in rational self-regarding conduct may have that conduct interfered with only to the extent that the attainment of competence is effectively promoted (Mill 1859, p. 224).

A number of late nineteenth-century liberals (e.g., Green 1881, pp. 51–53; Ritchie 1894, pp. 138–39) expressed their dissatisfaction with "negative" accounts of freedom of the kind so far outlined. They considered freedom from interference to be of little value in the absence of some positive power or capacity to use it in the service of one's ends. In this they were undoubtedly correct. But they spoke of this power or capacity as "positive liberty," and gave it argumentative precedence when discussing the value and limits of freedom. In so far as freedom from interference ("negative liberty") was justified, it was believed to be because it enabled a person to exercise his powers to make the best of himself.

Whatever the wisdom of their nomenclature (see Weinstein 1965, for a critique), these later liberals were drawing attention to a serious deficiency in much liberal writing. This was the tendency to forget an underlying and controlling conception of Man or ideal of a personal development in terms of which freedom as liberty could be provided with a principled defense. Mill speaks of it as the ideal of individuality, though we might just as well speak of it as an ideal of personal autonomy, and it is in terms of the conditions for its realization that his *principle of liberty* is to be understood. What the cultivation of individuality requires, as an internal prerequisite, is a developed capacity for rational choice (or, as Stanley Benn calls it, "autarchy" [1975–76, pp. 112–17]). It is for this reason that those who as yet lack this capacity do not come within its purview; though it is in order that they might that interferences with their self-regarding behavior can be justified. Where that capacity is already possessed, any interference not directed to the protection of others subverts the goal of individuality by negating a precondition for its realization. What the later liberals were concerned to emphasize was the *insufficiency* of noninterference, of *laissez-faire*. The (absolute) principle of liberty was based on the hidden and often false presumption that in social interactions, generally construed in contractual terms, people with equally developed capacities for rational choice also possessed equal bargaining power. What was freely (i.e., without interference) entered into might nonetheless be unfair and therefore a candidate for outside intervention. By losing sight of the ideal of personal autonomy, earlier liberals lost the perspective that was essential to a defensible principle of liberty.

We can sum up so far. Liberals have traditionally focused on an account of freedom as noninterference. This is "liberty," and either in itself or as embodied in a principle constitutes the principal weapon of liberal social criticism. But freedom as liberty depends for its moral force on an underlying conception or ideal, the central thrust of which is the most complete and coherent development of capacities and powers. This personal development, also frequently seen as a kind of freedom, can be characterized as "autonomy." The ideal of autonomy does not justify liberty without exception, a point reflected in Mill's principle of liberty. For Mill, only the self-regarding conduct of a person possessing "autarchy" or the developed capacity for rational choice is to be accorded absolute liberty. Even this, however, may be too permissive, in the absence of a certain equality of bargaining power in social relations.

We have, then, three kinds of freedom—liberty, autonomy, and autarchy—and much of this and subsequent chapters will be given to the detailed articulation of their relationships. In so far as paternalistic impositions involve a constraint on freedom, any one or all of these freedoms may be intended. Liberty may be curtailed; the capacity for rational choice may be ignored; autonomy may be overridden or undermined. For liberals, the latter constitutes the most serious intrusion, since the ideal of autonomy is central to the liberal vision of Man, and, in so far as constraints on liberty or the failure to recognize autarchy interfere with the realization of that vision, the burden of justification is equally heavy. However, at least in the case of invasions of liberty, autonomy may not always be threatened, and to that extent liberals have not set themselves against all paternalism. What we have referred to as weak paternalism need involve no threat to autonomy, since the conditions for its realization no longer or do not yet exist. The position is more problematic in the case of interferences with autarchy, for this is foundational to autonomy. Thus liberal writers have often treated the nonrecognition of autarchy as tantamount to a threat to autonomy.

A useful entrée to the next bracket of problems we must consider is the observation that "free" is sometimes used as an all-or-nothing predicate, sometimes as a predicate admitting of degrees. X's freedom to pursue a may be an all-or-nothing matter, but X's freedom, *simpliciter*, is often said to be a matter of degree. If X is not permitted to pursue a, then X's freedom (in general) is to that extent diminished: X is less free. In some cases, such comparative judgments are relatively unproblematic. If, at t_1, X is at liberty to do a, b, c, and d, but at t_2 at liberty to do only b, c, and d, then we can say that X is freer at t_1 than at t_2. X has more options or, alternatively, can satisfy more wants at t_1 than at t_2. However, the use of comparative judgments of freedom frequently goes beyond such uncomplicated cases. They are not uncommonly employed when, at t_1, X is at liberty to do a, b, c, and d, and at t_2 at liberty to do d, e, and f. Can we say in this case that X is freer at t_1 than at t_2? The situation is even more problematic when interpersonal comparative judgments are made. If X is at liberty to do a, b, c, and d, and Y is at liberty to do c, d, e, and f, are they equally free, or is one freer than the other? Or if both are at liberty to do a, b, and c, but X wants only to do d whereas Y is really happy about being able to do b, are they equally free? Our judgments here often presume that freedom is susceptible to "overall" assessments, that the liberty to do a, b, c, etc., can be compounded into a sum of freedom, in virtue of which X can be said to be freer at t_1 than at t_2 or freer than Y.

Where our judgments of *freedom in general* are transformed into judgments of *overall freedom*, there is presupposed some currency of comparison in terms of which it can be said, aggregatively, that a person at liberty to do *a*, *b*, *c*, and *d* is more (or less) free than one at liberty to do *c*, *d*, *e*, and *f*. It is presupposed, in other words, that these liberties are commensurable. And this is what makes them highly problematic. Can we say that a person who is free to move house and job but not to criticize the incumbent government is freer (or less free) than one who is not free to move house and job but is free to criticize the incumbent government? Or can we say only that one person is free in one respect, whereas the other is free in another respect? The problem is well-expressed by Joel Feinberg:

> The difficulty in striking . . . totals of "on balance freedom" derives from the fact that the relation among the various "areas" in which people are said to be free is not so much like the relation between the height, breadth, and depth of a physical object as it is like the relation between the gasoline economy, styling, and comfort of an automobile. Height times breadth times depth equals volume, a dimension compounded coherently out of the others; freedom of expression times freedom of movement yields nothing comparable (1973, p. 19).

The difficulty with judgments of overall freedom is not simply their lack of amenability to precise quantification, but the apparent incommensurability of their elements, thus making quantification impossible. Like aggregations of utility, aggregations of freedom appear to depend more on customary intuitions than on any genuine comparability of their components.

But this judgment may be premature, as even Feinberg recognizes (cf. also Swanton 1979). In a later discussion, he is more hopeful that in at least some everyday contexts judgments of overall freedom might be rationally made (1980a, pp. 30–44). He sustains this via an elaboration of the "options" account of liberty. We can, he suggests, think of life analogously to a maze of railroad tracks, which at various points are connected by switches. These tracks represent life's options and access to them depends on whether the switches at the junction points are open or closed. Not all tracks are equally "fecund," so far as options are concerned. Some will lead to many new options, others to deadends. Control over the switches may lie with a variety of agencies. Parents, governments, and other institutional bodies may be considered (within limits) as having a legitimate switch-opening and closing function. But others may also operate them: bullies, criminals, and resistance movements.

It is not too difficult to see how many of the things that we might be free to do or not to do can be recast in terms of the options that are opened up or closed off. And this might be seen as a common currency in terms of which freedom can be aggregated or quantified. But, as Feinberg himself realizes, this strategy will take us only part of the way toward commensurability. The railroad model is best suited to what we can broadly speak of as liberty of movement, but "is difficult to apply to liberty of expression and opinion, or to 'passive liberties' like the freedom to be let alone" (1980a, p. 37).[1] Moreover, the maze of life's railroad is not determinate, like the map of a railroad system, but capable of an indefinite number of extensions, not all of which are foreseeable at a particular point of time. What appears from the switchpoint to be a deadend may turn out to have all sorts of unexpected posssibilities attached to it.

But the problems in calculating overall freedom via an assessment of the fecundity of options are even more intractable than the foregoing deficiencies suggest. One general difficulty concerns the individuation of options. If an option is thought of as an action lying open to a person, even a relatively unexciting liberty such as the liberty to move around a room without hindrance will leave a person with an almost indefinite number of options. Of course, they will be restricted so far as their variety is concerned, but nevertheless remain distinct options. If this appears to multiply options beyond necessity, we must then provide some criterion for distinguishing significant options, in which case it will not be so much the number of options that is likely to be important, but their natures. This may then move us back in the direction of the "desires" view, where "options" are determined by reference to the desires of the agent.[2] The person who is most free will be the person whose most important desires are most nearly satisfied. But, as we have already observed, the desires view has problems of its own.

At this stage, it is not necessary that we pursue these matters further, since in the eyes of many liberals there is something else profoundly troubling about judgments of overall freedom. It is argued that liberalism is not committed to a maximization of some overall freedom, but to the securing of certain basic freedoms. Talk of overall freedom obscures the virtual sacrosanctity of these. If I am not permitted to drive on whatever side of the road I want, or to construct on my property whatever kind of dwelling I want, my liberty is limited in certain ways. Such limitations may be justified in terms of public convenience, the character of an area, and so on. In these cases, even if I want to do what I am forbidden to do, I am unlikely to consider the forbidden options as something I had a special claim to. But if what is prohibited are public assemblies, criticism of the incumbent régime, or access to what others wish to communicate with me, I may well complain that a different ball game is being played. These are my *civil liberties*, and even if I do not particularly care to make use of them, they are not up for trade-off in the same way as other freedoms. They constitute a distinct category of freedoms, and it is the protection of these to which liberalism is committed. Here the issue is not one of the *amount* of liberty to be gained or lost, but the *kind* of liberty. Some liberties, unlike others, have a special immunity to interference. This view is deeply embedded in the liberal tradition. Although Mill sees all restraint as an evil, requiring justification, he does not stop there. There are some liberties that stand apart, and, if compromised at all, must be done so only for the most compelling reasons. He writes:

This, then, is the appropriate region of human liberty. It comprises, first, the inward domain of consciousness; demanding liberty of conscience in the most comprehensive sense; liberty of thought and feeling; absolute freedom of opinion and sentiment on all subjects, practical or speculative, scientific, moral, or theological. The liberty of expressing and publishing opinions may seem to fall under a different principle, since it belongs to that part of the conduct of an individual which concerns other people; but, being almost of as much importance as liberty of thought itself, and resting in great part on the same reasons, is practically inseparable from it. Secondly, the principle requires liberty of tastes and pursuits; of framing a plan of our life to suit our own character; of doing as we like, subject to such consequences as may follow: without impediment from our fellow-creatures, so long as what we do does not harm them, even though they should think our conduct foolish, perverse, or wrong. Thirdly, from this liberty of each individual, follows the liberty, within the same limits, of combination among individuals; freedom to unite, for any purpose not involving harm to others: the persons combining being supposed to be of full age, and not forced or deceived (Mill 1859, p. 225–26; cf. Rawls 1971, p. 61).

What Mill here outlines as "the appropriate region of human liberty" is not so much some generalized commodity, capable of aggregation, but rather a set, system, or cluster of basic liberties or freedoms. And these, in their core or central applications, have a certain priority, so far as interpersonal behavior is concerned.

Now it is in virtue of these liberties that Mill (along with other liberals) is minded to reject all strong paternalism. What it is incumbent on us to do is to discover why these liberties are accorded such importance, and whether the reasons given serve, as they are intended to, to rule out all strong paternalism.

Justifying Freedom(s)

The importance of freedom, and in particular the liberties to which we have referred in the preceding discussion, is variously defended within liberal thought. We may, in somewhat Kantian fashion, see in autarchy—the capacity for rational choice—a basis for respect, a recognition of the equal standing of other rational choosers, violation of which would contravene the terms of the categorical imperative.[3] But for the time being, it is not the Kantian path that I want to follow. It is the route marked out by nineteenth-century liberalism, and particularly by John Stuart Mill. Kant is not too far away, but there are, as I shall indicate, certain advantages to the Millian approach.

The nineteenth-century liberals who opposed paternalism in the name of freedom had as the context for their stand a certain conception of human personality and its development. This functioned as their *terminus a quo*. An insight into it is given by two quotations from Baron Wilhelm von Humboldt, both of which are to be found in Mill. In the pivotal third chapter of *On Liberty*, Mill refers with approval to von Humboldt's assertions that

> "The end of man, or that which is prescribed by the eternal or immutable dictates of reason, and not suggested by vague and transient desires, is the highest and most harmonious development of his powers to a complete and consistent whole"; that, therefore, the object "towards which every human being must ceaselessly direct his efforts, and on which especially those who design to influence their fellowmen must ever keep their eyes, is the individuality of power and development"; that for this there are two requisites, "freedom and variety of situations"; and that from the union of these arise "individual vigour and manifold diversity", which combine themselves in "originality" (Mill 1859, p. 261; von Humboldt 1854, pp. 11, 13).

And as the epigraph to *On Liberty*, he uses the following quotation:

The grand, leading principle, towards which every argument unfolded in these pages directly converges, is the absolute and essential importance of human development in its richest diversity (Mill 1859, p. 215; von Humboldt 1854, p. 65).

What we have here is an ideal of human personality articulated in terms of "individuality" or personal autonomy—"the highest and most harmonious development" of a person's capacities, so that they come to form "a complete and consistent whole." This is a process that, because of their natural differences, will work itself out in different ways for different people. It could also work itself out in different ways for the same person. Most of us have more capacities than we have time and opportunity to develop, and which combination of capacities and what degree of development is optimal may vary with place and circumstance.

Freedom is seen as both a constitutive feature and as a causal prerequisite of this ideal of human personality. It is freedom in the sense of autarchy that is seen as a constitutive feature, and freedom as liberty that is seen as the causal prerequisite.

When nineteenth-century writers speak of natural capacities—capacities whose development is integral to the achievement of autonomy—they have in mind not just intellectual capacities, but also volitional and emotional ones. Further, they have in mind those capacities that set human beings apart from other animals, and whose development makes them "a noble and beautiful object of contemplation" (Mill 1859, p. 266). Creativity, aesthetic and emotional sensitivity, self-control, initiative and foresight, independence, judiciousness, moral and religious discrimination, and so on, belong, if not exclusively, at least distinctively to human beings. And they are possible only to the autarchic person. As Mill puts it, "the human faculties of perception, judgment, discriminative feeling, mental activity, and even moral preference, are exercised only in making a choice" (1859, p. 262). The refusal to recognize this—shown by interference with a person's liberty—constitutes a "pauperization" or "degradation" of that person. "It is," Mill writes, "the privilege and proper condition of a human being, arrived at the maturity of his faculties, to use and interpret experience in his own way" (ibid.) Not to accord a person that "privilege" or to acknowledge his "proper condition" is to treat him as less than a human being; it is, as Rawls would express it, to disregard and undermine the bases for self-respect (Rawls 1971, p. 544ff.).

There is a double aspect to this argument. The achievement of autonomy or individuality is possible only for the person whose beliefs and actions reflect a background of deliberation and choice—autarchy. Instrumental to the maintenance of the latter is an environment in which certain liberties are acknowledged. These liberties are just those that accommodate the requirements of autarchy and thus preserve the essential prerequisite for the achievement of individuality. We are not that far away from the Kantian conception of Man as a rational chooser, whose character as such is respected to the extent that he is permitted to direct his life by means of a self-prescribed *nomos* or standard. The form of justification is different, but the conclusion so far as the status of individual freedom is concerned is much the same.

For Kant, the principle of respect for persons articulates a status which we have in virtue of our capacity as rational choosers. It denies to one individual the standing to use his or her chosen ends as reasons for frustrating others in the pursuit of their own chosen ends. The nineteenth-century liberals come to much the same conclusion, not by means of some Kantian deduction, but because individuality has choice as one of its chief constituents, and liberty safeguards choice. Where the nineteenth-century liberals have an advantage over Kant is in their particularism. Kantian respect for persons is essentially impersonal. It is in view of the humanity in one's person (i.e., rationality) that Kantian respect is demanded. It is not because one's choices are *one's own* but because they are the choices of a rational being that forbearance is required. But for Mill it is because of the particular capacities, interests, and values one has—albeit the expression of a being with the capacity for rational choice—that liberty is mandated. There is a nonsubstitutability about Millian regard that is absent from Kantian respect.

In addition to the foregoing, nineteenth-century liberals have other arguments for liberty. These arise out of their conception of individuality as an ideal toward which we may progress, an ideal whose realization may be fostered in various ways, and whose dynamic character makes continuing demands on our initiative and resources for choice. Mill speaks of individuality analogously to bodily fitness. Regular exercise is needed if the muscles—mental and moral as well as physical—are not to atrophy (Mill 1859, p. 262).

One common argument premises itself on the supposition of diverse natures. The end of development—individuality—is not the same for everybody. There is no single way of harmonizing individual powers and capacities, and the most favorable balance for any particular individual will depend partly on the resources that his or her social situation is able to make available, and partly on his or her native endowments. Mill writes:

> If it were only that people have diversities of taste, that is reason enough for not attempting to shape them all after one model. But different persons also require different conditions for their spiritual development; and can no more exist healthily in the same moral, than all the variety of plants can in the same physical, atmosphere and climate. The same things which are helps to one person towards cultivation of his higher nature, are hindrances to another. The same mode of life is a healthy excitement to one, keeping all his faculties of action in their best order, while to another it is a distracting burthen, which suspends or crushes all internal life (1859, p. 270).

We need not get into the quicksand of the nature-nurture controversy to appreciate the substance of this argument and its implications for liberty. Where one person imposes on another a particular pattern or mode of living, the odds are that it will be unsuited to the nature of the individual, or, if not unsuited, imposed in a manner out of keeping with that individual's own rhythm and pace. The individual is not only "the person most interested in his own well-being," but in relation to it "has means of knowledge immeasurably surpassing those that can be possessed by anyone else" (Mill 1859, p. 277). Even if the individual's self-knowledge leaves much to be desired, it is still better, once the capacity for appraising and learning from experience has been acquired, that he or she not be taken in hand, for it is through participation in a variety of "experiments in living" (Mill 1859, p. 281) that the pattern best suited to his or her nature is most likely to be found.

This sort of probabilistic argument is likely to be at its strongest where legal or institutional intervention is contemplated. For it is characteristic of such interventions that attention is paid to generalities rather than particularities. In cases where there is a strong personal bond between the parties concerned, there may be a much greater sensitivity to the finer nuances of individual character. But are we justified in thinking that liberty will, on the whole, lead to greater self-awareness and increasing understanding of how native capacities can be best and most coherently developed? We may have strong doubts. When left to their own devices, individuals do not have a strong record so far as their self-knowledge and knowledge of means is concerned.[4] More than this, however, is required to subvert the argument, for even if individuals are notoriously lacking in self-perception, they do not have a more favorable record in the correction of others, and the balance may well be thought to tip in favor of liberty. It is not, after all, as though individual liberty requires that people be "left to their own devices." We can still benefit from the perceptions of others, as they are brought to bear on our own perceptions and misperceptions. On more than one occasion Mill regrets the lack of concern that individuals show to each other—their "selfish indifference" (1859, p. 276). He allows that where an individual purposes to act in ways that will be detrimental to him, "considerations to aid his judgment, exhortations to strengthen his will, may be offered to him, even obtruded upon him, by others" (1859, p. 277). But the final judgment should be left up to him: "The interference of society to overrule his judgment and purposes in what only regards himself, must be grounded on general presumptions; which may be altogether wrong, and even if right, are as likely as not to be misapplied to individual cases" (1859, p. 277).

Although the supposition of diverse natures is common to nineteenth-century liberal thought and provides the basis for an epistemic defense of basic liberties, there are other defenses for which this supposition is not required. Bad decisions do not always represent a total loss. The mere fact that we have chosen, albeit badly, has a developmental spinoff that would be frustrated were we to be diverted from our ill-judged choice by a paternalistic hand: "the mental and moral, like the muscular powers, are improved only by being used" (Mill 1859, p. 262). Even if our choices are not optimal, the act of choosing exercises our capacity to choose. While it is possible that a person "might be guided in some good path, and kept out of harm's way" without exercising choice, to give that sort of guidance will be to undercut the development of those capacities for choice on which individuality depends. And concerning such a person we might ask: "What will be his comparative worth as a human being? It really is of importance, not only what men do, but also what manner of men they are that do it" (Mill 1859, p. 263).

We have, then, at least three arguments for the recognition of basic liberties. The first sees in the nonrecognition of such liberties a violation of autarchy and sapping of individuality, the second argues that the individual is likely to be best positioned to judge of the pursuits through which individuality will be expressed, and the third claims some positive value for the act of choosing, so that even bad choices have a role to play in the development of individuality.

Paternalism and Freedom(s)

Given the foregoing arguments for freedom, or at least the basic liberties, it is not too difficult to see why liberals find paternalistic impositions problematic. They constitute an invasion of just that sphere of conduct that it is the purpose of those arguments to secure against imposition. Let me spell this out in further detail.

THE ARGUMENT FROM OPPRESSION OF INDIVIDUALITY

Although individuality is to be construed as an ideal to be cultivated rather than as a possession to be preserved, its key requisite is possessed by all who have reached "the age of discretion." This is the capacity for rational choice, or what Mill variously speaks of as "the capacity of being improved by free and equal discussion," or "the capacity of being guided to their own improvement by conviction or persuasion," or the capacity "of being acted on by rational consideration of distant motives" (Mill 1859, pp. 224, 282). It is a capacity, however neglected or abused, for self-evaluation and self-determination. Individuality is an elaboration of this capacity and thus constraints that do not have as their end the protection of others constitute oppression— in which the individual is impressed into the service of alien ends.

Although nineteenth-century liberals defend liberty in the name of a certain conception of human development, the crucial place of choosing to that development leaves them within walking distance of Kant. The language is different, but the drift is much the same. For Kantians, the capacity for choice marks out the individual as a distinct source of reasons, an end rather than merely a potential instrument to someone else's ends. The capacity for choice constitutes the individual an object of respect—demanding our forbearance— even if not, until that capacity is sufficiently refined and creatively employed, an object of worth.[5] The capacity for choice gives the individual standing, an equality of position with others in virtue of which his or her judgment and projects may not be subjugated to theirs. This Kantian version we may call the Argument from Disrespect for Persons.

Paternalism, then, is seen as a violation of the demands of individuality, or as a usurpation of the standing properly belonging to a chooser. In paternalism, one party imposes upon another his or her own conception of a path to good. Some part of the paternalized party's life-plan or pattern is made the construction of others.

THE ARGUMENT FROM PATERNALISTIC DISTANCE

Mill, like other nineteenth-century liberals, has no doubt that there are certain "distinctive human endowments" of which we are all the actual or potential possessors, and which constitute us a class apart. But despite this, there is no single best pattern for the development of these "endowments"; rather, there are a large though not indeterminate number of them. Though we all have feet, a shoe that fits one will pinch another, and a shoe that fits one person at one time will not fit that person at a later time. Even though shoe sizes vary within a fairly determinate range, it may nevertheless cause great discomfort if the particular shoe does not fit. Shoe purchasing is a highly individual matter: others cannot buy our shoes for us; we have to go for fitting ourselves (cf. Mill 1859, p. 270).

This variability provides the background to one of the most commonly employed arguments against paternalism—the Argument from Paternalistic Distance (cf. Bentham 1789, p. 319; Sidgwick 1891, p. 37). It is not, perhaps, crucial to the argument that our natures be diverse, though the presumption that they are adds a good deal to its persuasiveness.

On Mill's account, the paternalist is distanced from the object of concern in two ways. First, the paternalist's concern for the other's good is not likely to match that individual's concern for him- or herself. "Except in cases of strong personal attachment," Mill observes, "the interest which any other person" can have in that person's well-being "is trifling, compared with that which he himself has." The exceptive clause is understandable, for where there is strong personal attachment, the interests of the second party have become an important interest of the first—maybe even more important. However, where the paternalistically inclined party is not some strongly attached other but "society" or "the authorities," the interest is likely to be very remote: in such cases "the interest which society has in him individually (except as to his conduct to others) is fractional, and altogether indirect" (Mill 1859, p. 277).

Second, the paternalist's knowledge of the other's good is not likely to match that of the other. This is partly because of deficiencies in the paternalist. The latter is likely to interpret the other's good in ways that reflect his or her own conception of the good—if not with respect to its components, then with respect to their ordering or ranking within the other's life-pattern. But it is also partly because of the advantageous position of the person whose good is in question. As Mill writes: "with respect to his own feelings or circumstances, the most ordinary man or woman has means of knowledge immeasurably surpassing those that can be possessed by any one else" (1859, p. 277). The individual has a certain privileged position so far as the details of his or her good is concerned. This he makes clear when considering the person who, even after being warned, chooses to cross a dangerous bridge: "no one but the person himself can judge of the sufficiency of the motive which may prompt him to incur the risk" (1859, p. 294).

So much for the argument's strengths. But, as Mill and others who have deployed it have been aware, its force is primarily statistical. What may be true in general may not be true in particular cases, and what may be true with respect to some interests may not be true with respect to others. If we are often affronted by the presumption of paternalists, we ought to be no less astonished at the carelessness, thoughtlessness, and stupidity of people with respect to the unelevating character or self-destructive potential of their self-regarding behavior. For rational beings, we do some pretty irrational things. The "we" here refers not simply to isolated individuals, but to the generality of people, especially when the consequences are likely to be temporally remote. Mill himself was troubled by this phenomenon. In the *Principles of Political Economy*, he spells out in some detail the deficiencies that frequently attach to people's self-regarding judgments (1848, pp. 947f, 953), a concern reflected also in *On Liberty* (1859, p. 280).

But troubled though he is, Mill is reluctant to allow the inadequacies of the Argument from Paternalistic Distance to constitute an argument *for* paternalism. In *Principles*, his concern is with culture—with those commodities "which are chiefly useful as tending to raise the character of human beings." He allows that "any well-intentioned and tolerably civilized government may think, *without presumption*, that it does or might possess a degree of cultivation above the average of the community which it rules, and that it should therefore be capable of offering better education and better instruction to the people than the greater number of them would spontaneously demand." But he eschews any positive paternalism that this might appear to support. At best, a government may subsidize, with taxpayers' money, the continued *availability* of such character-raising enterprises. People should not be required to participate in them. Subsidization is justified because "a thing of which the public are bad judges may require to be shown to them and pressed upon their attention for a long time, and to prove its advantages by long experience, before they learn to appreciate it, yet they may learn at last; which they might never have done, if the thing had not been thus obtruded upon them in act, but only recommended in theory" (1848, pp. 947–48).

In *On Liberty*, the case for paternalistic intervention might seem to be stronger, for there it is not positive but negative paternalism that is at issue. It is not the imposition of some (partisan) positive conception of the good, but protection from "things which have been tried and condemned from the beginning of the world until now; things which experience has shown not to be useful or suitable to any person's individuality." In such cases, "it is merely desired to prevent generation after generation from falling over the same precipice which has been fatal to their predecessors" (1859, p. 281). This is a harder case, just because the failings not only contribute nothing to the advancement of individuality, but actually impede it. Nevertheless, Mill refuses to take the paternalistic way out. He argues that society has itself to blame if some of its number "grow up mere children, incapable of being acted upon by rational consideration of distant motives." The period of childhood provides ample opportunities for developing in such people a more prudent and rational outlook. "Society" has no business seeking to extend the powers that it has used so inefficiently (1859, p. 282).

Mill's argument here is not altogether convincing. "Society" may well have itself to blame for the personal deficiencies of its members, and it may consider itself duty-bound to improve the quality of early upbringing. But that doesn't settle the issue of what it should do with those who, for whatever reason, have grown up without a proper sense of their own welfare. Why shouldn't there go hand-in-hand with the implementation of a more adequate program of education, measures designed to protect the members of society from the worst consequences of their carelessness, imprudence, or stupidity? The answer to this question is to be found in Mill's other arguments against paternalism rather than the one under consideration.

THE ARGUMENT FROM THE DEVELOPMENTAL VALUE OF CHOICE

That we can sometimes know better than others what is good for them is not, for Mill, a strong enough reason for imposing on them. For, even if they do not make the best choices, there is a value in choosing that will be lost if others intervene to set them right. This is one reason why Mill will go so far as, though no further than, the subsidization of "cultural" activities. It is important that options be available, but it is also important that choices not be predetermined. The practice of choosing is itself a means to the development of individuality, independently of what is chosen. Paternalism, for all its benevolence, ultimately erodes the qualities that are distinctive of "character" (cf. 1859, pp. 264–65). What it seeks to preserve it also causes to decay.

This argument is at its strongest when directed at a generalized paternalism in which the intention is to ensure that all a person's decisions affecting his or her good are the best that they can be. Its force diminishes when the paternalism is strictly limited, designed to curb only self-destructive or severely damaging behavior, and then only by means that are not excessively intrusive.

We can push Mill's analogy with physical exercise a bit further than he was prepared to. If we do not exercise our muscles regularly they will lose their strength and tone, or even atrophy. But we can sometimes overdo the exercise or seek to undertake maneuvres that threaten to be permanently disabling. It can hardly be argued that the demands of fitness require that we be able to do these things, or that if they are not open to us our fitness will be lost. Likewise the exercise of our "mental and moral powers" does not require that every self-regarding possibility remain open to us.

True though the foregoing may be in theory, it is likely that at this point the antipaternalist will fall back on the Argument from Paternalistic Distance. Can we have any assurance that those who would intervene on our behalf are better placed than we are with respect to determining whether our decisions will cohere with our good? Here we need to remember that the good in question is neither reducible to nor as simply determinable as physical good, but must take account of that complex of goals, beliefs, attitudes, and so on that constitute a person's life-plans.

To some extent, the Arguments from Paternalistic Distance and the Developmental Value of Choice reinforce each other, though neither alone nor jointly are they sufficient to exclude all strong paternalism. Ultimately the weight must rest on the Argument from Oppression of Individuality, or its more Kantian version, the Argument from Disrespect for Persons.

I have focused attention on the foregoing arguments because they are grounded in the importance of freedom, and thus possess a generality lacking in other critiques of paternalism. Nevertheless, some of these other arguments have a part to play when specific kinds of paternalism are considered, and need to be accommodated if a case for paternalism is to have anything more than theoretical significance. Against legal paternalism, for example, it is often argued that the law will be brought into disrepute, that the corrupting tendencies of power will be accentuated, that valuable social resources will be diverted from more worthwhile ends, or that effective enforcement will cause disruption to unconnected activities. Some of these additional concerns will emerge more clearly in Part Two.

Of the three arguments considered, only the Argument from Oppression of Individuality presupposes autarchy. It is best seen, not as an argument for some bare freedom or general liberty of action, but as an argument for certain basic liberties, attaching to autarchic persons, and central to the requirements of individuality. The Arguments from Paternalistic Distance and the Developmental Value of Choice might equally be employed in respect of those not yet capable of rational choice, as a warning against careless benevolence or as a reminder of the merits of the dictum "Freedom begets freedom." Weak paternalistic impositions are not justified merely because their beneficiaries lack autarchy. As Mill makes clear, such impositions must be directed to the "improvement" of those on whom they are laid, and must be of a kind that "actually effect that end" (1859, p. 224). In the case of children, this must mean the development of those capacities that will enable them to make rational decisions of their own. It will not do to bring up a child as one might bring up a pet—treating it "kindly" but not developing its native capacities. In other words, the end of weak paternalism must be autarchy. The Arguments from Paternalistic Distance and the Developmental Value of Choice function to limit weak paternalistic impositions to those most conducive to autarchy and hence to the development of autonomy. Obviously this will hold only in those cases where autarchy/autonomy is possible. In the case of the very severely retarded, where this may not be a reasonable prospect, the claims of liberty are likely to be overshadowed by the claims of humanity—to avoid cruelty and minimize suffering.

Self- and Other-Regarding Conduct

The liberal critique of paternalism is grounded in an ideal of individuality or personal autonomy. It is by reference to this ideal that certain liberties are differentiated and defended. They secure against invasion what Mill speaks of as "that portion of a person's life and conduct which affects only himself, or if it also affects others, only with their free, voluntary and undeceived consent and participation" (1859, p. 225). But this distinction between "self-regarding" and "social" (or "other-regarding") conduct[6] troubles not only Mill, but also his commentators. Immediately after introducing it, Mill registers his own unease: "When I say only himself, I mean directly, and in the first instance: for whatever affects himself, may affect others through himself "(1859, p. 225), and a substantial part of Chapter 4 of On Liberty is taken up with the objection that it invites:

> How (it may be asked) can any part of the conduct of a member of society be a matter of indifference to the other members? No person is an entirely isolated being; it is impossible for a person to do anything seriously or permanently hurtful to himself, without mischief reaching at least to his near connexions, and often far beyond them (1859, p. 280).

In this chapter Mill concedes a good deal to his critic, but insists that his basic distinction still holds. But how well? Is it really possible to differentiate some conduct as self-regarding, and thus "out of bounds," or does what we do to ourselves so affect others that the question of intervention can always be raised?

The simplest way of making the self-/other-regarding distinction is to posit as self-regarding act-instances or act-kinds whose performance does not affect others in any way. Those falling within "the domain of inward consciousness, the thoughts and feelings" (Mill, 1848, p. 938) would seem to satisfy this requirement. But even if this is so, they hardly secure as much of a person's conduct from possible imposition as Mill is seeking by means of his distinction. So there is also included "as much of external conduct as is personal only, involving no consequence, none at least of a painful or injurious kind, to other people" (1848, p. 938). The point of the distinction, then, is not to separate out a realm of conduct having no causal impact at all on others, but at most to distinguish conduct in which certain kinds of effects on others are avoided—e.g., pain and injury. Even this, however, sanctions more extensive impositions than most liberals, including Mill, are willing to accommodate. For it appears to allow that if my life style is deeply upsetting to you, there exists a reason for your interfering with it. I may not flaunt my proclivities, but the fact that you know about them and my expression of them may be greatly disturbing to you. Bentham, it is true, does not seem to mind how pain is caused for it to figure in calculations about the wisdom of intervention (Bentham 1789, ch. 5; cf. Sartorius 1975, p. 161; Long 1977, pp. 106–8, 116–17; Ten 1980, ch. 2). He is prepared to take the risk that the costs of interference in such cases would be prohibitive. It is in virtue of this that penalties would be "unmeet." Mill, however, takes a much stronger stand: with "the personal tastes and self-regarding concerns" of individuals, the public has "no business" interfering (1859, p. 285), even though they may constitute "an outrage" to its feelings, be viewed with "unaffected disgust," or be found "really revolting" or "a scandal" (1859, pp. 283, 284, 285). "There is", he writes, "no parity between the feeling of a person for his own opinion, and the feeling of another who is offended at his holding it; no more than between the desire of a thief to take a purse, and the desire of the right owner to keep it" (1859, p. 283).

The distinction, then, is not simply between conduct that does or does not cause others pain, or even between conduct that does or does not cause others a lot of pain. We get a clue to its character when Mill distinguishes those acts that affect others "directly" and those in which they have only an "indirect interest" (1859, p. 225), or those that do and those that do not "affect" (he means affect prejudicially) others' "interests" or "injure" them. The point is partially obscured by an ambiguity in his use of "interest" and "injury." Here, to affect others' interests is not simply to thwart their desires but to infringe upon their legitimate concerns; to injure them is not merely to cause them some damage but to violate something to which they have a valid claim. It is to wrong them. We become answerable to others only when our conduct impairs their interests, "or rather certain interests, which, either by express legal provision or by tacit understanding, ought to be considered as rights" (1859, p. 276).

But this will not do either. For, as it now stands, the distinction is articulated in terms of the very considerations it is designed to determine. If conduct is self-regarding, then we are not answerable to others for it. But what constitutes it as self-regarding is not the absence of pain, distress, or damage to others, but the fact that no legitimate interests or rights are violated. Thus, rather than enabling us to tell whether a particular imposition would illegitimately invade another's domain, the self-/other-regarding distinction presupposes that that issue has already been settled. It provides us with no help in determining the limits of legitimate interference. Why is it that the distress that knowledge of my life style causes others does not constitute a legitimate ground for their interference, whereas the offense caused by my flaunting it in front of them, or the suffering caused by my attempts to impose it upon them, does constitute such a ground? It is not enough to say that if the former did constitute such a ground it would sanction massive and unacceptable invasions of freedom, for what we are trying to determine is what makes for an unacceptable invasion of freedom. It is all very well for Mill to say that there is "no parity between the desire of a thief to take a purse, and the desire of the right owner to keep it," for the question of rightful ownership has been predetermined. But does Mill have any ground for saying that "a person's taste is as much his own peculiar concern as his opinion or his purse"? Are we *entitled* to whatever tastes that we have? We cannot settle the matter of entitlement by saying that tastes are self-regarding, for we can determine their self-regarding character only by appealing to our entitlements. Mill is rightly concerned that we may become subject to massive encroachments on our freedom if *any* effects that our conduct may have on others can be taken into account in determining whether or not we should be permitted to continue in it. And he is rightly suspicious of the Benthamite belief that a utilitarian calculus will favor the person whose conduct distresses others only because they have knowledge of it and not because it is in some sense directed at them. But his attempt to circumscribe a type of conduct that does justice to the concern for individuality begs the very point at issue.

The same problem emerges even if we start from Mill's *terminus a quo*— the ideal of individuality, the full and harmonious development of our varied capacities. Liberty is essential to this development, and there is a case for maintaining that each individual ought to be permitted whatever liberty is necessary for its realization, consistent with a like liberty for others. Given this, it can be plausibly argued that if the suffering that mere knowledge of someone's life style causes is a ground for interfering with that life style, little room will be left for the development of individuality (cf. Hart 1963, pp. 46–47). Unless the individual is allowed a reasonably broad and clearly defined area within which to discover and exercise his or her capacities, the likelihood of individuality developing to any worthwhile extent will be extremely small. But where should the line be drawn?[7] It will not do to invoke the distinction between self- and other-regarding conduct, since that distinction presupposes rather than provides the criteria that we are seeking.

What is clear is that a line needs to be drawn somewhere. Might it be a line, not between kinds of conduct but between kinds of reasons for interference? Is the problem with paternalism not that it constitutes an imposition on self-regarding concerns, but that it is an imposition motivated by a concern for the other's good *as an end*? Does it involve one person's imposition on another for the other's good, without regard to that other's capacity to determine such matters for him- or herself? If that is so, paternalism may be seen as a denial of individuality—a refusal to acknowledge the conditions under which individuality is possible.

This way of positing the antipaternalist position does not require that we distinguish conduct into self- and other-regarding. It is enough that we can distinguish reasons for interfering with others into those that are directed to their good as an end and those that are directed to the good of third parties. This much might be inferred from Mill's later discussion.

In Chapter 4 of *On Liberty*, Mill considers the objection that, because "no man is an island," the self-/other-regarding distinction is bogus:

> If [a person] injures his property, he does harm to those who directly or indirectly derived support from it, and usually diminishes, by a greater or less amount the general resources of the community. If he deteriorates his bodily or mental faculties, he not only brings evil upon all who depended upon him for any portion of their happiness, but disqualifies himself from rendering the services which he owes to his fellow-creatures generally; perhaps becomes a burthen on their affection or benevolence; and if such conduct were very frequent, hardly any offence that is committed would detract more from the general sum of good. Finally, if by his vices or follies a person does no direct harm to others, he is nevertheless (it may be said) injurious by his example; and ought to be compelled to control himself, for the sake of those whom the sight or knowledge of his conduct might corrupt or mislead (1859, p. 280).

Mill's response is not to deny "that the mischief which a person does to himself may seriously affect, both through their sympathies and their interests, those nearly connected with him, and, in a minor degree, society at large" (1859, p. 281). But he distinguishes two kinds of effects—those which "violate a distinct and assignable obligation" to others, and those which do not. Where the former occur, "the case is taken out of the self-regarding class, and becomes amenable to moral disapprobation in the proper sense of the term" (1859, p. 281).[8] However, what the person is answerable for is not the self-regarding failing but the other-regarding one—not, say, extravagance, but the failure to provide for his or her family. In other words, the self-/other-regarding distinction does not require that we posit two quite separate kinds of conduct. Rather, so far as reasons for interfering with a person's conduct are concerned, only other-regarding failings may be taken into account.

This suggests that the "no man is an island" objection is irrelevant. Mill is not interested in securing certain act-instances or act-kinds against invasion, but only in morally discounting certain kinds of reasons for such invasions— e.g., concern for a person's good, as an end. However, this may not represent more than a Pyrrhic victory, unless it can be maintained that in a significant number of cases self-regarding failings are not also associated with significant other-regarding failings. It would be no great victory for freedom were the abandonment of paternalism not accompanied by an increase in liberty, on account of the other-regarding effects of self-regarding failings. True, interferences with freedom would not have the patronizing overtones so often associated with paternalism, but Mill and most liberals have believed that much more would follow. Liberals have not usually wanted to argue that each person's good is so importantly bound up with the good of others that efforts may justifiably be made to secure it for the latters' sake. But they cannot simply assume that this tight interwining does not exist.

This concern is prompted in part by Mill's own discussion, for he allows that we have not only negative but also positive duties to others:

> There are also many positive acts for the benefit of others, which [a person] may rightfully be compelled to perform; such as, to give evidence in a court of justice; to bear his fair share in the common defence, or in any other joint work necessary to the interest of the society of which he enjoys the protection; and to perform certain acts of individual beneficence, such as saving a fellow-creature's life, or interposing to protect the defenceless against ill-usage, things which, whenever it is obviously a man's duty to do, he may rightfully be made responsible to society for not doing (1859, pp. 224–25; cf. p. 276).

If Mill is right about this, it will have the effect of extending significantly the impact of self-regarding failings. Admittedly, he finds the extension troubling. He acknowledges that in such cases "a much more cautious exercise of compulsion" is required. Nevertheless, because he believes that we have a duty to prevent evil, and that we may cause evil to others not only by what we do but also by what we fail to do, he also believes that the case for recognizing such duties is a strong one.[9] But even if we can speculate that there are many self-regarding failings that will not breach other-regarding duties, we are still left with the problem of separating out merely self- from other-regarding failings in a nonquestion-begging way. Mill writes that "with regard to the merely contingent, or as it may be called, constructive injury which a person causes to society, by conduct which neither violates any specific duty to the public, nor occasions perceptible hurt to any assignable individual except himself; the inconvenience is one which society can afford to bear, for the sake of the greater good of human freedom" (1859, p. 282). The problem is: how are we to distinguish effects that violate an assignable obligation from those that do not? Why should the revulsion that others feel toward my life style be considered merely a "contingent" effect of my behavior?

The upshot of this discussion, then, is that the liberal critique of paternalism, particularly as it finds expression in Mill, does not depend on our being able to separate out two kinds of *conduct*—self-regarding and other-regarding. It is rather two kinds of *failings* that are to be distinguished, and only one of these, the other-regarding, is appropriately appealed to as a ground for interference. Cruelty of disposition, malice, dishonesty, insincerity, vindictiveness, selfishness, and lack of conscientiousness are "fit objects of moral reprobation, and, in grave cases, of moral retribution and punishment" (1859, p. 279). But imprudence, depraved taste, intemperance, extravagance, rashness, obstinacy, self-conceit, laziness, and cowardice, "to whatever pitch they may be carried, do not constitute wickedness" (1859, p. 279). This is not to deny that self-regarding failings may result in some actionable breach of duty or obligation to others. It is simply to maintain that when they do, it is because of the breach of obligation to others and not the self-regarding failing.

Mill's language here is not always helpful to his cause. It is clear enough from his account that other-regarding failings necessarily result in or threaten some injury to others. What is not so clear is whether he sees self-regarding failings as those that *do not necessarily* or *necessarily do not* result in or threaten injury to others. Mill seems to vacillate between the two. The former view is more plausible, but sits awkwardly with their characterization as "self-regarding". Taylor and Wolfram suggest that so-called self-regarding faults are better seen as failures to overcome the temptation or inclination not to do some action for whose performance there is believed to be some overriding reason (1968a). There is nothing especially "self-regarding" about them, for they can manifest themselves in one's relations with others no less than in relation to oneself. Indeed, as Taylor and Wolfram go on to suggest, what are often occasions for the display of other-regarding virtues are equally occasions for the display of self-regarding ones. This is because, associated with the demand for some other-regarding virtue to be exhibited, there will also be a temptation to do otherwise. Without the self-regarding virtues, there may not be much to show by way of other-regarding virtue. That being so, the appropriateness of interfering with "self-regarding" failings ought not to be ruled out too quickly.

If we want, therefore, to get to the heart of liberal antipathy to paternalism, we do better to consider not a distinction between kinds of conduct nor even a distinction between kinds of failings but rather the distinction between kinds of motivations for interference. It is the supposedly debasing character of imposing on others simply for their own good that puts it beyond the liberal pale. As an empirical point, liberals believe that it would make "a vast difference" not only in our attitudes to, but also in our dealings with each other, were such paternalistic concern not shown (Mill 1859, p. 279). They may be right about this, but to show it, more than an appeal to the distinction between self- and other-regarding conduct/failings is needed. Until we know how to determine which of our behavior's effects on others are to be accorded public significance, the distinction possesses little more than rhetorical value.

Notes

1. Even in the case of liberty of movement, there are serious complications (Feinberg 1980a, pp. 37–38).

2. This of course is not the only possibility. Another is to limit options by reference to conventional expectations—options valued by/in a particular society.

3. For a modern version, see Benn (1975–76; esp. pp. 117–22).

4. In *Law, Liberty and Morality*, Hart observes that "if we no longer sympathize with [Mill's protests against paternalism] this is due, in part, to a general decline in the belief that individuals know their own interests best, and an increased awareness of a great range of factors which diminish the significance to be attached to an apparently free choice or to consent" (1963, pp. 32–33). However, in *Principles of Political Economy*, Mill is less than confident about this. He observes that "the uncultivated cannot be competent judges of cultivation. Those who need to be made wiser and better, usually desire it least, and if they desired it, would be incapable of finding their way to it by their own light." He is similarly pessimistic where "an individual attempts to decide irrevocably now what will be best for his interest at some future and distant time. The presumption in favor of individual judgment is only legitimate, where the judgment is grounded on actual, and especially on present, personal experience; not where it is formed antecedently to experience, and not suffered to be reversed even after experience has condemned it" (1848, pp. 947f, 953).

5. In relation to the distinction between respect and worth, I have benefited greatly from discussions with Stanley Benn (see Benn 1981, p. 103).

6. The term "self-regarding", which Mill sometimes uses, is found in Bentham (1789, ch. 13), and it was no doubt from there that Mill derived it. He does not speak of "other-regarding" conduct, though he sometimes refers to it as "social." The popular description of conduct for which sanctions might be considered as "other-regarding", has its origins in J. F. Stephen's reference to "acts which regard others" (1874, p. 28). Mill had good reason not to contrast "self-regarding" with "other-regarding" conduct, for he was not attempting to divide *all* conduct into two classes, but to distinguish *all* self-regarding conduct from at most *some* "other-regarding" conduct, namely, that conduct in which others' *interests* were *deleteriously* affected.

7. In *Principles* Mill writes: "That there is, or ought to be, some space in human existence thus entrenched around, and sacred from authoritative intrusion, no one who professes the smallest regard to human freedom or dignity will call in question: the point to be determined is, where the limit should be placed; how large a province of human life this territory should include" (1848, p. 939).

8. Taylor and Wolfram (1968) argue that Mill's discussion of the self- and other-regarding failings is not wholly consistent, in that he oscillates between the position that self-regarding failings are necessarily noninjurious to others and that in which they may sometimes be injurious to others (in which case they are liable to be punished). See the discussion below on p. 36.

9. This causal thesis is controversial. I have defended it in Kleinig (1976, pp. 391–97), but see the subsequent reply by Mack (1980) and rejoinder by Harris (1981). There is still more to be said on this matter.

3

Approaches to Justification

Of the various objections to paternalism considered in the last chapter, the most powerful relates to what is regarded as its insulting, demeaning, or degrading character. By appearing to dismiss the capacity of an other to determine and choose for him- or herself what to do with his or her life, the paternalist undermines the other's individuality, effectively making him or her a means to ends of the paternalist's making, rather than being recognized as the source of his or her own ends.

Yet despite this powerful criticism, paternalism has not been without defenders, including some within the liberal tradition. Absolute opposition to all paternalism, even to all strong paternalism, is seen as a doctrinaire and uncompassionate overreaction, contrary to our humanitarian impulses and good sense. Paternalists, after all, are not generally or at least obviously out to advance their own interests, except in so far as they have the interests of others as one of their interests. And that would appear to be a morally commendable interest. Moreover, those toward whom they act paternalistically often seem petty, careless, silly, or stubborn in their preference for risky or nonbeneficial courses of action, allowing themselves to be actuated by reasons altogether insufficient for or unworthy of a rational being.

There is another factor that has contributed significantly to the attractiveness of what, within liberalism, tends to be seen as paternalism. This is the sense of connectedness between individuals. "None of us lives unto himself"; "No man is an island"; "Self and other exist in mutual interdependence"; and so on, are assertions that call into question the liberal dichotomy between the harm principle and the principle of paternalism. To the extent that recent liberal theory has moved in the direction of a greater communitarianism and communitarian doctrines of various kinds have engaged the modern imagination, what is condemned as paternalistic by some liberals is advocated by others as a proper recognition of our interdependence (cf. Green 1881).

In this chapter I will examine first those arguments that might be described as moving paternalism toward a new patriarchalism or, alternatively, toward subsuming it under the harm principle. Various consequentialist arguments for paternalism are then considered, followed by arguments that endeavour to give greater weight to the Argument from Oppression of Individuality (or

Disrespect for Persons). One argument, the Argument from Personal Integrity, I judge to provide a valid but not necessarily sufficient reason for strong paternalism, though clearly its force needs to be carefully circumscribed. Factors bearing on the latter are considered at the end of the chapter.

Arguments from Interconnectedness

There is a strand within liberalism in which the individual is regarded as an essentially asocial being, defined independently of social life, and entering into social relations only through choice. Such a position is very difficult, perhaps impossible to sustain (Provis 1975). We are inevitably social beings. We are born into an ongoing community, with its language, culture, and traditions, and our individuality can be understood and achieved only through participation in it. Most liberals have appreciated this, though there is considerable diversity in their understanding of how tightly and deeply these social interrelations are to be conceived. Are they sufficiently close to transform paternalism into patriarchalism or so loose that self-destructive activity will endanger little more than self-assumed obligations? Perhaps there is no general answer to this question. Communities vary in their degree of integration and fragility, and what at one place and time might represent a disastrous social loss could at another place and time be barely noticed—indeed, even be socially beneficial. Still, there is a point in looking at some of the possibilities, for they indicate the parameters within which Arguments from Interconnectedness must work.

Three general ways of conceiving the interconnectedness between individuals are here considered. First, and most radically, I examine the view that individuals are so deeply immersed in the community that their concerns are *ipso facto* community concerns. Second, and most minimally, I consider the possibility that the community has no more to offer than conditions for survival. And third, an intermediate position, in which the community is seen as the context for human flourishing, is explored.

THE SELF AS OTHER

According to one view, our self-realization is not constituted by some progressive differentiation from the society or community of which we are a part, but rather by our increasing immersion in its traditions and structures. It is not in some anomic individuality but in close community that we find ourselves and realize what our natures are capable of. On our own we are nothing. When embedded in the community's myriad ways, its complex conventions and fraternal relations, we become bearers of a personality—recognized and recognizing. Thus our good is not to be adjudged by reference to some individual nature of our own, but rather by reference to some generic nature whose individual characteristics are determined by their location within the ongoing demands of the community. On this view, self-destructive behavior that is not sanctioned by the transcendent purposes of the community does not constitute an act of merely self-regarding significance, but is first and foremost a violation of the community's prior claims. Our lives, therefore, are not our own to dispose of as we see fit, but differentiations from and subordinate to the community in which we live, move, and have our being.

Extreme though this position is, we ought not to overlook the truth that it contains. We are indeed creations of social relations. Our linguistic and social skills, our development as emotional, sensitive, and rational beings, our abilities as imaginative and forward-looking agents, owe much to the social environment in which we have been nurtured, and to some extent depend on its continuation for their maintenance and vitality. But this truth is not reducible to the view that only through subordination to the ideas and practices of our community can its and hence our interests be safeguarded and accommodated. No doubt some ways of looking at the world and the forms of behavior that follow from them are essential to social cohesion and thus to our own well-being. Most societies, moreover, embody cultural traditions that are able to stimulate creativity and individuality. But where this is so it is precisely because they do not demand subjection to the *status quo*. Nor are such traditions fixed, but progressive and adaptive. It is not so much diversity and change, but certain kinds of diversity and too rapid change that jeopardize social existence (cf. Hart 1967; Feinberg 1981).

Beyond what I have called our generic nature, those capacities for development that link us with other human beings, we also have individual talents, aptitudes, and temperaments, and it is an important function of community life to call forth and develop those individual characteristics, within the framework provided by our more general human nature. To do this, a relatively stable social life is necessary, but if it is too rigid, too enclosing, it will stifle those individual tendencies and abilities that are important to our particular identity—our individuality. Individuality ought not to be conceived of individualistically, but neither can it flourish in a closed community. It is not as we become bearers of community roles, but as we conceive and fulfill goals and roles of our own that we establish our individual identities.

Though we may be deeply indebted to social traditions and structures for a framework and the resources in terms of which we can develop into individual selves, there is nevertheless more to individuality than determination by a social milieu. Where the self is no more than a reflection of some social environment, it possesses no identity, no individuality of its own. Only as it comes to express determinations of its own, a prerequisite for which is liberty, can self-realization, so seriously misconceived by this radical position, be achieved. Individual good, though not unconnected with social good, cannot be resolved into it.

OTHERS AS NECESSARY TO SURVIVAL

Toward the other end of this spectrum of interconnectedness, there is an argument based on the recognition that survival is not a solitary but a social venture (cf. Turnbull 1973). Production and reproduction are necessary to human survival, and these are effectively accomplished only where there is cooperation and mutual aid. Further, there are many whose continued survival, or at least protection from serious harm, is dependent on the positive contributions of others. Infants, those who are severely retarded or badly injured, and certain others will not find it possible to survive unless they are aided in some way. This aid may not be forthcoming where those who might have rendered it have foolishly disabled themselves. From this it might be argued that people have an enforceable duty to ensure that they remain capable of contributing where the survival needs of others demand it.

But as an argument for "paternalism" this has more than its share of problems. There is, first of all, the difficult question of a duty to aid. Some relations carry with them a responsibility to ensure that others come to no harm or at least are rendered assistance where harm has already been caused. Parent-child, doctor-patient, carrier-passenger relationships have traditionally had this character: if, in the course of his or her duty the parent, doctor, or carrier acts in such a way that he or she is incapable of rendering needed aid, he or she may be held liable. This, however, is far from a general argument for requiring that people look after themselves. Once we move beyond duties to aid based on role responsibilities, they become much more difficult to establish. I happen to think that we do have such duties—of a limited kind—even to strangers, and that they can be enforced (Kleinig 1976; cf. Weinrib 1980). But even if the case for an enforceable duty to aid can be made out, it is a further, bigger step to require that people maintain themselves in such a way that they are able to give aid when it is needed. Even those who have role responsibilities cannot straightforwardly be regarded as having a duty to ensure their well-being when they are off-duty. Again, I do not want to insist that no duty to ensure our capacity to render aid when it is needed exists, only that the problems encountered in establishing it are considerable. There is a somewhat better case for claiming a general social (as distinct from individual) duty to ensure that the needy are attended to and that the social resources for this not be allowed to become too depleted. But a social duty of this kind can be met without individuals being required to maintain their capacity to render aid.

OTHERS AS NECESSARY FOR FLOURISHING

The value that we place on survival is largely instrumental. Survival is a precondition for the development and expression of those purposes and goals, those qualities of life and personality, that characterize a distinctively human existence. Achievement of the latter is not guaranteed by survival. It is no natural outcome of biological maturational processes, but arises through the interplay of the individual with his or her social environment. Human flourishing is not like that of a tree, genetically determined, needing only heat, light, moisture, and nutrients as catalysts for the unfolding of its potentiality. Human flourishing is, to a significant extent, learned. Not only does the individual person come to have a sense of him- or herself as an "I" through a process of comparison and contrast with other "thous," but also the particular "I" he or she becomes depends significantly on the relational and other resources of the society of "thous" in which his or her development takes place (cf. Wood 1972, ch. 2). This is the context in which the harm principle is to be understood. When others violate our rights or impair our welfare interests, they interfere with the development or expression of our capacities, capacities requisite to our identity as objects of respect and worth.

The question to be considered here is an extension of this: Do we have a sufficiently transparent and important interest in others' development that a ground for imposing on them would exist were they to jeopardize that development? At first blush, this is an outlandish question, since an affirmative answer would presage something like Johann Peter Frank's *A System of Complete Medical Police* (1777–1817; cf. Baumgartner and Ramsey 1933). But it does help us to focus on an important facet of later liberal thought, present in Mill, but even more evident in writers such as Green and Dewey (cf. Struhl

1976; Gaus 1983: chs. 2–3). This is the extent to which the flourishing of one individual may be instrumental to the flourishing of others. We can isolate five respects in which this is so.

Others as Inspiration. Once a certain level of personal development has been reached—what we have referred to as autarchy—we can oversee our own further growth in individuality. Even so, it is through observation of or interaction with others that this is best accomplished. Their example may inspire us or enable us to discover similar capacities in ourselves. Their criticism and encouragement may provoke us and their perceptiveness and concern may stimulate us to reassess our goals, projects, and priorities. Their inspiration may be individual or come through their participation in various collective enterprises—universities, orchestras, teams, etc. Mill's support for the public subsidization of cultural activities may be seen in this light. Recognizing that the popular taste is more easily satisfied by pushpin than by poetry, and that were a *laissez-faire* approach to be taken, poetry would vanish from the marketplace, Mill suggests that some taxation revenues be used to keep before the public eye those artistic and cultural activities that will be elevating to the character (1848, pp. 947–48).

Just as we may be inspired by others, we may also be depressed and demoralized by them; they may cause us to stagnate or wilt. Their degraded life style, the impoverished character of their collective activity, may infect all who come within its ambit. T. H. Green is clearly disturbed by this phenomenon when considering the proliferation of drink shops in working class areas (1881, pp. 69–71). The social ethos caused by habitual drunkenness he believes to be so dispiriting and suffocating that measures to ban such shops would be justified, at least until there should come about a rekindling of the spirit of independence, self-reliance, and self-respect. It is doubtful whether Green views such interventions as paternalistic in any strong sense. Their purpose is, as Bosanquet was later to put it, to be a "hindrance of hindrances" to freedom—a removal of barriers to people's capacity to make the best of themselves (Bosanquet 1899, pp. 177–87).

Others as Partners. Among the various social activities that may contribute to our flourishing are what Stanley Benn calls transcendent collective enterprises (Benn 1982, p. 47f), in which some valued endeavour can be realized only through collective activity grounded in common concern. Among his suggested examples are orchestras, scientific research institutes, religious orders, and revolutionary parties. Participation in such collective activities may constitute a source of stimulation and fulfillment, an incentive to the development of our powers, but their success depends on the cooperative, collaborative involvement of others. This includes the quality of their individual performances. If the first violin is outstanding or the second horn plays off-key, this will have a marked effect on the musicality of the outcome. What can be achieved will also depend on the availability of resources. If no cellists are available, or if the only cellist is an alcoholic, this will also limit the capacity of the orchestra. To the extent, then, that we have an interest in the sorts of endeavours that can be pursued only through participation in a transcendent collective enterprise, we also have an interest in the flourishing of other parties or likely parties to that enterprise. If they needlessly jeopardize or neglect their talent, they also hamper others in the pursuit of their joint goals. In some cases, of course, the effect of ruination will be miniscule.

Where there is a reasonable abundance of skill or talent, the loss of one participant can easily be made up; but where a particular talent is in short supply, the effect could be quite substantial.

Others as Instruments. Though we may have a certain admiration for Robinson Crusoe, most of us would not find the life to which he had to adjust himself a particularly desirable one. Too many of the pursuits through which we can express and extend our creative, affective, and intellectual powers would be rendered inaccessible to us. Most of us, in order to pursue our interests, need to avail ourselves of the services of others—whether it is to grow and process our food, build and service various communication channels, or to provide the resources required to satisfy those interests.

Sometimes, of course, our dependence on others is contractualized, and where this is so we have some claim against them should they fail us; on other occasions, the dependence is less obvious and less explicit. Nevertheless, even on these occasions we often have an interest in the flourishing of others, so that we can make use of their achievements.

Others as Alter Egos. We develop a conception of ourselves as persons through membership in a human community. Therein we learn not only to differentiate ourselves from others, to see ourselves as distinct centers of consciousness and possibilities, but also to identify with others, to see them as centers of consciousness and possibilities like ourselves. Through identification we come to feel a certain sympathy for and with others, so that their flourishing becomes a source of joy to us, and their sufferings a source of pain. Though those feelings of sympathetic identification are likely to be strongest where others suffer through no fault of their own, even where imprudence has caused their downfall, we may feel a keen sense of loss. Our identification with them as fellows, capable of a similar kind of feeling, capable of both flourishing and withering, gives us an interest in the former, a satisfaction in their highest and most harmonious development.

Others as Completion. There is no reason to think that for each of us there is only one desirable pattern of development. We are, for the most part, overdetermined with respect to our varied capacities and will be able to develop only some of them to their limits. The constraints of time and circumstance will ensure that there are talents and aptitudes that remain only partially developed, or not developed at all. The time, effort, and resources required to develop some capacities may rule out the full development of others.

Later and contemporary liberals have seen this surfeit of and competition between capacities as a potential source of frustration. It may be alleviated to some extent by the encouragement of broad and open capacities. But more importantly, they have seen in the development of others' excellences a source of vicarious satisfaction—a completion of our own incompleteness. Rawls makes the point as follows:

> Human beings have various talents and abilities the totality of which is unrealizable by any one person or group of persons. Thus we not only benefit from the complementary nature of our developed inclinations, but we take pleasure in another's activities. It is as if others were bringing forth a part of ourselves that we have not been able to cultivate. We

have had to devote ourselves to other things, to only a small part of what we might have done (1971, p. 448).

Given, then, that through the development of others' talents, our own lack of opportunity can to some extent be made up, the dissipation or neglect of those talents by others may make us more vulnerable to the frustration prompted by our own incompleteness.

It is clear from the foregoing that there are several respects in which we have an interest in the flourishing of others and can lose out if by virtue of their choices, whether deliberately willed or the consequence of negligence, they harm themselves or fail to develop their capacities as they might. Then is there not a case for ensuring that others do not put their good at risk—based not on strict paternalistic grounds, but on other-regarding considerations? Liberals, particularly those from Mill and Green on, have been aware of the interconnections that I have been outlining; despite this, however, they have been very reluctant to see them as an argument for strong "paternalism." Only in farily limited cases have they been prepared to countenance impositions. It is important to see why this is so. At least three factors seem to be involved.

First, the connection between self-regarding failure and other-regarding detriment is not straightforward, except in certain limited cases. Where that is so there may well be a ground for intervention, but this does not constitute a reason for some general requirement to look after and develop our potential. If Fred drinks himself into oblivion, that is a great pity. There is much that he could have contributed to the world, much that I had hoped for and would have gained from him. But there is still Gilbert, Henrietta, and Ivan, and the world is not too diminished by Fred's self-destructive behavior. The situation changes somewhat if Gilbert, Henrietta, and Ivan also become inebriates, for what we now have on our hands is not merely a personal tragedy but a social problem. What in isolation may cause barely a ripple on the surface of society, can be disruptive and costly if it occurs with great frequency. True, more may be required if intervention is to be justified, but the question can at least be raised when a certain level of self-destruction or disablement is reached. That such a level has been reached is sometimes argued by proponents of seat belt and safety helmet legislation (see below, pp. 94–95).

Secondly, despite the difficulties it involves, it is necessary to distinguish between the failure to receive a benefit and being harmed. There are many things that could contribute to our flourishing but that, if we do not obtain them, constitute no harm. Generally, where others fail to ensure their own flourishing, we lose out on a benefit rather than suffer harm. Except where those who stand to benefit are, like children, unable to improve themselves, there is at best a weak case for seeing the benefiting of others as an enforceable duty. To argue otherwise is to underrate the claims of individuality. The case is improved if others are harmed as a result of some self-regarding failing, though, as we have already noted, the causal impact of failure is disputable.

Finally, and most importantly, there is a serious misunderstanding involved in seeking to enforce flourishing. For the flourishing with which we are concerned, and that inspires or completes us, must be a voluntary achievement. It is because what others accomplish is their own creation that it has worth and exemplary value. Those who seek to compel improvement in the name of social good no doubt benefit some social enterprises; but they evacuate them of the human worth that constitutes their *telos*. "Mechanical virtues" are virtues only in name.

But even here something may be said for a more modest claim—viz., that impositions be directed, not to "ensuring" that people flourish, but to keeping them from choices that would make their flourishing impossible. This was part of T. H. Green's concern. Curbing the sale of liquor in working class areas was not intended to force on that class a set of values alien to them nor to force their individual natures into some uniform or preconceived mold, but to keep them from an influence that was sapping "the spirit of self-reliance and independence," dissipating their "moral energies," and disabling them from developing and exercising their native faculties and talents. There was, of course, more to Green's argument than this, in particular the disadvantageous "bargaining" position of working class people and the exploitation of this by liquor sellers, and this no doubt plays an important part in his reasoning. Nevertheless, the incapacitating consequences of drunkenness, their frequency, and the social effects of this, also figure significantly in his case. His solution may be dated, but the issue remains (cf. White 1972; Popham Schmidt, and de Lint 1976).

In sum, the various Arguments from Interconnectedness have at best a limited validity, carrying some weight in contexts where an assignable duty to others can be established, but otherwise coming into contention only where self-regarding failure occurs on a large scale. It is not surprising that liberal writers have been able to acknowledge the importance of such interconnections while remaining generally suspicious of "paternalism."

The Argument from Future Selves

We have already had occasion to observe that some liberals are troubled by the consequences of an antipaternalistic position. Were the choices people make always their best choices, the product of settled preferences and cool reflection on alternatives, it would be difficult to justify the intrusions of others. But they are often stupid and ill-considered, the outcome of temporary concerns or a lackadaisical attitude. What is stubbornly insisted upon today is regretted tomorrow: "If only I had listened . . . "

A way out of this dilemma has been suggested by the work of Derek Parfit (1971; 1973; 1976). His proposals for a rethinking of our notion of personal identity allow for apparently paternalistic impositions to be subsumed under the harm principle, or at least so several writers have thought (Regan 1974; 1983; Kogan 1976; cf. Goodin 1979 for a different use of Parfit's thesis). Parfit takes as his point of departure puzzles that arise if personal identity is seen as an all-or-nothing matter, something independent of certain (bodily and) psychological continuities, the latter being matters of degree. This "Simple View" generates paradoxes when the hypothetical cases of fusion and fission of individuals are considered. As an alternative, he proposes a "Complex View," according to which personal identity consists in (bodily and) psychological continuities of an appropriate kind, and is therefore to be viewed as a matter of degree. When considering the moral relevance of this shift he sets aside bodily continuity as morally unimportant and distinguishes the two kinds of psychological "continuity." The first of these does not admit of degrees: Albert in 1980 is psychologically continuous with Albert in 1950, though not with Alberta. This is a matter of survival. The second, which

Parfit speaks of as "connectedness," is a matter of degree: the psychological make-up of Albert in 1980 is not closely connected with that of Albert in 1950. On the Complex View, we have reason to say that Albert in 1980 is a later self of Albert in 1950. The shift is not morally neutral. It would, Parfit suggests, help to explain why we are less inclined to punish people for offenses committed many years before, where there has been a substantial change of character. To do so would be tantamount to punishing a later self for the offenses of an earlier self.

Why should we accept Parfit's account? For Parfit, it provides a solution to certain philosophers' puzzles—those generated by the possibility of fusion and fission. Regan is more impressed by the way the Complex View handles the "old offense" case, and offers a justification for limited "paternalism." But its attractiveness depends substantially on the unavailability of alternative accounts and the absence of unacceptable consequences. And in these respects it leaves much to be desired. For example, our reluctance to punish someone for an old offense is not because "the criminal is no longer accessible to us," but more plausibly because, in our treatment of people, a change in character is a morally relevant factor.[1] It constitutes a ground for mercy or forgiveness, in which desert and hence continuity of identity is presupposed. As to unacceptable consequences, Bernard Williams has persuasively argued that the Complex View, if taken seriously, undermines the whole practice of promise keeping, including its legal expression in contract (Williams 1976, p. 203).

To spell out these points in more detail, let us look at the application made to "paternalism." It is not implausible to predict that a person who, prior to an accident, is careless about wearing a safety helmet, is likely to undergo significant psychological changes as a result, and that among those changes will be a disposition to be more careful about his or her welfare. A proponent of the Complex View may argue that there will come into being a later self, one that has been injured by the actions of an earlier self. Regan does not demand as much as Parfit and Kogan before he is prepared to indulge in talk of earlier and later selves. Whereas the latter writers seem to envisage a substantial and wide-ranging disconnectedness as the basis for saying that another self has come into being, Regan allows that someone may be a later self in some respects but not in others. Take a person, who, at the time of embezzling money, also commits an unrelated aggravated assault. Ten years later, he is no longer disposed to embezzle, but still has no control over a volatile temper. "In such a case, I think we might hold it inappropriate to punish the embezzler now for his embezzlement, but appropriate to punish him for the assault" (Regan 1974, p. 205; cf. 1983). But this leaves Regan in a very curious position. For, by virtue of their occupancy of the same body, what is done by way of punishment to oneself will also affect the "innocent" other. Maybe Regan could reply that this is not too different from the case in which a criminal's family suffers when he or she is punished, something to be regretted, and maybe taken into account, but not allowed to weigh too heavily. However, a criminal's family has a rather better chance of escaping the consequences of his or her behavior than does the later self from the earlier self. More importantly, we need not follow Regan in making sense of the idea that punishment is appropriate for one offense, but not for the other. It is less paradoxical to maintain that although the criminal is deserving of punishment for both offenses, he or she has changed in certain relevant respects, and that in respect of one of the offenses it would be morally legitimate (or called for) to show mercy. Desert is, after all, just one, albeit important, consideration to be taken into account in deciding whether or not to punish a person.

Proponents of the Argument from Future Selves claim that it justifies just those "paternalistic" impositions for which we are likely to have an intuitive attraction—e.g., the compulsory wearing of safety helmets. Because of the seriousness of the damage that an accident is likely to cause, we can predict with reasonable certainty that those who ride without helmets would change their minds were they to become involved in an accident. Kogan cites evidence for a much more comprehensive personality change. This being so, it is argued, we owe it to the future person not to do him or her any reasonably avoidable harm. There is a certain counterintuitiveness about this conclusion. It suggests, for example, that if we were reasonably sure that the consequences of an accident involving a nonhelmeted rider would be death or a permanently comatose state, interference would not be justified. But those who are attracted toward mandatory helmet laws are usually just as concerned about senseless deaths as they are about injured future selves (cf. Ten 1980, pp. 121–22).[2]

To add to the problems of this position, we need to be reasonably confident that the person *will* be involved in an accident if a helmet is not worn. It is all very well to say that *if* a person who doesn't wear a helmet gets caught in an accident *and* survives in a self-conscious state *and* undergoes the relevant kinds of personality changes, he or she will be harming some future self which the accident has brought into being. But if only 10 percent of those who ride without helmets fall into this category, are we justified in preventing the other 90 percent from continuing as they are? Regan prescinds from this question by insisting that he is talking only from the point of view of an "ideal paternalist" who knows that the cyclist will be injured and also relevantly changed by the experience, but in view of the practical conclusions he wants to draw (to confirm "our" intuitions about the justifiability of mandatory helmet legislation), such a disclaimer is hardly in place. There is a further point. Regan appears to premise his argument on the effects of an accident on a nonhelmeted rider. There the trauma can be expected to bring about appropriate personality changes. But if his argument is not to generate further paradoxes, he needs to assume that those who are required to wear helmets will also change with respect to their concern for personal safety. Otherwise, who is it that is being protected from injury? No actual person, but only a hypothetical one, one who might have been brought into being had a helmet not been worn.

What is perhaps most puzzling about the Argument from Future Selves is why we should be attracted to the view of personal identity that underlies it. In Parfit's case, at least, we can see how it might accommodate certain philosophers' puzzle cases, though how seriously we are supposed to treat these possibilities, or what conclusions we are supposed to draw from them, is not at all obvious (see, on contrived examples, Goodin 1982, pp. 8–12). But in Regan and Kogan's case, the only purpose in accepting the Complex View seems to be that it offers us a possible way of accommodating restrictions on some "ultra-risky" actions. It suffers from a certain ad hocery, especially in view of the counterintuitiveness of some of its extensions. Parfit, it is true, tries to show how the Simple and Complex Views might support different moral conclusions on some issues, the balance being in favor of the Complex View; but, as we have briefly noted, the balance has been artificially rigged, since the moral intuitions in question can be supported without the Simple

View being abandoned. Of course, it may be, as Parfit suggests, that the Complex View fits in better with a fairly radical utilitarianism, but this constitutes a plus only if there is some reason to accept that form of utilitarianism. And this can be doubted.[3] The Complex View may help to explain such a position, but this is not to justify it. Fascinating though the speculative possibilities of the Complex View may be, it is hardly secure enough to support the kinds of practices it is intended to.

Consequentialist Arguments for Paternalism

It is probably no accident that liberalism has been closely associated with consequentialism. The Enlightenment belief in and commitment to progress sat more comfortably with "forward-looking" theories of ethics and politics than traditionalist and natural law theories, and, for some writers at least, utilitarianism, when cashed out in terms of pleasure and pain, harmonized with the demands of a dominant empiricism. But there are many varieties of consequentialism, some monistic, others pluralistic, some clearly distinguishable from deontological theories, others not obviously so. Not surprisingly, they show some variation in the standing given to freedom, and hence to paternalism. Several variants repay attention.

THE ARGUMENT FROM THE INSTRUMENTALITY OF FREEDOM

According to one version of the Argument from Paternalistic Distance (pp. 28–30, above), there is some ultimate value (or set of values) that is likely to be realized more effectively and fully if individuals are permitted to order their own lives as they see fit, without interference by others. Maximum plausibility is given to this position if the ultimate value or end is some "mental state," such as the satisfaction of desire, or, on certain accounts, pleasure or happiness. In such cases, we can presume that the person concerned will have a greater commitment to the realization of this end than others and, moreover, will be in a privileged position with respect to the choices most conducive to it. The rebuttable nature of this presumption provides the room needed for the Argument from the Instrumentality of Freedom.

Despite the interest that people have in their well-being, there is ample evidence that they are often poor judges of it. Some of the reasons for this stem from a lack of motivation—the failure to keep long-term goals and remote effects consistently before their eyes; some stem from defects in knowledge or rationality—an inadequate appreciation of subtleties, hasty and ill-considered inferences, culpable ignorance, and so forth. For all the talk of our being "rational animals," we show a disturbing capacity for irrationality, which, though under our control, is not removed simply by correction (Stich 1983). It is not that such claims about our irrationality are especially controversial, for they are not. It is rather that, individually, we do not make very good use of the powers that we have. The value of wearing a seat belt when traveling in a car is clear when the statistics are considered, yet a large proportion of drivers and travelers neglect to avail themselves of them, unless compelled to do so. "Belt-up" campaigns have been remarkably ineffective in producing long-term changes to habits, even where people are persuaded of the value of belts. There is always a tendency to rationalize, to make an exception of oneself, without there being any good reason for doing so.

It is not too difficult to spell out cases of this kind, and where we can do so, there would seem to be strong consequentialist grounds for limiting liberty. True, we would need to take into account the disutility of coercive measures, though on the other side there would be the misery avoided and most probably the gratitude of those whose lives had been saved from serious injury or loss as a result.

An argument of this kind is likely to attract two kinds of replies. The first kind of reply is that the calculation of utilities is arguably much more complex and uncertain that I have made it appear. This kind of response is outlined and criticized by Rolf Sartorius (1975, ch. 8). Defending Mill against the simple criticism that a utilitarian defence of liberty can hardly justify total opposition to paternalism, Sartorius suggests that Mill is to be understood as being absolutely opposed only to paternalistic *legislation*. In individual cases, paternalistic interference might indeed maximize utility, but this cannot be concluded so far as paternalistic laws are concerned, because of the problems involved in providing and applying criteria for identifying those classes of behavior in which the benefits of intervention would outweigh the evils.

We might reasonably question Sartorius's interpretation of Mill. Although he is correct to see that translating what is permissible at an individual level into public policy complicates the utilitarian picture, we have no reason to think that Mill was utilizing this when opposing paternalism. His opposition is much more general. Moreover, as Sartorius himself goes on to argue, it would still amount to no more than a strong presumptive argument against paternalistic legislation. Legislators ought to be extremely cautious about introducing such legislation; even so, occasions for it may be indicated:

> There are instances in which it is empirically demonstrable that people will act against their own interests if not coerced into acting otherwise; thus statutes making compulsory the wearing of protective helmets by motorcycle-riders, and others prohibiting swimming after dark at un-guarded beaches. Where identifiable classes of individuals can be shown to be likely to manifest choice behavior inconsistent with their preferences as those preferences can be unproblematically attributed to them, the odds may change in favor of interfering with their personal liberty, if necessary, in order to protect them against themselves. Mill's principle can and should be modified accordingly (Sartorius 1975, p. 157).

In making this rejoinder, Sartorius appears to slide from a "mental state" to an "ideal" utilitarian position, for he points out that the paternalistic imposition must be in line with individuals' preferences "as those preferences can be unproblematically attributed to them." How can this be if coercion is required? We shouldn't need to be coerced into acting on our preferences! Two responses might be suggested. First, we could distinguish, with Sartorius, between stable preferences and choice behavior, or, perhaps, between settled and temporary or passing preferences. Second, we could identify certain "objective" interests as essential to the execution of preferences, whatever those preferences may be (Foot 1958–59). Though neither of these moves would be unproblematic, they provide an explanation of how, on "mental state" utilitarian grounds, it might be possible to justify a limited measure of paternalism. Where the utilitarianism is of an "ideal" kind, the epistemological difficulties may not appear so pressing, for the claim to a privileged access to one's good is not so easily sustained.

The second kind of reply to this consequentialist argument for paternalism takes up and questions the assumption that freedom is simply an instrumental value. Freedom, it may be claimed, is not merely a means to the satisfaction of our preferences, but is itself a source of satisfaction—a major one at that (cf. Sartorius 1975, p. 152). Paternalistic interferences therefore, even if they help to achieve some of the ends to which freedom is normally a means, will nevertheless frustrate one important end, freedom of choice.

But, as stated, this does not pose an insuperable problem for the consequentialist case. For, though the abrogation of freedom can represent a real loss, it may be counterbalanced by satisfactions not otherwise securable. Should it be claimed that the freedom to choose is one of our most important sources of satisfaction, perhaps even the most important, this may still not be decisive in cases where the freedom lost is small and the other ends secured are substantial. After all, it is not as though the person who is paternalistically imposed upon loses all freedom. The only freedom lost would be that which would have led to the closing off of other important sources of satisfaction.

The contours of this instrumental account of freedom and the space it provides for a limited measure of paternalism can be appreciated more easily by reference to Joel Feinberg's discussion of liberty as an *interest* (1980a, pp. 30–44, esp. 40ff.) Three kinds or levels of interest are distinguished. First and foremost is a welfare interest in freedom, an interest in that level of liberty necessary to sustain personal life. Unless we are permitted a certain freedom with respect to our thoughts, tastes, and choices, we will not be able to express those characteristics that distinguish genuinely human life, nor be able to relate to each other in a truly personal way. Like the inhabitants of *Brave New World*, we will be "programed" to respond, think, and act in certain ways, devoid of creative and self-critical capacities, incapable of taking real responsibility for what we do, whether as achievement or failure—beyond praise and blame. We might, of course, like robots, be able to accomplish valuable tasks but, also like robots, credit would lie with the programmer rather than its executor. And we might, like the inhabitants of *Brave New World*, be susceptible to feelings of pleasure and pain, but the "happiness" or "unhappiness" associated with such capacities would not be recognizably human. We identify with John the Savage rather than the Director, or, in more Millian terms, with Socrates dissatisfied rather than the pig satisfied. Understood as a welfare interest, liberty is clearly of enormous instrumental value, and encroachments on it will be exceedingly difficult, if not impossible, to justify. Enforced slavery of a very limiting kind, the sort of possibilities for genetic and social manipulation speculated on in *Brave New World*, and the omnipresent monitoring, coerciveness, and reconstructive character of Newspeak in Orwell's *Nineteen Eighty-Four* are meant to illustrate the effects of the welfare interest in freedom denied.

But it is not obvious that all strong paternalism would amount to a denial of our welfare interest in liberty. If paternalistic interventions are limited to negating only those choices that would severely limit or destroy our capacity to make rational choices, a case based on our welfare interest in liberty, though strong, would not be compelling.

The interest in liberty is not confined to our welfare needs. Feinberg distinguishes two further interests, a security and an accumulative interest, that extend beyond the minimum threshold required to satisfy our welfare interest.

Many of us believe it important, once we have developed our capacities and established an identity and life-plan, to be able nevertheless to accommodate unexpected contingencies or even changes of interest. Life is not so secure that, once we have set ourselves on a particular course, it will not be interrupted or diverted; moreover, with the progress, development, and unfolding of our capacities and perhaps the discovery of new talents, we may find that the course upon which we originally embarked, or the persons we at one time believed ourselves to be, will change in significant ways. We will want the freedom to respond productively to such contingencies. Unlike our welfare interest in freedom, this security interest may never be resorted to. It may be like money put aside for the rainy day that never comes. Nevertheless, as Feinberg observes, it is of some importance to us that it is there and known to be there. Life is much too unpredictable to dispense with it, and even if it were, happily, more predictable in certain respects, we would still not want to 'lock ourselves into' routines and pursuits that allowed for no shifts of interest or developments of talent.

But for all that, the security interest in liberty is not of such centrality that it would be unreasonable to sacrifice at least some part of it to other interests. If Arthur's security interest in freedom (represented, let us say, by the $50,000 he has saved) is all but expropriated in order that he may undergo a life-saving operation that will enable him to continue in the occupations in which he is presently engaged, he has not been too badly done by. Considered as a security interest, his liberty was not likely to be so important as to make such a trade-off unreasonable.

Unlike the welfare and security interests in liberty, the accumulative interest is noninstrumental. It involves a desire for liberty as an end, liberty for its own sake. Like Jonathan Livingston Seagull, one may get a sense of uplift, of euphoric exultation, from the contemplation of one's liberty, an urge to preserve and expand it, as a precious and self-sustaining pursuit.

The accumulative interest in freedom has some claim to our recognition, but its claims are markedly weaker than those of the welfare and security interests. Certainly a person could become so engrossed in the enterprise of expanding his or her options that the accumulation of options came to assume the character of a welfare interest, but this would not seem to be typical. Most of us can do with fewer options than we presently have without being substantially affected. We value our liberty but do not feel we have to cling to every bit of it. If some of our options are foregone to improve our health or safety, the balance may well lie in favor of health or safety. Of course, matters are never quite as simple as this, but in general terms at least, there would seem to be less against paternalism where the interest in liberty is an accumulative one.

The two replies so far considered do not exhaust those available to us. But before we look at a more substantial objection to the consequentialist case for paternalism, it will be useful to consider a further consequentialist strategy.

ARGUMENTS FROM FREEDOM ENHANCEMENT

There are weak and strong versions of this argument. The weak version, which I shall call the Argument from Freedom Promotion, presupposes some defect in capacity or situation on the part of those who are interfered with and attempts to justify paternalism as a means of remedying that defect or situation, so that they can become responsible choosers. It is, in essence, an argument for weak paternalism. The strong version, which I shall call the Argument from Freedom Protection, acknowledges that those for whom it is intended may be autarchic, but attempts to justify paternalism as means whereby that autarchy, or perhaps only liberty, may be preserved.[4]

What gives these arguments their special attractiveness is their attempt to come to terms with the privileged position of freedom within liberalism. Other consequentialist arguments, like those previously considered, risk sacrificing freedom to some other value—pleasure, happiness, or whatever. The Arguments from Freedom Enhancement, however, claim that it is only for the sake of freedom that freedom can be constrained.

The Argument from Freedom Promotion. When Mill enunciates his principle of liberty, he excludes children and "barbarians" from its purview. To such as these, "liberty, as a principle, has no application." They lack the competence to improve themselves "by free and equal discussion," and paternalistic interferences may be justified so long as they are effectually directed to rectifying that lack. Behind this allowance of weak paternalism there is Mill's ideal of individuality, a desire to develop the individual's capacity "to use and interpret experience in his own way" (Mill 1859, p. 262), so that he may progressively and coherently develop his various powers.

The limit to such weak paternalism is reached with the achievement of autarchy (cf. D'Agostino 1982). Once autarchy (the capacity for "spontaneous progress") has been reached, paternalistic interference must cease, even though this falls short of individuality. Autarchy is essential to autonomy, and the use of paternalistic power beyond the point necessary to produce or restore autarchy will subvert the end of individuality.

However, determining criteria for autarchy is no simple matter, as is clear from the "antipsychiatry" debate. Judgments of competence cannot be detached completely from cultural expectations, and there is a tendency to read any marked deviation from convention as evidence of incompetence. Nevertheless, Stanley Benn's six conditions for the indentification of an autarchic person provide a useful starting point:

1. it must be possible to identify a single person corresponding over time to a single physically acting subject;
2. he must recognize canons for evidence and inferences warranting changes in his beliefs;
3. he must have the capacity for making decisions when confronted by options, and for acting on them;
4. changes of belief must be capable of making appropriate differences to decisions and policies;
5. he must be capable of deciding in the light of preferences; and
6. he must be capable of formulating a project or a policy so that a decision can be taken now for the sake of a preferred future state (Benn 1975–76, p. 116).

These are, of course, fairly formal requirements, and it is at the level of application that many of the problems arise. Among these is the fact that autarchy is not a simple all-or-nothing matter. Autarchy with respect to some kinds of decisions does not mean autarchy with respect to all decisions. We may be capable of deciding when to cross the street before we are capable of deciding whether or not to take up smoking. Some of these issues will confront us, and will need to be addressed, in Part Two.

The Argument from Freedom Protection. Donald Regan detects an argument of this kind in Mill's nonrecognition of voluntary slavery contracts. Mill's claim that "the principle of freedom cannot require that [a person] should be free not to be free" (1859, p. 300) is interpreted to mean that where a person's exercise of liberty is likely to lead to a substantial diminution of future options, there is good reason to act paternalistically. Justice is thereby done to the liberal commitment to freedom in a way not possible with the Argument from the Instrumentality of Freedom. The latter argument fails to give freedom the priority it warrants, overrating its importance to ends such as happiness. Even versions that see in freedom a source of satisfaction, as well as a means to it, are believed to fall short of elevating freedom to the key place it has in liberal thought. The Argument from Freedom Protection, on the other hand, by allowing interferences only for the sake of freedom, does not compromise the latter even though it provides for paternalism in cases where it has seemed to have some intuitive acceptability. The sorts of cases Regan has in mind are bans on smoking and the use of narcotics, and the compulsory wearing of seat belts or safety helmets. In claiming that paternalism can be justified where the purpose is to protect or maximize freedom, Regan does not wish to imply that it always is justified in such cases. There are other values besides freedom that have a claim to our recognition, and in particular cases, the costs of paternalism might be too great. A mountain climber, for example, is likely to have a substantial portion of his or her identity invested in that occupation, and its paternalistic prohibition would be unacceptably intrusive. Smoking, on the other hand, does not qualify as an occupation in the same way, and might be banned without causing undue hardship, although Regan allows that exceptions might have to be made for some who, "if they could not smoke, would be so persistently wracked by nervous tension that they could not otherwise assuage, that they would be fit for no other activity" (Regan 1983).

At this point we will leave to one side the adequacy of Regan's interpretation of Mill and focus on more pressing difficulties. One concerns Regan's presumption that freedoms can be compared and aggregated, a thesis we have already had occasion to question. He is aware of the problems but believes them to be no more intractable than those involved in utility-aggregation. Since it is common for people to give the aggregation of utilities some role in their thinking, there should be an equal willingness to allow for freedom-aggregation (Regan 1974, p. 194; 1983). But this will fail to satisfy the many liberals who are no more wedded to utility-aggregation than to freedom-aggregation, or whose opposition to strong paternalism is based on deontological grounds. As an accommodation, it could be argued that the freedoms to be secured would be of greater importance than the freedoms abrogated by paternalistic interference. But this would show a serious misunderstanding of the Millian tradition, in which it is just those freedoms invaded by paternalism that have the greatest claim to our recognition. I shall return to this soon.

A further difficulty for Regan's position arises out of his fairly exclusive focus on liberty-protection/maximization. His concern is with the number and quality of options available to a person in the long term. But he acknowledges that others might be more concerned with autarchy-protection/maximization—with optimizing a person's capacity for making and keeping to rational choices. A commitment to the latter might work against a commitment to the former, for reasons articulated in the Argument from the Developmental Value of Choice. Regan does not dispute this, but believes that in the sorts of cases he has in mind, viz., smoking, safety helmets, etc., his conclusions would not be seriously affected. He may be right, for, as we saw earlier, the Argument from the Developmental Value of Choice does not by itself rule out all paternalism. We are much more likely to learn from our mistakes if their deleterious consequences are relatively immediate or not catastrophic, and in these cases those conditions are not likely to be satisfied.

A third difficulty relates to the assumption that if smokers, etc. are not stopped, they will suffer from serious freedom-diminishing disabilities. There is, of course, a fair bit of statistical information linking cigarette smoking to lung cancer, emphysema, etc., enabling us to claim with some confidence that the probability of a smoker's succumbing to them is substantially higher than that of a nonsmoker. But is this sufficient for the purposes of the argument? Might it not be said that unless the person *would have* suffered from the freedom-diminishing ailments had he or she not been imposed upon, the imposition will turn out to be freedom-diminishing rather than freedom-protecting/maximizing? One response to this could be that what is true in particular cases is false in general and that having an antismoking policy would do more for freedom than not having one. But this is not a route that Regan can take, since he eschews interpersonal freedom-protection/maximization (Regan 1983).

The foregoing difficulties, however, are merely preliminary to what is surely the most serious difficulty confronting not only the Argument from Freedom Protection but also that from the Instrumentality of Freedom. This is its failure to come to terms with the special claims of the Argument from the Oppression of Individuality, or its Kantian counterpart, the Argument from Disrespect for Persons. What paternalism does, even when motivated by a concern for freedom-protection/maximization, is to undermine individuality. A person is made to act in a way that no longer reflects his or her own judgment and choice, but the determinations of an other. With respect to his or her well-being, the individual is treated as if lacking in the capacity for rational choice. In a more Kantian mode, paternalism denies a person's status as an agent, as a source of reasons for action to whom respect is due. While others may dislike or object to the individual's choices, considering them stupid, self-destructive, or freedom-diminishing, it is not for them to interfere, not for them to superimpose their own judgements. Failure to observe this constraint is, in effect, to "depersonalize" the person, to ignore his or her standing as an end and not merely the instrument of others' evaluations and determinations.

The point of these objections is not blunted by the comparatively small "sacrifice" of freedom involved and the potentially large gains to be made. A consequentialist "calculus" may work strongly in favor of intervention. The point is that people are dispossessed of their choices, are made subservient to others' determinations, and not treated as a source of evaluations and determinations. Admittedly, their choices may not be as good as the choices of others, but this is not the point, which is that the choices be *their* choices. Joel Feinberg gets close to the heart of the objection when he writes that

> When a mature adult has a conflict between getting what he wants and having his options left open in the future, we are bound by our respect

for his autonomy not to force his present choice in order to protect his future "liberty". His present autonomy takes precedence even over his probable future good, and he may use it as he will, even at the expense of the future self he will one day become. Children are different. Respect for the child's future autonomy, as an adult, often requires preventing his free choice now. Thus the future self does not have as much moral weight in our treatment of adults as it does with children. Perhaps it should weigh as much with adults pondering their *own* decisions as it does with adults governing their own children. In the self-regarding case, the future self exerts itself in the form of a claim to prudence, but prudence cannot rightly be imposed from the outside on an autonomous adult (1980b, pp. 127–28).[5]

To treat an adult paternalistically is tantamount to treating that adult as one who is still normatively a child, as yet incapable of prudence. It is the implied insult in this that consequentialists overlook or fail to appreciate when arguing for paternalism, albeit on freedom-maximizing grounds.

We might, in conclusion, question whether consequentialist attempts at justification are really concerned with paternalism. As we earlier characterized them, impositions are paternalistic to the extent that they are designed to secure a person's good, as an end. But it is not someone's good, as an end, that constitutes the focus of much consequentialism. It is a more general, impersonal end, such as happiness or freedom which is the end, and to which a particular person's good is the means or in which it is at best an ingredient. Where this is so, consequentialist arguments fail to offer a motivation appropriate to paternalism. Although they suggest reasons for imposing on individuals for their own good, it is not, in the very nature of the case, *their* good *as an end* that is sought. Of course, consequentialism may be individualized, so that the happiness or freedom which it is proposed to maximize is the happiness or freedom of the individual who is imposed on. But in such cases we may wonder about the 'purity' of the consequentialism (cf. Mill 1859, p. 224).

Consent-based Arguments for Paternalism

As we have seen, the apparently demeaning or degrading character of strong paternalism constitutes its great stumbling block. An autarchic individual is denied the opportunity to make his or her own choices, thus violating the claims of individuality. To many liberals, this decisively rules out any legitimate strong paternalism. Yet, as we noted at the beginning of this chapter, total opposition has its counterintuitive aspects. In an effort to accommodate this, and to dissipate or alleviate liberal concern, there have been various attempts to argue that where the case for paternalism carries intuitive plausibility, the authorization or consent of the paternalized person can be taken as read. By virtue of some actual or hypothetical, past or future consent, these paternalistic impositions can be understood as sanctioned, licensed or justified. The claims in terms of which paternalism is judged to be objectionable are thereby waived. Here I distinguish five consent-based arguments, commencing with a version that has strong claims to our assent, and then passing on to several common extrapolations.

THE ARGUMENT FROM PRIOR CONSENT

In its simplest form, this argument begins with a recognition of weakness—
usually of lack of resistance to temptation in areas where our settled interests
may be jeopardized. To secure ourselves against the conequences of such
weakness, we may request or authorize others to intervene when lapses are
likely to occur, to ensure by whatever means seem necessary and appropriate
to the case that these interests are protected or even promoted. So, to take
a well-worn example, Odysseus, conscious of the entrancing Sirens' song and
of the dire consequences of falling under its spell, yet desirous of indulging
himself, ordered his men to tie him to the mast and to respond to his pleas
and commands to be set free by binding him even tighter, until they had
passed beyond its sound (Homer *Odyssey*: xii; cf. Dworkin 1971, pp. 119–20).
To the extent that the actions of Odysseus's men were motivated by a concern
for his good, we may see them as paternalistic; to the extent that they were
prosecuted with his consent, we may see them as authorized;[6] and to that
extent we may consider them justified. More mundane examples come readily
to mind. If Mary knows that she is likely to act foolishly under the influence
of alcohol, taking dangerous risks with her welfare, she may, before indulging,
ask her friends to ensure that she doesn't do anything hazardous, even if at
the time she protests at their interference. Or, if Neville believes smoking is
bad for his health, he may ask his family and friends to prevent him from
purchasing cigarettes or smoking them, when he is tempted and likely to do
so.

There is some dispute as to whether these cases are genuinely paternalistic.
Donald VanDeVeer, for example, argues that in all these cases the risk-taking
behavior arises out of "episodic" rather than "settled" wants, and that the
interference does not therefore conflict with the person's "settled determination." It is seen as "cooperative" rather than "coercive" interference, and
thus not paternalistic (VanDeVeer 1979, pp. 635–37). I am not sure that
there is more than a verbal point at stake here.[7] For the sort of reasons I
outlined in Chapter 1, I find it useful to cast the net widely rather than
narrowly, including within the scope of paternalism benevolently motivated
impositions that have been sought as well as those that have not. For, in so
far as there has been an imposition, there is a justificatory question to be
answered. That it can be answered relatively easily in these cases is not
sufficient reason for refusing to call them paternalistic. However, I do not
want to make too much of this point. Whether or not we regard them as
"genuinely" paternalistic, they belong on a continuum of cases, some of which
are most definitely paternalistic, and they are frequently appealed to as a
model in terms of which other cases can be justified.

The apparently simple Argument from Prior Consent is not quite so simple
when we look at some of the uses to which it is put. Olga is anxious to lose
weight, and so she enters into a contract with O-So-Slim Clinics, by the terms
of which she forfeits certain surrendered items of value if her progress in a
specified weight reduction program is inadequate. Once in the program, she
is committed to its terms for the duration of the contract (cf. Mann 1972).
Pedro is a narcotics addict in search of treatment. It is a condition of his
admission to a state-run institution that he agrees to remain there for a
specified period of time. That agreement will be enforced (cf. Wexler 1972,
pp. 330–31; Dresser 1982, p. 820f.) Quentin suffers from manic-depressive

fluctuations of mood that are becoming more extreme. During a period of calmness and lucidity, he draws up a contract enabling others to institutionalize him, against his expressed wishes, for a limited period of time, when the swings threaten his welfare (cf. Culver and Gert, 1981; 171; Howell, Diamond, and Wikler, 1982; Dresser, 1982).

It is arguable that the cases of Olga, Pedro, and Quentin represent instances of paternalism with prior consent, and are, to that extent, justifiable. But they differ in a number of ways from the cases of Odysseus, Mary, and Neville. In the earlier cases, a reason for believing that no wrong has been done is our recognition that the behavior interfered with springs from uncontrollable or barely controllable episodic wants rather than voluntary settled wants. As Dworkin writes of Odysseus: even if, in his pleas and demands, he claimed to have changed his mind, his men would have been justified in ignoring him, "since it is *just* such changes that he wished to guard against" (1971, p. 120). But in the latter cases, this presumption cannot be so easily sustained. Though there may be occasions on which the penalized or prevented behavior expresses a merely episodic want, it may also turn out that the person's settled wants have changed.[8] Perhaps Olga has experienced a shift in perspective that causes her to lose her self-consciousness about her weight; maybe Pedro has come to believe (what was not at all visible from the outside), that "the cure is worse than the disease"; possibly Quentin has seen a side to the commitment contract that he did not fully appreciate when he entered into it. Either the consent once given is withdrawn, or, it could perhaps be argued, consent was not given to constraints on settled wants. Consent is not to be construed after the manner of an irrevocable contract but as an ongoing commitment that may be reassessed and given up. Where given up, it may be appropriate to exact some form of compensation, but this is to be distinguished from holding the parties to its terms.

One other form in which the Argument from Prior Consent is sometimes found deserves comment. Traditional liberal democratic theory legitimates civil society by appealing to the consent of the governed, be it their "tacit" consent as expressed in the continuing enjoyment of its benefits, or their "express" consent to a particular governing régime as signified through periodic voting. Now it may be argued that where an administration so elected introduces paternalistic measures (say seat belt and safety helmet regulations), and particularly where it continues in power through a further election, those measures can be said to have had prior consent, a consent confirmed by subsequent electoral success. However, this form of the argument possesses too many special difficulties to be viable, at least without substantial reconstruction. If it is intended to indicate actual consent to the various regulatory measures that follow in its wake, then there are serious problems about the appropriateness of the motions to which it appeals as vehicles of consent; even if we can reach agreement on that, there is a gap between theory and practice that goes a long way toward undermining their efficacy. The actual practice of voting in liberal democracies is poorly suited to gauging consent with regard to individual regulatory measures. And even as a gauge of agreement to broad policy matters it leaves a lot to be desired (see further, Kleinig 1982, pp. 107–9).

But even if a majority can be said to have given prior consent to some paternalistic measure, there is a residual difficulty of great importance. The liberal criticism of legal paternalism is that it illegitimately treats as a public interest what properly belongs to the private domain. Paternalistic interventions, it is claimed, do not justifiably belong in the public sphere, and even if introduced via a fairly conducted vote, cannot rightly be said to have the indirect consent (i.e., to the outcome, whatever it is) of the dissenting minority. Of course, as we have seen, there are difficulties in distinguishing between a public and private domain; nevertheless, majoritarian decisions might be said to have as their sphere of legitimacy only conduct that touches substantial public interests. This issue has not yet been squarely addressed.

THE "REAL WILL" ARGUMENT

Idealist philosophers have sometimes attempted to keep up the appearance of actual consent to paternalism by appealing to a distinction between the person's "real" and "empirical" will. Even though a person manifestly wants to do *A*, it may be claimed that what he or she *really* wants is *B*. Because priority is given to the latter, interferences with the former are not considered to be a violation of freedom.

Claims based on the "Real Will" Argument are variously grounded. They range from those previously expressed preferences of the individual that are constitutive elements in his or her life-plans to some general theory about human nature and its tendencies or strivings.[9] Their function is to enable a discounting of the individual's presently manifest or empirical wants in favor of what are called his or her "real" ones. However, it is one thing to discount a person's empirical wants; it is quite another to term those considerations on the basis of which they are discounted that person's "real" wants (cf. Berlin 1969, pp. 133–34). Whatever might be said in favor of overriding a person's manifest wants, it is a subterfuge to argue that these considerations are appropriately described as his or her "real" ones. It is a subterfuge because a matter of individual freedom is made to appear as something else.

Although the "Real Will" Argument is usually seen as the preserve of Idealist philosophers, Bosanquet and Day believe that even Mill appropriates it on occasion (Bosanquet 1899, pp. 64–5, 90, 110; Day 1970). This, it is claimed, can be seen when he argues that where there is no time to warn a person that he is approaching an unsafe bridge, he may be prevented from crossing "without any real infringement of his liberty, for liberty consists in doing what one desires, and he does not desire to fall into the river" (Mill 1859, p. 294). Mill's wording may suggest a certain awkwardness on his part. Given the general proposition that "liberty consists in doing what one desires" and his claim that, in the case of the man halted at the unsafe bridge, there is no "real infringement of his liberty," we might have expected him to say that this person "desired not to fall into the river." But this, it is suggested, would have been almost certainly false. The man was otherwise preoccupied. So Mill draws back and says only that "he does not desire to fall into the river." But, it is then maintained, this is not sufficient, on his account, to show that there was no real infringement. An infringement there is: the man wants to step on the bridge and he is prevented from doing so. It will not do to argue that, because a consequence of the man's stepping on the bridge is that he will fall into the river, and he doesn't want this, he therefore doesn't really want to step on the bridge. Wanting is referentially opaque.

However, interesting though this interpretation of Mill is, it relies too heavily on a view of desires as occurrent states. Desires may equally well be seen as dispositions, and, given that this is so, we may see in the episode, not an interference with someone's actual will in the name of his real will, but a person who is probably acting on incompatible desires and who is having this drawn to his attention, since it is most likely that he does not realize it.

Versions of the "Real Will" Argument have been invoked in legal contexts. There are cases in which, in order to curb their spending habits, the relatives of elderly people have successfully initiated guardianship proceedings. Although there is a strong case for seeing such proceedings as an attempt by heirs to secure their interest in the elderly relative's estate, they have been defined as attempts to "preserve the integrity of the ward's intent": "The ward would not want to act 'foolishly' and the court aids him in fulfilling his desire" (Anon. 1964, p. 688). The basis for this attribution of intent is presumably the elderly persons' inclusion of the relatives in his or her will. "Unwise" spending or property alienation is thought to be incompatible with an adequate realization of this intent, and, since the latter is for various reasons identified with the person's "real" intent, it is used to override the former. A similarly motivated but differently grounded argument is sometimes used to show testamentary incapacity. If a decedent omits from his or her will those who are deemed to be "the 'natural' objects of his or her bounty," he or she may be judged "mentally incapable of having drawn a valid will" (ibid). Here there is no previously established life-plan to which appeal is made, but certain generalizations about "natural affections" (cf. Guttmacher and Weihofen 1952, pp. 197–99). What it is "natural" to will is what is really willed, and this takes precedence over what is manifestly willed.

These examples begin to illustrate what political theorists such as Berlin have seen as the totalitarian tendencies in the "Real Will" Argument (1969, pp. 131–34). Not only does it represent as "real" what can at best be inferred, but it opens the door to reconstructions that permit the overriding of any actual desire by a fictional one with a quite different character. Admittedly, in those cases where the real will is determined by reference to a person's well-established life-plans, these tendencies are considerably diminished (and, as I shall later argue, provide some sort of a base for paternalism). Nevertheless, there is an obscuring of the issues if what is inferred from these life-plans is called the person's "real will."

The Arguments from Prior Consent and the "Real Will' endeavor to show how, by virtue of their being consented to, some acts of paternalism involve impositions that do not violate or override a person's basic freedoms. This is because the restrictions are seen, in effect, as self-prescribed. Responsibility for them resides with the individual. As we have seen, such arguments do not always deliver as much as they promise. Nevertheless, their character is quite different from those we now turn to; although they appeal to the notion of consent, it does not have its normal function of signifying a responsible participation in the initiatives of an other (Kleinig 1982), but figures as a normative explanation for what are believed to be justifiable impositions. Indeed, if the point of consent is to express a person's participation in the initiatives of an other, that point would seem to be pre-empted where those initiatives are followed through beforehand.

THE ARGUMENT FROM ANTICIPATED CONSENT

Circumstances sometimes arise in which those in need of care have not had the opportunity to consent to it. Nevertheless, their previous behavior may have provided good reasons for thinking that they would have consented, had they been able to. Suppose Sylvia and Cynthia are working on a joint project involving experiments with a toxic, delirium-producing gas. Though they have taken precautions to avoid inhaling it, Sylvia accidentally does so and becomes wildly delirious. Cynthia rushes to her aid, and, despite Sylvia's strong resistance, forces the appropriate treatment on her. Here, although Sylvia's consent to treatment has not been obtained, we have good reason to think that, had she been in a fit state to give it, she would have done so. What we know about Sylvia and her life-plans strongly indicates that her resistance was "out of character" and that treatment was much more likely to have been in keeping with it.

It is most likely that we would consider Cynthia justified in treating Sylvia as she did, even though she acted paternalistically. But it is not because of some actual or supposedly implied consent on Sylvia's part. That we have reason to think Sylvia would have consented is not to say that in some sense she did. So what is it that leads us to think Cynthia was justified in imposing on Sylvia? We can get somewhere, I believe, by appealing to the notion of *personal integrity*. What I mean here by "integrity" is closely related to wholeness—that complex of beliefs, dispositions, attitudes, goals, relations, and life-plans that together constitute someone as the particular person he or she is. What we can say in this case is that even though Sylvia does not consent to the interference, her integrity is not violated. What Cynthia does for her meshes in with the kind of person she has, until that point, shown herself to be. Her protests can be explained as an effect of the gas and not as an alteration in the direction of her moral convictions, settled desires, or life-plans. Thus no violence is done to *her* in interposing. Rather, the interposition is directed to the restoration or preservation of her integrity.

Normally, we respect people's integrity by refraining from interfering with or otherwise imposing on them. But there is no necessity about this. Sylvia's case is a pretty clear exception. Her wild protests are merely episodic; they do not reflect the wants of a responsible (as distinct from nonresponsible) individual, and the wants they reflect are quite uncharacteristic. But what about cases where the wants are those of a competent person, albeit one who is acting in a thoughtless or foolish manner? Might we intervene in the name of that person's integrity, even though the person could be held responsible for the consequences of his or her acts? Might we argue that such thoughtless or short-sighted behavior is so out of keeping with other long-held and strongly expressed wants, it could reasonably be anticipated that in a cooler, more reflective hour the intervention would be appreciated? I do not believe there is any decisive theoretical objection to this. People frequently act on the basis of desires that do not "belong" to them in an ongoing sense. They may belong to them in the way that moments of weakness belong—something for which they can be held responsible, but not something they desire to own further. These desires are something they seek or could be expected to seek to eliminate from their constellation of desires. If acting on them would have seriously interfered with the satisfaction of their more significant desires, we might expect them to appreciate our intervention. Obviously, though, a good deal of care and sensitivity would be required were we to interfere.

The legal equivalent of the Argument from Anticipated Consent is the Doctrine of Substituted Judgement. This doctrine is at present employed exclusively in cases where the person to be imposed on is judged to be incompetent, and it represents an attempt to resolve treatment decisions by determining what the particular individual would have decided for him- or herself were he or she *compos mentis*. Obviously its employment requires a fairly close acquaintance with the individual concerned—something that can be very difficult to achieve. The doctrine also has a limited scope, being only marginally applicable in the cases of young children or the severely retarded where there is as yet no pattern of settled wants or clear identity, or where there is not likely to be. In such cases, there is a drift in the direction of two further arguments, the Argument from Subsequent Consent and the Argument from Hypothetical Rational Consent (with its legal equivalent, the Doctrine of Best Interests).

There is much more to be said about the issues I have raised here, and some of the more pressing ones will be taken up again when I develop the Argument from Personal Integrity. My more immediate purpose has been simply to point out that the so-called Argument from Anticipated Consent does not rely on any actual consent for its plausibility. There is no waiving of rights, no exercise of rational choice on the part of the person interfered with, only an expectation that what is done will be appreciated or approved. What is at issue is integrity rather than consent. Anticipated consent cannot be construed as a kind of actual consent, with all the moral implications of the latter.

THE ARGUMENT FROM SUBSEQUENT CONSENT

Liberals who believe that only consent can justify paternalistically motivated impositions (Dworkin 1971, p. 119; Carter 1977, pp. 133, 135), sometimes believe it sufficient that the consent be subsequently given. Dworkin conjectures that parental paternalism (which he considers unproblematic) is morally limited

> by the notion of the child eventually coming to see the correctness of his parent's interventions. Parental paternalism may be thought of as a wager by the parent on the child's subsequent recognition of the wisdom of the restrictions (1971, p. 119).

In speaking of parental paternalism as a "wager," Dworkin implies that it may turn out to be incorrect, and therefore unjustified. How far Dworkin is prepared to take this is not clear, because he does not distinguish carefully enough between the Argument from Subsequent Consent and the Arguments from Anticipated and Hypothetical Rational Consent. There is, however, nothing in the argument to restrict it to children.

Even as a justification for parental paternalism the Argument from Subsequent Consent runs into problems. Tommy's parents may wager that he will eventually appreciate being made to do his homework before going out to play, even though Tommy's inclination is to play. Do they lose their wager if Tommy suddenly dies, in advance of the time when his "consent" can be expected? Were they unjustified in making him do his homework? (Cf. VanDeVeer 1980b, p. 194; Husak 1981, p. 33.) The Argument from Subsequent Consent hardly allows that they would have been justified, although it might be argued that the circumstances were such as to make their failure excusable. Even so, this is an odd result. It is more plausible to argue that contingencies such as Tommy's untimely demise would not affect the justifiability of his parents' demands. Rosemary Carter, who appeals to the Argument from Subsequent Consent, rightly claims that occurrences of the sort outlined would be "arbitrary from a moral point of view and should not render unjustified a paternalistic act which would otherwise be justified" (1977, p. 135). Indeed they should not, but the Argument from Subsequent Consent cannot provide for this. Her own suggested modification, viz., reference to a "disposition to consent," isn't broad enough to accommodate cases like Tommy's.

Even more troubling are the argument's manipulative possibilities. One way in which (barring accidents) we can come close to ensuring that we will win our wager is by structuring our children's social conditions so that they will almost certainly come to welcome what we in our wisdom choose for them (cf. Elster 1979, p. 47). The possibilities are even more unacceptable if we contemplate cases in which competent subjects are taken and manipulated (by means of hypnosis, subliminal propagandizing, or brainwashing) into "consenting" to what they had not given their prior consent to (cf. Murphy 1974, p. 482; also pp. 214–16 below).

Proponents of the argument have not been wholly insensitive to the difficulty. Rosemary Carter draws attention to three kinds of cases in which what poses as subsequent consent will not qualify: where the paternalistic act is causally sufficient to guarantee the subject's "subsequent consent" (as in the case of brainwashing); where the "consent" results from a distortion in the subject's values, beliefs, or desires; and where it would have been withheld or withdrawn upon the receipt of a piece of relevant information (1977, pp. 136–38). Her response to this, however, is simply to build them into her account as exceptions. But more is needed if the charge of ad hocery is to be avoided, and some brake is to be put on exceptions. In addition, the exceptions themselves embody a problematic vagueness. Talk of consent resulting from distortion presumes that an acceptable account of distortion can be or is provided. But this is not so. There is only an appeal to our intuitions: a child who is brought up "to approve of the pressures used to force him into the mold of a narrow religious sect which forbids the development of certain artistic or intellectual skills, because he now accepts the tenets of the religion, and has been trained to be the kind of person who does not value these things" (Carter 1977, p. 137). Perhaps there has been a distortion of preferences. But is there any less (except less obvious) distortion if Ulrich's parents, dedicated empiricists, bring him up to approve of his consequent lack of religious feeling; or if Vera is brought up to see herself as someone to be desired by men, and is appreciative of the habits, attitudes, and life-style that have resulted; or if Walter, trained to see his future in the commercial world, finds its cut and thrust exciting and challenging, and feels indebted to his parents for preparing him for it? There are difficult normative issues here, but Carter provides little help in resolving them.

There is something paradoxical about the Argument from Subsequent Consent: if subsequent "consent" alone can justify interference, how can we know in advance that it will be given and that we are justified in going ahead with it? Obviously we cannot, and this is the point of calling it a wager. Of course, as Carter points out, we can have more or less reason to believe that "consent" will subsequently be given, and she notes several factors relevant to determining this (1977, p. 139). Even so, it is odd to make the justifiability of the interference dependent on "consent" subsequently given rather than on the reasonableness of thinking that it will be given. But maybe a liberal would be happier with a theory that allows, at best, for the excusing of a loser.

More problematically paradoxical are the theoretical underpinnings of Carter's position. Consenting to interference, she believes, is generally sufficient to waive ("alienate") one's right to noninterference. This holds equally of "subsequent consent." What would otherwise have been a violation of rights is transformed into an acceptable intrusion by the "consent" subsequently given. But this is a *non sequitur*. If any rights were violated, they were violated, not when consent was not subsequently given, but when the person was initially interfered with. The so-called subsequent consent does not alter that, for it is not, in any nonpersuasive sense, a form of consent. Approval it may be, even gratitude, but that is a different matter. At best it shows that the person interfered with will not hold it against the interferer (cf. VanDeVeer 1979, p. 638).

THE ARGUMENT FROM HYPOTHETICAL RATIONAL CONSENT

It is here that the fixation with "consent" reaches its most extreme form. In order to escape the limitations or deficiencies of the Arguments from Prior, Anticipated, and Subsequent Consent, any pretense of an actual consent is abandoned and replaced by what is effectively a concern with rationally justifiable interferences. For this is what the argument reduces to. "What fully rational individuals would accept as forms of protection" (Dworkin, 1971, p. 120) is presumably no more and no less than "what forms of protection it would be rational to impose on individuals."

But what forms of protection would rational individuals accept? As most of its proponents realize, the problems confronting this argument overlap substantially with those confronting some versions of the "Real Will" Argument: what the individual "really wills" is couched in terms of what the "rational" individual would accept. There is a tendency for the rational individual to reflect the understanding and values of upholders of power or the dominant ideology. It is therefore prey to idiosyncrasy and partisan constructions. How can this be avoided? Dworkin believe that good progress can be made by limiting protective impositions to securing

> "goods" such as health which any person would want to have in order to pursue his own good—no matter how that good is conceived. . . .
> [T]he attainment of such goods should be promoted even when not recognized as such, at the moment, by the individuals concerned (1971, pp. 120–21).

This proposal is not unattractive—if it can be made to work. A difficulty arises where basic goods come into conflict, for example, where the relief of pain would most probably shorten a person's life or the administration of life-saving treatment would violate a person's religious convictions. There is no obvious way of ordering such goods independently of people's ongoing life-plans, and Dworkin appears to believe that where decisions are made on the basis of those life-plans they ought to be respected. But if life-plans can figure decisively at this level, why should they not always be determinative? Dworkin believes that the considerations that motivate some actions depart so significantly from what an "average person" might contemplate, that they can be deemed irrational in a sense that justifies prohibition. The person who refuses a blood transfusion on religious grounds is thus to be distinguished from the person who prepares to jump from a high window ledge in the belief that he can fly. Somewhere, no doubt, there is a distinction to be drawn. The difficulty is to know how to draw it without importing distorting factors. Appeals to the "average person," for example, offer little protection against cultural idiosyncrasies, and Mill for one was as much concerned about this form of authoritarianism as about that associated with particular individuals.

A somewhat more subtle version of the Argument from Hypothetical Rational Consent can be extracted from John Rawls's *A Theory of Justice*. Rawls's discussion of paternalism borrows heavily from Dworkin's; but by placing it in a wider theoretical context he gives it a coherence and plausibility that Dworkin's account lacks.

It is Rawls's view that principles governing legitimate interferences can be determined by a consideration of what a group of rational, generally informed individuals would adopt as rules of social order from behind a "veil of ignorance" with respect to their own and others' particular characteristics. This strategy is intended to facilitate decisions that are not biased in favor of any particular society's or individual's characteristics. All that is assumed of individuals behind the veil is that they are rational (in the sense of being capable of developing life-plans, capable of understanding and taking the most effective means to their chosen ends, and committed to integrating these ends into a coherent framework of ends or life-plans), and motivated by the need to secure (and augment) their "primary goods." The latter are prerequisites to achieving the self's heterogeneous aims (Rawls 1971, p. 554), or as he more commonly expresses it, they are things which "it is rational to want whatever else one wants" (1971, p. 253; cf. pp. 249, 260). Included are "natural" goods, such as health and vigour, intelligence and imagination, and "social" goods, such as self-respect, rights and liberties, powers and opportunities, income and wealth. Against this background, Rawls believes that individuals in the original position would agree to two lexically ordered principles of social organization: first, each person is to have an equal right to the most extensive total system of equal basic liberties compatible with a similar system of liberty for all; and second, social and economic inequalities are to be arranged so that they are both (a) to the greatest benefit of the least advantaged, and (b) attached to offices and positions open to all under conditions of fair equality of opportunity (1971, pp. 302–3).

It is not our purpose here to enter into the debate engendered by *A Theory of Justice*, though it bears noting that some doubts have been expressed concerning Rawls's success in abstracting his individual choosers sufficiently from the predilections of a particular cultural tradition (cf. Teitelman 1972; Schwartz 1973). More to the present point is Rawls's application of his general strategy to paternalism. It turns out that Rawlsian individuals would be willing (i.e., consider it rational) to accept a limited measure of paternalism, for, knowing in general the diverse conditions of life,

> they will want to insure themselves against the possibility that their powers are undeveloped and they cannot rationally advance their interest, as in the case of children, or that through some misfortune or accident they are unable to make decisions for their good, as in the case of those seriously injured or mentally disturbed. It is also rational for them to protect themselves against their own irrational inclinations by consenting to a scheme of penalties that may give them a sufficient motive to avoid foolish actions and by accepting certain impositions designed to undo the unfortunate consequences of their imprudent behaviour (1971, p. 249).

What we have here, within the broad framework of an Argument from Hypothetical Rational Consent, are several of the arguments already discussed. Children, and perhaps those who are seriously injured or mentally disturbed, are accommodated via the Argument from Freedom Promotion, though as a "fall back" position there would appear to be an appeal to the Doctrine of Best Interests. The situation of those who act foolishly or imprudently is more complicated. At one point, on the basis of the *hypothetical* original position, Rawls is moved to claim that "others are *authorized* and sometimes required to act on our behalf and to do what we would do for ourselves if we were rational" (1971, p. 249, emphasis added), a phrasing that strongly suggests some actual prior consent. But he soon goes on to speak of the "requirement that the other person in due course accepts his condition" (1971, p. 249), a claim much more at home in the Argument from Subsequent Consent. This, however, should not be taken at face value, for it follows immediately after a sentence in which he asserts only that "we must be able to *argue* that with the development or recovery of his rational powers the individual in question will accept our decision on his behalf and agree with us that we did the best thing for him" (1971, p. 249, emphasis added). Only the Argument from Anticipated Consent is intended. This is reinforced by his later claim that the Argument from Hypothetical Rational Consent (i.e., the original position) requires "two further stipulations":

> paternalistic intervention must be justified by the evident failure or absence of reason and will; and it must be guided by the principles of justice and what is known about the subject's more permanent aims and preferences, or by the account of primary goods (1971, p. 250).

We can probably reconstruct Rawls's position in the following way. People in the original position, behind the veil of ignorance, would not be aware of their own personal characteristics and circumstances. They must devise principles of social organization without knowing whether they are young or old, rich or poor, strong or weak, competent or incapacitated. In the event that they should turn out to be children, they would sanction paternalistic principles likely to secure their primary goods, in particular, their self-respect. This would require that paternalistic impositions contribute to the development of autarchy (cf. 1971, pp. 514–16). In the event that temporary incapacity should befall them, they would sanction paternalistic principles that would first give effect to what is known of their "more permanent aims and preferences," and beyond that would secure their primary goods, since "the parties want to guarantee the integrity of their person and their final ends and beliefs whatever they are" (1971, p. 250). In the event that they do not fall into the categories mentioned, any paternalism will need to come before the bar of the principles of justice (particularly the first one), thus giving priority to the individuals' more permanent aims and preferences. Does this leave any room for strong paternalism? Some of Rawls's remarks suggest that the answer is "no"' e.g., his claim that "paternalistic intervention must be justified by the evident failure or absence of reason and will" (1971, p. 250). But the notion of a "failure . . . of reason and will" is not very precise. Other remarks suggest a more affirmative answer: e.g., his claim that parties in the original position will "protect themselves against their own irrational inclinations by consenting to a scheme of penalties that may give them a sufficient motive to avoid foolish actions," etc. Does he have in mind here seat belts and safety helmet legislation?

Obscurities apart, what is interesting about Rawls's use of the Argument from Hypothetical Rational Consent is its accommodation of the Arguments from Freedom Promotion and Anticipated Consent. The Doctrine of Best Interests, which has a central place in the Argument from Hypothetical Rational Consent, is interpreted in terms of the liberal ideal of individuality, thus giving due weight to the promotion of autarchy and the individual's own "more permanent aims and preferences." Individuals in the original position would consider their interests best served if paternalistic interferences were to take into account and accord with their settled wants, in so far as these could be known. This represents a significant advance on the Doctrine of Best Interests as it is usually employed in legal contexts; there, unmoderated by a concern for the existing life-plans and desires of the person in need of paternalism, the doctrine allows for the imposition of alien values and purposes. Within Rawls's schema, the "unmoderated" doctrine is operative only where the settled determinations of the person concerned are not known, and even then, where feasible, the development of autarchy is of prime concern.

I have suggested that the status of strong paternalism is not altogether clear within Rawls's schema. It is tempting to see it excluded: after all, to interfere with people's voluntary conduct is to override *their* judgment. But the matter is not quite as simple as this, for there is an underlying assumption that when people are permitted to exercise their judgement, it will also be their *best* judgment. It may not be *the* best judgment, but it is at least *their* best judgment. But when people act carelessly or imprudently, when they stupidly succumb to temptation or passing desires, they are not even acting on their best judgment. It is not unreasonable to surmise that when Rawls states that people in the original position might "consent to a scheme of penalties that may give them a sufficient motive to avoid foolish actions," etc. he has in mind the hiatus between judgments that are one's own and judgments that are one's best. If this is so, then there is some room here for strong paternalism, room allowed by the ideal of individuality. I shall endeavor to elaborate this further in considering the final argument, the Argument from Personal Integrity.

In various ways, the five consent-based arguments I have canvassed attempt to find space for some paternalism within a framework that is genuinely liberal. They try to do this, I have suggested, by trading on the significance given to consent within that tradition: *volenti non fit injuria*, to the one who consents no wrong is done. Even where consent is not actual but only anticipated or hypothetical, there is an attempt to capitalize on this significance—to see it as "licensing" or "authorizing" paternalistic intervention. We are encouraged to believe that by virtue of the anticipated or subsequent consent, or the consent of some hypothetical rational person, there has been, after all, no violation of freedom but something more closely akin to a self-prescribed limitation. My response has been to argue that only in the case of the Argument from Prior Consent (and then only in some of its applications) can the waiver effected by consent be appealed to, and that in the remaining cases, whatever their merits, the appeal to consent has no direct value. This is not to argue that where consent-based arguments are employed an unjustifiable intrusion takes place. Obviously, where the person concerned is incompetent, there is no autarchy to be violated, and so the demand for consent is inappropriate. In other cases, however, the requirements of autarchy are infringed, and this is not altered by the fact of some anticipated, subsequent, or hypothetical rational "consent." Any justificatory argument needs to take a different form. This I shall now attempt to provide.

The Argument from Personal Integrity

I have already foreshadowed some of the factors that bear on this last, and I believe most promising, argument for paternalism. It seeks to accommodate the attractive features of other arguments we have considered while avoiding their defects.

To see how it does this, we need to go back to the conception of human nature that informs liberal theory. What we find is not a single, fixed blueprint, intended as a pattern for all development, but something far more complex and varied. Within certain broad limits, we differ from each other in our capacities, and even when our capacities are similar, they are likely to differ in their potential for development. Even for any particular individual there is no single developmental path. Most of us possess more capacities than we can possibly develop, or develop to their fullest extent, and so the formation of a life-plan is not a simple matter of "letting nature take its course," but rather an ongoing enterprise requiring deliberation, experimentation, and accommodation. The human individual does not come into the world a fully formed personality, but a bundle of undeveloped and uncoordinated capacities. We acquire a specific personality, a specific identity, through learning. This is not to be conceived on the model of a jigsaw puzzle, in which the variously shaped pieces are fitted together into a predetermined whole. It is more like the construction of a coherent and cohesive unity out of a large assortment of blocks, some of which are identical, but many of which differ in shape, color, or texture. For each of us, there is a somewhat different assortment from which to work.

In our early years, we lack the ability to form these blocks into complex, coordinated structures. Our hands need to be held or steadied and guided. But as we gain better control over our movements, as we come to appreciate what might be involved in shaping a unified configuration and acquire an interest in its realization, as our confidence increases and our imagination is stimulated, we are able to build using our own initiative, creating a structure that has "our own stamp" upon it. Building is a lifetime process, though it is quite likely that the general shape will become evident after several years. Obviously, how it ends up will depend partly on the adequacy of our early training, partly on the numbers and kind of blocks available to us, and partly on our building environment. Although some people manage to create complex yet tightly integrated and stable structures, most of us find ourselves with something less coherent and cohesive. Although we have arrived at a stage in our development where responsibility for the structure of purposes, attitudes, interests, beliefs, desires, values, and so on that constitute our identity and life-plans devolves upon us, our "ownership" of some of these elements may be equivocal or a matter of embarrassment or regret. Our lives do not always display the cohesion and maturity of purpose that exemplifies the liberal ideal of individuality, but instead manifest a carelessness, unreflectiveness, short-sightedness, or foolishness that not only does us no credit but also represents a departure from some of our own more permanent and central commitments and dispositions. That is characteristic of the self-regarding vices, and most of us are prey to some. On many occasions, the consequences of such lapses and deviations will not be serious, and we must wear them as best we can. But sometimes because of our actions, consequences of a more catastrophic kind may become inevitable or considerably more probable, consequences that would be quite disproportionate to the conduct's value for us. This we may fail to appreciate, not because we are incapable of it, but because of our lack of discipline, our impulsiveness, or our tendency to rationalize the risks involved. It would not take much to act more prudently, yet we are inclined to negligence.

It is against this background that the Argument from Personal Integrity operates. Where our conduct or choices place our more permanent, stable, and central projects in jeopardy, and where what comes to expression in this conduct or these choices manifests aspects of our personality that do not rank highly in our constellation of desires, dispositions, etc., benevolent interference will constitute no violation of integrity. Indeed, if anything, it helps to preserve it. Though it acknowledges the liberal ideal of individuality, it works with a more differentiated and less abstract conception of the self than is customary in liberal thinking. Not only do we have a diversity of aims, preferences, wants, and so on, but they vary in the status we accord them so far as our core identity and life-plans are concerned. We can differentiate passing and settled desires, major and minor projects, central and peripheral concerns, valued and disvalued habits and dispositions. Our conduct and choices may reflect any of these, though not necessarily in a way that matches their ranking in our hierarchy of values and concerns. The settled may give way to the passing, the major to the minor, the central to the peripheral, the valued to the disvalued. The argument in question maintains that where a course of conduct would, in response to some peripheral or lowly ranked tendency, threaten disproportionate disruption to highly ranked concerns, paternalistic grounds for intervention have a legitimate place. Strong, no less than weak, paternalism may thus find a toe hold.

So much for the argument's general outline. We can flesh it out by considering some of the objections it is likely to attract. For a start, adherents of the Argument from Oppression of Individuality will want to complain that it flies in the face of the very ends it proclaims. To interfere with a person's voluntary conduct for paternalistic reasons is to supplant that person's own judgment, it is to set his evaluations and determinations at naught, to treat him merely as an instrument, a vehicle for the paternalist's altruism, and not as a project-maker in his own right. So it will be claimed. But in this form the charge is somewhat unfair. From the fact that the paternalist has an interest in the other's interests, it does not follow that the other's interests are being made subservient to the interests of the paternalist. For the paternalist may be motivated and directed by a concern for the *other's* relatively permanent and highly ranked projects, and not by his or her own conception of what would be in the other's best interest.

A defender of the Argument from Oppression of Individuality is not likely to be convinced by this disclaimer, for it will be rejoined that by intervening the paternalist *is* thwarting at least *one* of the other's projects, the one that is believed to be jeopardizing the rest. This can be admitted. But it will be counterclaimed that in interfering the paternalist is doing no more than reflecting a tension that already exists between the other's projects, in which the pursuit of one is placing the others at risk. Further, it will be insisted that the direction taken by the intervention accords with the other's ordering (even if not present choice) of projects. There is, therefore, no violation of integrity or life-plans. The paternalist is neither determining what ends are constitutive of the other's good nor ranking those ends, but giving them effect in the face of certain character failings. Although the person interfered with can be held responsible for such failings, preventing them from having their worst effects does not violate that person's integrity. The paternalism here is not moralistic. No alien values are imported.

At this point the opponent of strong paternalism may suspect that the Argument from Personal Integrity gets what force it has by describing cases of strong paternalism in a manner more appropriate to weak paternalism. After all, it is being suggested that in virtue of certain deficiencies a person departs from his or her established priorities to engage in conduct which risks undermining their later fulfillment. However, I wish to resist this suggestion. It rests on a confusion of two senses of voluntariness, one comparative and the other absolute (cf. above, pp. 9–10). On one view, voluntariness is an ideal to which our decisions and conduct more or less approximate. Thus Joel Feinberg characterizes a "fully voluntary" assumption of risk as one that

> one shoulders . . . while fully informed of all relevant facts and contingencies, with one's eyes wide open, so to speak, and in the absence of all coercive pressure or compulsion. There must be a calmness and deliberateness, no distracting and unsettling emotions, no neurotic compulsion, no misunderstanding. To whatever extent there is compulsion, misinformation, excitement or impetuousness, clouded judgment (as e.g., from alcohol), or immature or defective faculties of reasoning, to that extent the choice falls short of voluntariness (1971, pp. 110–11).

It is clear that few of our decisions and acts will qualify as "fully voluntary" on this account. The sorts of deficiencies we have referred to as providing a basis for paternalism will be among those that detract from full voluntariness. But failure to realize this ideal of voluntariness does not render decisions and acts nonvoluntary in the sense appropriate to weak paternalism. For that is a threshold conception, in which all that is required is (roughly) a level of decision-making ability and freedom from internal and external pressures sufficient for a person to be held accountable for his or her decisions or acts. Voluntariness in this sense is an all-or-nothing matter. Decisions or acts will need to be very substantially less than fully voluntary (in the comparative sense) before they fall below the threshold of voluntariness (in the absolute sense).

Now the kinds of character deficiencies of which I have been speaking in outlining the Argument from Personal Integrity represent a falling short of full voluntariness in the comparative sense, but do not (necessarily) divest one of responsibility in the absolute sense. More often they render us objects of legitimate criticism. If, through carelessness or weakness of will, we come to grief, it might properly be said that we have only ourselves to blame. The responsibility is ours; the deficiency explains but does not excuse. Certainly we may become objects of others' sympathy rather than condemnation if the consequences of our shortcomings are very serious, but this is because the consequences are out of all proportion to the failing. Even though they have only themselves to blame, there is something callous about saying of motorcyclists who kill themselves or suffer massive injuries through not wearing a helmet that it "served them right."

In suggesting that paternalistic intervention might be justified where, as a result of some character deficiency, a person places his or her life-plans in jeopardy, it is not my intention to imply that grounds for paternalistic intervention would exist only rarely. All too often the carelessness or impulsiveness that jeopardizes a person's projects has gained a firm albeit somewhat unwelcome foothold in a person's character, and may display itself with some frequency. This does not mean that a strong ground for paternalism exists in every case, for it is often better, so far as the person's own development is concerned, that he or she bears the cost of failure to bring projects to completion. But sometimes the consequences of failure may be so serious that something stronger than persuasion might be called for. The student who is strongly tempted, just before his or her final exams, to "throw it in," may need to be "sat upon" rather than simply advised and pleaded with. If we know, as we may, that the failure to go through with the exams would be a source of serious and continuing regret and considerable personal loss, something stronger than rational pressure may reasonably be called for.

This, no doubt, will trouble the antipaternalist. Why not accept people as they are with all their complexities and internal tensions, regretting the mess they sometimes make of their lives but not intruding to the point of liberty-diminishing interference? Does it really show respect for their integrity, their individuality, if only part of their person is permitted to express itself? These are serious questions, and a defender of the Argument from Personal Integrity cannot brush them aside. There is a cost involved in strong paternalism—the paternalist takes a moral risk, and the demand for justification is an especially strong one. But it may be met. For the person who is interfered with, the proper response may be gratitude rather than resentment or forgiveness—a recognition that the intrusion expressed a sympathetic identification with his or her core aims and attitudes rather than officious intermeddling or disguised manipulation. While it is true that respect for a person's integrity or individuality must allow for the fragile complexity that this sometimes involves, it needs also to recognize the hierarchy of values through which this complexity is mediated. It is one thing to interfere with a person whose twin ambitions are excellence as a philosopher and mountain climber; it is another to interfere with a person whose philosophical (or mountain-climbing!) ambitions are put at unnecessary risk because he or she can't be bothered to put on a seat belt. It is cases of the latter rather than former sort that fall within the purview of the Argument from Personal Integrity.

Nevertheless, as I have stated, there is some cost involved, just because a constraint has been placed on voluntary conduct. It would be a better world were such paternalism not necessary, just as it would be a better world were punishment not sometimes called for. Paternalism is not something to be evangelistic about. It is not a substitute for persuasion and education, but a strategy of last resort. Like punishment, it is something that, though justified, we would like to see less of, something there are strong moral reasons for seeking to eliminate the need for. However, provided that it is limited to those character deficiencies, and those expressions of them, that place at unnecessary risk the aims and activities that are intimately connected with our self-identity, its use can be justified.

But there is still more to be said on the antipaternalist side. It may be granted that paternalism can accord with a person's settled and long-term interests and thus not undermine individuality. Nevertheless, the person interfered with may feel peculiarly put out by the imposition: "Who do you think you are?" "By virtue of what right or authority do you decide what I shall do?" "What is your standing, such that you can impose on me?" "What business is it of yours?" "What has it got to do with you?" Just as the person who deserves to be punished may feel offended that some particular person should take it into his or her hands to inflict it, a similar offense may be felt by the person on whom some paternalistic constraint is placed.

There are weak and strong versions of this objection. According to the weak version, the issue is one of the precise relationship between the paternalist and paternalized. Where there is some sort of close relationship between them—as in friendship—there has been an acknowledgment of goodwill and concern. Even though paternalistic intrusions have not been written into such relationships in the form of prior consent, they might nevertheless constitute an acceptable expression of the values embodied in the relationship. It is one thing for one's wife to take a paternalistic interest in one's diet (cf. Husak 1981, p. 45); it is another for a stranger, however well-meaning, to do so. In the first case, a relationship has been entered into, and a certain complex of values realized thereby; if the intrusion undermines those values or disrupts them too much, the relationship may be weakened or terminated. This is a risk that the paternalistic party must take. In the second case, there are no bonds of affection to sustain and give redeeming significance to the interference, no inbuilt sanctions that would discriminate it from officious intermeddling, and if the paternalistic agent is as powerful as the state, there may be no escape or redress.

The weak version demands, but does not preclude the possibility of, standing. However, it severely circumscribes it. Friends, lovers, and those to whom one stands in a fiduciary relationship may be morally positioned to take such risks; strangers will not. The situation of the state is morally ambiguous, and our understanding may be dependent on both circumstance and background understanding. Those of a Bosanquetian bent may grant it standing (cf. Bosanquet, 1899, pp. 186–87); those possessing a more individualistic metaphysic may see the state as little more than an alien other. To choose between these (and various other) positions would take us too far afield, though perhaps that is not the most helpful way to think about the issue. In so far as the state is seen as a locus of both authority and power, its standing may be ineliminably ambiguous.

The strong version denies the possibility of standing, except where consent has been given. Whatever the wisdom or benefit of intervention, strong paternalism is seen as an inexcusable (though not necessarily unforgivable) moral trespass, an unjustified violation of individual rights. On this view, the standing that is acquired by virtue of the capacity to determine and pursue one's own good is like that acquired when the title to a piece of land passes into one's hands: there is a boundary that may not be crossed save by invitation of the title holder. So long as the property is not used in a manner detrimental to others' interests, the boundary acts as a "side constraint" (Nozick 1974, ch. 3) on their conduct. This standing does not operate simply as a consideration to be taken into account by others, to be weighed or played off against, and perhaps overridden by, other considerations, such as beneficence, but it functions as a restriction on their reach. It is part of what it is to be a person in a world of persons that entry into this sphere may be made only with consent. The paternalist is to be charged with confusing a legitimate concern for others (which may lead to and justify admonition or remonstration) with a respect for their sovereignty (which limits the expression of concern to conduct falling short of imposition).

It is, however, one thing to assert individual sovereignty, with its implication that enforced benevolence would be morally *ultra vires*. It is another to establish this role for it. It is one thing to assert that this sovereignty is warranted in virtue of the individual's capacity to make his or her own choices, and that this is in *no way* contingent on what is chosen (so long as it is self-regarding). It is another thing to explain why *no* exceptions are endurable. Is it part of the very meaning of "sovereignty"? In that case, why does the capacity for self-development demand sovereignty over self? Is it because choices have a value in their own right? Dworkin suggests as much, when interpreting Mill: "To be able to choose is a good that is independent of the wisdom of what is chosen" (1971, p. 117). But if that is so, the capacity to make one's own choice does not generate a side constraint on the conduct of others, but functions simply as an independent value, possibly to be outweighed by the unwisdom of what is chosen. Antipaternalists have wanted it to carry more weight than that—to see it as not just a value but a principle, constituting a framework within which the balancing or trading off of values can take place. But can the standing this demands for individual choice be sustained?

There is a very important insight informing the strong account of standing. It is that morality is not chiefly concerned with the realization or maximization of values or something of that sort, but with the quality of relationship that exists between persons, whether individually or collectively. A "morality" that takes as its fundamental commitment the maximization of utility or value views the individuals who are bearers or creators of that utility or value as essentially anonymous, potentially replaceable instruments in its realization. They are no longer personalized individuals, and the relations they bear to each other are not judged in terms of the quality they have as relations between persons, but in terms of the utility or value realized. The individual persons vanish, to be replaced by some value, which, it so happens, requires as the precondition for its realization its origination (for the most part) in free choice.

The standing that one has in virtue of the capacity to make one's own choices thus reflects a profoundly *moral* attitude. It recognizes the fundamental concern that morality has with personal relationships. Yet even so, it is not obvious that the demands of autarchy/autonomy constitute a strict *side* constraint. For what is it that one respects when one respects the individuality of an other? Is it any and every free choice, or is it those free choices that manifest the other's established and valued concerns—the other's integrity? It is not to voluntary choices as such that liberalism is committed, but to the persons who express themselves in their choices. Where choices having marginal significance to a person's settled life-plans and values threaten serious disruption to their realization, we do not violate their integrity in interfering with them. This, admittedly, is a risky business, for, as we have already observed, people are generally better placed to know what accords with their own conception of good and their voluntary choices provide strong evidence that what they are doing will further it. Nevertheless, the evidence is not decisive, and risking unjustifiable offense may be called for. Relationships without risk are likely to be relationships without moral depth.

I have argued that proponents of the Arguments from Oppression of Individuality and Disrespect for Persons tend to see the individual too monochromatically. We can add a further dimension to this criticism by reflecting on the "ontology" of the individual person. There is a tendency[10] for defenders of these arguments to see people in terms of their immediate presentation, and to abstract expressed desires from the individual of whom they are an expression. There is a tendency to give full sovereignty to the present free decision, no matter how badly it sits with the individual's other pursuits, ideals, beliefs, and plans. But individuals are continuants—existents who persist through time, having a past and future as well as a present. This is not simply a function of their physiology but of their personal life, which does not (usually) focus exclusively on the present, but reaches backward and forward in expectations, ongoing projects, life-plans, and so on. Recognition of the individuality of others, then, is not some respect for bare voluntary choices or rational choosers in an abstract sense, but for continuants whose capacities have found concrete expression in ongoing projects, life-plans, etc., and who in day-to-day decision-making can be expected to work within the framework they provide. But as we know, sometimes to our continuing regret, we are often disposed to act in ways that are perilous to the projects and plans that are partially constitutive of our identity. Where this is so, paternalism may not be violative of integrity.

It is a corollary of the Argument from Personal Integrity that any impositions it sanctions will be relatively minor (cf. Weale 1978, pp. 170–71). Though they will impede or even prevent the risk-taking activity, they will not interfere with the individual's significant pursuits. It is for this reason that seat belt and safety helmet legislation has found considerable support (cf. Dworkin 1971, p. 125; Greenawalt 1971, p. 470 n. 21). But, as we shall see in more detail later (below, pp. 88–90), we need to be careful when making claims of this kind. Whether a restriction is trivial is not independent of the beliefs, purposes, temperament, life-plans, etc. of the person interfered with. What is seen as a minor inconvenience by one person may be taken as a major intrusion by another. For most English people, the requirement to wear a safety helmet when travelling on a motorcycle was at worst a nuisance, but for the local Sikh population it was viewed as a serious encroachment on religious freedom. Hence Mill's comment, in relation to the person who, after warning, still chooses to cross the unsafe bridge, that "no one but the person himself can judge of the sufficiency of the motive that may prompt him to incur the risk" (Mill 1859, p. 294). Though Mill overstates the point, it provides a salutary warning against the assumption that judgments of triviality can be made without regard to people's life-plans. What may be said in favor of seat belt and safety helmet legislation is that they are unlikely to provide a substantial impediment to most people's pursuits, and that where they do, it should be possible to make legislative provision for this.

One interesting consequence of the Argument from Personal Integrity is that the ardent antipaternalist may be spared its paternalistic conclusion. If it is of great importance to a person that his or her liberty be maximized, then any paternalistic imposition will be experienced as a gross intrusion, not because of what it directly requires or prohibits, but because it violates a central commitment. With such a person it may not be legitimate to do more than remonstrate.[11]

Limits to Paternalism

In this chapter I have endeavored to create some moral space for paternalism, including strong paternalism. Lest it be thought that a Pandora's Box has been opened, it is appropriate that I conclude by addressing more explicitly some of the limitations that need to be placed on the appeal to paternalistic considerations. The limiting maxims that follow are to some extent independent of each other, and trade-offs may sometimes be required.

THE LEAST RESTRICTIVE ALTERNATIVE IS TO BE PREFERRED

Some end, say, the securing of A against physical injury, may be achievable with roughly equivalent effectiveness by two alternative means, say x and y. If x is less or nonrestrictive of A's freedom—if the freedoms it diminishes are less significant, or it does not diminish them to the same extent (degree and time)—then, *ceteris paribus*, x is to be preferred. This doctrine is not limited to paternalism, but makes good sense in that context. If one of the things that bothers us about paternalism is the constraint on freedom that is involved, there is clearly something to be said for less as against more intrusive impositions (see Wormuth and Mirkin 1964; Struve 1967; Chambers 1976; Dresser 1982, pp. 805–8). Paternalistic measures are not desirable in themselves but only as a benevolent response to certain failings, and they ought to be directed to their overcoming. Paternalism is not something we can happily live with, as an intrinsically valuable part of our daily life; the sooner we can acquire the wisdom and discipline to make it unnecessary the better. In some cases the learning process is best accomplished if people are permitted to make their mistakes and put their losses down to "experience," but not all mistakes allow for a future in which what is learned can be put into effective practice. Opponents of paternalism rightly worry about a steadily increasing use of paternalistic measures, the growth of a society in which adults are more and more treated as though they were young children, and in which people are increasingly encouraged to rely on external motivations in preference to developing and executing a proper regard for their own welfare. The principle that we should prefer the least restrictive alernative thus functions to caution against the indiscriminate use of paternalistic measures in the first place, and to contain such measures once they have been implemented.

Although the doctrine of the least restrictive alternative is a general limiting consideration, there are certain areas in which its invocation is particularly important. Where weak paternalism is involved—as in the treatment of children and others considered incompetent—it is common to find abuses of paternalistic privilege. Parents frequently extend childhood (in a normative sense) beyond the time when it should be necessary. Childhood is seen not as a stage of development to be passed through as soon as possible, but as a state of being to be cultivated and preserved, whose passing is to be viewed with regret (cf. Kleinig 1976a, pp. 3–5). With the perpetuation of childhood has gone extended opportunities for indoctrination in docility, the evidences for which are clearly seen in the schooling system. Those committed to institutions are often worse off. Children generally grow up despite efforts to keep them young, but people committed to total institutions often find the institutional ethos destructive of efforts to develop coping skills. The doctrine of the least restrictive alternative would often mandate much less intrusive therapeutic or supervisory measures.

THERE IS A PRESUMPTION IN FAVOR OF THOSE PATERNALISTIC IMPOSITIONS THAT ACCORD WITH THE RECIPIENT'S OWN CONCEPTION OF GOOD

Paternalistic interventions ought not to be seen as occasions for manipulation in alien ways of life. Yet this is what they may well become if their reference point is not the person concerned's own conception of good. What secures the acceptability of a nonmoralistically, as distinct from a more explicitly moralistically, paternalistic imposition is its promotion of already existing goals, projects, and life-plans. Generally it requires that we do not interfere with what people voluntarily desire for themselves. But this is based on the rebuttable presumption that even if people's self-regarding decisions are not (in some "objective" sense) the best decisions they might make, at least they are *their best* decisions. However, our frailties are such that this is not always the case. Our voluntary conduct is marked by weakness of will, indiscipline, haste, carelessness, irrationality, impulsiveness, thoughtlessness, and so on. And we voluntarily go against even our own better judgment. The person who believes that wearing a seat belt is a very sensible thing to do, may adopt a "can't be bothered" attitude when he or she gets into a car.

We do not, of course, always have a clear idea of others' conceptions of their good. They may be unconscious or otherwise incapable of letting us know, or, as in the case of young children, they may as yet not possess a clear and reasonably stable conception of their good. Where this is so, a number of subsidiary maxims will diminish the likelihood of that good being undermined or corrupted.

In general, negative paternalism is to be preferred. Where a paternalistic imposition is directed to securing a person's welfare interests, there is less chance of his or her good being violated. For welfare interests function as prerequisites of whatever pursuits we have. More or less. A person may give some project priority over what we would consider to be his or her welfare interests, but we can generally presume that the projects people have will require the satisfaction of their welfare interests as a precondition for their successful prosecution. Negative paternalism minimizes the likelihood of manipulation. In the case of children, however, paternalism is likely to have a more positive aspect, since they need to acquire the wherewithal for forming a conception of their own good. Even so, the emphasis is not to be on securing for them someone else's conception of their good (although to some extent that will inevitably be involved), but on enabling them to determine their own.

In general, the "weaker" the paternalism, the more likely it is that it can be justified. Although we have employed an absolute distinction between weak and strong paternalism (see above, pp. 9–10), the considerations in terms of which that distinction is made are matters of degree. People have greater or less control over their behavior, even their voluntary behavior. Where the factors influencing a person's risky choice detract from its full voluntariness, paternalism will pose a less serious threat to that person's integrity than would be the case were they expressive of cool deliberation. This, however, does not license us to read less than full voluntariness from risky choices. They may raise the question for us, but they cannot be taken to settle it.

In general, the more serious the threatened detriment to welfare, the more likely it is that paternalism will be justified. Although our welfare interests function as prerequisites to the pursuit of our other interests, not all detriment to the former will seriously impede the latter.

In general, the higher the risk involved, the more compelling the case for paternalism. Most activities have some degree of risk associated with them. There is always a chance that one will get food poisoning or will be knocked over crossing the road. But some harms are more probable than others, and a concerted effort to eliminate all risk would be both futile and oppressive. There are other factors to be taken into account, such as the importance of the risky pursuit to the person concerned, and the ease with which the risk might be reduced. In assessing risk, there are both absolute and comparative factors to be taken into account. Some activities are inherently high-risk activities—boxing, speedway racing, mountain climbing, etc. Others are not in themselves high-risk activities, but the risk that they do involve can be substantially reduced with a minimum of effort. For example, crossing the road may not be a high-risk activity, yet the risk that it does involve may be substantially reduced (and with a minimum of effort) if people refrain from jaywalking and observe crossing signs at crossroads.

In general, the more difficult it is to repair the harm or detriment, the more likely it is that paternalism will be justified. If, say, boxing is likely to lead to bruises and broken bones, this might well be thought worth the risk. Broken bones heal, and one can expect to be able to take up boxing again, along with other valued activities. But if there is a high probability that one will be killed or suffer irreversible brain damage, this is a different matter. On its own it may not be a strong enough reason for outlawing boxing, but it is a factor that might reasonably be taken into account.

THE MORE EFFECTIVE IMPOSITION IS TO BE PREFERRED TO A LESS EFFECTIVE IMPOSITION

We characterize an imposition as paternalistic if it is directed to securing someone's good, as an end. It is not essential that it achieve that end. Yet this can hardly be irrelevant to its justification. Misguided though good intentions may not even be excusable, let alone justifiable. So there is reason to expect (1) that a paternalistically motivated imposition be likely to accomplish what it is intended to, and (2) that preference be given, *ceteris paribus*, to the imposition most likely to achieve that end. There are various ways in which an imposition may fail to achieve the end to which it is directed. It may not be tailored to a particular end, in that there has been a failure to appreciate the causal connections involved. Or it may be tailored to the end but have counterproductive side effects. Opponents of fluoridation often claim that though artificially added fluorides decrease the incidence of dental caries, they increase the likelihood of other health problems. This may not be correct, but were it so, it would have a bearing on the justifiability of paternalistically motivated interference. The notorious Volstead Act no doubt diminished the availability of alcohol, but it did so in a way that proved counterproductive.

As T. H. Green had wisely observed some forty years before its enactment: "To attempt a restraining law in advance of the social sentiment necessary to give real effect to it, is always a mistake" (1881, p. 70).

SOCIAL SPINOFFS ARE TO BE TAKEN INTO ACCOUNT

Although it is not the purpose of paternalistic impositions to achieve socially valuable ends, it is likely that they will have certain social benefits and costs attached to them, and these may be given a secondary role in their justification. Seat belt and safety helmet regulations, for example, are likely to have some effect on the availability, cost, and quality of medical and welfare resources, and these may be taken into account when considering such legislation. At the same time, account will need to be taken of various costs of regulation: to motorists, in ensuring that helmets are purchased and seat belts fitted and kept in good working order; and to the community, in the costs of enforcement, and so on.

Because of the sensitive character of paternalistic impositions, there are strong reasons for providing opportunities for their debate and their removal or revision where it is proposed to give them legal effect. The foregoing maxims and considerations indicate some of the factors that will be relevant to that debate, and, if taken seriously, ought to ensure that the likelihood of unacceptable violations of basic liberties will be minimized.

Notes

1. A person may be filled with remorse immediately after committing the offense, and be moved to repentance. Although we may want a time lapse "to be sure," it does not seem necessary. Statutes of limitations are grounded on other (e.g., evidential) considerations.

2. The Argument from Future Selves allows mandatory helmet legislation but does not sanction state interference with (attempted) suicide, since, (if successful) no new self comes into being. Terry Kogan welcomes this consequence (1976, pp. 841–42). But should he? We may consider criminal statutes against (attempted) suicide to be inappropriate, but it is not intuitively clear that all interference should be eschewed.

3. It is all very well to say that personal identity is a matter of connectedness. But how much connection should there be for it to be reasonable to speak of two time-slices of selves as time-slices of the *same* self? As Regan himself poses it: Why not "go the whole way and say that the cyclist is a different person at every moment of time" (1974, p. 205)? Regan's only response seems to be that the consequences would be counterintuitive: "it would seem to undermine our whole concept of freedom" (1974, p. 206). Parfit is rather more willing to grasp the nettle (1973, pp. 154–60). What he sees as a possible consequence of his position, that we should come "to focus less upon the person, the subject of experience, and instead focus more upon the experiences themselves" (1973, p. 160), is both revealing and troubling, for it suggests that a radical utilitarianism is less concerned with people and their relationships with each other than about pleasures and pains (or whatever). It is this that tempts one to regard it as an amoral doctrine. For a different approach, which also finds depersonalized moralities problematic, see Stocker (1976).

4. Another version, the Argument from Freedom Maximization, gives a positive twist to the Argument from Freedom Protection. For present purposes they can be considered together.

5. Cf. Stanley Benn: "Assuredly, valuing a person and concern for his continuance as a rational chooser *can* be a reason for action of forbearance; but it is a different

one from respect: that looks to his future, this is exhausted altogether in recognizing his *present* moral status. My claim is that where considerations of respect for that present status block interference, concern for his future, even his future as a person, will not license it" (1981, p. 107).

6. In Odysseus's case, talk of consent may seem out of place, since consent is normally given to the initiatives of another. However, as I have argued elsewhere, this awkwardness does not affect the argument (Kleinig 1982, pp. 96–97).

7. For reasons given in Chapter 1 (above, pp. 5–6), I would dispute VanDeVeer's characterization of paternalism as coercive, a point he appears to acknowledge in a later article (1980b, p. 206, n. 16).

8. Reliance on the vocabulary of "episodic" and "settled" wants is not altogether satisfactory. As I've stated the distinction, it has heavily psychological overtones. But this is not the only, and may not be the most appropriate way of construing it. Alternatives would be to distinguish wants that are integral to a person's identity or life-plans from those that are not; or wants that are open to rational consideration from those that are not. Sartorius, as we have seen (above, p. 49), distinguishes between stable preferences and choice behavior. But none of these alternatives is without its difficulties (cf. Elster 1979, p. 84f).

9. For writers like Bosanquet, the "real" will or self is identical with the developed and coherently organized self, and the "manifest" will is distinguished as those indulgences and inclinations that are out of tune with or pull against it. Mill, however, seems to be less committed to cohesion and consistency as requirements for selfhood, and would have found greater difficulty in making the distinctions that Bosanquet recognizes (see Gaus 1983, ch. 5).

10. I say "tendency" because some opponents of strong paternalism, such as Mill, take a more extended view by insisting on the importance of taking a (noncoercive) interest in the self-regarding conduct of others (Mill 1859, pp. 276–77; cf. Struhl 1976).

11. I say "may" because if (a) it is very difficult in practice to separate those whose protest is serious from those whose protest represents no more than a passing insistence, and (b) there is reason to believe that a large majority of those who would be affected belong to the latter category, we may, for their sake, not permit exceptions to be made.

Part Two

Applications

4

Physical Protection

If paternalism of a strong kind can be justified at all, it is most likely to be justified in cases where bodily integrity is at risk. Serious physical injuries constitute impediments to most of our important personal projects or life-plans, their presence is easily determined, and they are often easily preventable. Laws and regulations requiring the use of seat belts in motor vehicles and safety helmets on motorcycles are paradigmatic instances of such apparently strong paternalism, and will provide a test case. Laws proscribing suicide or attempted suicide are less easily classifiable, and will be discussed in the latter part of the chapter.

However, it is well to remind ourselves at the outset that these constraints represent only few of a potentially large number designed in part to protect the individual from self-induced physical injury. We might also take into consideration laws or regulations requiring the use of seat belts during aircraft take-off or landing; the use of protective helmets, safety belts, and/or goggles by construction or industrial workers; the wearing of life preservers by water skiers or brightly colored jackets by hunters; the fitting of boats with life preservers, or the provision of safety nets for acrobatic and other aerial performances. Consider, too, laws and regulations limiting or prohibiting dangerous sports or pastimes (e.g., hang-gliding, boxing, squash, whitewater rafting, scuba diving, skiing, motor racing, parachuting, mountain climbing, abseiling, bull fighting, daredevil, and other endurance feats); or forbidding doubling on bicycles, riding on any part of a vehicle other than that designated for the use of passengers, attaching a mounted motorcycle to any other vehicle on a public highway, jaywalking, and swimming outside the limits of safety flags or when lifeguards are not on duty. Further possible examples include laws or regulations outlawing duelling; those making it illegal for women or children to work at certain physically exacting jobs; prohibiting suttee or the handling of venomous snakes during religious ceremonies; forbidding vol-unteering for dangerous experiments; and criminalizing self-mutilation, may-hem, and euthanasia. Naturally it would be rash to treat all of these actual or potential regulatory provisions as though they were on a par, or even as standing or falling with the cases relating to seat belts, safety helmets, and suicide. Nevertheless, paternalistic considerations are often included in their rationales: they testify to the large range of formal measures having physical self-protection as one of their ends.

Seat Belts and Safety Helmets

Although I shall be treating these together, they have not been treated equally by the same legislatures. Since 1966, many states in the U.S. have had safety helmet legislation, but seat belt legislation has never been introduced.[1] Mandatory helmet legislation was introduced into the U.K. in 1973, but seat belt legislation has only just come into force.[2] In Australia, the two have gone hand in hand, commencing with Victoria in 1970. Generally, legislatures have been much more favorable to safety helmet than to seat belt legislation, though the latter can now be found in New Zealand, France, Spain, Israel, Czechoslovakia, Belgium, the Netherlands, Sweden, Malawi, Denmark, Finland, Germany, the U.S.S.R., Switzerland, and some of the Canadian provinces (cf. Wakeling 1977, pp. 106–7).

It is not altogether clear why this legislative difference should have existed. No doubt the death and serious injury statistics for motorcyclists are substantially worse than those for car travellers. In addition, there is a greater optimism in the case of motor vehicles, that alternative safety measures can be developed (via improvements in vehicle design, the fitting of air bags, seat belt warning devices, etc.). Some commentators believe that seat belt laws, unlike safety helmet regulations, would be difficult to enforce. But undoubtedly one of the main reasons for the differential treatment has been the lobbying power of the respective groups.

There is little doubt that one of the prime motivating factors in the introduction of belt and helmet legislation has been the enormous toll, in injury and death, exacted on the roads (see Purver 1970, pp. 1271–72). There is, further, statistical evidence to suggest that a substantial reduction in this toll can be achieved if belts and helmets are worn (see Roethe 1967, pp. 292–93; Henderson and Freedman 1974; Countermeasures Development 1974, pp. 1–4; Vaughan, Wood, and Croft 1974, pp. 103–24; Hoglund and Parsons 1974, pp. 4–5; Kraus 1975; Watson et al. 1980; 1981). Yet mandatory use is vigorously opposed. It is maintained that, whatever the wisdom of such arrangements, making them compulsory lies outside the proper sphere of authority. The principle of individual liberty limits legitimate interference to contexts in which the interests of *others* are jeopardized. But here public authority has no jurisdiction, for the only person to be injured is the nonwearer.

Such is the strength of this liberal heritage that judicial defenses of seat belt and safety helmet legislation show considerable coyness. Paternalistic rationales are clearly an embarrassment, and strenuous efforts are usually made to provide a nonpaternalistic justification. Various *public* interests are said to be threatened by the failure to wear seat belts or safety helmets. Nonusers are said to constitute a danger to others, to run the risk of becoming public charges, or to place in jeopardy their publicly valued productive capacity. Alternatively, the road toll is argued to have reached the proportions of a public disaster. But as we shall see, it is only with some difficulty that these considerations, taken individually or together in some combination, can sustain belt and helmet legislation, and there is often a surreptitious appeal to paternalistic reasons. It would clearly be of some advantage of defenders of this legislation if a legitimate niche for paternalism can be found. In order to determine whether this is so, I shall first explore the ramifications of four paternalistically oriented arguments before passing on to a brief examination of arguments invoking some public interest.

PATERNALISTIC ARGUMENTS FOR SEAT BELT
AND SAFETY HELMET LEGISLATION

Of the four arguments to be considered here, the first two have little to be said for them, which is not to say that they are only rarely heard. The remaining two are potentially more interesting.

The Argument from Privilege. Put crudely, the principle of liberty affirms a right to freedom from interference in matters that are private to the individual. Thus the owner of private property is (on one account) entitled to conduct him- or herself as he or she wishes with respect to that property, so long as the rights of others are not violated. So far as access to property is concerned, discretion rests with the owner. Others may be excluded, or granted entrance on conditions determined by the owner. Their access is a matter of privilege, not right.

In several U.S. court cases, involving challenges to safety helmet legislation, and in some of the supporting literature for seat belt legislation, the distinction between a right and a privilege is claimed to justify paternalism on public roads and highways.[3] Briefly, it is maintained that public roads and highways do not constitute the private property of their users. They are not theirs to use and regulate as they wish; they are public property, and using them is a matter of privilege, not right. That being so, it is for the public, through its agent, the state, to determine the conditions under which users should travel. And if paternalistically motivated constraints are included, there is no ground for complaint. As the court in *Odegaard* declared, in such circumstances "the state can adopt reasonable measures for the promotion of safety upon public highways in the interests of those who use them." A similar argument has been deployed in the Canadian debate over seat belt legislation. Responding to the claim that the government has no business protecting personal safety in an automobile, it is maintained:

> The logic behind this argument is simply faulty. Highways built with tax-payers' money are public property, driving one's automobile on them is a privilege, not a right; the government which represents the best interests of the people, the collective "owners" of the road, has the authority and duty to see these public highways used in a manner that contributes to the public safety and welfare (Countermeasures Development 1974, p. 17).

Despite the rhetoric of "public safety and welfare" resorted to in this quotation, the Argument from Privilege fails at a crucial point. Whereas the private owner of property might be acknowledged to have reasonable latitude in the conditions under which people are permitted access to and use of that property (enough latitude to legitimize paternalistically motivated restrictions), in the case of public property, limitations on access and use have to be justified in terms of the public interest.[4] That being the case, it is difficult to see what room an argument of this kind could leave for paternalistically inspired legislation, for, *ex hypothesi*, the interests in question are private, not public.

There may, of course, be a public interest served by seat belt and safety helmet regulations, but its justification will not require an appeal to privilege. So far as the safety of travellers on public roads from self-induced injury is concerned, the Argument from Privilege has nothing to say.

The Argument from Paternalistic Precedent. A common procedure for evaluating rationales is to trace out their implications, to see whether they are likely to have unacceptable consequences. If so, the rationale must be modified or abandoned. The Argument from Paternalistic Precedent is a variant on this. It is maintained that the "extreme" antipaternalism involved in opposition to seat belt and safety helmet legislation, if followed through, would require the repeal of much other legislation, more than could be reasonably countenanced. So argued the court in *Bisenius* v. *Karns*:

> If the public interest were indeed the test to be used in determining the validity of a police power statute, a considerable number of statutes here and elsewhere would become suspect, including laws requiring hunters to wear brightly coloured jackets, prohibiting riders on motor driven cycles from attaching same to any vehicle on a highway, prohibiting persons other than employees from riding upon any part of a vehicle not designated for the use of passengers, requiring boats to be equipped with life preservers, prohibiting aerial performances without a net, requiring persons to wear life preservers while riding on water skis, requiring tunnel workers to wear protective helmets and other types of industrial employees to wear protective goggles.[5]

The implication here is that there is much common sense embodied in these regulations, and that we would be considerably poorer without them. So, if we are to oppose (in this instance) safety helmet legislation on the ground that "it is my neck and I have a right to risk it when and where I please" (ibid), we must also be prepared to dispense with numerous other established, common sense legal requirements.

But this won't do. If the argument is to work, it must be shown either that the rationale employed is equally necessary to the other pieces of legislation, or that the supposed implications are unacceptable. Otherwise, we have no reason either for treating it similarly or for not repealing its analogues. We cannot assume that the common-sense nature of the regulations is sufficient for either of these purposes. The sympathy we may have for the content of these regulations does not necessarily attach to their form—that is, their embodiment in legislation. And that is what here needs to be justified. From the fact that we would be poorer if people did not take the sorts of precautions embodied in these pieces of legislation, it does not follow that we would be poorer without the legislation. For it may be argued that legislation would intrude unjustifiably on what is spoken of as a "zone of privacy" surrounding the individual.

Whether safety helmet legislation is on a justificatory par with the other examples may also be questioned. Industrial employees, for example, may be covered by a no-fault compensation act, which provides that injuries received in the workplace be compensated without regard to responsibility. In these circumstances, it may be reasonable to require that protective helmets, goggles, or other clothing be worn. And the act itself may be justified, not in paternalistic terms, but by reference to the costliness, wastefulness, and difficulty of administering a fault-based system. We may thus find, in some cases at least, that the supposed analogues do not stand or fall together and that the case for safety helmets is being illegitimately "carried" (cf. Royalty 1969, pp. 372–74).

The Argument from Weak Paternalism. Where, at the time of a physically dangerous act, there is good reason to believe that a person is subject to some responsibility-defeating condition, it is generally conceded that paternalistic intervention may be permissible.[6] It is sometimes argued that most of those who fail or even refuse to wear a seat belt or safety helmet fall into this category. Various reasons are given for this. The refusal of many motorcycle riders to wear helmets is sometimes attributed to peer group pressure—pressure to live up to a "macho" image. The words of one ice hockey player are apposite: "It's foolish not to wear a helmet. But I don't—because the other guys don't. I know that's silly, but most of the players feel the same way. If the league made us do it, though, we'd all wear them and nobody would mind" (quoted in Schelling 1973, p. 381). Sometimes car drivers refuse to wear belts because of phobias about being trapped inside a burning or sinking car. C. Edwin Harris, Jr. argues that belt and helmet legislation is designed to "protect people from their own foolhardiness, lack of sufficient forethought and lack of discipline," claiming that the "irresponsible actions" to which these failings give rise "are close enough to nonresponsible or involuntary actions" to be covered by the arguments for weak paternalism. They are "substantially less than voluntary" (Harris, 1977, p. 88–89).

The foregoing represent something of a mixed bag and call for a varying response. But one general reaction might be to deny that claims of this kind would account for most nonwearing. Some who refuse to wear belts or helmets do so as a matter of deliberate policy. Harris, for one, concedes this and allows that, if practicable, exemptions should be made for such people. However, if it is not practicable, then "the state would have to make a choice between caring for those who are not in fact making informed and free decisions in this area, and forcing those who do not want to be part of the system to be a part anyhow" (Harris 1977, p. 80). If it is reasonable to assume that those who would oppose the wearing of protective equipment as a matter of strong principle comprise only a small minority of those affected by the legislation, it is arguably better that they should be required to suffer that (in most respects) minor inconvenience than that, out of deference to them, large numbers of people, albeit as a result of their own "irresponsibility," should be exposed to unnecessary and serious risks. Here a collective good argument is used to justify interference with those whose opposition stems from principle.

However, all this is premised on the assumption that the sort of "irresponsibility" of which Harris speaks, and which others imply, is tantamount to "substantially nonvoluntary behavior." This assumption is implausible—at least in many of the cases to which it is applied. We can grant that voluntariness is a matter of degree, and that only a small proportion at best conforms to Feinberg's standard of "full voluntariness" (1971, pp. 110–11). But do the failings referred to by Harris belong so far down the scale to justify "rectification" in the name of weak paternalism? Not really. True, there is some evidence indicating that a good proportion of those who fail to wear belts or helmets favor being made to do so (see Henderson and Freedman 1974, pp. 13–14; Hoglund and Parsons 1974, p. 15, n. 52; *The Times*, 12 Jan. 1973, p. 3c; 13 June 1974, p. 35a; 23 Feb. 1976, p. 13c). This suggests that the failure is as often as not a consequence of thoughtlessness, laziness, or rationalization as of principle. And it might also be granted that certain features of our culture militate against properly informed and carefully weighed appraisals of the value of and need for belts and helmets. The mass media have "anesthetized" us against some of the horrors of physical injury in general, and the road toll in particular. We are constantly encouraged to focus on the present and to give less than due consideration to the possible future consequences of our actions. Our cultural role models, moreover, tend to exude invulnerability as they go about their risk-defying ways. But this does not really add up to a case for saying that our responsibility for failure to wear belts or helmets has been alienated.

John Hodson might disagree. He argues that in cases where a person's decisions are "encumbered," one of the conditions for justifiable (i.e., weak) paternalism is satisfied. Encumbered decisions are characterized as those "made in circumstances which are known to affect decision-making in such a way that the person making decisions sometimes comes to believe that the decisions are mistaken or unfortunate" (Hodson 1977, p. 65). This would certainly allow us to claim that many decisions not to wear a seat belt or safety helmet were encumbered, but as a condition for weak paternalism it is surely too permissive. It appears to sanction paternalism in any case where the circumstances are of a kind that would lead to decisions being made that would be likely to be regretted later. Brock remarks of this concept of encumbrance that it "is such that it includes, either already or by a natural and plausible extension, all decisions and decision-making made in circumstances that do not result in the maximally best decision" (1983). This, perhaps, overstates the problem, since Hodson might reply that where a suboptimal decision represents the best we can do at the time, later events will not necessarily lead us to think of it as "mistaken or unfortunate." Even so, Hodson's account would allow interference with a much wider range of conduct than Mill (whose position Hodson is seeking to defend) would have countenanced. Though we may wish to see thoughtlessness, laziness, rationalization, and so on as detracting from "full voluntariness," they do not take us below the threshold of competence that would justify calling any paternalistically motivated interference with their consequences "weak." Carelessness and indiscipline are vices rather than mere defects.

The Argument from the Relative Value of Freedom.[7] Benjamin Franklin's dictum that "they that can give up essential liberty to obtain a little temporary safety deserve neither liberty nor safety" (1759, p. 289), is usually taken to imply that in any conflict between freedom and other values, freedom takes priority. But it may be read in another way. Arguably, the force of Franklin's claim rests on a contrast between "essential freedom" and "temporary safety" rather than freedom and safety *simpliciter*. If this is so, seat belt and safety helmet legislation has some claim to be exempted. Although the use of seat belts or safety helmets offers only limited protection in limited circumstances, the dangers from which one is protected in these limited ways are very substantial. It would be misleading to characterize what they provide as merely "a little temporary safety." On the other hand, to see such legislation as an infringement of "essential freedom" seems excessive. It overlooks the variable intrusiveness of infringements, and treats a minor limitation as though it were a major assault. If liberty is looked at as a piece of territory over which we have jurisdiction, a clear difference can be discerned between a temporary trespass that does not interfere with any or any significant projects of the occupier and the permanent alienation of a substantial part of that territory. Equally, there is a clear difference between an interference intended to prevent an occupier from planting a crop and one intended to prevent the occupier from rendering the land permanently useless. Seat belt and safety helmet requirements, it may be argued, do not violate "essential freedom," since they leave an agent's significant projects virtually untouched. If anything, they are advanced, since the protection they afford increases the probability of their being realized.

In this form, however, the argument is not likely to carry conviction. For the antipaternalist will respond along the lines of the Arguments from Oppression of Individuality/Disrespect for Persons. Liberty, it will be argued, is not simply a value, to be put in the balance with other values, but a principle grounded in a recognition of individuality or of a person's status as a chooser—capable of forming and pursuing his or her own plans and purposes. This status constitutes a "moral trump card" vis-à-vis the intrusion of others. The paternalist confuses a legitimate concern for others (which may justify remonstrating or arguing with them) with a respect or regard for them (which functions to limit the reach of concern). Whereas concern arises out of a certain valuing of others, respect is not a value. It is a principle that limits the commitments consequent upon the ascription of value and is consistent with an absence of value. Respect or regard is due even to those we do not value, by virtue of their capacity to initiate their own projects and form their own plans.

Powerful though this riposte may be, it does not completely dispose of the version of the Argument from the Relative Value of Freedom under consideration. For a proponent of the latter may press the antipaternalist to show why it is that the liberty of a chooser has the status of a principle rather than a value (albeit an important one). More incisively, it might be claimed that it is only in virtue of certain values that liberty has its status as a principle. Should a person's conduct threaten to undermine these values, liberty's claims lose their otherwise compelling character.

How might an argument of this kind be run? The following is a sketch. There are many things that we value—trees, sunsets, food, some peace and quiet, cars, our work, political freedom, love, friendship, and so on. We do not have to produce any single or even completely compatible list. What is more important is the fact that we value some of these things more than others, and further that some of those things we value most are expressions of human activity and valued in part because they originate in the free initiatives of individuals. It is for this reason that fettering a person is likely to deprive the world of a *potential* for great value, for there is no other way in which those values can be realized other than via the unconstrained activity of rational persons. Herein lies the justificatory source of the standing that freedom has as a side constraint. If we do not respect others as ends or have regard for their individuality but view their liberty simply as a value along with other values, then we undercut or destroy the conditions under which those most highly prized values can be conceived. Now, although this would rule out most paternalistic interference, it would not necessarily rule out some—for example, where the consequences of a person's decisions would significantly jeopardize his or her future value-realizing capacities.

Should this line of argument be accepted, it would preserve a distinction between valuing and respecting or having regard for a person, since it does not require of the person who is to be respected that he or she possess anything more than the *potential* for value-creation. But it does not preserve the same distinction as the one initially proposed. For what the relativist is putting forward is an argument for preserving opportunities for value-creation, and it just so happens that this requires "unconstrained activity" (by and large). This is not the point of respect for persons or having regard for individuality and, indeed, differs significantly from them. Consider a situation in which five hospitalized people are likely to die unless they receive organ transplants. In the same hospital there is also a wastrel, receiving treatment for a broken nose, but otherwise in good health. If what sustains the principle of respect or regard is potentiality for value-creation, a case could be made for dispatching the wastrel and dividing up his organs among the other five. Admittedly, the wastrel's potential, such as it is, will be lost, but the potential of the five others will be preserved. We may not know for sure that these five would have more to offer than the wastrel, but it would be worth a wager. Perhaps the consequentialist defender of this argument would attempt to avoid this possibility by drawing attention to the unwelcome side effects it would have. But even if this could be sustained, it would still support a very different kind of principle from the one we began with. Supporters of "respect for persons" would not even countenance the kind of possibility I have been exploring. For the point of the principle is to secure an equality of standing among choosers, and this is undercut by the proposed rationale. There would be a similar refusal on the part of those whose concern is individuality. It is because the wastrel has purposes and projects of his own (however unworthy) that it would be unconscionable to sacrifice him.

The problems confronting the Argument from the Relative Value of Freedom can be seen in somewhat clearer focus by taking a closer look at the assumption that is made in the present context, viz., that seat belt and safety helmet legislation constitutes only a minor infringement of freedom. As we have already noted, judgments of the triviality or seriousness of impositions are relative to individual value structures, and what is seen as a trivial invasion in terms of one person's hierarchy of values may be accorded great significance in relation to another's. Those who claim that belts and helmets are at worst a minor inconvenience are, in effect, observing that, in terms of their own values and goals, it makes little difference. They may have no business assuming that the same would be true for others. As C. L. Ten observes, many who object to such legislative measures will claim,

> with some justice, that they value not wearing seat belts much more than is made out. By rejecting their own assessment of their values we run the risk of evaluating the benefits of an activity by our own standards. . . . Where we disapprove of an activity, or cannot appreciate it, we tend to think that the agent himself derives little benefit from it. In these ways the practice of paternalism easily becomes a cloak for the imposition of our values on those who are coerced (1980, p. 116).

Ten believes that we frequently distinguish risk-taking activities that we are prepared to tolerate from those that we are not. We admire mountain climbers and those who attempt to sail solo round the world, and can appreciate the position of those who continue to work in defiance of doctor's "orders." But we are prepared to penalize those who object to wearing a seat belt or safety helmet. This distinction, he claims, is possible only if we "allow paternalism to slide into the enforcement of our values" (1980, p. 117).[8]

Obviously there is something to be said for this objection. To assess its force, it will be helpful if we distinguish two ways in which people may see the matter of belt and helmet wearing as nontrivial. First, they may regard the protective devices as serious impediments to the realization of some of their highly valued ends. Motorcyclists, for example, have sometimes made a great deal of the sensations involved when the wind beats in the face and rushes through the hair—its almost sensual quality, the feeling and celebration of independence, a sympathy with nature or a sense of striving against it. Ten further notes that "the desire to seek danger is often the product of a certain type of personality and temperament that some people take pride in cultivating. To interfere with their risky conduct is to deny them the opportunity to pursue their own plans of life" (Ten 1980, p. 117; cf. Tribe 1978, pp. 939–40). So, whereas for some riders not wearing a helmet has a significance independent of the risks involved, for others the risk is integral to that significance. But we should not assume that interference would be less intrusive in the former case than in the latter. This can be seen when we consider the vigorous opposition to helmet legislation mounted by the Sikhs in the United Kingdom, with many Sikhs claiming in the strongest possible terms that the requirement went contrary to the tenets of their faith.[9] In addition, it has sometimes been claimed that the helmets themselves are hazardous because they affect the rider's hearing and peripheral vision, are liable to "fog up", and are generally distracting. Seat belts also come in for this sort of criticism—they are said to be accident-inducing and, in the event of an accident, injury-producing; moreover, some people find them claustrophobic: they are gripped by the fear that, should there be an accident, they will be trapped in a burning or submerged vehicle.[10]

Although some of the claims made against seat belts and safety helmets are undoubtedly exaggerated, it would be wrong to underestimate the intrusiveness that legislation sometimes involves. Nevertheless, the balance might still remain on the side of legislation. If we can assume that most of those who fail to wear belts or helmets do so for marginal reasons (laziness, forgetfulness, rationalization, and so on), requiring them to wear one will leave their integrity intact. For the rest, some form of exemption may be possible. In England, for example, Sikhs are no longer under a legal duty to wear safety helmets. It may be possible to provide for other grounds of exception as well. However, there is a difficulty here. Laws need to be clear, predictable in their application, and enforceable, and these requirements may lead to fewer exemptions being made available than the "nontriviality" criterion would foreshadow. This is a cost that would need to be taken into account. It is to be noted, however, that in these cases the imposition would not have a directly paternalistic justification but an administrative one. The point would not be to impose on those with strong objections to the use of belts and helmets an alien conception of their good, but to administer a system of regulation in which those who, through indiscipline, rationalization, and carelessness, fail to wear a belt or helmet, would be provided with sufficient motivation to act in ways compatible with their significant projects and life-plans. If this seems an unacceptable trade-off, one mitigating factor might be the likelihood of a change of mind should the risk later materialize. A motorcyclist who objects to being forced to wear a helmet is likely to be less critical if he or she becomes a beneficiary of the requirement (cf. Mooney 1977, p. 101; Goodin 1982, pp. 45–47).

The second way in which seat belt and safety helmet legislation may assume great importance for the objector is a consequence of the maxim implied— viz., that "self-regarding" conduct is not immune to legal interference. A significant number of people, including some who regularly wear a belt or helmet, believe that self-protective legislation violates a central tenet of liberalism—viz., that individuals should be left free from interference in matters that do not unreasonably intrude upon the interests of other people. So, although the interference is not significant in itself, the principle that it violates is.

This takes us back to what is usually seen as the central problem, though here the focus is on its subjective or psychological rather than moral dimensions. Clearly, if people feel strongly that in being required to wear a seat belt or safety helmet a crucial liberty is being seriously eroded, then, whether or not they are right to think that, they will feel seriously aggrieved if compelled to wear one. They will feel that even if they ordinarily wear one. Such feelings cannot be ignored in the political process. Whatever the merits and justification for belt and helmet legislation *in vacuo*, if in the existing social environment it is likely to offend against strongly held beliefs, its promulgation may prove self-defeating. Lest such legislation prove unwarrantedly distressing, there is an onus on its supporters to provide assurances that the invasion of liberty is not unprincipled and escalatory. The limiting maxims discussed at the end of the last chapter are intended to provide some of that assurance.

Be that as it may, the Argument from the Relative Value of Freedom underrates the force of the Argument from Oppression of Individuality. To see the issue as one of balancing a potentially great gain against a minor restriction is to distort it. What is at issue is recognition of the individual's standing as a source of reasons and projects, reasons and projects that are invested with a special moral significance just because they are *that individual's* reasons and projects. It is that standing that seat belt and safety helmet legislation symbolically threatens, and the matter is not improved by talk about the relative value of freedom or the relative importance of restrictions and gains. For it is in relation to that particular individual's own projects and life-plans that these restrictions and gains have the importance they do.

We do better, I suggest, to come at the issue via the Argument from Personal Integrity, for this is designed to give moral space to paternalism without transgressing the requirements of individuality. The Argument from Personal Integrity claims that seat belt and safety helmet legislation may be justified because the reasons why many people fail or even refuse to wear them do not accord with their own acknowledged goals, purposes, attitudes, and values—or at least not those they value highly. If what causes people not to do what they themselves recognize to be worth doing is laziness, indiscipline, lack of forethought, absent-mindedness, weakness of will, care-lessness, and even cussedness, compelling them to do it will involve no serious intrusion. It is this that makes the restriction only a trivial one. And it is because reasons of this kind generally do lie behind the failure to wear seat belts and safety helmets, that legislation makes serious sense. But by the same token, just because we cannot presume that all people will construe their good in the same way, or even have the same good, any such requirement will need to accommodate exceptions.

The Argument from Personal Integrity provides us with a reason for seat belt and safety helmet legislation. It may not be a sufficient reason, and it is therefore worth considering more briefly what else may be said on its behalf. This returns us to the public interest arguments that I initially canvassed.

PUBLIC INTEREST ARGUMENTS FOR SEAT BELT AND SAFETY HELMET LEGISLATION

Mill argues that where a person's risky acts threaten not only his or her own interests, but also the interests of others, they are "taken out of the self-regarding class" and into the public domain of other-regarding behavior (Mill 1859, p. 281). The failure to wear a seat belt or safety helmet is sometimes claimed to fit this pattern. Four arguments can be distinguished. The first two I consider to be implausible, but some weight must be given to the remaining two.

The Argument from Danger to Others. The courts have sometimes claimed that motorcyclists (and their passengers) are particularly vulnerable to injuries and distractions that could cause them to lose (or cause loss of) control of their vehicles and thus endanger other road users or pedestrians:

> Cyclists generally keep to the right of the road where stones and gravel are found which could be propelled by the delicately balanced wheels into the head of the cyclist or passenger, causing distraction and loss of control.

> One reads or hears about instances where cyclists have been hit with hard-shelled beetles or bees and have lost control of their bikes, causing damage and injuries to others.[11]

A similarly imaginative scenario has been painted for the failure to wear a seat belt. It is claimed that

> far more easily than the experienced racing driver, the average motor vehicle operator may lose control by being thrown from the wheel by a spin, violent evasive action or sudden braking. A similar loss of control may be precipitated by the sliding or unseating of a passenger flung by inertial or centrifugal forces against the operator. The innocent motorist requires and deserves protection from the spectre of an oncoming, careening automobile whose driver has been jostled from its controls (Hoglund and Parsons 1974, p. 17; cf. p. 4, n. 11).

There is little evidence, other than of a hearsay kind, that any significant number of accidents originate in these ways. It is one thing to say, as did one member of the judiciary, that it "does not tax the intellect to comprehend" that such a conjunction of events could occur;[12] it is quite another to say that it is likely to occur. Until that is established, there is no reason for giving effect to judicial imagination.

The Argument from Loss of Productivity. Society is not a mere aggregation of isolated atoms. Its members bear certain relations to each other, and their individual well-being is to some extent dependent on those relations being maintained in certain ways (see above, pp. 40ff). Courts have sometimes argued that there are social obligations in these dependencies and benefits, and that our capacity to fulfill them is jeopardized if we fail to take reasonable self-protective measures. So *Carmichael*:

> It is in the interest of the state to have strong, robust, healthy citizens capable of self-support, or bearing arms, and of adding to the resources of the country.[13]

As we have already seen, this claim to the positive contribution of citizens, though controversial, is not foreign to the liberal tradition (Mill 1859, pp. 224–25). But how far can it be stretched? Might an individual's duty to "bear his fair share in the common defence, or in any other joint work necessary to the interests of the society of which he enjoys the protection," extend to the wearing of a seat belt or safety helmet? Mandatory seat belt and safety helmet wearing is not the same as forced labor. The former does not require that an active role be played in the workforce or other socially important activities. It does not imply, as was stated in *American Motorcycle Association* v. *Davids*, that "people exist for the state rather than that the state exists for the people."[14] What it does is to help protect people from harms that would render them incapable of fulfilling their allegedly positive social duties. But this is to weaken the causal connection excessively, at least when taken at an individual level. Perhaps it could be argued that collectively, the incapacitation caused by the failure to wear seat belts and safety helmets puts an unacceptable strain on the social fabric, but this now shades into the Argument from Public Disaster, to be considered later. The Argument from Loss of Productivity has too many controversial features to be safely used in support of seat belt and safety helmet legislation.

The Public Charge Argument. Injuries received in road accidents may have costly consequences not only for the victim but also for others. The victim may be incapacitated for a considerable period of time, requiring the use of scarce medical resources and possibly made dependent on public funds for support. It has sometimes been claimed that the available funds are already stretched to the limit and that additional demands would unfairly burden the rest of society.[15] This unfairness is said to be a function of the size of the tax demand and/or the easy avoidability of the injuries. Not only the victims, but also their dependents, may be cast on the public purse. Spouses and children may have both a financial and psychological stake in the victim's continued well-being, and the collapse of this may lead to their becoming charges on the community. It was put this way by the Federal District Court of Massachusetts:

> While we agree with the plaintiff that the Act's only realistic purpose is the prevention of head injuries incurred in motorcycle mishaps, we cannot agree that the consequences of such injuries are limited to the individual who sustains the injury. . . . The public has an interest in minimizing the resources directly involved. From the moment of the injury, society picks the person up off the highway; delivers him to a municipal hospital and municipal doctors; provides him with unemployment compensation if, after recovery, he cannot replace his lost job, and if the injury causes permanent disability, may assume the

responsibility for his and his family's subsistence. We do not understand
a state of mind that permits plaintiff to think that only himself is
concerned.[16]

The argument applies, naturally, only in respect of injuries that would not
have been received had the victim been wearing a seat belt or safety helmet.
These may not be easy to calculate, though this does not seriously weaken
the injury-diminishing claims made for these protective devices. The legislative
conclusion, however, does not uncontroversially follow. It is arguable that
many, if not most vehicle drivers should be able to accommodate the costs
of their treatment and hospitalization within their existing resources (either
private means or through their membership of a health fund). And should
it turn out that a sizable proportion of them are not covered in this way,
proof of medical insurance could be made a prerequisite of their vehicle
registration (Royalty 1974, pp. 370–71). This would be a less restrictive
alternative. In some courts it has been claimed that mandatory medical
insurance does not shift the burden adequately, since it is reflected in increased
insurance premiums.[17] But this could be handled by means of differential
premiums. All such strategies assume that accident victims consume a sizable
proportion of public resources, and this too may be challenged (Royalty 1974,
p. 371). It is arguable that, if there is substantial unfairness in the tax burden
that people are asked to bear, its source lies elsewhere in the welfare system.
We can afford to bear the costs of those whose injuries stem from failure to
wear a seat belt or safety helmet. I raise this point not because I am convinced
of its correctness, but because it indicates that cost-benefit analyses are more
complex than we can expect to handle via an appeal to our intuitions.

But becoming a public charge is not simply a matter of economics. I have
already referred to the psychological costs that friends and relatives of the
accident victim may have to bear. These costs do not stop there. Think of
the witnesses, of the driver/passengers in any other vehicle that may have
been involved, of those who have to care for the victim, and of ourselves,
should the details of the accident be reported in the media. The effects may
be traumatic. Of course, wearing a seat belt or safety helmet won't necessarily
prevent an accident from happening, but it may prevent injuries of the more
horrific kind from occurring. What is more, these psychological effects "extort"
from us assistance that the failure to wear theoretically passes up.[18] For the
person who deliberately chooses to travel without a belt or helmet is telling
us that what he does with his life is his business, not ours. But it is ours, in
more than one way. We cannot turn aside and deny assistance should it be
required. And we cannot escape the psychological shock. Perhaps we *could*
inure ourselves to the frightful mess and its aftermath, but is it fair that we
should be expected to? Do we want to become people who remain impassive
in the face of avoidable tragedy?

Once again, it is not clear that we have anything like a decisive argument.
Like it or not, the world has so much suffering in it that we are forced to
develop accommodating mechanisms. What is the road toll compared to the
bloodshed in Lebanon, South Africa, Northern Ireland, etc.? It's closer to
home, perhaps, but it is not as though it places any more strain on our
emotional capacities than other events in the world. Even the financial argument
is a bit thin, since it is likely that some of our taxes are being used to support
the grisly "cause of justice" in other places.

There is a further source of difficulty for the Public Charge Argument, one that applies to both economic and psychological versions. It is that if an argument of this kind is admitted, it will open the door to "unlimited paternalism" (broadly understood). In *American Motorcycle Association* v. *Davids*, the court argued, as a *reductio*, that if the state's exercise of police power[19] was able to encompass safety helmet legislation, it was also broad enough to require car drivers to buckle up their seat belts! It would also permit the state to forbid smoking or to require that people go to bed at 10:00 P.M.[20] The problem, as one dissenting opinion put it, is that if the safety helmet requirement

> is based upon the possibility that [motorcyclists] may become hospitalized, or on welfare, that opens a wide door indeed to paternalistic controls over innumerable aspects of human conduct as to what may or may not be good for one's individual health, morals or safety. The difficulty is that if the obliteration of individual rights is permissible whenever there is the possibility, even indirect or remote, of injury to the public, then the line of demarcation as to the permissible intrusion of law, and its implementing functionaries, into conduct which should be one's private and personal concern becomes blurred almost to vanishing point.[21]

The plausibility of this attempted *reductio* depends on our taking the possibility of becoming a charge on the public purse or psyche as the sole ground for legislation, unconstrained by considerations of probabilities and onerousness. But this would involve a caricature. The costs of interference have to be taken into account no less than the costs incurred by the risky conduct. It is precisely because the costs are believed to favor intervention that the Public Charge Argument is advanced in the case of seat belts and safety helmets, and not in some of the other cases believed to lie on the slippery slope. The slippery slope has always been the refuge of a conservative.

The Public Disaster Argument. To say that the cry of "slippery slope" is a refuge is not to deny that it is ever justified. But it needs to be justified and not merely intoned. One problem with the Public Charge Argument may be that it does not provide sufficiently explicit safeguards against unwarranted extensions and erosions of legitimate liberties. The Public Disaster Argument is an attempt to provide an additional check. It focuses not on the effects of individual injuries, but on the social impact of those injuries viewed aggregatively. Their number and rate of increase are said to have combined to constitute them a "public disaster" (Royalty 1974, pp. 374–77; cf. R. N. Harris 1967, p. 593). To put it in the words of the court in *Anderson*:

> Death on the highway can no longer be considered as a personal and individual tragedy alone. The mounting carnage has long since reached proportions of a public disaster. Legislation reasonably designed to reduce the toll may for that reason alone be sufficiently imbued with the public interests to meet the constitutional test required for a valid exercise of the State's police power.[22]

There are similarities between this argument and that advanced by Lord Devlin against a firm distinction between private and public morality (Devlin 1965, p. 14). The Public Disaster Argument, however, possesses an important advantage. Whereas Devlin's argument was premised on the *possibility* of public detriment through an aggregation of "private" harms, the present argument has the *already existing* road toll as its starting point. Like "Keep off the Grass" signs in public parks, which have as their justification not merely the reasonable belief that many feet will damage what one or two will not, but the reasonable belief that without the sign many feet will indeed walk on the grass, the Public Disaster Argument works not with bare possibilities but high probabilities.

But there is a catch. How do we determine when some social occurrence constitutes a public disaster? It is not too difficult to tell when the grass has been killed off. It is not so easy to determine what number of serious injuries and deaths is needed before one has a public disaster. The notion of a public disaster is none too clear. But even if we are prepared to buy the view that the road toll constitutes a public disaster, it does not follow that the failure to wear seat belts and safety helmets is responsible for this. No doubt the failure to wear them contributes to the situation, but if, as seems probable, it accounts for at most 10 to 20 percent of the social and economic costs, legislation might not be thought warranted. Other, less restrictive ways of dealing with the toll may be thought preferable. This is frequently argued. The following alternatives are suggested:

(a) In a dispute between the U.S. Federal Department of Transport and the State of Utah in 1975, the latter proposed, as an alternative to requiring the use of safety helmets, a program involving "public information, increased inspection, speed law enforcement, cyclist education and improved licensing procedures" (Anon 1975, p. 4). The emphasis is on education in preference to compulsion. Salutary though that may be, such programs have a poor record (McCarthy 1973; Hoglund and Parsons 1974, p. 6, n. 17: Countermeasures Development 1974, pp. 7–8). Even though people are generally persuaded of the value of helmets and belts, they are often not sufficiently motivated to wear them. Laziness, the attitude that "it won't happen to me," the rationalization that one isn't going far, aesthetic quibbles, and so on, all interpose themselves. "Education" has been tried and found wanting.

(b) It has been argued that a better procedure is to place the safety burden on manufacturers of motor vehicles. This could include the incorporation of passive restraint systems such as airbags, the fixing of seat belts to all new cars, the attachment of a warning device that is activated when the ignition is turned on, or wiring the ignition system so that the car cannot be started until the seat belt is clipped in. It is argued that these alternatives are preferable because they do not constitute paternalism so much as an imposition on the manufacturer in the name of public safety (B. I. Kogan 1969, pp. 109–10). Here the assumption is that people want their cars to be made safe in some of these ways, but will not be able to obtain them at reasonable cost unless they become standard fittings. A "collective good" argument is used to justify their inclusion (and the costs associated with that) in cases where people would prefer to go without. The trouble with these strategies is that they are significantly less effective than worn seat belts (Hoglund and Parsons 1974, p. 7, n. 21; Countermeasures Development 1974, p. 3).

(c) An alternative means of encouraging motorcyclists and car occupants to use self-protective devices is to allow nonuse to bear on the apportionment of damages arising out of accidents.[23] Where a belt or helmet is not worn, there will be a discounting for negligence. It is understandable how a strategy of this kind might be adopted as a way of securing a certain kind of justice.

What is less clear is its deterrent value. To attribute that to it is to assume that the same factors that operate to produce the current situation in which, despite the risks, travellers neglect to use safety devices, will not continue to operate as powerfully and effectively where a comparative negligence standard operates. That assumption I find implausible. Road users do not have a realistic estimate of the risks they run: accidents are assumed to happen to "the other guy"; long-range costs are obscured by conveniences of the present, etc. (Calabresi 1970, pp. 55–58).

What I have attempted to do in this discussion is to bring out some of the complexities that are involved in the debate about seat belt and safety helmet legislation, complexities that are not obvious if it is characterized and then dismissed as "paternalistic." Some paternalism probably is involved, yet I do not believe that paternalism—even strong paternalism—is all of a piece. Those who invoke the Argument from Oppression of Individuality have an important point to make, but they tend to operate with a somewhat idealized conception of the normal personality, which gives their claims a rigid and doctrinaire, almost callous quality. Yet they are rarely willing to follow through the logic of their own position, leaving the careless and short-sighted to bear the full weight of their stupidity. I have wanted to claim that a revision of the Argument from the Relative Value of Freedom, what I discussed in Chapter 3 as the Argument from Personal Integrity, gives us enough room for some strong paternalism without compromising the insights that are embodied in the Argument from Oppression of Individuality.

But there is more than paternalism involved in the case for seat belt and safety helmet legislation. There are also public interests involved, and though I have indicated some of the problems involved in establishing these interests and the weight they are to be accorded, I believe that, taken together with the paternalistic considerations I defended, they constitute a strong enough case for seat belt and safety helmet legislation to be justified. I should, however, add two final qualifications. First, just because legislation is intrusive and easily insensitive to particularities, its introduction should be preceded by open debate in which objections can be freely expressed and allowed to carry their due weight, and its subsequent implementation (presuming that comes about) should be responsive to the lessons of experience. And second, where it is clear that the legislation infringes on stable and strongly held commitments, every effort should be made to create an exemption or otherwise modify its impact.

Attempted Suicide

Although travellers who fail to wear a seat belt or safety helmet may often be said to display a reckless or negligent disregard for their own safety (quite apart from any social obligations or duties they may have), it would not be plausible to say that they intend or will the death (or damage) that their failure may produce, at least in most cases. Paternalistic impositions are based on the (generally reasonable) assumption that they desire to continue living, and in circumstances that will enable their significant plans and projects to be prosecuted. Interferences with suicide attempts are not so clear-cut. For here, almost by definition, there is an attempt to bring about death (Holland 1969, p. 74f). But only "almost." For many so-called "attempted suicides" are better seen as dramatic attempts to draw attention to and to precipitate change in what is experienced as an unbearable situation. We are likely to characterize deaths resulting from such attempts as "accidental" rather than "deliberate" suicides. Death is a second-best. In this respect attempted suicide differs from daredevil conduct. Although the latter involves flirtation with death, death, if if eventuates, does not constitute a second-best.

Death through suicide is not uncommon. Some 500,000 suicides occur each year, and the number of attempts is several times that figure. It evokes no uniform moral or legal response. By some it has been viewed as an honorable and fitting way of departing this life (cf. Seneca *Epistulae Morales*: LXXVII). Not so, by others. Augustine believed that suicide violated the Sixth Commandment against murder, that it permanently deprived the person of opportunities for repentance, and that it was an act of cowardice (*City of God*: I.16–28). Aquinas claimed that it went against our "natural" (and hence proper) inclination to self-love, that it injured the community of which the suicide was a part, and that it violated a prerogative of God (*Summa Theologiae*: 2a2ae, q.64, a.5). It attracted ecclesiastical sanctions following the Council of Arles in A.D. 542, sanctions that continued spasmodically in England until the nineteenth century. Secular statutes against suicide go back to the ninth century in England, where the Roman penalty of forfeiture of possessions, imposed on those who committed suicide to avoid trial or conviction, was taken over and applied more generally. This practice ceased with the Forfeiture Act of 1870. In England, attempted suicide was not made a criminal offense until 1854, but both it and suicide were decriminalized in 1961. In the United States and Australia, some jurisdictions still keep the offense of attempted suicide on the books, though it is rarely invoked. It is now more common to see the person who attempts to commit suicide as suffering from psychiatric disorder than possessing criminal tendencies. Civil rather than criminal action is taken, though this does not necessarily indicate any melioration.

Before considering some of the arguments for intervening in suicide attempts, it is important to be aware of the great variety of reasons prompting such attempts. Many, as we have noted, attempt suicide in response to an unbearable situation. But unbearability can have many sources. It may be a failed love affair, a long-term psychotic condition, the onset of Huntington's chorea, loneliness, the pain of terminal cancer, the fear of being found out, or apparently unmanageable debts, to mention some of the possibilities. There are other reasons, too. Consider the practice of *suttee*, which was outlawed in the middle of the last century, the self-immolation of Buddhist monks during the Vietnam War, the Jews at Masada, those who have acted on the belief that by age sixty-five one's social usefulness has ended, etc. The catalogue of reasons should make us wary of oversimplified reactions.

Arguments about the morality of suicide frequently appeal to theological and natural law considerations (cf. Battin 1982, ch. 3). In a pluralistic society, these are not likely to weigh strongly in a case for legally sanctioned intervention. Public Interest Arguments are more apposite, but they have usually been bolstered by arguments possessing a more paternalistic ring. The former have not seemed capable of bearing the weight alone. Here I briefly canvass those arguments, before turning to the paternalistic rationales.

PUBLIC INTEREST ARGUMENTS
FOR INTERVENING IN SUICIDE ATTEMPTS

Several arguments are comprehended in this section. Here I shall consider just four of them.

The Argument from Violated Obligations. Few of us live in isolation from others. Generally we belong to and have commitments within interlocking networks of relationships. Sometimes suicide represents an opportunity to escape from such commitments; sometimes the failure to honor them is simply a consequence of suicide. A parent with dependent children who commits suicide in order to escape from gambling debts wrongs both his or her creditors and the children. In the latter case, the obligations are not merely economic but social and emotional. A suiciding relative may leave deep emotional scars on other members of a family.

There is some mileage to be gained from an argument of this kind, though whether the action taken should take the form of requiring performances of the obligations in question is doubtful. Intervention to prevent the suicide would at least have *prima facie* justification. Only *prima facie*, however. For the person may be a burden to others in a way that prevents the obligations from being fulfilled, and suicide may benefit them more than it injures them. Be that as it may, an argument based on assumed obligations is too narrow to support any general case for intervention. Some of those who commit suicide are scrupulous in seeking to meet their outstanding obligations.

The Argument from Loss of Productivity. In the sixteenth-century case of *Hales* v. *Petit,* Justice Dyer argued, *inter alia,* that suicide was an offense "against the King in that hereby he has lost a subject."[24] In so arguing, he was reflecting a position going back to Plato and Aristotle, in which the community is seen as having some claim upon the individual's labor and talents.

This argument, however, shares the weaknesses of the various Arguments from Interconnectedness considered in Chapter 3. Although social circumstances can be envisaged in which the loss caused by suicide would be great enough to warrant intervention, these would only rarely be present. Interdependence would need to be so tight that even migration could not be tolerated, for that is one way of looking at suicide.

The "Infectious Disease" Argument. The King, argued Justice Dyer, must, as governor of the people, "take care that no evil example be given them." If suicide goes unchecked, it may "catch on." Counterintuitive though this may seem, it is not completely fanciful (cf. Battin 1982, pp. 88–90, 95). Mass suicide is not unknown—Jonestown, Guyana being a recent example (Kilduff and Javers 1978; Knerr 1979). Gore Vidal's novel *Messiah* (1954) depicts a plausible scenario for the marketing of a suicide cult. It might therefore be argued that even if no proscribable social damage is caused by a few cases of suicide, it would be a very different matter were it to become prevalent. Some deterrence, therefore, is justified.

But for the infectious disease analogy to hold we need to have some reason to think that if unchecked, suicide would attain epidemic proportions. Unlike the Public Disaster Argument, in which a manifest social impact grounds the intervention, in this case the impact is only speculative. "What if everyone did the same?" constitutes an argument for intervention only if there is reason to think that there *are* many who want to do the same.

The Argument from Social Subversiveness. In Fedden's classic survey of suicide, it is suggested that the suicide, by opting out of life altogether, "shows contempt for society." Or, as Chesterton puts it, "The man who kills a man, kills a man. The man who kills himself, kills all men; as far as he is concerned he wipes out the world" (1909, p. 130). Whereas civil disobedience and even rebellion acknowledge some future for social relations, the extreme individualism of suicide throws doubt on this.

> Seeing a man who appears not to care for the things which it prizes, society is compelled to question all it has thought desirable. The things which make its own life worth living, the suicide boldly jettisons. Society is troubled, and its natural and nervous reaction is to condemn the suicide. Thus it bolsters up again its own values (Fedden 1938, p. 42).

Such a reaction is taken to be not merely "natural" but proper, a justifiable response to subversion of a radical kind. Not to respond is to confess that society does not carry within its own resources the means for resolving problems occurring within it.

An argument of this kind depends heavily on a certain reading of suicide. If not in intention, at least by implication, suicide must be interpreted as a vote against society. But is it? On occasions that may be so, but not as a rule. And even if it is intended as a protest, this is not in itself a sufficient reason for intervening. It is one thing to protest; it is another for the protest to be justified. And unless the social substructure is very unstable, there is no reason why every criticism demands a response. Even if the protest is soundly based, that may not be a reason for intervening, only for seeking to ensure that some improvements are made.

Although it is possible to tell stories in which the four Public Interest Arguments just considered would carry enough weight to justify legally sanctioned intervention, these stories would need to posit social conditions rather different from those with which we are familiar. It is not surprising, then, that arguments for suicide intervention tend to be, if not moralistic, then paternalistic.

PATERNALISTIC ARGUMENTS FOR INTERVENING IN SUICIDE ATTEMPTS

Although there are a number of paternalistic arguments for suicide prevention/ punishment, I shall here focus on the three that have the largest following. The first concentrates exclusively on the harm that death is assumed to be, the second on the decision-making capacity of the potential suicide, and the third on the meaning of suicide attempts.

The Argument from Harm Prevention. Death, whether it is brought about by others or through one's own acts, is usually thought to be a harm. This is because it brings to an (apparent) end all of an individual's projects and plans, and severs irrevocably all his or her valued human relationships. That being so, its prevention is often considered to be a justifiable social interest. So the court claimed in *Root*: "The policy of the law is to protect human life including the life of a person who wishes to destroy his own life."[25] Even more explicit is *Mink*: "The life of every human being is under the protection of the law, and cannot lawfully be taken by himself, or by another, with his consent, except by legal authority."[26]

Perhaps the first point to be noted is the particular notion of harm that is under consideration. It is claimed in this argument that there is a social interest in "harm prevention." It is to be observed, however, that as it is here understood "harm" is not to be equated with "the violation of rights" as in the harm principle, but with "damage" or "the impairment of welfare interests." The paternalistic Argument from Harm Prevention cannot be subsumed under the harm principle. The question then arises as to whether there is a *social* interest in harm prevention beyond that which is encompassed by the harm principle. The Argument from Harm Prevention tends to assume rather than argue that there is. While it is true that there are apparent precedents for such an interest (consent is no defense to a charge of assault), these precedents may show only that the law intrudes elsewhere where it ought not (though see Kleinig 1979).

It can, moreover, be questioned whether suicide always does constitute a harm, or if, when it does, it would constitute a greater harm than would be involved in preventing it. It is not, perhaps, usual to think of death as a benefit, though it is not impossible to think of it that way. More frequently, however, death can be seen as a means whereby certain harms might be nullified. Where a life offers no real prospects for the advancement of a person's core interests (as, perhaps, in the case of a terminal illness or severe disablement), death may be viewed as a release. The act of committing suicide may be the only way left whereby a person's individuality can be expressed. To interfere in such cases will constitute a violation of that individuality, made all the more gross because no other means remain whereby it may be expressed. No doubt there is something tragic about a situation in which death is the only thing left, but that is no reason for adding to the constraints.

Even where suicide would close off many of a person's ongoing options and projects, interference with it may constitute a serious violation of individuality. For the decision to suicide may be designed to further a project that is of fundamental importance to the person. The Buddhist monks who burned themselves to death in protest against the Vietnam War considered that protest to be more important than the alternative that would have remained to them had they stayed alive. A similar claim might be made about the kamikaze pilots in World War II. Whatever our views about the rightness of the causes for which people are prepared to sacrifice themselves, that they should be able to do so accords with a central commitment of liberalism. Something more than the damage people will do to themselves is required if paternalistic intervention is to be justified.

The Argument from Weak Paternalism. The "something more" is generally said to be some form of psychological debilitation. If, as it is sometimes claimed, we naturally seek our own good, then the decision to die must be actuated by factors beyond our control. Such is the contemporary wisdom. Whereas an earlier generation saw the decision to commit suicide as a sinful act of rebellion, the present one sees it as the product of a disordered mind. Not punishment but therapy is called for. If this is the case, if suicide attempts do not express the authentic desires of those who make them but alien compulsions, then the case for paternalistic interference is a strong one. For the problem confronted by the Argument from Harm Prevention is now circumvented. It represents no violation of individuality, no usurpation of a person's own projects, if a suicide attempt is thwarted, because the attempt does not belong to that person in the way in which our autarchically chosen projects do. To interfere is to take steps to release the person from hostile forces, so that he or she may reassume control over his or her life.

The relation between attempted suicide and the judgment that there is a responsibility-defeating disorder is not always easy to determine. On some views about the ends of human action, suicide attempts are *ipso facto* pathological. No one in his or her right mind would seek death. Such a priorism, however, has little to commend it. More commonly, the desire to commit suicide is taken as evidence for or symptomatic of a disordered mind. But this is not much more satisfactory, since it begs the question at issue. In other statements of the relation, suicide attempts are highly correlated with some previously diagnosed psychiatric condition, and for that reason taken to be expressive of it. However, not even this will do. Let us see why.

There is, first of all, a problem about psychiatric diagnoses. Although we will explore this in greater detail later, it bears pointing out at this stage that judgments of psychiatric illness are notorious for their variability. Though I would not be prepared to claim that psychiatric disease does not exist, there is a very wide penumbra surrounding what we would generally be inclined to see as paradigmatic cases. It is to that penumbra that most ordinary judgments of psychiatric disorder belong. Theoretical accounts of psychiatric disease are not much help here, for they are both abundant and varied. Resolving disputes is a bit like resolving disputes in ethics, except that there seem to be even fewer touchstones to work with. The point, again, is not to eschew such judgments, but to draw attention to the risks involved in appealing to them as a basis for interfering with people's self-regarding decisions.

But suppose that we can diagnose someone who wants to commit suicide as psychiatrically disordered. What follows from this? Of course it depends on the particular account given of psychiatric disorder. But on most accounts it would not follow that the person was suffering from some responsibility-defeating incapacity. It is altogether possible that because of the disorder the person wants to end his or her life, but the decision to end it may be a lucid and rational response to the disorder, not a manifestation of it. Even if it was a manifestation of it, it would not by virtue of that be beyond the person's control.

The weak paternalist may not be convinced. For, it can be claimed, even though there is no decisive reason for thinking that the person wanting to commit suicide is suffering from a responsibility-diminishing disorder, nevertheless, the desire to commit suicide is sufficiently bizarre to create a presumption that that is so and that the desire does not reflect a settled interest. The presumption, of course, would be a rebuttable one. But since there is such a presumption, we would be justified in intervening just as long as it is necessary to determine whether suicide is authentically desired or reflects only the influence of alien forces. Of course, to justify intervention, it is not sufficient that the desires be "bizarre"; it needs also to be damaging to the person.

We need to be aware of the costs that would be involved in a policy of this kind. Unless we can presume that a large number of those who want to commit suicide suffer from responsibility-defeating disorders, substantial encroachments on freedom will be involved. They might be minimized if there is a strict limit on the length of time that a person attempting suicide can be detained or restrained. Nevertheless, given the importance that a decision of this kind is likely to have for a person, any forced delay would represent a considerable encroachment. The presumption, however, that many of those who desire to commit suicide suffer from some responsibility-defeating disorder is a contentious one. True, the desire to commit suicide is a pretty radical and unusual one. But to call it bizarre is to go a long way toward begging the question at issue. Whether it is bizarre depends on the reasons for it, and not simply on its content. Given that there are many reasons why a person might intelligibly desire to commit suicide, it would be wrong to presume that it reflects the workings of a disordered mind.

The "Desperate Play" Argument. It seems to me that there is very little solid evidence to show that most of those who attempt suicide lack control over what they are doing. I say this, not simply because the notion of mental disease is a contested one, as are the conclusions drawn from its attribution, but because many who attempt to commit suicide appear to be quite clear about what they are doing. Suicide is a deliberate, planned response to the situation in which they find themselves, and intelligibly related to it. However, I do not believe that it follows from this that paternalistic intervention in such attempts would be unjustified.

Most suicide attempts do not result in death. Is this due simply to ineptitude? I do not believe so. Is it, then, that those who attempt to commit suicide do not really want to die, that their behavior is a charade? That is an oversimplification. It would be closer to the mark to say that death is not what those who attempt to commit suicide *most* want. Nevertheless, in a situation in which what they most want is unattainable through their own efforts, death is seen as the only option. It is the one way they see of exercising control over their lives. Yet it is not just that. A suicide attempt is also a dramatic way of drawing attention to the fact that no viable options remain. It thus raises the possibility that others might be able and willing to restructure the conditions of their world in such way that worthwhile life-options again become (visibly) available. This is no bluff. The person who attempts to commit suicide is not merely pretending to attempt to commit suicide. Nevertheless, there is frequently a genuine ambivalence in suicide attempts. The person would like to continue living, but only in significantly changed circumstances. And the change lies beyond that person's power to bring about. Does this make attempted suicide a form of blackmail? It may sometimes be. But for the potential suicide the situation is more serious than that. While there may be hope that something will happen to make for a better future, there is also the conviction that this cannot be achieved through one's own initiatives. The potential suicide has no hold over others. While I do not want to argue that this account accommodates all those who attempt to commit suicide, I believe that it includes a substantial majority and provides a better account of their actions than does the account that emphasizes mental disorder. Attempted suicide is a "desperate play" (cf. Greenberg 1974), the last move available to a person in the game of life. Whichever way it goes, one will have done all one can. At least one will have done what one wanted to do.

Where does this leave a potential rescuer? Does the fact that intervention would frustrate what was a responsible and deliberate, if desperate, act make it an unacceptable violation of individuality? I do not believe it would have to do so. But this requires some spelling out. One tempting explanation of why intervention could be justified is supplied by the "Real Will" Argument. We are inclined to argue that the person does not really want to die, that the attempt is simply an aberration, a chimera, a passing impulse. And in some cases this may be true. But I do not believe that an argument of this kind serves to capture enough cases; if it does, it does so because its idealist tendencies are being exploited (cf. above p. 59). Nor do I think the fact that there is a sense in which the person also wants to live can be read as prior consent to intervention. Attempted suicide is too deliberate for that. Both the "Real Will" and Prior Consent Arguments underestimate the authenticity of the desire to die.

Once again, I believe that we can profitably appeal to the Argument from Personal Integrity. Not only does it allow that the suicide attempt may reflect the act of a responsible being, but it also provides a way of limiting such interventions. If, as I have suggested, suicide attempts display some genuine ambivalence, intervention will not necessarily violate the potential suicide's integrity. But this will hold *only* if there is some commitment to altering or seeking to have altered the existing conditions of that person's life. As I have pointed out, the person who attempts to commit suicide is not usually rejecting life on any terms, but only on the terms on which it is presently experienced, terms that the person believes he or she has no power to change. But what the person him- or herself cannot change, others may be able to or at least seek to initiate, and there is reason to believe that this would sit well with the rescued person. A very large proportion of those who attempt to commit suicide do not do so again, and there is reason to think that this is largely because the dramatic nature of their previous choice has helped to stimulate changes in their situation, improving it to the point where the satisfactions of living are sufficiently strong to outweigh the frustrations that previously made death a reasonable option.

The "Desperate Play" Argument is not of course intended to accommodate all cases of attempted suicide. It is statistically based. With the Argument from Weak Paternalism it creates a strong presumptive case for intervention in suicide attempts. Unlike the Argument from Weak Paternalism, however, it does not justify the more extreme forms of restraint (e.g., civil commitment) that might otherwise seem to be indicated. The "Desperate Play" Argument justifies intervention (if at all) only for long enough to determine what is going on and whether changes can be made to a person's circumstances that would render them tolerable. In some cases this might not be possible (cf. Tuker 1961, pp. 56–61), and where this is so there should be as little impediment as possible placed in the person's way. This category would not necessarily include all and only those with terminal illnesses. For some such people, access to a hospice environment might make a considerable difference to their assessment of the days or months ahead. But there would also be those with the prospect of many years ahead of them, years divested of the means of pursuing any of the projects that have come to reflect and structure their identity. The intervention justified by the "Desperate Play" Argument might also be sufficient to determine whether some of those restrained would more appropriately come within the purview of the Argument from Weak Paternalism. Although that argument is not strong enough on its own to create a presumption in favor of intervention, where intervention can be supported on other grounds, it can be applied as a subsidiary ground. In this context it does not constitute an unacceptable constraint on individuality.

In limiting the "Desperate Play" Argument to contexts in which there is some preparedness to do something about the life-circumstances of the potential suicide, there is a recognition of the seriousness with which a decision to die is taken. People rarely attempt to commit suicide for what are to them frivolous reasons. The decision to commit suicide, although often ambivalent, reflects deeply felt concerns, and if we ignore these concerns we show scant respect for their individuality. This points to a further advantage over the Argument for Weak Paternalism, which has often sanctioned virtual incarceration without treatment. Unless there is some willingness to seek to alleviate the potential suicide's situation, intervention will constitute a gross violation of individuality. This is a respect in which suicide decisions generally differ from decisions not to wear a seat belt or safety helmet. The latter, generally, do not manifest serious deliberation but only a casualness that generates unnecessary risk.

Notes

1. The impetus for safety helmet legislation was the U.S. Federal Highway Safety Act (1966), which made the provision of highway funds conditional upon its enactment. By 1975, all but three states had complied. However, in 1976 the nexus between funding and the statutes was broken, and since then over half the states have repealed their laws, bringing in its train a marked increase in deaths and serious injuries. For developments, see Graham 1980, pp. 233–40, and on the effects of repeal, Anon. 1977a, pp. 11–12; Watson, *et al.* 1980; 1981. In view of its history, it might be more accurate to say that it was the Highway Safety Act, rather than the statutes of individual states, that was paternalistically motivated. However, some of the judicial dicta that followed challenges to these statutes were also paternalistic.

2. On 1 February 1983. For some of the background, see Anon. 1981, p. 10.

3. These cases include *People* v. *Bielmeyer*, 54 Misc. 2d 466, 282 N.Y.S. 2d 797 (1967); *People* v. *Schmidt*, 54 Misc. 2d 702, 283 N.Y.S. 2d 290 (1967); *People* v. *Newhouse*, 55 Misc. 2d 1064, 287 N.Y.S. 2d 713 (1968); *Everhardt* v. *New Orleans*, 253 La. 285, 217 So. 2d 400 (1968); *Connecticut* v. *Burzycki*, 37 U.S. Law Week. 2448 (1969, Conn.); *State* v. *Odegaard*, 165 N.W. 2d 677 (1969, N.D.).

4. The justifiability of restrictions attaching to privileges is discussed in Reich 1964, and Alstyne 1968. The argument goes back to Oliver Wendell Holmes, Jr. In *McAuliffe* v. *Mayor of New Bedford*, 155 Mass. 216, at 220 (1892), where the petitioner was a policeman dismissed for violating a regulation concerning political activities, he asserted: "The petitioner may have a constitutional right to talk politics, but he has no constitutional right to be a policeman."

5. *Bisenius* v. *Karns*, 42 Wis. 2d 42, 165 N.W. 2d 377, at 382 (1969).

6. I say "may," not only because interference may be counterproductive, but also because the person may have previously expressed a desire not to be hindered should such a conjunction arise.

7. In developing the various facets of this argument, I received much critical stimulation from Stanley Benn and Gerald Gaus.

8. Cf.: "Most cyclists agree that wearing a helmet takes much of the enjoyment out of riding a motorcycle. Helmets are a nuisance when the cyclist reaches his destination, and their required use often prevents a cyclist from taking riders since they seldom have a helmet available. This result infringes the cyclist's right to the use of his property. The law deprives the cyclist of his freedom to choose what risks he will take, and if and how he will guard himself from these risks. These infringements may seem trivial to the non-cyclist, but if helmets were required for all motorists, these and other 'trivial' infringements would suddenly become very important" (Anon. 1969, p. 326).

9. In the English debate, it was far from clear *how* helmet legislation violated the requirements of Sikh religion. See *The Times* 1 March 1973, p. 5d; 25 June 1973, p. 5h; 13 August 1973, p. 2c; 27 August 1973, p. 7d; 28 August 1973, p. 13g; 31 August 1973, p. 13f; 3 September 1973, p. 13e; 6 January 1975, p. 2e; 11 January 1975, p. 13a. However, the important consideration would appear to be that the Sikhs sincerely believed helmet-wearing would compromise their position.

10. Generally, the fears associated with the wearing of seat belts are groundless. Injuries caused by them can of course be documented, but statistically, a belt wearer is much better off (see Birenbaum 1983). Seat belts are said to be accident-inducing by virtue of encouraging a feeling of invulnerability. Or, as one opponent put it, "if

motorists were obliged to sit on the front bumpers of their cars there would not be many smashes" (*The Times* 1 July 1971, p. 29a; cf. Anon. 1968, p. 389; Peltzman 1975, p. 7). the injury-producing possibilities are usually advanced as a reason for exempting pregnant women from the requirements—though there is some evidence to suggest that more serious injuries are occasioned to both the mother and her unborn child by the failure to wear a belt (see Hoglund and Parsons 1974, p. 6, n. 16 and references). The point at issue, however, is not whether belt wearing can lead to injury—it obviously can—but whether the incidence of serious injury is significantly diminished by the belts, which it is.

11. *People* v. *Bielmeyer*, 54 Misc. 2d 466, at 469, 282 N.Y.S. 2d 797, at 800 (1967). In *State* v. *Odegaard*, 165 N.W. 2d 677 (1969, N.D.), "fallen objects such as windblown tree branches" were added to the fantasy (cf. Hisert 1970, p. 620).

12. *State ex rel. Colvin* v. *Lombardi*, 241 A. 2d 625, at 627, 32 A.L.R. 3d 1265 (1968, R.I.). In *State* v. *Babbs*, No. 80–330 (Fla. Martin City Court, 5 September 1968), at 2, this reasoning was held to "torture logic beyond its limits." There is, however, another way in which a helmetless cyclist or unbelted vehicle occupant might pose a threat to others, and which I do not consider here. In the event of an accident, a negligent driver may face a manslaughter rather than some lesser charge. This possibility deserves more attention than I have given it.

13. *People* v. *Carmichael*, 55 Misc. 2d 388, 288 N.Y.S. 2d 931 at 935 (1968).

14. Reply Brief of Plaintiff at 2, *American Motorcycle Association* v. *Davids*, 158 N.W. 2d 72 (1968).

15. *People* v. *Newhouse*, 55 Misc. 2d 1064, 287 N.Y.S. 2d 713 (1968); *State* v. *Odegaard*, 165 N.W. 2d 677 (1969 N.D.); *State ex rel. Colvin* v. *Lombardi*, 241 A. 2d 625, 32 A.L.R. 3d 1265 (1968, R.I.). Cf. Childress 1981, p. 147.

16. *Simon* v. *Sargeant*, 346 F. Supp. 277, at 279 (1972, Mass.), *affirmed* 409 U.S. 1020 (1972).

17. *State* v. *Anderson*, 3 N.C. App. 124, 164 S.E. 2d 48 (1968). Cf. Royalty 1974, p. 369; Anon. 1969, p. 323; Tantlinger 1969, p. 195.

18. An argument of this kind is persuasively developed by Joel Feinberg (forthcoming, ch. 15).

19. This U.S. legal notion is generally characterized as "the power vested in the legislature by the constitution, to make, ordain and establish all manner of wholesome and reasonable laws, statutes and ordinances, either with penalties or without, not repugnant to the constitution as they shall judge to be for the good and welfare of the commonwealth, and of the subjects of the same" [*Commonwealth* v. *Alger*, 61 Mass. (7 Cush.) 53, at 85 (1851)]. Note the following appeal to police power: "The physical welfare of the citizen is a subject of such primary importance to the state and has such a direct relation to the general good as to make laws tending to promote that object proper under police power" [16 Am. Jur. 2d *Constitutional Law* §308 (1964)]. Cf. Rubinow 1969, p. 154.

20. *American Motorcycle Association* v. *Davids*, 158 N.W. 2d 72, at 75–6 (1968). Cf. Hisert 1970, pp. 615–16.

21. *State* v. *Acker*, 495 P. 2d 1038, at 1042 (1971).

22. *State* v. *Anderson*, 164 S.E. 2d 48, at 50 (1968, N.C. App.).

23. The use of a comparative negligence standard (in preference to the contributory negligence standard or doctrine of avoidable consequences) is discussed at length in Hoglund and Parsons 1974, pp. 14–27.

24. *Hales* v. *Petit*, 75 Eng. Rep. 387, at 400 (C.B. 1562).

25. *Pennsylvania* v. *Root*, 191 Pa. 238, at 244, 150 A. 2d 895, at 900 (1959).

26. *Commonwealth* v. *Mink*, 123 Mass. 422, at 425 (1877).

5

Health

Until the early part of this century, most people died from some form of communicable disease. Infant mortality rates were high, and even for those who survived the perils of childhood, premature death was common. Growing acceptance of the germ theory of disease enabled very significant improvements to be made. The transmission of disease via water and milk supplies was substantially decreased. The connection between adequate nutrition and resistance to disease was recognized, and the improvements consequent upon this were reinforced by the development of vaccines and the implementation of immunization programs. Although there was some initial resistance to the efforts of public authorities in the health field, much of it was due to skepticism with respect to the efficacy of the mandated measures. For the most part, the conflict was not one of principle. Once agreement was reached on the causes of disease and the suitability of the recommended measures to its eradication or prevention, most opposition vanished. Public health measures could be justified by appeal to the harm principle.

Not only did the germ theory of disease enable a very significant impact to be made on the incidence of serious communicable disease, but it also provided a handle for cure. The last fifty years have witnessed some stunning developments in drug therapy—e.g., sulfonamide, penicillin, isoniazid, etc. Despite this, the incidence of chronic disease and death from "unnatural causes" remains very high, and health costs have increased enormously. There are two, interconnected reasons for this. First, the germ theory of disease tells only one part of the disease story. In developed countries, environment and life style are also important contributors. This has become increasingly evident. The major causes of ill-health and death are no longer communicable diseases but heart disease, cancer, and strokes. These have their source, not in the invasive agency of germs, but more significantly in life patterns. These can be viewed broadly—taking account of environmental pollution—or narrowly, in which the focus is on individual and group preferences. Overrefined, artificial, and fatty foods, coupled with a sedentary life style and high levels of use of and dependence upon drugs (pills, nicotine, alcohol) have contributed to a situation in which the increasing resources devoted to health care have not been reflected in a corresponding improvement in the health of individuals.

Not that significant advances are absent—there has been a marked decrease in deaths from coronary heart disease. Developments in medical technology and changes in personal behavior have had a marked impact, though at enormous cost.

But (and this is the second reason) unlike the situation with communicable diseases, it has proved very difficult to alter unhealthy life styles at the level of public policy. Broad environmental factors, such as atmospheric pollution, have until recently been very difficult to control because of legal conventions about causation and identifiable victims. The narrower life-style factors are said to lie outside the public domain. If it is my own smoking habit and penchant for fatty foods that has led to or is likely to lead to my chronic health problems, then it is not clear, at least within our current ideological climate, that this is anybody else's business, even though we do complain about health costs.

My concern in the first part of this chapter will be with health-related factors in individual life styles, to consider whether, in view of future costs (the credit-card mentality) and the difficulties involved in maintaining the health system on which we depend, there might be some room for the regulation of our life styles. To some extent, of course, the discussion follows on from that in the previous chapter. Seat belt and safety helmet legislation constitutes a form of life-style regulation. Nevertheless, my concerns in this chapter tend to be more problematic. For whereas seat belt and safety helmet legislation does not generally interfere with our significant concerns, many of the life-style factors that I have here in mind—particularly our dietary and exercise habits—could not be changed significantly without considerable personal upheaval. In various ways these life styles have become bound up with our self-identity, and sudden change in respect of them would be disruptive. Their pleasures or the remoteness of the risks may seem adequate compensation or a reasonable cost. A vehicle accident can happen at any time, but chronic life-style diseases belong to a more distant future—perhaps ten, twenty, or thirty years hence—when we may have already completed our major goals in life. And even if we haven't, the effect of the disease may be only to slow us down and not to thwart them.

Health regulations tend to be preventive rather than curative, yet our mental set tends to be curative rather than preventive. Good health is something that we take for granted; we attend to our health only when it starts to break down, even though it is often too late to restore it completely. So, much of our thinking about health and the limits of health care occurs at the interface of doctor and patient. It is this that will occupy us in the second part of the chapter, for it has proved fertile ground for paternalism. Professional expertise has traditionally been advanced as a reason for leaving health care decisions in the hands of doctors, even though it is the patients who will have to live (or die) with these decisions. Is this paternalism justified?

Regulating for Health

Life styles are alterable. Many of our health problems would be substantially diminished were our life styles different. In some cases, changes could be brought about with the willing cooperation of those concerned, since their persistence in an unhealthy life style is due not to choice but to circumstances. Poverty and ignorance combine to perpetuate it. What these people need is not the constraint of regulation but improved living conditions and access to information. But there are many others for whom an unhealthy life style is a matter of habit and choice rather than necessity. They have come to desire and perhaps to identify with patterns of living that in time will probably exact a heavy physiological and psychological cost. In some cases, a vivid educational program might influence them to change. Confronted with the costs of their choices in ways that do not obscure or dilute them, they may be moved to make progressive adjustments to their life style, diminishing their susceptibility to debilitating ailments or premature death. However, such programs have usually had only a limited effect, even though they are sometimes conducted in a manipulative manner (cf. Wikler 1978a, pp. 327–29). A variety of more intrusive measures have therefore been contemplated and sometimes instituted (see Wikler 1978a, pp. 329–32; 1978b, pp. 236–40; Bonnie 1978, pp. 210–14).

One common form of regulation has consisted in a tax or additional taxes on goods possessing a high health-risk factor. Tobacco and alcohol are the main targets; some have suggested salt and sugar. One idea is that these taxes function as a deterrent on consumption, without making it impossible. Rationing could also serve to diminish consumption, though it would function in a more egalitarian manner. An indirect strategy is to accommodate medical insurance premiums or health tax levies to life styles: smokers might pay a surcharge, teetotallers might receive a rebate. A more indirect form of constraint is to ban the advertisement of health-compromising products. Cigarette advertisements have been the main target to date. Some of the support for this is due to the belief that such advertising is often manipulatory: its banning, therefore, is thought to promote rather than threaten an environment for free choice. Even more restrictive than the foregoing are laws that ban health-threatening substances altogether (narcotics, for example) or make them available only on prescription (therapeutic drugs). In some cases, people are required to submit to health-promoting régimes (fluoridation of the water supply).

Justifications for regulating health vary. As with seat belt and safety helmet legislation, there is a tendency to favor arguments in which some public interest can be discerned and appealed to, though there is also a noticeable dependence on considerations of a more paternalistic kind. Though they do not exhaust the range of arguments used, I shall first consider two paternalistic arguments for healthy life-style regulations, and then pass on to arguments in which some public interest is said to be involved.

PATERNALISTIC ARGUMENTS FOR
REGULATING IN FAVOR OF HEALTHY LIFE STYLES

Although it is sometimes considered that the self-endangering character of certain habits constitutes a self-evidently sufficient reason for interfering with them, most paternalistic arguments for health regulations recognize that the claims of individual freedom are sufficiently formidable to require something more. Two strategies are common. Either it is claimed that people do not freely choose or choose to persist in unhealthy habits, or that regulation represents something like an "Odysseus contract."

The Argument from Weak Paternalism. Strongly paternalistic arguments for the regulation of individual life-styles are usually confined to their more peripheral features, and even then mostly where the likelihood of harm is high and the harm is serious. That is so with seat belt and safety helmet legislation. Where more deeply entrenched and deliberately pursued patterns and practices are involved, and the harms temporally remote, the situation is significantly altered. In these circumstances, strong paternalism looks too much like the sort of thing against which the Argument from Oppression of Individuality is directed. There is, therefore, a strong temptation to claim that the unhealthy life styles to which people are committed lie outside their power to change. Hence the need for intervention. No violation of autonomy will be involved.

The Argument from Weak Paternalism can be developed in a number of ways. Smoking provides a useful base example. Many who smoke develop the habit while they are still young and impressionable—too young, perhaps, to appreciate the long-term consequences of what they are doing and easily influenced by social pressures and media manipulation. By the time they gain a proper perspective on the practice, they are hooked and unable to give up the habit even if they want to. Regulations designed to curb smoking do not, therefore, interfere with voluntary commitments.

The argument might be extrapolated to other aspects of our life styles. We acquire our taste for artificially salted and sugared food when very young, so that by the time we learn of the effects of overindulgence, our taste-preferences have been fairly firmly fixed. There is not, perhaps, the same physical dependence that is associated with tobacco and alcohol, but it takes a good deal of effort to alter one's eating patterns. Some sort of "prodding" may stimulate us to do so. The penchant for fatty and high cholesterol foods and overreliance on pharmaceuticals may be explained in much the same sort of way.

Appealing though such an argument is, it faces several substantial problems. As a first move, it can be pointed out that even people who are in some sense trapped by their habits may reflect upon them and assess the importance they have for them. Even though they may not have the power to break the habit, they do have the power to decide whether or not it should be broken. Should they decide to break the habit, then they may voluntarily seek help for that purpose. Regulation is not required. If, on reflection, they prefer to persist with the habit, despite their knowledge of what it will do to them, then any attempt to regulate them out of it will violate their individuality.

Obviously an argument of this kind cannot be ignored. While it may contribute to a person's better health if he or she does not smoke, this does not exhaust the factors relevant to the determination of his or her good. To rank that person's health so highly that his or her reflective decision to persist in the habit is overridden, is not only to presume that one knows better, but also to make that person subservient to one's own ends and values. Nevertheless, more is required if the argument is to stick. There are hidden complexities. If as a result of early socialization, peer group pressure, or media manipulation, a person has come to be addicted to some habit, the decision to persist in it may not reflect the judgment that life with the habit is better than life without it, but that the *costs of change* (withdrawal and adjustment) are too daunting. Can we say that the person freely chooses to persist in the habit? Had the habit not already been formed, the person would not have chosen to form it; however, having acquired it (ignorantly, under duress, or whatever), he or she now chooses to continue in it because breaking it would be painful. Is such a choice free? It might be better to say that it has been rigged. However, it is not clear that a paternalistic imposition would be justified. It would be unfair to impose such a high cost on persisting in the habit that its abandonment would become preferable. More appropriate would be the development of ways of breaking the habit that diminished the costs of change.

There is another way in which a constrained persistence in the habit may be handled better by nonpaternalistic means. It is sometimes pointed out that although adult smoking has shown some decline, this is not reflected in the poor. One possible reason for this is that the extra years of health that might be expected as a result of giving up smoking have no special attraction for the poor. Growing old has little to offer if you are poor. For such people, the answer lies not in paternalistic regulation but in the improvement of their living conditions and future security.

Another way of setting up the Argument from Weak Paternalism is by attending to the difficulties in dispelling ignorance about unhealthy life styles. We can grant that people often persist in unhealthy life styles because of ignorance. What they basically need is education, not regulation. But it is arguable that the difficulties in disseminating adequate, intelligible information without it being "snowed" by political or commercial interests, so that people can give it the consideration it deserves, are so formidable that some kinds of regulation are necessary. We are not faced with a simple either/or. Clearly the preferable course is to educate, so that people can adjust their life styles to their major goals and values. And this may be helped by certain kinds of regulation: requiring cigarette manufacturers to indicate the hazardousness of smoking and the tar content of particular brands; banning advertisements that give a misleading picture of the healthfulness of the products concerned. Whether more restrictive kinds of regulation would be justified would depend on the effectiveness of this sort of educational program in increasing appreciation of the hazards involved. Even though it could be expected to bring about significant changes in life styles, it wouldn't guarantee them. For whatever reasons, people may still choose to persist in their old ways. Any further regulation in these circumstances would need to be justified, if at all, by reference to the sorts of considerations that inform the Argument from Personal Integrity.

In the case of unhealthy habits, the Argument from Personal Integrity is likely to have less bite than it did in the case of seat belt and safety helmet legislation. For here our "weaknesses" and vices may be associated with significant pleasures, and to interfere with them will violate concerns of real importance to the individual. What is more, the effects are likely to be temporally remote. A gourmet may realize that his or her life style is likely to result in premature death, but believe that its enjoyments will more than compensate for the few years lost. Overindulgence, unlike the failure to wear a seat belt or safety helmet, is much more likely to mesh with a person's life-plans and values. We may not approve of such conduct, but unless we disregard the other's personal autonomy, we must confine ourselves to remonstration or exhortation.

The Argument from Prior Consent. As I have already pointed out, it does not follow from the fact that people are habituated to unhealthy life styles and unable to give them up voluntarily, that they come within the purview of the Argument from Weak Paternalism. They may still be free to determine whether they wish to persist in them, and to seek appropriate help if their answer is in the negative. Suppose a substantial percentage of the population, including the smoking population, came to the view that smoking is bad for health and not worth persisting in. To give effect to this, they advocate and institute a variety of public measures designed to make them desist. Possibilities might be stomach-turning advertisements on TV, a trebling of the excise on tobacco, a restriction of outlets to pharmacies, a limit on the number of packets that can be purchased at any one time, a large hike in health fund premiums for smokers, the banning of smoking from public places, and so on. Would such measures be justified?

At first blush, no problem presents itself. The measures are democratically determined. What cause is there for complaint? But the matter is not so simple. Should the majority be permitted to impose its views on the minority in a matter such as this? Should the weakness of some be made a cost to others? One response is that in cases where the many can achieve a beneficial end only by including everyone within the terms of their arrangements, such constraints would be justified. This is commonly argued in relation to compulsory participation in retirement schemes and product-safety legislation (see below, pp. 165–67, 191–92). But to sustain this conclusion we must suppose that the measures proposed constitute the least restrictive alternative. And it is not clear that they do. Why not instead sponsor programs for those who wish to give up smoking, in which they can enroll themselves and that will then act coercively only with them (cf. Elliott and Tighe 1968; Winnett 1973)? For many, however, such programs may be impracticable and, it may turn out, repressive (cf. Dresser 1982). Nevertheless, unless or until there is substantial support for deterrent measures of the kind suggested from the affected population, individual arrangements may be all that the argument will support.

Though not wholly lacking in credibility, paternalistic arguments do not provide strong support for life-style regulation. If there is to be regulation in that regard, the main weight will need to be borne by public interest considerations.

PUBLIC INTEREST ARGUMENTS FOR
REGULATING IN FAVOR OF HEALTHY LIFE-STYLES.

Although we are inclined to see our life styles as private matters that others have no business interfering with, there is no reason why this should be so. Our lives intersect with those of others in many different ways, and sometimes our style of life may impinge on their protectable interests. Here I consider three possibilities.

The Argument from Hazardousness. There was a time when nonsmokers put up with smokers, accepting smoke fumes as one of the nuisances that belong to the give-and-take of social life. Public attitudes are changing, and smoking in public places is now commonly seen as an offensive nuisance. It is seen as an unacceptable distraction, a source of sore eyes, headaches, malodorous after-effects, and so on. There is, moreover, some evidence to suggest that nonsmokers may be susceptible to the health-diminishing consequences of other's smoking activity (Department of Health, Education, and Welfare 1972; World Health Organization 1975). These considerations might be advanced in support of a ban on smoking in enclosed public places. There is in addition a fire hazard involved in smoking. In theaters and lecture rooms, or places where flammable materials are kept, there may be a public interest involved in prohibiting smoking. Obviously, different considerations would need to be advanced in relation to other life-style factors.

There are the beginnings of an argument here, though only the beginnings. Offensive nuisance arguments have to be carefully articulated, lest they become the occasion for covert moralism (see Feinberg 1980a, pp. 69–109; Bayles 1973; VanDeVeer 1979a). And there needs to be a balancing of harms and risks before restrictions can be implemented. Even so, these would fall far short of a regulation of unhealthy life styles. At best they require that that kind of life style be pursued in surroundings where others are not offended or endangered. Just as drunk-driving laws can hardly be seen as an attempt to curb an unhealthy life style, neither can restrictions on the places in which one can smoke.

The Argument from Public Welfare. Debilitating diseases and early death are said to constitute social harms. Workdays lost through sickness are economically costly, diseases induced by unhealthy life styles strain medical resources, and overindulgence causes an unacceptable drain on food resources and fossil fuels. Early death deprives the community of valuable intellectual and productive input. The argument gets its force not from a consideration of isolated cases, but rather from the accumulation of loss. It can be seen as an amalgam of the Arguments from Loss of Productivity and Public Disaster already canvassed in our discussion of seat belt and safety helmet legislation.

The Argument from Public Welfare has both the strengths and weaknesses of the arguments it resembles. It cannot be simply assumed that we ought to be required to contribute to society what we might be able to contribute. Positive, as distinct from negative, social duties are problematic and, if admitted at all, require careful circumscription if they are not to be occasions for unacceptable encroachments on individuality. There is, furthermore, not the same social loss in the case of unhealthy life styles as there is in the case of seat belt and safety helmet negligence. The "social investment" in individuals (through education, etc.) is more likely to have been matched by the individual's own contribution where the loss is brought about as the result of an unhealthy life style. Nevertheless, statistics detailing the social cost of unhealthy life styles are disturbing, especially when hidden, noneconomically assessable costs are taken into account (cf. Department of Health, Education, and Welfare 1979).

But even the "Public Disaster" aspects of this argument are not as strong as they are in the case of seat belts and safety helmets. Restrictions on unhealthy life styles are likely to constitute a more serious qualification to autonomy than belt and helmet regulations, and although the community cost is substantial, it is arguably bearable for the sake of individual freedom.

There are, in addition, further dimensions to the employment of the Argument from Public Welfare that need to be taken into account. It is arguable that the focus on unhealthy individual life styles deflects attention from other, politically sensitive and possibly more important contributors to debilitation and early death—environmental pollution, unsafe working conditions, stress induced by economic and commercial factors, poverty, and so on. It also tends to breed "a 'blame-the-victim' mentality, which could be used as a pretext for failing to make curative services available" (Wikler 1978a, p. 306; cf. D. Beauchamp 1980, p. 135; Meenan 1976, p. 45; Crawford 1978). Though this does not undermine the argument, it points to an aspect of its use that needs to be recognized and taken into account.

There is, further, some uncertainty about the causal relationships between life style and disease. Although some connections are fairly well established (e.g., between smoking and respiratory problems, lung cancer; alcohol and cirrhosis of the liver), other connections are not as clear-cut (e.g., between fatty foods and heart ailments), and there is some real danger that regulation will be half-cocked (cf. Leichter, in Bayer et al. 1981, p. 35; Meenan 1976, p. 46). It is becoming clearer that many of the factors which contribute to ill-health do not function in isolation, but as elements in causal complexes, and that some who indulge in so-called unhealthy practices may escape their consequences because other causal pre-conditions (e.g., a stressful and sedentary life-style) are missing. There is therefore a danger that regulatory agencies will misidentify or misrepresent the causes of disease, and thus unfairly impose on people.

The Argument from Distributive Justice. This is a variant of the Public Charge Argument considered earlier in connection with seat belt and safety helmet legislation (cf. Wikler 1978a, pp. 317–25; 1978b, pp. 232–34). Arguably, the escalating cost of health care is related to conditions brought about as a result of unhealthy life styles. But these costs are not confined to those who suffer from these conditions; they are reflected in the premiums or taxes that we all have to pay. They would be even heavier were it not that some are more careful about their health. To that extent, those indulging in unhealthy life styles are free riders, unfairly benefiting from the prudence of others. As a matter of distributive justice, therefore, these people should be made to pay— either by means of heavy excises, which are then devoted to the stabilization of health costs, or higher medical premiums. Where the health system is funded out of general taxes, other ways of making it harder to indulge in a life style of that kind may be explored. Should it be asked why these people should pay, rather than others who suffer from expensive disabilities, the answer is that they, unlike these others, can be held responsible for their situation. They are at fault (cf. Veatch and Steinfels 1974).

Superficially, at least, this argument is very attractive, though the possibilities for its political exploitation need to be kept in mind. It is unfair that some should make others pay for their avoidable, unwise living habits. But there are contentious factual premises that need to be substantiated. Is the escalation of health costs the result of (or at least disproportionately the result of) conditions precipitated by unhealthy life styles? Would a move in the direction of more healthy life styles have economic benefits for the community?

Some writers have suggested that we have reason to believe that social costs would not be diminished by greater prudence. As Wikler poses the issue:

> It is not enough to point to the cost of medical care for lung cancer and other diseases brought on by individual behavior. . . . [O]ne must also determine what the individual would have died of had he not engaged in the harmful practice, and subtract the cost of the care which that condition requires. There is no obvious reason to suppose that the diseases brought on by self-destructive behaviour are costlier to treat than those that arise from "natural causes" (1978a, pp. 318–19).

Even if the prudent are not as prone to expensive diseases, their greater longevity may cost the community in other ways, such as pension payments and rate rebates:

> It may turn out, for all we know prior to investigation, that smoking tends to cause few problems during a person's productive years and then to kill the individual before the need to provide years of social security and pension payments. From this perspective, the truly burdensome individual may be the unreasonably fit senior citizen who lives on for 30 years after retirement, contributing to the bankruptcy of the social security system, and using up savings that would have reverted to the public purse via inheritance taxes had an immoderate life-style brought an early death (Winkler 1978a, p. 319).

These are serious questions and obviously need to be addressed. There is some evidence to suggest that so far as social security payments are concerned, a substantial decline in smoking would, over a period of twenty years, lead to a massive increase in social security payments (Leichter, in Bayer et al. 1981, p. 36). This is one reason why governments are unwilling to confront the issue head-on—not to forget their reliance on duties exacted from the sale of tobacco, alcohol, and other hazardous products. But the issue is not quite as simple as this, for many of the problems caused by indulgent living manifest themselves during a person's working life and significantly diminish productivity.

If nothing else, the Argument from Distributive Justice needs the support of extremely complex factual judgments, which are very difficult to be confident about. For that reason, therefore, it would be risky to place too much reliance on it. Like most arguments that rely heavily on economic predictions, its suasiveness either way depends on which of a large number of variables are kept constant, variables whose constancy cannot be uncontentiously presumed.

Even if it is conceded that the argument has more to be said for it than against it, it is not easy to propose fair strategies in response. This is because only a proportion of those who indulge in unhealthy life styles contract the ailments that unfairly impose upon others. Increased taxes on the "unhealthy" ingredients (tobacco, alcohol, etc.) affect all consumers of those items alike. It is true that the most indulgent will probably be at greatest risk and will therefore be paying more by way of excise. But this may still be thought unfair to the economically less well-off. A form of proportional taxation could be instituted were there a national health system, funded through a taxation levy. But even this is considered problematic by those who find nationalized health unacceptable. Wikler puts it in the following terms:

> Two classes of acts must be distinguished: the acts constituting the life-style that causes the disease and creates the need for care; and the acts imposing financial shackles upon an unwilling public. Unless the acts in the first group are voluntary, the argument for imposing behavior change does not get off the ground. Even if voluntary, those acts in the second class might not be. Destructive acts affect others only because others are in financial relationships with the individual that causes the medical costs to be distributed among them. If the financial arrangement is mandatory, then the individual may not have chosen that his acts should have these effects on others (1978a, pp. 321–22).

Rather more is required to sustain this response. The case for giving all citizens access to adequate health care is a strong one. Economic factors should not function as a barrier. Within such an arrangement, itself a collective good and manifestation of social justice, those persisting in an unhealthy life style could foresee that their behavior would impose a cost on others. The mandatoriness of their involvement would constitute no excuse. Perhaps there is no way of distributing health costs that escapes some measure of injustice. But if so, it is better that the injustice be shouldered by those who have the greatest maneuverability.

As the foregoing discussion has indicated, the arguments for regulating allegedly unhealthy life styles are not, taken individually, strong enough to support any very restrictive practices. There is a little to be said for some paternalism—mainly weak—but not much. And the various public interest arguments are either very limited in scope or premised on complex and controversial factual claims. This would seem to be an area in which benevolence is probably best expressed through a more intensive education and a removal of some of the social factors that make the choice of an unhealthy life style more attractive than it should be, given an understanding of the risks and costs involved. Resistance to strong paternalism shouldn't debar action against manipulative advertising; nor should it encourage complacency with respect to social conditions that give unhealthy life styles a "structured reasonableness."

Medical Paternalism

The term "medical paternalism" refers to a subset of the set of impositions directed to the bodily and/or psychological welfare or health of individuals. The boundaries of medical paternalism are largely set by the nexus of doctor and patient, though this is at best a rough-and-ready circumscription. Instead of doctors we may substitute nurses and other health care providers, and on the other side we are not limited to patients but may include those close to them, such as their families. The paternalism, moreover, may express itself in structurally diverse ways. It may be direct (as in cases where the doctor withholds information from a patient) or indirect (where treatment is authorized by a court order, a hospital committee, or the relatives of a patient, or where there is a regulation banning a putative therapy).

To some extent, "the problem" of medical paternalism arises out of the meeting of two competing (though not necessarily incompatible) traditions that belong to our recent cultural history. One is a narrowly liberal tradition, the tradition of individuality and individual liberty, in virtue of which individuals are left or encouraged to take responsibility for the development and direction of their own lives, and others are discouraged from interfering except in very limited circumstances. The other tradition is that of the expert, a product, by and large, of the enormous advances in technology and knowledge and the concomitant division of labor that have come about over the past few centuries. With the division of labor there has come specialized expertise, with specialism there has come professionalization, and with professionalization there has come a view that certain decisions (including decisions that bear directly on what others must do or suffer) belong properly or especially to "professionals." Although there is no inexorability about it, these two traditions have tended to work against each other, and what is often seen as "the problem" of medical paternalism is in large part the problem of reconciling them or at least of alleviating some of the tensions brought about by their juxtaposition.

The professionalization of medicine, like that of law, predates the boom of the past few centuries and its intensification in recent decades. But it has been shaped by that boom, and some of its manifestations directly result from it. The vocabulary and grammar of medical discourse is opaque to the average patient, and many doctors experience great difficulty in communicating their knowledge in a manner that is informative and assimilable. This may not matter too much if the relationship of doctor and patient is thought of as being essentially paternalistic, for in that case what is important is that the doctor understands what he or she is doing. The patient is mostly the passive subject of the doctor's attention. I have no doubt that there are doctors who see their relationship with patients primarily in paternalistic terms. They see themselves as committed by their professional calling to oversee their patients' "best interests," and they interpret the fact that patients come to them as a recognition of this and as a surrender to their professional judgment. But there are many doctors who would not go so far as this. They understand that their patients have lives of their own to live, that their cooperativeness requires that this be taken into account, that there are various alternative therapeutic paths that may be followed, and that which one is followed is best determined in consultation with the patient. However, this group of doctors does not wish to rule out all paternalism. There are circumstances in which, "in their professional judgment," it is best to proceed without the patient's consent or at least informed consent. There may be considerable disagreement about when those circumstances prevail; nevertheless, the paternalistic privilege is to be jealousy guarded. There is, finally, a third group of doctors, much smaller, I suspect, who believe that paternalism in doctor-patient relations is never justified, or, if justified, is not really thought of as paternalism. What I have in mind are cases in which the patient is brought in unconscious and there is no way in which his or her wishes in the matter can be determined. For this third group of doctors, therapeutic decisions, when they can be secured, are always patient decisions. And they remain that, even if they manifest an exasperating stupidity. If the patient chooses a frivolous or unreasonable option, that is the patient's business. The doctor may not take any positive steps in the patient's behalf, but neither will he or she stand in the patient's way.

If, as I believe, most doctors belong to that somewhat amorphous and varied central group, which is neither unabashedly paternalistic nor resolutely set against anything that smacks of paternalism, we face the problem of articulating and justifying an understanding of doctor-patient relationships within which there is enough, not too much or too little, room for paternalism. That is no easy matter. One of the virtues of extreme positions is consistency. They usually reflect the single-minded and undeviating application of one principle. If other principles are acknowledged, they must always bow to it. The middle ground is much messier, and consistency much more difficult to achieve. Yet we often feel that only if we remain somewhere on that middle ground can the complexities of situations be properly appreciated. The problem is to do that in a principled way. The middle ground covers a wide range of possibilities; traversing it in a principled manner, however, is like threading one's way between swamp and quicksand.

In an effort to characterize and to some extent vindicate the doctor's position vis-à-vis his or her patients, various models of doctor-patient relations have been proposed. While I am not altogether convinced that this is the most fruitful way of mapping out an ethically acceptable path for those relationships to take, and am even less convinced that any one model is adequate to the task, there is nevertheless some heuristic value in spelling out and comparing them, for they bring out some facet of those relationships. In working through them, I shall be particularly concerned to explore the extent to which paternalism might be indicated. On completion of that I will then consider a number of situations in which medical paternalism is commonly defended—in decisions to withhold information from patients, to administer life-saving treatment, to sterilize, and to commit people to or retain them in institutions for the mentally ill. These do not exhaust the situations in which paternalistic decisions are made or mooted, and to some extent they deflect attention from its more frequent mundane occurrence in the surgery or hospital bed. Nevertheless, they help to bring out with some clarity the complex issues involved.

THE DOCTOR-PATIENT RELATIONSHIP.

Doctors have been likened to artisans, mechanics, priests, vendors of health services, trusted friends, and philanthropists, to name just a few of the models used to illuminate the character of doctor-patient relationships. They have not all been used to the same end. The models of mechanic and priest, for example, have been used both to commend and condemn that relationship. Here I shall consider just four models, chosen because of their capacity to throw into clearer focus the issue of medical paternalism. Two of these models, the Authority and Free Market Models, stand in strong opposition to each other, and to some extent represent extreme positions. The other two models, the Fiduciary and Contractual Models, represent compromise positions, in which there is some effort made to accommodate the ambiguity of the doctor's position.

The Authority Model. This, I guess, has been the dominant and most pervasive model of doctor-patient relations. It is implicit in the Hippocratic Oath and features prominently in nineteenth-century codes. For example, the 1847 American Medical Association *Code of Ethics* directs that

> the obedience of a patient to the prescriptions of his physician should be prompt and explicit. He should never permit his own crude opinions as to their fitness, to influence his attention to them. . . . A patient should after his recovery, entertain a just and enduring sense of the value of the services rendered him by his physician; for these are of such a character that no mere pecuniary acknowledgement can repay or cancel them (American Medical Association 1848: I.II.6).

For their part, doctors are enjoined to study, "in their deportment, so to unite *tenderness* with *firmness*, and *condescension* with *authority*, as to inspire the minds of their patients with gratitude, respect and confidence" (1848: I.I.I). The focus in this model is on the doctor's professional expertise, and on the power that ought to follow from it. The doctor is taken to have a special competence and, barring negligence and ill-will, can be expected to do what will, so far as the present state of knowledge is concerned, be most conducive to the patient's health. The patient ought therefore to be prepared to accept the doctor's judgment and treatment, shifting to the latter the locus of decision-making responsibility.

We can get a better sense of the strengths and weaknesses of this model and of its implications for medical paternalism by contrasting it with what I call the Free Market Model.

The Free Market Model. Here the focus is on the doctor as a resource to be drawn upon as the need arises. The stage is populated with free and equal individuals, with their distinctive projects and possessions, seeking to advance those projects in the most advantageous way. The doctor represents a source of information and services so far as the individual's bodily and/or psychological well-being is concerned. Should the patient so desire it, he or she may consult a doctor in the expectation of gaining information relevant to some future course of action and/or receiving some bodily/psychological treatment determined in relation to his or her wider purposes. On this model, unless the doctor acts negligently or maliciously, responsibility for any untoward consequences of the transaction will lie with the patient.

It is tempting to express the difference between the Authority and Free Market Models as a disagreement about how to determine *what is the best thing to do.* Proponents of the Authority Model maintain that doctors are professionally committed (by virtue of their ethical codes) to providing the best care they can for their patients and, moreover, are prepared by their training to give it. In contrast, advocates of the Free Market Model maintain that the patient has a much greater stake in the matter and is in a better position to determine and mediate between the various relevant considerations.

But this way of formulating the difference is not altogether satisfactory. The assumption that both models concern the same question—viz., What is the best thing to do?—and differ only in respect of who is better placed to answer it, is misleading. The form of words, "What is the best thing to do?" conflates two distinct questions, and what gives each model its plausibility is its suitability to the particular version to which it addresses itself. The Authority Model focuses primarily on a medical matter—on what, in the circumstances, would be most conducive to the patient's bodily and/or psychological well-being. And it is very often this that proponents of the Authority Model, usually doctors, assume that patients have uppermost in their minds when they seek medical counsel or treatment. The very fact that the patient presents him- or herself is taken to constitute consent to whatever therapy the doctor considers most appropriate.

Now, to the extent that the medical question is uppermost in the patient's mind, it may be that the doctor is peculiarly well placed to answer it. Though something more than a *caveat* is also in order. Medical judgments are a matter of probability, and in some areas, at least, the level of misdiagnosis, misprognosis and misprescription is fairly high. A patient cannot assume that twelve doctors good and true will coincide in their judgments. Unfortunately, these uncertainties tend not to display themselves in the doctor-patient confrontation. Doctors are encouraged by their professional socialization to exude an aura of confidence. To do so is thought therapeutically beneficial, especially when so much treatment is of an alleviatory rather than curative character. There is good reason for an individual to shop around, even at the level of medical judgments. This is not to doubt the doctor's professional authority, substituting for it one's own, but rather to recognize that no particular doctor's authority is decisive so far as medical judgments are concerned. What is accessible to doctors and not to the lay person is not necessarily the possession of any particular doctor.

The Free Market Model, on the other hand, is geared to something wider than a medical question. What it is concerned to safeguard is a "whole-of-life" decision, that is, a decision that takes into account as many of the circumstances of life as the patient counts important. This has medical dimensions, of course, but it sets these into a multi-dimensional context in which economic, religious, social, moral, and other considerations also play a more or less important part. The amalgamation of these different considerations into a practical decision is the preserve of the individual patient rather than the doctor. The doctor's medical expertise has no special claim here.

Separating out these two kinds of questions (medical and whole-of-life) helps to explain some of the antipathy that exists between advocates of the two models—proponents of the Authority Model accusing defenders of the Free Market Model of incompetence, and proponents of the Free Market Model countering with the charge of arrogance. As Franz Ingelfinger put it, "the arrogance of expertise" is matched by "the arrogance of ignorance" (1980, pp. 1508–10). Although these charges are sometimes, probably too often, justified, they are frequently misdirected, since the accuser wrongly assumes that the other is addressing the same question.

But even if some of the antipathy between advocates of the two models has been based on misunderstanding, there might still be reason for giving one model priority over the other at the doctor-patient interface. Supporters of the Free Market Model argue, to some effect, that their own approach has the stronger claim, since it explicitly recognizes that the patient is a person—a complex agent-subject, and not merely a bodily or psychic object in need of repairs. Although as the Authority Model opines, it may reasonably be assumed that patients, by consulting a doctor, are thereby investing their bodily and/or psychic health with a reasonable degree of importance, its preeminence for them cannot be presumed. The medical judgment has to be set in the context of nonmedical factors to which it is conjoined in the life experience of the individual patient.

However, I believe that a defender of the Authority Model is unlikely to be convinced by this argument, at least as it stands. There are two reasons for this, a positive one and a negative one. The positive one is that the doctor's presumptions are not unreasonable. Bodily and psychological health are important welfare interests. They are included in those basic requisites of life by means of which we can pursue our varied purposes, projects, and life-plans, whatever those may be. They are Rawlsian "primary goods"— "things which it is supposed a rational man wants, whatever else he wants" (Rawls 1971, p. 92). Doctors, then, have every reason to presume their preeminence and, therefore, the appropriateness of the Authority Model. If we go further and argue with Nicholas Rescher that these primary goods or welfare interests cannot be traded off or compensated for, but belong together like the links in a chain, the claims of the Authority Model are further enhanced (Rescher 1972, p. 5).

The weakness of this set of claims is that it is, at very best, presumptive. Even if we allow that bodily and psychological health constitute primary goods and that doctors have some acceptable way of determining them, it has to be recognized that their realization is a matter of degree, and that situations in which conflict arises between supporters of the two models are generally ones in which there *is* a clash between primary goods: one *has to be* traded off against the other. The most usual cases are those in which the patient is faced with a choice between therapies that prolong life but limit opportunities, and those that leave a person's capacities relatively unaffected while doing little to prolong life; or between those that prolong life but also pain, and those that diminish pain but do little to improve life expectations. Supporters of the Free Market Model argue that these sorts of choices can be made only if the patient's total set of values can be brought to bear on them,

The negative reason for staying with the Authority Model is provided by deficiencies in the Free Market Model, or at least in the assumption it makes about the decision-making ability of patients. There are two aspects to this. First of all, many of the decisions to be made in this area are quite complex, and for most patients they will be novel. Given our propensity for invalid inference even at the best of times, there is a strong likelihood that, left to him- or herself, the patient will choose badly or not at all. The doctor, it might be argued, is at home in this context. He or she brings to the situation not merely an easy familiarity with the technical aspects, but also a long experience with patients that enables him or her to make a reasonable prediction about the best course for the particular patient. Thus, while it is true that the doctor's expertise is medical, nevertheless, because he or she is constantly dealing with patients, he or she also has a wealth of whole-of-life experience to contribute. Second, patients tend to be vulnerable in a way that doctors aren't. They tend to be troubled by their conditions and beset by fears, and these detract from their ability to perform in the manner presupposed by the Free Market Model. As Engelhardt has put it, "a physician is not usually in as pressing a need for a patient, at a particular time, as a patient is for a physician" (1978, p. 16). Added to this, patients often suffer the disability of an educational or linguistic background that does not prepare them for an intelligent discussion and decision concerning their options.

A defender of the Authority Model may wish to press the critique of the Free Market Model even further by arguing that much of its attractiveness stems from a tacit acceptance of constraints derived from the Authority Model. The requirement that doctors be licensed not only limits the availability of certain kinds of medical services, but serves to protect consumers of those services from at least some catastrophic treatment. Those who advocate a Free Market Model in doctor-patient relationships thus get their appeal at the cost of consistency.

I shall have more to say about this last contention in Chapter 7. But for the most part I want to go along with the critique of the Free Market Model. It operates with an unrealistic picture of the patient-consumer. For a variety of reasons, patients do not relate to their doctors as equals in a bargaining situation (cf. Masters 1975; Dresser 1982, p. 827). To grant this, however, is not to advocate the Authority Model. That would be a *non sequitur*. We need to find some other model.

The Fiduciary Model. Deficiencies in the two models I have so far explored have pushed a number of writers in the direction of what I call the Fiduciary Model.[1] Here there is envisaged a certain sort of partnership between doctor and patient, a partnership in which the establishment and maintenance of mutual trust is seen as central.

What is it for mutual trust to exist between two people? There is generally a presumption that each will act in ways that have some bearing on the other, and that in so acting each will act in a way that takes full account of the other's welfare and interests. But there is more to trust than a prediction that this will be so. We may be able to predict accurately that others will recognize our welfare and interests without trusting them. Our prediction may be based on a close investigation of their prior behavior and the pressures to which they are subject. In mutual trust, there is a commitment of the parties to each other, such that they can rely on the respect and/or beneficence of the other without there being, in the particular instance, direct evidence for it. Trust is therefore frequently shown by taking others at their word. This is not mere gullibility, for trust normally needs to be established and the process of establishing trust is in large measure one of finding out whether others can be taken at their word.

Proponents of the Fiduciary Model claim that if the relationship between doctor and patient is one of mutual trust, then the deficiencies of the Authority and Free Market Models will be overcome. For the doctor will no longer be just a medical expert, but also a friend and confidant, someone whose actions and recommendations will show due regard for the patient's person and life circumstances. And the patient will not be left to make complex decisions on his or her own, without the balance that comes from a sympathetic and informed partner. The doctor will be able to trust the patient to inform him or her of all considerations relevant to the case; the patient will be able to trust the doctor to give them the weight that he or she would want them to have. Although the doctor's role is primarily a medical one, the bearing of other factors on the medical decision is recognized and taken into account at every point in the interchange.

There is something very attractive and reassuring about the Fiduciary Model. It finds its closest exemplification in the tradition—largely vanished—of the family doctor. If there is some pressure to revive it, it is partly because the model has so much to offer. Within its framework, the Hippocratic dictum, "Do no harm," is unlikely to come into serious conflict with patient autonomy, for the doctor would recognize that harm might be done in more than one way. Not only might it come about through carelessness in treatment, but also through a violation of the relationship of trust, by imposing on the patient treatment that would not accord with his or her serious and established desires. This contrasts with the Authority Model, in which commitment to the Hippocratic requirement is taken to license a paternalism that downgrades the patient's desires.

The point is not that the Fiduciary Model rules out paternalism, whereas the Authority Model does not limit it; it is rather that they provide different grounds for any paternalism they sanction. The Authority Model licenses paternalism where it is believed to be "in the patient's best interests"; the Fiduciary Model, however, will license it only where it would accord with "the patient's own best judgment." That would normally require the doctor to leave any decision up to the patient, ensuring only that the patient is fully informed of factors that materially bear on it. But what is normally the case is not necessarily always the case. Our voluntary decisions may not be our best decisions, and in such cases it may be an expression rather than a denial of the basis of trust that exists between patient and doctor if the doctor withholds information or otherwise acts to secure the patient's good without consent. Of course, the doctor takes a risk in acting against the patient's judgment and expectations, and he or she must be prepared to accept responsibility if the paternalism is misguided. But sometimes such risks are just what fiduciary relationships require.

But for all this, there are grave problems with the Fiduciary Model—problems not unlike those confronting the Free Market Model. The practice of medicine does not operate in a Garden of Eden but for the most part in a depersonalized technological jungle. Medical practice has become increasingly specialized and formalized. Group practices have largely replaced the family doctor, home visits are a rare luxury, time as well as service enter into fee setting, the costs of care have skyrocketed, and the multiplicity of treatment options has become bewildering. Added to that, the doctor has sinned, and we cannot ignore his or her nakedness. Iatrogenic disorders can no longer be seen as exceptional, Hippocratic high-mindedness is all too frequently tempered by greed, ambition, and all the other failings that infest human life, and even the effectiveness of official medicine is being called into question (cf. Illich 1976; Kennedy 1982). There is competition from a burgeoning radical health movement that claims, and in some places is being given, the same recognition as has traditionally been accorded to doctors (cf. Webb 1977).

Ironically, the disenchantment with official medicine has gone hand-in-hand with its increasing professionalization. Law, education, and social work are well down the same road and experiencing the same problems. Professionalization is a modern form of gnosticism. Certain kinds of knowledge and expertise are made the preserve of a self-regulating élite. Those outside that élite are not considered competent to question either the bounds or the content of that knowledge. The first of these disqualifications is particularly important, for professionalization tends to be an aggrandizing process. Professions have a tendency to increase rather than decrease their spheres of professed competence. This is not surprising, for professionalization is a form of institutionalization, and institutional success has power as one of its prerequisites.

At the interface of doctor and patient, professionalization has resulted in depersonalization and structured inequality. In Brian Clark's play, *Whose Life Is It Anyway?* (1978) what stands out is not any particular incompetence on the part of the professionals involved (Dr. Emerson, Mrs. Boyle), but their unwillingness or inability to relate to Harrison in anything but a depersonalized way. There is a professional approach that has to be maintained, even where the situation has been individualized. There is no real room for Harrison the person, only Harrison the patient. This I think is crucial to the play—even more crucial than its author realizes. The play asks us to accept that Harrison's decision to leave the hospital for a certain death should take priority over Dr. Emerson's Hippocratic determination to keep him alive. What it does not probe is whether Harrison's decision would have been the same had the inequalities not been so rigidly structured. Frequently, of course, doctors can get their way. The aura of the professional is able to beguile or intimidate. But Harrison is articulate and clear-headed. He does not merely ask but insists that his own concerns be taken into account in any treatment decisions that are made. And so, to the professional, he is a nuisance, to be sedated and even certified.

Professionalization, I am suggesting, has worked against the Fiduciary Model, and I see no way of realizing it on a large scale. It was probably never the dominant model, but now that much of the trust that there was has been eroded, it will be difficult to restore even what there was. Some steps, however, can be and have been taken through the employment of a fourth and final model.

The Contractual Model. The Fiduciary Model finds its home in the *Gemeinschaft*— a community bonded by ties of affection, shared goals, and mutual concern. But in Western society the *Gemeinschaft* has become privatized in the family. Public life, which includes the health care system, is more closely aligned to a *Gesellschaft*, an institutionalized structure in which roles and responsibilities are allocated in accord with publicly recognized and enforceable rules and procedures (Tönnies 1887). This has generated a Contractual Model of doctor-patient relationships, arguably more appropriate to the prevailing social situation than the Fiduciary Model.

We should not, perhaps, contrast the Fiduciary and Contractual Models too starkly.[2] The Contractual Model represents a formalized modification of the Fiduciary Model, rather than its abandonment. It is recognized, for example, that illness is a function not only of physiological factors, but also, and often more significantly, of socio-psychological ones. And so it is important, if a doctor is to provide adequate therapy, that some understanding of the patient's personal and social situation be obtained. To some extent this is shown and preserved in the continued commitment to confidentiality in doctor-patient relationships. What the Contractual Model does is to insert into the operation of the Fiduciary Model various institutional constraints, designed to ensure that the patient's integrity is safeguarded at points where it has proved vulnerable.

Perhaps the most striking and significant safeguard has been the development of the legal doctrine of informed consent. This doctrine, which requires that, prior to the commencement of intrusive (and some other) procedures, patients be intelligibly informed of whatever would be materially relevant to their making the best decision concerning them, is a reaction against the abuse of a privileged position. It attempts to ensure that certain of the prerequisites of the fiduciary relationship are secured within the therapeutic (and/or experimental) situation. To do this most effectively, however, it must not be construed on the simple model of a contract for the exchange of goods. There, consent is construed as a single act, signified in some conventional manner—the signing of a document, or something of that sort. Informed consent in medical contexts has an ongoing character. As Alexander Capron puts it, it should not be viewed "as a single act but as a process of contracting, negotiating, and reconstructing." It is not "a highly formalized event through which the physician-investigator insulates himself from liability, but an on-going process through which the physician-investigator and patient-subject . . . continually rededicate themselves to their joint endeavour or withdraw from it if they wish" (Capron 1975, p. 364). Though not, perhaps, "highly formalized," the doctrine of informed consent is sufficiently formalized to provide patients with a means of redress should they find that the natural inequality of their position is the occasion for abuse; it thus acts as a deterrent to doctors who are inclined to substitute their authority for the trust that is placed in them.

It is usually considered that the Contractual Model is incompatible with any strong paternalism. Since the function of an informed consent requirement is to apprise the patient of as many facts as are materially relevant to the making of informed decisions relating to treatment or its outcomes, thus removing any "advantage" that the doctor may have, there would seem to be no place for the privileged judgment of which paternalism smacks. As a generalization this is correct and constitutes one of the reasons why doctors have been unhappy with the requirement. But it does not rule it out altogether. The difficulties involved in securing an ongoing and fully informed consent have led to the creation of contractualized space for paternalism. Patients may, after consultation, agree not only to a specified set of procedures, but also to other (unspecified) procedures that become indicated in the pursuit of certain agreed upon ends. The extent of surgery required is not always evident prior to its commencement, and a patient may be asked to trust the doctor's discretion with respect to any additional treatment that appears necessary. However, the Contractual Model requires that this discretion be limited, lest it subvert the intentions of the informed consent provision. Any paternalism will thus be firmly bounded (cf. Engelhardt 1978, p. 18; *pace* Marsh 1977, p. 135). If the additional surgery that appears to be necessary would be massive and debilitating, it may be wrong for the doctor to presume that it would accord with the patient's life-plans and expectations, even though it would be life-prolonging. On the other hand, a patient who definitely wants to get well but doesn't want a needle may have to be held still or even deceived in order that desired therapy can go ahead.

The weakness of the Contractual Model is a consequence of its strength. Just because the relationship marked out by the Contractual Model is legally configured, it shares the weaknesses as well as the strengths of that configuration. The legal doctrine of informed consent attempts to ensure an equality between doctor and patient, but it can do this only by laying down certain general requirements. These requirements, though they may usually operate to ensure for the patient an environment in which he or she will be placed to make his or her best decision, will not always do so. Information is not an inert object that can be passed from one person to another without changing its character. It is volatile and in certain environments may be explosive. A doctor who wishes to carry out tests that, among other things, will show whether or not a particular hunch he or she has is correct, may not wish to disclose that to the patient if the disorder in question would be particularly distressing (cf. Hoffmaster 1980, p. 200). The situation would of course be different if the tests proved positive. Even here, however, there may be cases in which informing the patient would be destructive (see below, p. 128). The Contractual Model cannot easily accommodate the sort of fine-tuning that morally sensitive relationships require. The Fiduciary Model is better fitted for that. But the Fiduciary Model, as we have seen, is too prone to abuse in contemporary medical practice.

Where does this leave us, so far as the doctor-patient relationship is concerned? As I have indicated, the relationship is a particularly sensitive one, partly because of the intimate connection we have to our bodies, and the bearing that our health has on the prosecution of the various projects and purposes that express our particular identities. It is sensitive also because of certain inequalities that exist between doctor and patient, rendering the latter vulnerable either to exploitation or to invasions of integrity. This may occur even if the doctor is possessed of altruistic intentions.

It is the sensitivity of the doctor-patient relationship that prompts the promulgation of various models designed to circumscribe it in an ethically acceptable manner. Yet it is that same sensitivity that renders these models inadequate as a total representation of the relationship. The only comparable relations—those between lawyer and client, teacher and student, priest and congregational member, husband and wife—comparable, that is, so far as the sensitivities involved, themselves stand in need of careful delineation in order that proper boundaries are observed and responsibilities discharged. Proper boundaries, I have suggested, do not exclude paternalism, but its occasions and limits are not satisfactorily indicated and safeguarded by recourse to any one model. Ultimately we need to fall back on what should never have been forgotten, namely, that in dealing with doctor-patient relationships we are dealing with two social beings whose standing as persons is the same.

MEDICAL DECEPTION

In passing, I have already suggested that in certain circumstances doctors may be justified in withholding information from their patients. But this needs a more detailed discussion than I have so far accorded it. A closer look will enable us to delineate more concretely some of the sensitivities involved in the doctor-patient relationship.

It bears observing at the outset that to talk of medical deception is not to talk of any uniform phenomenon. The administration of placebos, the withholding of information from a patient (or perhaps others closely associated with the patient), and directly lying to the patient all come within its ambit. Because each has its own moral nuances, I shall concentrate on cases in which information is withheld from a patient. These are, perhaps, the easiest cases, but even so, in the view of most antipaternalists, indefensible.

There are many ways in which, other than by means of an outright lie, information may be withheld from a patient. The patient may be told nothing at all or only part of the story, or relevant information may be couched in technical or euphemistic language, calculated to deceive. Any of these may be done in the name of the patient's good.[3] Of course, that is not the only reason why they may be done. There is some reason to think that what sometimes poses as paternalistic is in fact done for less high-minded reasons. Perhaps a mistake has been made or the doctor does not want to be confronted with a situation he or she finds hard to handle. Nevertheless, in so far as the motivation has been paternalistic, some withholding of information has had widespread support in the medical profession. Indeed, what most traditional codes of medical ethics require of doctors is a concern for the well-being of their patients, and this is not constrained by the demand for truthfulness. In some cases it is even suggested that truthfulness could be a bad thing. The 1847 AMA *Code of Ethics* requires that the doctor "should not fail, on proper occasions, to give to the friends of the patient timely notice of danger, when it really occurs; and even to the patient himself, *if absolutely necessary.*" In this latter connection it is observed that

> The life of a sick person can be shortened not only by the acts, but also by the words or the manner of a physician. It is, therefore, a sacred duty to guard himself in this respect, and to avoid all things which have a tendency to discourage the patient and to depress his spirits (1848: I.I.4).

Even the 1973 American Hospital Association's *Patient's Bill of Rights* allows that it might not be "medically advisable" to give the patient "complete current information concerning his diagnosis, treatment and prognosis," though it provides that in such cases "the information should be made available to an appropriate person in his behalf" (in Reich 1978, vol. 4: 1782). It is only very recently that the situation has shown any radical change. The American Medical Association's 1980 *Principles of Medical Ethics* marks this by counselling: "A physician shall deal honestly with patients and colleagues, and strive to expose those physicians deficient in character or competence, or who engage in fraud or deception" (American Medical Association 1982, p. ix). This is interpreted to "require a physician to make relevant information available to patients . . . [and] to properly inform the patient of the nature and purpose of the treatment undertaken or prescribed. The physician may not refuse to so inform the patient" (p. 28). Still, many doctors will not be happy with this requirement, since they maintain a Hippocratic self-conception. Responsibility for the patient's welfare does not always coincide with disclosure.

In order to assess the discretion sought by many doctors, it will be useful to rehearse briefly the case in favour of truth-telling. Its central plank is the ideal of individuality—the development of a person's distinctively human powers to the fullest extent consistent with their forming a coherent and consistent whole. This, as we have already seen (pp. 41–46, above), does not happen "naturally," in isolation, but in the context of social relationships. An important requisite of sociality, particularly if it is to be of a kind conducive to the growth of individuality, is trust, particularly in the realm of communication. If our social intercourse is to be autonomy-enhancing, we must be able to place a reasonable degree of reliance on the sincerity of others. If we are not able to do this, the fabric of trust and sociality will disintegrate, and with it, personality. As a further articulation of this, it can be claimed that the kinds of activities that characterize our lives as human beings and enable us to take responsibility for what we do are dependent on our obtaining information, and for this we are importantly reliant on the resources of others. If our decisions are to be informed, if we are to be accountable for what we decide to do, then we must be able to take it that what is said to us by others is, for the most part, said in good faith. The person who fails to be truthful shows scant regard for those whom he or she attempts to mislead. Instead of relating to them in a way that acknowledges their standing as accountable beings having projects of their own, the deceiver manipulates their decisions to ends of his or her own devising.

This is a powerful argument for truth-telling in general and in particular for truth-telling in medicine. The condition of our health has an important bearing on our capacity to prosecute our life-plans and may require that we make important modifications to them. If we are not apprised of our prospects or of the various therapeutic alternatives we have, we are divested of a certain control that we may still have over the direction and development of our lives. Even at the best of times illness functions to limit us in the assertion of our individuality. If in addition we are not informed about the nature of our condition and the treatment options, the threat is intensified.

But many doctors will argue that this is an oversimplification, and that account needs to be taken of other factors, such as the wishes of patients and the effects of information. I shall consider arguments based on three such factors (cf. Buchanan 1978; Bok 1978, ch. 14).

The Argument from Harm Prevention. As reflected in the various codes, it is a common belief amongst medical practitioners that information can be bad for patients. To tell a patient the truth about his or her prognosis may cause depression, fear, and anxiety, all to no avail. Better that the patient be able to enjoy what time he or she has, freed from the oppressiveness of such information. Even if the prognosis is not bad, the treatment régime may require cooperation and positive psychological participation, both of which may be jeopardized if the patient is confronted with the true gravity of his or her situation. Many doctors would go along with Alexander Guiora's belief that

> Information is medicine, very potent medicine indeed, that has to be titrated, properly dosaged based on proper diagnosis. Diagnosis of course in this context means an assessment of how information will affect the course of illness, how much and what kind of information is the most therapeutic in face of the patient's preferred modes of coping (Guiora 1980, p. 32).

So seen, information is part of the therapeutic régime, to be dispensed by the doctor with the same authority as "other medicine."

To some extent an argument of this kind turns on empirical considerations. And here, if treated as a general argument for withholding information from patients, it is not very strong. Painful though it may be, patients are generally in favor of being told the truth about their condition (cf. Veatch 1978, pp. 1678–79). There are various reasons for this. Uncertainty and confusion can often be more unsettling than the truth. Knowledge concerning one's condition is crucial to the restoration of some control over one's affairs—whether it is to decide on submission to certain alleviatory régimes, to set one's affairs in order, or to realize some long-standing desires. And so on. But we do not need to take the Argument from Harm Prevention as a general argument for nondisclosure. Although it may once have been the case, as Katz suggests, that for doctors the "modal policy is to tell as little as possible in the most general terms consistent with maintaining cooperation in treatment" (1972, p. 693), this view is now less common. It is now generally believed that patients are better off knowing where they stand, what the options are, what risks will be involved, etc. However, the Argument from Harm Prevention is still advanced in favor of a discretionary power for doctors. There is a big gap between a policy of nondisclosure and mandatory truth-telling, and the Argument from Harm Prevention operates within that gap. Doctors will argue that whatever the merits of a general policy of truth-telling, there will be occasions on which, in the best interests of the patient, the withholding of information or deception as to condition will be indicated.

This, however, will not satisfy an opponent of paternalistic deception. The main reason is parallel to that used by Mill to oppose censorship. Let us grant that information may sometimes have unwanted and deleterious effects. But who are doctors to judge when that will be so? Not only are doctors fallible beings, but the judgments in question are "psychiatric" in character and lie outside even their professional competence (Buchanan 1978, p. 379). Add to that the fact that the constraints of contemporary medical practice are such that doctors rarely possess an intimate knowledge of their patients and their circumstances, and the judgment about potential harmfulness becomes highly speculative (Buchanan 1978, pp. 381–82). Now, I believe that it would be wrong to underrate the importance of these counterconsiderations, particularly in view of the paternalistic tradition that has prevailed in the medical profession. Doctors are likely to interpret the discretionary view of the Argument from Harm Prevention in an unacceptably liberal way, and there are strong reasons for adopting a policy of truthfulness. It may be too weak to see medical fallibility simply as a *caveat* against withholding information. Doctors ought to tell the truth to their patients.

Nevertheless, to see truth-telling as rigid dogma seems to be as wrong in medical contexts as it is in other areas of life. Central though truth-telling may be to social life, it does not follow that exceptions can never be made. Consider the case of a seventy-four year old patient, Mrs. P., who was admitted to hospital for a herniorrhaphy. During surgery a gonad was removed, and tests showed that it was an atrophied testis and 46XY karyotype. That is, she had male hermaphroditism. Mrs. P. was happily married, had not realized that she had a false vagina, and had raised an adopted child. It was decided not to reveal to her her genetic maleness. In a clinico-pathologic conference following the operation, Dr. D., reflecting more generally on such patients, advised as follows:

> Although it is not established that there is an increased incidence of testicular malignancy in patients with testicular feminization, the recognized increase of malignancy in undescended testes makes it likely that this is so. Thus, most recommend that the testes be removed. Thus, since testicular estradiol is of value, gonadectomy can be delayed till after puberty and estrogen replacement given thereafter. Clearly the patient should not be informed of her genetic sex. Rather, she should be told that she will be sterile, that there is a gonadal abnormality associated with an increased frequency of tumour formation and that the gonads should be removed and that the hormonal product of the gonad can be given as a medication (Cryer and Kissane 1978, p. 519).

Although I am inclined to think that disclosure in such cases should be determined on an individual basis, it seems clear to me that in Mrs. P.'s case, Dr. D. made the correct decision. What purpose would have been served in informing her? It is clear from Dr. D.'s advice that there is no attempt to keep from such patients information that will be helpful to their future decision-making, but there is a judgment that some kinds of information are so unlikely to forward their ends that their communication would be inadvisable.

But there is a more fundamental reason why the antipaternalist might oppose nondisclosure. This is that it involves one person's determining for another what the other should know concerning him- or herself. What business does the doctor have deciding for the patient what the patient can bear or should know? The patient has "a right to know," as one of the rights of personality. In other words, the Argument from Oppression of Individuality reappears. The response to this is that where the patient's individuality is unlikely to be served by the communication of information—where, as in some of these cases, it is likely to be severely damaged—it is no violation of that individuality if information is withheld. Of course, as we have stated before in relation to the Argument from Personal Integrity (of which this is a variant), a doctor taking this path takes a moral risk, but it is a risk that would seem in some cases to be justified. This is not to give the doctor absolute discretion over what is told to the patient. If a patient is insistent on knowing all the details of his or her case, and if this insistence involves a preparedness for whatever might have turned up, then even though it may be hard for the patient to take, the doctor might disclose details that would otherwise have been withheld.

The Argument from Consent. There are several versions of this argument. Patients, it is sometimes said, don't really want to be told the details of their diseases or of the various treatment options. What they want is a recommendation. Alternatively, it is argued that when patients present themselves to their doctors, they commit themselves to the doctor's care and discretion, where this may involve the withholding of information. Or, somewhat more plausibly, it can be claimed that when patients authorize their doctors to do whatever they deem necessary (as they frequently do), they imply as part of this the possibility of the doctor's withholding information. Buchanan treats this as an argument for the general practice of withholding information, and then rightly criticizes it for its false initial premise, viz., the assumption that patients have such wishes or imply or give such authorization. But most proponents of the argument would not intend it so generally. All that needs to be argued is that where there is such a desire or authorization, it would be permissible for the doctor to withhold information. Even so, Buchanan would be skeptical of the argument's acceptability. He claims that an authorization that allows for the withholding of information would tend to undercut the patient's ability to determine whether or not contractual limits are being observed. The patient is potentially denied access to information that would be essential if he or she is to ascertain whether the best of care is being provided (Buchanan 1978, pp. 384–85). The authorization might act as a shield for negligence. But, as Donald VanDeVeer rightly insists, this criticism is misguided. For it is not to be supposed that the doctor, in being authorized to withhold information, is being given a *carte blanche*. The doctor is not being authorized to withhold whatever information he or she likes. Only certain kinds of information are in view, and this would be most unlikely to include information relevant to determining whether the terms of the agreement have been adhered to (VanDeVeer 1980a, pp. 202–3).

The Argument from Weak Paternalism. Sometimes doctors believe that their patients are incapable of dealing with the information relevant to their situation. Several reasons may be given. Either the information is too technical or the educational background of the patient is too inadequate or the patient is too emotionally involved to gain perspective (Buchanan 1978, p. 386). At best the argument could be employed in particular cases, though Buchanan appears to take the view that withholding would never be justified. To think otherwise will tempt doctors to abdicate their responsibility for disclosing relevant information. The doctor's duty is to make a reasonable effort to inform, not to ensure understanding. This is a fair point but does not settle the question of paternalism. That is simply pushed back one step. Having attempted to inform (but having good reason to think that those concerned have not been able to grasp the situation), does the doctor then go ahead with what they (appear to) want, or does he or she impose on them what appears to accord with their long-term interests? The latter would seem to be indicated, unless there is no need for haste and an extension of time would rectify the comprehension problem.

It is right that we should be concerned about the withholding of materially relevant information. The development and maintenance of our individuality depends on it. This does not mean, however, that in every instance we are well served by it or that our integrity requires it. The information we seek may destroy as well as build up, and were we to appreciate that it would do the former, we would most probably not wish to have it. For it was not with an end of that kind in mind that we sought it. Yet to leave such discretionary power in the hands of others is a risky business, and it needs to be carefully circumscribed. It is certainly not sufficient to claim, as has traditionally been done, that the doctor's primary duty is to benefit the patient. The patient is not there merely to be benefited but to be respected as an individual with life-plans and capacities of his or her own. Because that is so, the doctor's primary duty is to inform the patient—not in just any manner but with due regard for the patient's sensitivities and needs. When and how the patient is informed may vary from case to case. That much understood, there is then room to consider those problematic and rare cases in which informing the patient cannot but be destructive and in which the withholding of information would not violate the patient's integrity.

COMPULSORY LIFE-SAVING TREATMENT.

As we have seen, there is a strong presumption in favor of doctors informing their patients concerning their condition, prospects, options, and the attendant risks. In so doing, doctors acknowledge their patients' status as subjects, choosers with interests and ends of their own, to be formulated and prosecuted through their own determinations. Informed patients are not immune to mistakes in decision-making: although we may expect information to diminish the incidence of mistake, it is unlikely to eliminate it. As Capron expresses the point, the informed consent requirement "does not suggest that patient-subjects will not make 'mistakes' or pursue courses not 'in their best interests' but they will be *their* best decisions, challenged when necessary by medical opinion to the contrary" (1974, p. 393). It is certainly likely that the informed consent requirement will encourage people to make their best decisions, though as I have earlier argued, it does not guarantee this (see above, p. 66). What is *theirs* is not necessarily their *best* (and certainly not necessarily *the* best).

Patients sometimes choose to decline treatment, even though the likely outcome of this will be death. Sometimes this is understandable as in the case of a terminally ill or aged patient suffering acute pain. But in other cases such choices will be felt by others to be contrary to the patient's best interests. Where this is so, doctors will be strongly tempted to intervene or to continue treatment. Would its imposition be justifiable? Does patient sovereignty extend to such a drastic alternative?

Compulsory life-saving treatment might be contemplated in a variety of circumstances. Terminally ill patients may not wish to prolong their suffering—caused, say, by metastatic cancer or severe third degree burns. Nonterminally ill but severely handicapped patients may decline needed treatment because they do not consider their lives worth living. A prisoner (or free citizen) may refuse to eat and to accept medical aid when it becomes necessary. A patient with a correctible condition may refuse to accept some part of a therapeutic régime (e.g., a blood transfusion) or even all medical intervention, because it would violate a religious commitment. Essential therapy may be declined on the basis of a false belief (say, that a gangrenous condition won't spread or that a particular therapy is life-threatening). These are only some of the possibilities.

Not all arguments for imposing life-saving treatment on patients are paternalistic in character. It is sometimes argued that the value of life is of such importance, morally and socially, that compulsory life-saving intervention is justified. Or, in some cases, the particular obligations that the patient is said to have to others is made the ground for intervention. But paternalistic arguments are also common. Some of these derive from what is seen as the doctor's particular professional commitment to benefit his or her patients, but it is often believed that this professional "obligation" merely codifies a more general responsibility or at least liberty to ensure the welfare of others. Here I will confine myself to interventions on paternalistic grounds.

Weak Paternalistic Arguments. Perhaps the easiest and most natural move to make in circumstances where essential treatment is declined or at least not consented to is to question the person's competence to take responsibility for the outcome. There is something of a presumption that people wish to live, not simply because of some inborn "will-to-live," but because continued life is a prerequisite to almost all our valued projects. It is not immediately intelligible to us that a person would voluntarily choose to die. Choices are made in the pursuit of valued ends; choosing death seems to go contrary to this, since it involves a denial of the prerequisite for valued ends. There is therefore a strong inclination to believe that a person who declines life-saving treatment is actuated by other than rational motives. Paternalistic intervention would represent no violation of individuality.

There are no doubt cases in which the decision to administer life-saving treatment belongs most appropriately to others. (Whether it is the doctor, the person's family, a hospital committee, or the court is another matter.) If the patient is a young child or severely retarded or suffering from a psychological condition that renders him or her incapable of understanding or appreciating the nature of a refusal, others may act in a way most likely to be in accord with the person's established plans and values or, in the absence of that, the person's welfare interests. But the presumption that a competent person would choose life-saving treatment is only a presumption, carrying much of its plausibility through a conflation of biological and purposive life. Although biological life is indeed *a* prerequisite for most of our valued ends, its continuation is not sufficient for their pursuit. A person in the last stages of a terminal illness may be able to look forward only to a perpetuation of bodily functions, without any possibility of achievement of his or her own. The distinctively human qualities of life, if not destroyed, are not capable of materialization. If life has nothing to offer beyond biological functioning, death becomes an intelligible choice and the refusal of further treatment may be one of the only ways in which one can purposively assert oneself. To deny that choice will be to stifle the individuality that remains.

The intelligibility of refusing life-saving treatment is not simply a matter of seeing how biological life might become detached from purposive life. A range of positive values may be associated with such refusals. This is most clearly evident in cases where some "cause" is valued more highly than present life. Prisoners who go on hunger strike, refusing offers of life support, and Jehovah's Witnesses who refuse blood transfusions, intelligibly decline needed treatment, even if we do not sympathize with their values or the weight which they place on them. Self-interested action is not necessarily self-regarding action, and a person can intelligibly have interests that come into conflict with the demands of self-regard. Even self-regarding action does not demand the perpetuation of biological life, unless certain assumptions are made about the character or finality of bodily death. That these assumptions are disputed should not be seen as evidence of a responsibility-defeating incompetence.

The situation is altered, however, where proxy refusals are tendered—
say, by Jehovah's Witness parents on behalf of their non-competent children.
As a rule, we allow parents considerable discretion with respect to the nurture
and treatment of their children. This is variously grounded: in a recognition
of the importance of family life to the development of children, a belief that
parents have the greatest interest in the welfare of their children, and on
the assumption that they are best placed to discern and represent the particular
needs and interests of their children. But as we know all too well, parents
are not always interested or wise judges so far as the good of their offspring
is concerned. The difficulty is to know where to draw the line. It is easy
enough where parents grossly abuse their children. It is much harder in the
case of Jehovah's Witness parents who can be presumed to love their children
and to believe that what they are doing represents the child's interests. But
the refusal to consent can be said to represent the child's interests only if it
can be assumed that the child does or will see his or her interests from the
perspective of a Jehovah's Witness. That may seem a reasonable assumption,
given that we allow to parents the freedom to bring up their children in
their own religious tradition. However, there is nothing mechanical about
this. In allowing this liberty to parents, we do not imply a right to indoctrinate
or manipulate. It is assumed that children brought up in the faith of their
parents will adopt that faith freely. Its rejection, no less than its acceptance,
must remain a reasonable option for them. For this reason, it would be wrong
to assume, without some clear and competent indication from the child, that
the parents' refusal should be taken as the child's.

We can express this point by reference to the Doctrines of Substituted
Judgment and Best Interests. Where a patient lacks the competence to consent
to or refuse life-saving treatment, the decision where possible, ought to accord
with that person's dominant life-plans and values, as these are known. Where
they are not known, as in the case of young children or severely retarded
people, the decision ought to attempt to secure their welfare interests or
primary goods. Although this procedure will not guarantee that noncompetent
people will be safeguarded against the imposition of alien values, it will help
to minimize it. Although the interests of individuality dictate priority for the
Doctrine of Substituted Judgment, they are not furthered by "reading into"
the experience of those who have never developed settled plans and a structure
of values, plans and values which they have never had. An inadequacy in this
respect was evident in the *Saikewicz* case, for here the Doctrine of Substituted
Judgment was applied to a sixty-seven year old man with the mental age of
a two or three year old.[4] This makes nonsense of a valuable doctrine, in
much the same way as some of the consent-based arguments for paternalism
make nonsense of consent.

The Argument from Contingencies. This parallels the argument considered in
connection with suicide (pp. 102–4, above). As I have indicated, it is possible
for biological and purposive life to become dissociated, or for patients to
have values that override the value they accord to their individual lives.
Sometimes, however, the conflicts that lead to their manifestation in refusal
of life-saving treatment are artificial and unnecessary. With their resolution
there may come a reversal of decision.

Even terminally ill patients may find that their remaining days provide
them opportunities to express their individuality in ways they find satisfying.
Yet frequently the environment in which they are expected to spend those

days is inimical to satisfying expressions of individuality, and, instead of choosing to persevere in the face of the disease, they decide to take what steps they can to shorten their remaining time. The antiseptic and impersonal hospital environment often contributes significantly to this. Were the patient in hospicelike surroundings, the decision might be quite different. Where there is reason to think that the patient is responding (albeit voluntarily) to an environment that it is in the power of others to change, it would be permissible to delay the withdrawal of treatment while changes are made to the environment, giving the patient opportunity to reassess his or her position in more congenial surroundings. A delay would, I believe, have been permissible in the case of Ken Harrison, in *Whose Life Is It Anyway?*, provided that genuine steps were taken to repersonalize his environment. There is little doubt that his decision was influenced (though it is not clear how decisively) by the authoritarian and depersonalized attitudes of the key medical personnel; his desire to remove himself from this, even at the cost of his life, is understandable. A similar argument for treatment might be used in relation to a comatose hunger striker whose political demands are acceded to by the relevant authorities. Where the contingencies that help to inform a decision to refuse life-saving treatment will be altered immediately, it is permissible to delay the withdrawal or withholding of treatment.

The Argument from Marginal-because-False Beliefs. This presents much greater difficulty. Patients sometimes refuse what amounts to life-saving treatment for reasons that are almost certainly false. Yet such refusals are voluntary. In *Yetter*, for example, the sixty year old patient refused to consent to a breast biopsy because of falsely based fears about surgery (an aunt had undergone a similar operation some fifteen years before and had died, though from unrelated causes; she also believed it would affect her ability to bear children and to realize an ambition to be a film star).[5] In *Northern*, the patient refused to consent to the amputation of gangrenous feet because she believed (falsely) that their black color was caused by soot or dirt rather than infection.[6] Clarke et al. report the case of a forty year old man who refused surgery to repair a severed artery because some years before he had been partially disabled as the result of an operation (Clarke et al. 1980). Culver et al. discuss the case of a sixty-nine year old woman for whom electro-convulsive therapy seemed to be indicated, but who refused, giving as her unelaborated ground, "I deserve to die" (Culver et al. 1980).

The temptation in such cases is to claim that the patient is not competent to decide, a temptation succumbed to in *Yetter* and *Northern* (though with different legal outcomes). In the *Yetter* case, it was determined that although her decision "might be considered unwise, foolish or ridiculous," Mrs. Yetter's "constitutional right of privacy" gave her final say. In *Northern*, although it was acknowledged that Mrs. Northern was "an intelligent, lucid, communicative and articulate individual," it was claimed that, "because of her inability or unwillingness to recognize the actual condition of her feet which is clearly observable by her, she is incompetent to make a rational decision as to the amputation of her feet." A similar strategy was adopted in the case of Ms. D. in Culver et al. A temporary guardianship order was obtained and ECT successfully administered. This solution would also have been sought in the Clarke case, had not relatives succeeded in pressuring the patient into "consenting" to surgery.

Though easy, the weak paternalistic solution adopted in some of these cases is unconvincing. A stubborn refusal to reconsider erroneous beliefs may reflect a lack of competence, but it cannot be taken to do so without independent evidence. And in these cases such independent evidence appears for the most part to have been lacking. On the other hand, going along with the patient is hardly satisfactory either. One reason for this is that in at least three of the cases the patient does not want to die and believes that the chances of staying alive will not be lowered by the refusal to consent. In the case of Ms. D., the belief that she deserves to die is not tied up with some significant element in her personal history. Paternalistic intervention, I believe, is more honestly handled via the Argument from Personal Integrity. In none of these cases does the almost certain consequence of a refusal to consent comport with the patient's settled determination or life-plans. Nor does it reflect the best decision of which the patient him- or herself is capable. The patient's capacity to perform in other contexts gives us reason to think that with time and patience (more than the circumstances allow), the patient could be rationally persuaded to have a different view. Further, the immediate prognosis is such that we could anticipate that an intrusion would come to be appreciated by the patient. Because the patients' beliefs are groundless and clearly so, the overriding of a refusal to consent will not come into conflict with any of their long-term, settled goals.

Of course, we might be wrong. If so, we should be prepared to bear responsibility for the intrusion, as the Argument from Personal Integrity requires. That may not justify a massive civil suit, but there should be a penalty sufficient to ensure that a doctor who imposes in such cases does so with due care for the particularities of the patient's person, and not as the expression of medical imperialism or Hippocratic beneficence. Weak paternalistic arguments, in contradistinction, not only stretch the criteria for noncompetence to breaking-point, but also encourage doctors to abdicate their responsibility to their patients.

INVOLUNTARY STERILIZATION.

Early moves to provide for the sterilization of certain classes of persons were closely associated with the eugenics movement. It was believed that certain disabilities, in particular imbecility, were genetically transmitted, and that if unchecked would lead to widespread "social contamination" and an unacceptable drain on social resources. Thus, in a notorious but influential judgment, Justice Holmes argued:

We have seen more than once that the public welfare may call upon the best citizens for their lives. It would be strange if it could not call upon those who already sap the strength of the State to make lesser sacrifices, often not felt to be such by those concerned. In order to prevent our being swamped by incompetents, it is better for all the world that if instead of waiting to execute degenerate offspring for crime or to let them starve for their imbecility, society can prevent those who are manifestly unfit from continuing their kind. The principle that sustains compulsory vaccination is broad enough to cover cutting the fallopian tubes: "three generations of imbeciles are enough".[7]

This judgment has several problematic features, some general, some specific. It is not easy, for example, to sustain the analogies with wartime conscription and vaccination; mental retardation is not, for the most part, genetically transmitted; and there are significant doubts about the facts of the case (Macklin and Gaylin 1981, pp. 65–68). Nevertheless, reaction to the judgment has not been strong enough to bring about a substantial change in the legal position. At most the arguments have been modernized. The social costs are now articulated in terms of the interests of children who might be born to people unable to care adequately for them, the interests of parents or institutional guardians who have to oversee the activities of such people, and the interests of the taxpayer, who must finance their upkeep and that of any progeny.

However, there are also various paternalistic arguments for the sterilization of those who are in some degree mentally retarded. Here we shall look at just three.

The Argument from Enhanced Autonomy. It is claimed that many mildly retarded people not only desire sexual relations, but would find the opportunity to engage in them beneficial to their own personal and social development. But this, it is claimed, is contingent upon there being no offspring, since the physiological and psychological changes brought about by pregnancy (in the case of women) and the demands of parenthood would be beyond their capacity to handle. Normal contraceptive methods are said to be inadequate to their circumstances, since they are often incapable of taking adequate precautions. Sterilization thus presents itself as the only acceptable alternative (barring new developments in contraceptive procedures). It will enable the persons concerned to engage in sexual activity without the need for constant supervision to ensure that appropriate contraceptive precautions have been taken. It will also, in many cases, allow their deinstitutionalization (Macklin and Gaylin 1981, pp. 181–93).

On the surface this is an attractive argument. It promises substantial benefits so far as the development of an individual personality and life style are concerned. Yet the very irreversibility (for the most part) of the procedure and the options it eliminates are reasons for caution. Judgments of mental retardation are by no means fool-proof, and the inability of a mentally retarded person to handle more regular forms of contraception at puberty or, say, twenty-one, does not imply a continuing inability to handle them. Retarded people are slower in learning such procedures, but they are not necessarily incapable of learning them. Where possible, there is a strong argument for seeking some less intrusive alternative. This is strengthened by our growing knowledge of the capacity of retarded people to learn and of how that capacity might be tapped. Sterilization might simply function as an easy way out for those who have some kind of formal oversight over such persons. As Rosalind Petchesky suggests:

> More pertinent to "an active heterosexual life" for such persons would be commitment to programmes involving sex counselling, body awareness, sex-integrated activities, private bedrooms, and many other basic conditions that are presently inaccessible to many retarded people (1979, p. 38).

This response, of course, is not decisive against involuntary sterilization; it is best seen as an appeal to the doctrine of the least restrictive alternative. If, as is probably the case, a significant element in the incapacity of the mildly retarded has to be seen as a consequence of labelling and institutionalization, then we should not rule out the possibility that with changed attitudes and practices, such people may come to be able not only to control their own bodies but also to nurture children.[8]

The Protection from Exploitation Argument. It is probably fair to say that those suffering from retardation are more vulnerable than others to exploitation and abuse. And, at least in the case of mildly retarded women, these risks could be substantial. Involuntary sterilization has seemed a way out of this problem, particularly, though not necessarily exclusively, by the parents of retarded girls.

In responding to this argument, we need not deny that retarded people require some sort of protection against exploitation and its consequences. Sterilization, however, is of dubious suitability for this purpose. Although some of the possible consequences of sexual exploitation will be removed (pregnancy), the likelihood of exploitation and abuse is unlikely to be diminished thereby. Indeed, it may well be increased, due to the absence of "evidence" of exploitation. As with the Argument from Enhanced Autonomy, a more appropriate solution (at least in nonextreme cases) is likely to lie with improved counselling. This may be more difficult to administer, but it is also more sensitive to the potential and capacities of the retarded person.

The Argument from Inability to Cope. Retarded females may find various aspects of their sexuality very difficult to comprehend, and hence to cope with. Not merely the problems of nurturing children, but various aspects of pregnancy, childbirth, and even menstruation may overtax their capacities. Psychological trauma may be involved and also the risks of infection and discomforting illnesses. Sterilization may present itself as the safest and most practical way of circumventing these problems.

Without wishing to deny that there may be people for whom, on the grounds mentioned, sterilization would seem to be indicated, it is nevertheless important that the requirements of the doctrine of the least restrictive alternative be heeded. In most cases, particularly where the persons concerned are only mildly retarded, programs could be developed or techniques employed that would enable the mildly retarded to understand and cope with their bodily functions and changes. Because of its probable irreversibility, sterilization ought to be seen as a last rather than a first or early option.

Even though involuntary sterilization is not contemplated for or confined to the mentally retarded alone, the foregoing arguments have been structured for that context. But here too they will have varying appropriateness. Retardation is a matter of degree, and the arguments will be more appropriate to the moderately, severely, and profoundly retarded than they will be to the mildly retarded. Yet it is the mildly retarded who make up by far the largest proportion of the retarded and for whom sterilization is most commonly suggested. Even this does not provide us with a fine enough classification, for the mildly retarded themselves differ significantly in their educability. Some will be capable not merely of understanding the character and consequences of sexual activity, but also of giving or withholding informed consent to sterilization. Where that is the case, the case for involuntary sterilization will be at its weakest. Indeed, where informed consent could be given (or refused), it would almost always be wrong to sterilize without consent. Though their capacities for individuality may not be as great, mildly retarded people are nevertheless capable of having life-plans and a good of their own. The fact that they may be more heavily dependent on others in the realization of these is not sufficient reason for denying them the possibility.

It may not appear that there is any problem with sterilization in cases where the mildly retarded give their consent. But this would be premature. Where consent is given, it is often given in the context of what Petchesky calls "heavy structural contraints" (1979, p. 31). Where those concerned are already institutionalized, there is often a lot of overt or covert pressure involved. Whether it is the somewhat authoritarian atmosphere of the institution, the inadequacy of its facilities, or the veiled threat that release or favors will depend on compliance with recommendations, inmates will find it difficult to give a voluntary refusal. Where the person is not already institutionalized, there may be the threat of institutionalization or withdrawal of support in the event of noncompliance. This is not to say that the mildly retarded cannot, by virture of their circumstances, give informed consent, or that the prospect of (continued) institutionalization *ipso facto* negates an acceptably voluntary consent. For it may be that sterilization and institutionalization constitute the only reasonable alternatives. But it is more likely that contextual factors will be unreasonably skewed in favor of those recommending sterilization (cf. Kleinig 1982, pp. 100–102).

If there is a problem about the legitimacy of sterilization in cases where the mildly retarded appear to give their consent, there is a connected and no less serious problem in cases where they are deemed not competent to consent, and consent to it is given by others on their behalf. The determination of incapacity is problematic at the best of times, and there is ample evidence that sterilization has frequently been authorized without incompetency being properly established. Immaturity and incapacity have often been conflated in order that parents might be spared the problems of supervising their teenage daughters. Unless adequate criteria for incompetency can be produced and fairly applied, there is reason for eschewing the practice altogether, so far as the mildly retarded are concerned.

It is common these days to lay claim to a right to procreate, a right whose realization is jeopardized by involuntary sterilization. That there is a fairly widespread recognition of such a right does not of course substantiate it, though it strongly suggests that for many people procreation is closely associated with their welfare interests. Interference with the capacity to procreate, therefore, is likely to constitute a significant intrusion into their valued ends and life-plans. Yet procreation is not itself a welfare interest; it is not uncommon for people to alienate it by choice and, as "wrongful life" arguments suggest, it is more vulnerable than a welfare interest. This is not to downgrade the interest, but rather to suggest that the case for a total ban on involuntary sterilization overreaches itself. Nevertheless, because the interest in procreation is a significant one for many people, sterilization of the retarded, whether voluntarily consented to or involuntary, ought to be carefully monitored so that abuses or unwarranted intrusions do not occur. Not only do less restrictive alternatives need to be taken into account (including postponement), but also the actual wishes of the person concerned (including the proclivity for sexual activity) and the likelihood of a relationship coming into being in which adequate support for a child would be available.

INVOLUNTARY CIVIL COMMITMENT

Some of the problems confronting involuntary sterilization are brought into clearer relief by the practice of committing to institutions those who are deemed dangerous to themselves or others, where this dangerousness is the consequence of some incapacity, and the person is not considered competent to take appropriate evasive action (such as voluntarily admitting him- or herself to an institution or securing a guardian). For present purposes I shall leave to one side the civil commitment of those deemed dangerous to others, and shall focus instead on paternalistic civil commitment.

At first blush, involuntary civil commitment looks relatively unproblematic. Institutionalizing the incompetent as an act of weak paternalism should raise no liberal eyebrows. In fact, it is difficult to find a more controversial issue. The problems are theoretical as well as empirical, and illustrate some of the complexities involved in making even weak paternalism work. Several issues deserve attention.

Dangerousness. In my initial formula, I restricted the scope of a civil commitment provision to those "deemed dangerous to themselves (or others)." Many have considered this too narrow, wishing to include as well those "in need of treatment" or "unable to care for themselves," to cite just two common extensions. The problem with these broader descriptions is simply that they are far too elastic and provide too much opportunity for excessively moralistic paternalism. Even dangerousness has proved too elastic in legal practice (cf. Beaver 1968, p. 57; Dershowitz 1968, p. 374; Stone 1971, p. 36). Several questions have to be addressed if dangerousness is to function as a workable basis for interference. (a) What is the danger involved? Is it to one or more of the individual's welfare interests, or to some interest of less central significance, or to what is considered by others to be in the person's interests? (b) How likely is it that the particular harm or injury will occur if the individual is left alone or provided with alternative means of support or care? Psychiatrists have shown themselves to be very poor judges in this regard (cf. Dresser 1982, pp. 846–51). (c) How serious are the predicted harms? Severe self-mutilation will warrant more concern than clumsiness. How reversible are the harms in question?

It is rare for these questions to be investigated with the seriousness they deserve, and so civil commitment provisions have been vehicles not of beneficence but repression. That said, however, if involuntary civil commitment is to be justified on paternalistic grounds, then "dangerousness to self" is the best-looking candidate.

Dangerousness and Incapacity. People regularly engage in hazardous activities, but we do not contemplate civil commitment simply on account of this. Where the engagement in a dangerous enterprise reflects a firm and significant commitment, the product of forethought and deliberation, it would be grossly insulting to require the person's institutionalization. Dangerousness constitutes a ground for involuntary civil commitment only when it is caused by factors beyond that person's control. Being beyond that person's control, we have reason to believe that the hazardous activity is not integral to his or her life-plans and identity.

Incompetence. Perhaps the crucial element in justifying civil commitment is the determination of a person's competence or lack thereof. Even where the dangers to which a person is exposed result from some incapacity, we do not have a sufficient ground for committing that person to an institution. Certainly he or she may choose to safeguard him- or herself by entering one, but to commit the person to an institution merely because he or she has no control over the hazardous behavior is to make assumptions about the person's priorities and values that could be quite unjustified. Unless the person is incapable of taking evasive action with respect to the dangers to which he or she, through incapacity, is periodically subject, his or her position is not significantly different from that of the person who, in the pursuit of his or her ends, knowingly runs certain risks. A person whose incompetence is such as to subject him- or herself to danger, may nevertheless consider it preferable, in terms of his or her life-plans and goals, to run those risks than to guard against them via voluntary commitment to an institution. This is clearly the judgment made by most of those who suffer from epilepsy. But it may also be a reasonable choice where the risks are more frequent. A dramatic case is that of Mrs. Elizabeth Lake, who was involuntarily committed as an insane person because the "chronic brain syndrome" from which she was said to be suffering exhibited itself in memory lapses, personal neglect, and periodic wandering in the streets without a clear conception of who or where she was or of the elapse of time.[9] Mrs. Lake appealed her commitment because in her more lucid moments she clearly preferred the risks associated with her condition to a life of confinement. But the court agrued that even though her relatives were prepared to take some responsibility for her, this would not be sufficient to ensure her bodily health, and that she should therefore remain institutionalized. In deciding as it did, the court violated Mrs. Lake's integrity. She was capable of appreciating the alternatives before her and clearly preferred to run the risks of "life on the outside" to the lonely and suffocating safety of the hospital. Whether or not it was the best choice to make, it was her best one, one that reflected her most important and abiding concerns.[10]

But what does it mean to be incapable of taking evasive action? Dangerousness is not itself evidence of incapacity, nor does it create a presumption of incapacity, even though it may raise the question. Given the tendency of psychiatrists to overpredict dangerousness, the onus of proof should rest on those wishing to confine rather than on the endangered individual, and the dangerousness of nonconfinement should not be admissible as evidence of incapacity. For it is not the inability to avoid hazardous activities so much as the inability to determine whether or not to take evasive action with respect to such inability that is at issue.

We have already had occasion to notice the difficulties involved in determining incompetence. Here it may be useful to take that discussion a bit further. It has been common in psychiatric circles to make judgments of incompetence a natural outcome of diagnosis of mental illness. This runs into two difficulties. The first, discussed previously, is the *non sequitur* involved in concluding mental incompetence from mental illness. There are illnesses and illnesses, and only in some cases is decision-making incapacity involved. The second is the tendentious character of judgments of psychiatric illness. Thomas S. Szasz has developed this position most relentlessly (1961; 1970; 1970a). Broadly speaking, Szasz has claimed that most judgments of mental illness have a strongly ideological character: they tell you more about the values of the person making the judgments than about the condition of those in relation to whom the judgments are made. It is not that he rejects the notion of mental illness *tout court*, but he believes that such claims can be legitimated only if some responsible physiological malfunction, defect, or condition can be identified. Otherwise, they constitute not judgments of illness but of moral, social, or political unacceptability.

There is much to be said for Szasz's concerns. Psychiatric classification has an unhappy history of arbitrariness, and horror stories abound. Nevertheless, Szasz's own insistence that judgments of mental illness or mental incapacity be yoked to an identifiable physiological condition seems overly stringent. Herbert Morris is right to suggest that while Szasz is correct to see in psychiatrists "madness-mongering" tendencies, he is himself prone to "responsibility-mongering" (Morris 1971, p. 1166). His disdain for those who would "protect the patient from his own wishes" displays a somewhat simplistic acceptance of what people express as wishes. Szasz's proper concern about psychiatric moralism and authoritarianism needs to be counterbalanced by M. S. Moore's assessment: "The problem is that mental illness is not a myth. It is not some palpable falsehood propagated among the populace by power-mad psychiatrists, but a cruel and bitter reality that has been with the human race since antiquity" (1975, p. 1483). The deep and difficult problems engendered by psychiatric classification and judgment do not show mental illness to be a myth any more than the equally deep problems in moral theory and judgment show morality to be a chimera. While it is true that judgments of mental illness will almost inevitably have a normative dimension, this is not in itself sufficient to discredit them.

But even if mental illness is not a myth and the difference between mental illness and incompetence is noted, the justifiability of civil commitment may be questioned. It is claimed that the difficulties in accurately determining incompetence are so substantial that serious mistakes will be made. Some who competently refuse commitment will be involuntarily committed because others mistakenly judge them to be incompetent to decide. The seriousness of this injustice and the likelihood of its occurring tend to discredit the practice of involuntary civil commitment. In a slightly different context, Livermore, Malmquist, and Meehl put the argument as follows:

> Assume that one person out of a thousand will kill. Assume also that an exceptionally accurate test is created which differentiates with ninety–five per cent effectiveness those who will kill from those who will not. If 100,000 people were tested, out of 100 who would kill 95 would be isolated. Unfortunately, out of the 99,900 who would not kill, 4,995 people would also be isolated as potential killers. In these circumstances, it is clear that we could not justify incarcerating all 5,090 people. . . . If, in the criminal law, it is better that ten guilty men go free than that one innocent man suffer, how can we say in the civil commitment area that it is better that fifty-four harmless people be incarcerated lest one dangerous man be free? (1968, p. 84; cf. Sartorius 1980, pp. 143–44).

Unless our technique for isolating incompetence is virtually foolproof, many will have their persons violated, an injustice not compensated for by the small additional protection that society or the individual gains. However, as troubling as these possibilities are, it is not clear that abandonment of all involuntary civil commitment is the appropriate response. The argument might be better seen as a demand for much greater care and stringency in the use of tests to determine incompetence, and if some (suitably defined) dangerous behavior is made a *precondition* of the testing process, the likelihood of mistake will be greatly reduced. There is a certain artificiality about the way in which Livermore, Malmquist, and Meehl calculate the likelihood of error.

Commitment and Treatment. Even if it is established that a person is not competent to take evasive action with respect to self-harming conduct, it does not follow that involuntary commitment would be justified. Merely confining a person to an institution in order that he or she comes to no harm may be no better than confining a child to a cage for the same reason. The fact that a paternalistic imposition is weak does not mean that it is therefore morally unproblematic. There is a strong argument for making it a condition of commitment that the person so confined will be helped to recover his or her autarchy (cf. the Argument from Freedom Promotion, pp. 52–53). Even where a person has lost the capacity to make appropriate decisions of his or her own, his or her integrity requires that impositions acknowledge and advance it. The responsiveness to a person's integrity that weak paternalism may involve can be undermined if there is no intention and effort to restore autarchy. The paternalism of involuntary civil commitment must therefore have a positive as well as a negative aspect. It is not merely the protection from harm but the promotion of a capacity for self-direction that legitimates it. In the words of an Alabama court: "The purpose of involuntary hospitalization for treatment purposes is *treatment* and not mere custodial care or punishment. This is the only justification, from a constitutional standpoint, that allows civil commitments to mental institutions."[11] Although no direct violation of integrity is involved in interfering with the self-threatening behavior of a person lacking control over his or her actions, a continuation of this interference with the sole purpose of preventing the harmful behavior from reasserting itself constitutes neglect of the person who is, in a sense, trapped by alien tendencies and to whom we have undertaken a duty of care.

The situation is complicated somewhat where there is reason to think that competence has been permanently lost. This would not automatically disqualify involuntary civil commitment, since the harms of nonconfinement would not be voluntarily chosen. However, it is possible to imagine a situation in which confinement for merely custodial purposes would be unjustified. If what we know of the person's values and life-plans gives us good reason to think that he or she would have preferred the risks of nonconfinement to the indignity of permanent institutionalization, involuntary commitment would violate that integrity.

Alternatives to Commitment. We have not yet established a case for involuntary civil commitment. Even though a person may not be capable of deciding to take evasive action with respect to self-endangering conduct, institutionalization may represent an unjustifiable imposition. The reason is not that it would be ineffective (common though that may be), but that there are equally effective but less restrictive alternatives available. Involuntary civil commitment, just because it involves confinement within a total institution, ought to be seen as a last resort, rather than the first option. Yet all too often it has been resorted to as an easy way out, a means whereby relatives and social agencies can relieve themselves of the "costs" that care involves when the person in need of it cannot be "controlled."

There are various alternatives to civil commitment that are less intrusive and quite probably more effective, just because they provide greater scope for the recovery and exercise of rational capacities. For some of those presently confined in institutions, regular monitoring of their activities by social welfare personnel would be quite sufficient (home visits or their attendance at a community center); for others, some form of guardianship (limited or general) would suffice; only for the most intractable or urgent cases is the institutional alternative appropriate. Even then, there ought to be a regular review of patients to determine not merely whether they are ready for some less confining treatment, but also whether the treatment they are receiving is appropriate to their condition and directed toward the restoration of their capacity to determine whether or not to take evasive action with respect to the dangerous conduct that has precipitated their confinement.

Notes

1. I use the term "fiduciary" in its general rather than legal sense. It is intended to indicate a mutual rather than one-way trust.

2. As we might expect were we to follow Tönnies.

3. Although there are special problems in paternalistic deception, I do not want to suggest that there is some special connection between paternalism and deception. The truth may be told, as well as withheld, for paternalistic reasons. A doctor may want to make a patient to face up to his or her own situation.

4. *Superintendent of Belchertown* v. *Saikewicz*, 370 N.E. 2d, 417 (1977).

5. *In re Maida Yetter*, 62 Pa. D. & C. 2d, 619 (C.P. Northhampton County, 1973).

6. *Department of Human Services* v. *Northern*, 563 S.W. 2d, 167 (Tn. App., 1978), *cert. denied*, U.S. (1978).

7. *Buck* v. *Bell*, 274 U.S. 200, at 208 (1927).

8. Some of our difficulty here arises from the individualistic way in which we conceptualize family life and childrearing.

9. *Lake* v. *Cameron*, 364 F. 2d, 657 (D.C. Cir., 1966).

10. As it turned out, Mrs. Cameron probably knew better than the court what was good for her. She remained in hospital for a further five years, until her death, receiving no visitors in the last year.

11. *Wyatt* v. *Stickney*, 325 F. Supp., 381, at 384 (M.D. Ala., 1971).

6

Long-Term Welfare

As a matter of broad social policy, it is reasonable to assume that people's lives will span several decades, and that if they are to be characterized by a tolerable degree of dignity and purposefulness, various provisions will need to be made either by or for them. What is done now will have some bearing on the kind of life they can expect to have in the future. To some extent, this consideration has been operative in the previous two chapters. The person who fails to wear a seat belt or safety helmet now risks having no future or a future with markedly deteriorated possibilities. The person who eats unwisely now may have a shortened future or one beset with prematurely diminished capacities. But attention to safety and diet constitute only part of what is likely to be necessary if one's future is to be a source of fulfilled projects and expectations. Our welfare interests include, besides health, the development of our intellectual and emotional capacities, the fostering of significant relationships with others, and the accumulation of sufficient, stable resources to enable the execution of flexible life-plans (cf. Rescher 1972, ch.1).

These welfare interests are not secured in some automatic fashion, as the natural outgrowth of a maturational process (though maturational processes are not irrelevant to their acquisition). In large measure they come about through deliberate planning—either by ourselves or by others on or in our behalf. Nor, once secured, are these welfare interests automatically protected. They may be damaged or squandered; they may even atrophy through nonuse. The maintenance of welfare, no less than its initial procurement, requires foresight and planning—either by ourselves or by others on or in our behalf.

In the initial stages of an individual's life, his or her welfare interests will need to be both determined and secured by others. The infant enters the world helpless, barely able to make its needs known, urgently in need of protection and nurture by others. It is in virtue of this that parental paternalism is generally endorsed. It is believed and expected that parents will secure or provide for the securing of the child's physical and emotional needs, and will to some extent prepare the child for participation in the wider community. It is in that larger context that his or her life-plans and interests will need to be pursued and realized. But parents sometimes fall unacceptably short of the moral minima that limit their paternalistic role, and children sometimes rebel against the wisdom that is exercised on their behalf. And so the state also exercises a *parens patriae* function. Sometimes this compels parents to act in certain ways toward their children; sometimes it compels children to bow to the wisdom of their parents; sometimes it places protective constraints on the relations that children may have with other adults. Compulsory schooling regulations, fluoridation of the public water supply, the mandatory use of child restraints in cars, limitations on the age at which a child may leave school or home, and the fixing of an age of majority or varying ages at which consent may be given to various risk-bearing activities—sexual intercourse, therapeutic treatment, labor contracts, hire-purchase agreements, tattooing, and participation as an experimental subject—all these represent at least partially paternalistic constraints designed to benefit or protect children in the long term.

Long-term paternalism, or what I would include under that rubric, is not necessarily limited to children. Adults, too, are sometimes limited in ways which suggest a paternalistic concern. There are various informal limitations of choice, such as those that might occur between spouses, in which paternalistic motivations are involved: fatty foods are not served (even though they are liked); pills are hidden, lest they facilitate a possible suicide attempt; etc. But formal restrictions can be found as well. The refusal to recognize voluntary slavery contracts, compulsory participation in superannuation or retirement schemes, restrictions on what experimental projects a person may volunteer for, and, particularly in the case of the elderly, subjection to guardianship orders to ensure that they do not squander their assets and leave their interests unprovided for, all may have self-regarding good as (part of) their motivation.

Long-term paternalism may also take the more inclusive form I refer to as political paternalism. Here it is argued that the social traditions and political structures within which people construct and pursue their life-plans are so unpromising with respect to their well-being that large-scale control of their political and social environment is justified. Several varieties of political paternalism have found public expression. The activities of the nineteenth- and early twentieth-century colonial powers represent one example; it has continued to be a feature of certain revolutionary movements, and it is often present in the treatment of ethnic (or other) minorities.

In this chapter I discuss some representative examples of long-term paternalism, in the hope of rendering more sensitive the argumentative instruments developed in Chapters 2 and 3.

Children and Paternalism

The neonate is, to all intents, helpless: a living organism, capable, it is true, of breathing on its own and of giving expression to felt physiological needs by crying, sucking, and so forth, but in no serious sense able to make its own way in the world or to ensure that others will help it do so. If its survival needs are to be met, others will need to meet them.

But the human neonate is not just a biological organism with various "survival needs." It also possesses (or at least it usually does) an impressive range of capacities for development—physical, cognitive, affective, and volitional. The cultivation and improvement of these capacities, so that progress toward individuality can become the growing person's own project, is not entirely spontaneous but depends in some measure on the uninvited attentions of others. These others are normally its biological parents. There are other possibilities, but there is some reason to think that the developmental needs of children are likely to be met most successfully in an environment in which primary responsibility, and the authority that is derivative of that, lies with the parents. There are grounds for believing that parents, more than anyone else, will have the kind of commitment to their offspring that will safeguard and promote their welfare interests, and encourage the formation of an identity and life-plans compatible with their individual character, abilities, and talents. Parents, therefore, are permitted a wide range of discretion so far as the treatment of their children is concerned.

This discretion, however, is limited on two sides. On the one side, it is recognized that the presumption in favor of parents is only a presumption. Not all parents have a strong commitment to securing even the welfare interests of their children, or, even if they do, are capable of ensuring that they are met. They may need direction and support; in some cases, they may need to be relieved of the responsibility/authority that is vested in them. On the other side, the children themselves come to exert an increasingly strong claim to set their own course and the means by which and terms under which it is to be pursued. At some point, parental authority, at least so far as the child's self-regarding conduct is concerned, loses its special status, and parents stand in no more privileged relation to their children than anyone else. Only in exceptional circumstances (such as the adult child's noncompetence) will there be occasion for its renewed exercise.

The problem is to know where the lines are to be drawn: where parents fail in their responsibility to the extent that some form of outside intervention is required; and where children have developed to the point at which the responsibility for some decision should be theirs. I shall offer certain general criteria for determining these issues, and then apply them to some examples.

THE LIMITS OF PARENTAL AUTHORITY

Although there is historical support for the view that children are the property of their parents, there is not much else to be said in its favor. Even Locke, who grounds property rights in labor, resists the view that children are chattels. As he puts it, parents are but "the occasions of their being" (Locke 1690: I.54). Their life comes from God; they are God's workmanship and are thus, like their parents, only his property (II.6). The Law of Nature, which embodies God's will, requires that they "preserve, nourish and educate" their children (II.56). Whatever we may think of Locke's reasoning here, the general thrust of his position seems to be correct. That is, parents have, in the first instance, duties to their children, and any rights that they have with respect to them are secondary to these duties. Parental authority is an authority exercised on behalf of, more than over, children.

Locke says that parents must "preserve, nourish, and educate" their children, and that fairly well captures the range of parental duties. Children are highly vulnerable organisms, lacking the capacity to protect themselves against aggression, accident, and their own inexperience. This protection parents usually can and should provide. Not only are children vulnerable, but they are unable to provide for their bodily and psychological needs. Here, too, parents can be expected to contribute. Food and loving care are important if the child is to survive and be receptive to the various inputs that will constitute its education. Parental responsibility for education demands not that the parents themselves provide it, but that they ensure its provision.

For how long are parents bound by this role, such that they may exercise their authority over their children? The classic liberal answer is given by Mill, who claims that once children "are capable of being improved by free and equal discussion," then it is no longer permissible to impose on them for their own good. Once they have reached that stage, they are able to act in ways that are truly their own, creating for themselves the life-plans and identity that will be integral to their individuality.

But before I say more about this issue, I want to look briefly at some of the conditions under which we might want to say that the authority of parents to act for their children has been exceeded or abdicated. In general terms, this is not too hard to do. Since parental authority is secondary to parental duties, attempts to exercise that authority in ways that fall short of or violate those duties will call for, or at least provide a reason for intervention by others. Child abuse that threatens the child's welfare interests or primary goods is a clear enough case, though in practice it might sometimes be difficult to tell whether what is happening does constitute abuse of a kind warranting interference. If it arises out of an excess of concern rather than malice, we may be hesitant about intervening in a structure that is in general oriented to the child's development. But there are obviously limits. Jehovah's Witness parents who refuse to give consent to blood transfusions their children need are exceeding the bounds of parental authority. Even though it is important that the children continue to be accepted within the family environment, an environment that is committed to their nurture, nevertheless, in a case such as this the consequence would be their death. *Ceteris paribus*, it is difficult to see how this would be better for the children than intervention.

Incest is a more difficult case because it is not clear that incest *as such* has long-term deleterious consequences. Nevertheless, the likelihood of exploitation, the lack of any clear connection with the advancement of the child's welfare interests, and, at least in our culture, the risks of severe psychological repercussions, are likely to weigh in favor of its prohibition.

Another difficult case is provided by the offering of children as experimental subjects. Here it is not so much the child's individual benefit that is in view, but (presumably) some social benefit. I see no absolute objection to such offers, though as a safeguard it would probably be best to prohibit payment for such services. Where there is no risk to the child (say, the use of a urine sample), I see no objection to a parent consenting to his or her child's involvement. Indeed, doing so may be one of the ways in which the parent teaches the child a measure of social responsibility (cf. Gaylin 1982, p. 49; but see Bartholome and Gaylin 1982.) It is harder to justify when some risk to the child's welfare interests is present. Here we would need to take into account the social interests involved. Where they are very pressing and there is some recognizable connection between the research and those interests, some modest risks might be permissible. The reason for this is that the child's ends will ultimately be realized only in the context of the larger society, and to that extent he or she has a serious interest in and duty regarding it. In cases such as these, the cost-benefit ratios are not easy to determine, and my own inclination would be that so far as social policy is concerned, we err in favor of the child's welfare interests rather than the parent's derivative authority.

That, however, is easier said than done. One reason why we vest authority in parents rather than, say, the state, is that we presume that parents will both be more committed to and more aware of their children's welfare interests than some outside agency. This would not be so troublesome were we able to provide a nonideologically-loaded account of those interests. But we can't, despite Rawls's ingenious efforts to do so (Rawls 1971, pp. 92–5, 253, 260, ch.7). I do not think that this is a strong enough reason for not intervening when what are generally acknowledged welfare interests are at risk, but it reminds us that when we do intervene in such cases, we take a moral risk in doing so and ought to be willing to reconsider such decisions. We have no morally impregnable fortress to which we can retreat.

Where it is not the child's welfare interests that are at stake, then it is probably best that parents be left to exercise their authority without intervention. There are at least two reasons for this. The first is the greater likelihood overall of parents knowing what would be conducive to their children's good. Parents generally have a greater interest in and more intimate knowledge of their children than others. Exceptions can no doubt be found, but as a matter of social policy, the balance is probably best left in favor of the parents. The second relates to the importance of the family to the child. If children are to develop into beings with stable and cohesive interests, it is important that they be nurtured in a secure and integrated environment, where they are loved and cared for as intimates and not aliens. To interfere too much with parents' upbringing of their children is likely to destabilize the environment whose stability is of such importance to the children.

Again, this is easier said than done. Welfare and ulterior interests are not sharply separated. Inculcating in a child certain kinds of ulterior interests may in time be detrimental to the child's welfare interests. Creating in a child the love for sugary substances may cause serious health problems later on. Are we justified in interfering with the ulterior interests that parents inculcate because of what we believe will be the eventual effect on the child's welfare interests? Should a child be permitted to become an understudy to its prostitute parent? Should parents be permitted to withdraw their children from school (as did the Old Amish of Wisconsin)? Should a homosexual parent be permitted custody of a child? In cases such as these we see both the difficulty of clearly separating welfare and other interests, and the extent to which even the enumeration of welfare interests is infected by normative considerations.

Just in conclusion here, I need to add that it would be wrong to approach this issue in terms of only two options: parental authority vs. state authority. Where parental authority has exceeded its bounds or been abdicated, we might consider the appropriateness of a range of informal and formal intermediate interventions. Relatives, friends, and voluntary agencies may come to have certain discretionary powers recognized, on the understanding that they will be held accountable for their exercise.

THE DEVELOPMENT OF AUTARCHY

Were children born fully developed, the issue of parental paternalism would hardly arise. But they don't, and so parents have the duty to act toward them in a paternalistic manner: ensuring their good, even if it is not to their present liking. This, however, cannot go on forever, for one of the purposes of parental paternalism is to make itself redundant. Children are to be brought to a stage of development where they become capable of determining for themselves the details of their own good. The purpose of parental paternalism is not simply to secure for them a generalized good, as represented by their welfare interests, but to develop their capacities to a point at which they can place their own stamp on what they do, and can structure a conception of their good that accommodates the fruit of their own reflection: their attitudes, values, interests, and ends.

The development of children presents a problem for parental (and other) authority. For the achievement of autarchy is not an all-or-nothing affair, but a matter of ever-widening competence. What is more, because this development is not simply a matter of maturation but a product of learning, its accomplishment requires that children be given some scope for exploration and practice, some room for their own initiative. Unless we presume that we all have identical natures, the setting of directions cannot be determined prior to there being a form of interaction with the child in which it has the opportunity of articulating, to the extent to which it is able, its own understanding of its interests and temperament.

So far as social policy is concerned, we are inclined to approach the matter somewhat crudely. We nominate an age below which children may not act in their own right and above which they normally take responsibility for all that they do. Although the law was never quite as crude as this, many parents still act as though they retain full authority over their children until they reach the age of majority. This cannot be justified by the facts of child development. Given a relatively normal social environment, a child's development is gradual and progressive. This is not to deny that some periods may be more significant than others—say, the first five years, and then puberty. The point is that unless some impediment is placed in their way, children will increase in experience, in their capacity to understand what is happening to and around them, in their grasp of causal connections, in their sense of time, in their identification with and differentiation from others, in their ability to shape their environment, and in their capacity to evaluate themselves and the world they inhabit. At first, of course, their conceptualization and evaluation of experience will be almost wholly secondhand; but as it becomes more extensive, it will contain within it tools for reflection, tools that, we hope, they will eventually be able to use self-reflexively and self-critically, perhaps so that they will be refined or even replaced, but more importantly so that they will be genuinely their own.

This gradualist conception fits ill with an age-based one. It fits ill, not only because it is inappropriate, but also because children differ in their rates of development. Whereas eighteen may be appropriate for one, fourteen might be more to the point for another and twenty-one for a third. This, however, is not to suggest that there is nothing to be said in its favor. On the one hand, an age-based criterion of competence allows easy application, a positive virtue so far as public policy is concerned. Where standards are difficult to apply, uncertainty and confusion tend to be generated. On the other hand, an age-based criterion does not lend itself so easily to abuse. If eighteen is nominated the age of majority, then there is no excuse for continuing to act paternalistically toward someone who is twenty-three, on the grounds that he or she is not yet competent to make "adult" decisions. Some writers have considered that this counts decisively in favor of an age-based criterion (e.g., Schrag 1977, pp. 176–77; cf. Reed and Johnston 1980).

I believe that we do better through a combination of standards. First of all, what is at issue is the child's capacity to make its own decisions. In the beginning it is undeveloped, and others will have to make decisions for it. However, that opens the door to various forms of abuse, and those with oversight over it should be encouraged to be reasonably diligent in their efforts to bring the child to a point at which it can make decisions of its own regarding its goals and values. That is a reason for setting what I would call a presumptive age of decision. Better still, presumptive ages of decision. Let me spell this out in more detail.

What I mean by a *presumptive* age of decision is an age before which a person can be presumed not to be competent to make a certain kind of decision and after which a person can be presumed to be competent to make that kind of decision. Such presumptions are rebuttable, but the onus of rebuttal rests on a different party in each case. Before the stated age a person can be presumed not competent to bear responsibility for decisions of a certain kind unless he or she can show otherwise. After the stated age a person can be presumed competent to bear responsibility for that kind of decision unless others can show otherwise. Unless we have an age of this kind, there will be a temptation, at least in our present social environment, to extend the period of noncompetence, and by the same token to increase the opportunities for structuring a life in a way that limits the possibility for personal autonomy. There is reason to move the age down rather than up. If children have the capacity to make certain kinds of decisions when they are fourteen, there is no reason to delay their development of that capacity to make decisions of that kind until they are eighteen. In certain circumstances it might be found necessary to move the age up; this should not be done, however, because parents have been found slack in fulfilling their duties.

In saying that prior to the age of decision a person can be presumed not to be competent to make a certain kind of decision, I am focusing on the responsibility-bearing aspect of decision-making. I do not wish to suggest that children should not have some say with respect to the matters at issue. Their views should be taken into account, even if they are not determinative. Although parents can usually be presumed to know better than outsiders what will be best for their children, it should not surprise us if the children have knowledge about themselves and their good that is not readily accessible to their parents. In some cases it might be required that the views of children be taken into account before decisions are made on their behalf. This is now often done in custody proceedings and might also be required where major medical treatment is planned.

The reason for speaking of ages of decision is fairly simple. Self-regarding decisions are not all of a kind. They differ in their complexity, in the amount of experience they require, in the risks they involve, and in their long-term consequences. It is to be expected that we will learn to be able to make informed decisions about some matters earlier than others. Having a single age of majority obscures this variability and maintains the paternalistic yoke where it can no longer be justified. Many jurisdictions now recognize this variability, and give it statutory acknowledgement. So, consent to nonsurgical medical treatment might be recognized at fourteen, to marriage at sixteen, to hire purchase agreements at eighteen, and so on. Because statutory decisions on such matters often reflect pressures other than those relating to the capacities of children and are made in a somewhat piecemeal fashion, anomalies tend to be common (cf. Gaylin and Macklin 1982, pp. 8, 95–114).

What is it that people above/below a certain age are presumed able/not able to do? I have spoken in terms of their competence to make certain kinds of decisions. What does this involve? It does not require that the decision they make be seen by others as the correct one. Competence is not a matter of coming up with the right answers. We can competently make wrong decisions. It does require that the various options presented by some situation be understood. Their scope and consequences must be grasped. The person must possess canons for evidence and argument that would enable him or her to evaluate the options. And there must be a sufficiently settled and developed self-conception for any decision made to be that of an identifiable individual. It is not always easy to determine whether a person has developed the abilities that are constitutive of competence. We shall probably need to see how the person handles relevant information—whether it is allowed to mesh with his or her value system, whether the decision that results is backed up by reasons that are recognizably connected to it, and so on. And this opens the possibility of our impressing our own standards of correctness on the person. But I do not see how that is altogether avoidable. The proper response is to be aware of the danger and do the best one can.

It is one thing to talk about paternalism toward children in the abstract. The issue is more complicated when we look at particular examples of such paternalism. Here I shall consider just two.

Compulsory Schooling. As long as there have been schools, there has been compulsory schooling for some. Parents have sent their children to them, with or without the children's cooperation. Legal compulsion to attend school is relatively recent, most industrialized societies introducing it only in the latter part of the nineteenth century. The initial motivations for this appear to have been strongly ideological. Schooling was seen as a means whereby certain otherwise-threatened social values and practices could be preserved (cf. Kleinig 1981). But there were paternalistic arguments as well. Three have found fairly wide currency. The Protectionist Argument works from the vulnerability of children to self-induced harms and various forms of exploitation. Compelling school attendance is seen as a way of "keeping them out of harm's way." The Socio-Economic Argument works from an observed correlation between socio-economic status and schooling; it is argued that it will be better for children if they are made to attend school and to attend it for as long as possible. The Educative Argument sees in schooling the provision of some of a person's primary goods—the development of native capacities and the power of self-determination. The last of these arguments is probably the most attractive, and I shall concentrate on it (there is a preliminary discussion of the first two in Kleinig 1981, pp. 194–96).

An influential statement of the Educative Argument can be found in *On Liberty.* The base assumption is that the development of individuality cannot be expected to occur spontaneously. Compulsion will be needed (Mill 1859, p. 224). The responsibility for ensuring this falls, in the first instance, to parents. According to Mill, by bringing children into the world they have assumed responsibility for their nurture, and may intervene in their lives in order that and to the point where they can display the rational skills, emotional sensitivities, and resolution requisite for individuality (1859, pp. 301–2). As yet, this does not amount to an argument for compulsory *schooling* so much as for compulsory *education.* Further steps are required, which Mill saw being supplied by the social circumstances of his time. Although the Factory Act of 1833 had initiated a series of legislative reforms alleviating the conditions of children in industry, it was Mill's view that many parents lacked the inclination and/or ability to provide the wherewithal for an individuality-disposed autarchy. Only by the state enforcement of "education" could some of the important interests of children be advanced. Mill proposes that there be a series of public examinations that children would be required to pass, up to a certain level. Although this does not constitute a full-fledged argument for compulsory schooling (since the requisite standards could be reached through home-based learning), in practice Mill saw it working itself out via schooling. But there are certain dangers in this, which Mill underscores by distinguishing between "the enforcement of education by the State" and "State education." If Mill was skeptical about the fitness of parents to educate their children, he was no less skeptical about the motives of the state in taking it over. "A general State education," he writes,

> is a mere contrivance for moulding people to be exactly like one another; and as the mould in which it casts them is that which pleases the predominant power in government, whether this be a monarch, a priesthood, an aristocracy, or the majority of the existing generation; in proportion as it is efficient and successful, it establishes a despotism over the mind leading by natural tendency to one over the body (1859, p. 302).

Mill concedes that the state might set up a few schools—though only as "one among many competing experiments, carried on the purpose of example and stimulus, to keep the others up to a certain standard of excellence" (1859, p. 302). But beyond that it should provide only the means whereby parents could send their children to schools of their own choosing. It is not that Mill expected "independent" schools to be less zealous in seeking to mold students in partisan ways, but he believed that the meeting of diverse backgrounds in adult society would counteract indoctrination, and thus be subject to checks that would not otherwise operate.

Mill shows a salutary sensitivity to ways in which state schooling may become an instrument of state ideology. However, it might well be argued that he has misidentified "the enemy." The state does not constitute an autonomous source of influence, but is itself largely formed by and expressive of other social forces, and Mill's fears of ideological domination are not likely to be allayed by an insistence on the state enforcement of education as distinct from its control by the state. To loosen the state's hand on education is not necessarily to create more space for the individual to develop his or her own life-plans, or at least life-plans that give ample opportunity for the integrated development of his or her capacities, for the hand of a particular economic system may weigh more heavily on the formation of individual character than the institution that helps to maintain it. If something like that is the case, the answer to Mill's fears will have to take the form not of this versus that form of schooling, but of this versus that socio-economic formation (cf. Bowles and Gintis 1975).

The problem with the Educative Argument, then, is not that educational ends do not justify paternalism, but that compulsory schooling may not be conducive to educational ends. Although the ideology of schooling proclaims its educative value, there tends, on the one hand, to be a diffuseness about the understanding of education and, on the other, to be a domination of the school's educational ends by other competing social demands.

However, even if this criticism of the Educative Argument is justified, it will not follow that compulsory schooling is unjustified. What may follow is that within a particular, say, the present socio-economic formation, compulsory schooling cannot be justified *paternalistically*. In a different socio-economic formation, it may be justified on paternalistic grounds. But quite apart from that, there may be other grounds for persisting with the *status quo*, at least for the time being. It is at least arguable that the demands of social justice are better served within our present set-up by persevering with compulsory schooling than they would be by abandoning it. If our concern is with the inequalities of power distribution within the present social arrangements, the situation would almost certainly be exacerbated were the compulsory schooling requirement dropped. Those most likely to move out of the system are just those who presently lack social power, and their position would be made worse by their withdrawal. That of course is not an argument for conservatism, but rather an argument for not dropping the compulsory schooling requirement *in isolation*.

A rather different and less probing criticism of the Educative Argument is that compulsion sits uneasily with education. If education includes the development of a person's powers of self-determination, this is likely to be subverted by compulsion, since it will induce a merely extrinsic motivation for the activities that come to be embodied in projects and life-plans rather than one appropriate to a commitment to those activities (cf. Krimerman 1978, pp. 84–86). Only where spontaneity is encouraged—that is, only in an environment free from paternalism—can an authentic appreciation and commitment develop. Furthermore, it might be maintained, where there already exists an intrinsic interest in various enterprises, pursuing them within a framework of compulsoriness will subvert that interest, either killing or corrupting it.

Several problems weaken this argument. First, where capacities are not yet developed, it is not to be supposed that interests and competence are likely to develop spontaneously. The acquisition of a language may seem to run counter to this, and to some extent it does so. But this is because language acquisition is given an immediate relevance to the child's emerging self-consciousness. However, much of the information that a child will need to learn if it is to develop its capacity for individuality will relate to its future rather than present requirements. It is just because, as Mill puts it, the child is as yet "incapable of being acted upon by rational consideration of distant motives" (1859, p. 282), that some form of compulsion is necessary. Maybe some of these things would be picked up in the ordinary course of events, without compulsion, in a suitably rich environment, but such an approach would be too unreliable and most likely result in a dereliction of parental duty. The point of compulsion in these cases is not to provide an external reason for engaging in activities of certain kinds, but to ensure that there is some engagement so that the ends and standards intrinsic to those activities may be given opportunity to exert their own influence on the one who is required to participate in them. No doubt compulsion can be overdone. It can be necessitated by bad teaching or continued to the point where it becomes counterproductive. But this is another matter.

Second, the argument tends to confuse compulsoriness and coerciveness. Coercion, the achievement of some end by threat, may well be antieducative.

But compulsory schooling/education is not necessarily coercive, at least so far as children are concerned. Although compulsory attendance laws do not allow children the option of not attending, it does not follow that they are therefore coerced into attending. We may do willingly what we are compelled to do, whereas if we are coerced, what we do we do not do willingly but under threat. Even where compulsory attendance laws act coercively, the coercion may be on the parents rather than the children. By the same token, it would not follow from the absence of compulsory attendance laws that children would not be compelled or even coerced into attending school. For their parents may require that they go.

Third, even if compulsory schooling and the coercion that sometimes goes with it does not provide the healthiest of contexts for educationally valuable learning, it may be better than the alternatives. Consider the case where parents (perhaps with the understandable acquiescence of their children) propose to deny their children access to schools in order that they may inculcate in them what must appear to outsiders as a narrow and restrictive self-understanding and understanding of the wider world. This was one of the points at issue in the dispute between the Old Order Amish and the State of Wisonsin.[1] The Amish argued that secondary schooling would promote values, attitudes, and desires at variance with those upheld by their families and community. To require secondary school attendance would be destructive both to family and community life. On the other side, it was argued that the interests of children were not served by bringing them up with a "closed future"—a mental and social world so constricting that many of their capacities would remain undeveloped or stunted. In the event, the Amish won their case, but this was partly because of the relatively short period in dispute (two years). Had they opposed all schooling, the situation would have been "very different." For this would then have deprived the children of their liberal right to develop the capacity to choose competently between differing life-plans and thus to participate effectively as citizens in a democratic community (cf. Feinberg 1980b; Gutman 1980). As we have noted, parents do not have exclusive or overriding claims on their children. Children have welfare interests of their own that need to be acknowledged and secured, and, since they will also be citizens, the state too has certain legitimate expectations concerning the outcome of their nurture.

If the Educative Argument for compulsory schooling goes some way toward justifying a certain form of parental or even legal paternalism, it does not therefore justify the *status quo*. This is in part because of their ideologizing tendencies, but also in part because of the developing capacities of the children themselves. Whether children should not be permitted to leave school before they are fifteen (as is commonly the case) is by no means obvious. They are not completely lacking in independent interests until that age, and even though there may be no assurance that these interests have acquired a stable position in a reasonably cohesive life-plan, their wishes ought to be taken into account. Although they are still developing centers of self-consciousness, their sensitivity to their own needs is sometimes more acute than that of the adults who have responsibility for them but who have been indoctrinated with alienating interests and have lost perspective even on their own well-being.

Compulsory schooling, of course, usually involves more than compulsory attendance. A compulsory curriculum is often also involved, and here too there ought to be sensitivity to the diversity of children's natures. This is very difficult to achieve in a bureaucratized institution, where managerial considerations operate powerfully and there is likely to be a greater respon-siveness to other social and cultural demands (the needs of commerce and industry, for example). Perhaps the best that we can do in this context is to set up as a kind of benchmark, against which questions of curriculum can be focused, a generalized conception of the individual who it is hoped will emerge from the nurturing process. So far as the liberal tradition is concerned, this will be an individual whose capacities have been developed to the point where he or she is able to engage in the sort of reflective self-evaluation that is central to individuality, and can, in concert with others, set in motion plans and projects of his or her own. To the extent that schooling fails to encourage this kind of development, to that extent the Educative Argument may not be employed in its behalf.

Consent to Medical Treatment. The "age of consent," considered not in its more specialized use as the age at which a woman may legally consent to sexual intercourse, but in its more generalized employment, is a legal fiction aimed at demarcating an age before which the consent of a person to some specified act or activity will not be recognized. The theory behind it is that by virtue of their immaturity young people are not able to appreciate sufficiently what is involved in making a decision concerning the act or activity for any response to be *their own*, in any full-blooded sense. The conditions for autarchy are not yet present.

So far as medical treatment is concerned, the theory is outlined in *Bellotti v. Baird*, where the capacity of a minor to consent to an abortion without her parents' knowledge was at issue:

> States may validly limit the freedom of children to choose for themselves in the making of important, affirmative choices with potentially serious consequences. These [limitations] have been grounded in the recognition that, during the formative years of childhood and adolescence, minors often lack the experience, perspective and judgment to recognize and avoid choices that would be detrimental to them.[2]

In consenting to medical treatment, a person assumes responsibility for it. Where responsibility cannot properly be assumed, genuine consent cannot be given. It cannot be assumed where the person who assents does not understand either the nature or expectable consequences of the activity, or where there is duress or ratiocinative incapacity. Children are prone or subject to each of these responsibility-defeating conditions. In the early stages of their de-velopment, conceptualization, inference-drawing, and argumentation are at best embryonic, and their dependence and need for security make them highly susceptible to duress and other coercive influences. The general drift of *Bellotti* is sound.

But what conclusions may be drawn from this, so far as consent to medical treatment is concerned? As I have already indicated, it is not justifiable to treat children as though they have no capacity for consent until a certain "magic" age is reached, after which they have thrust upon them the whole burden of decision-making. The growth of experience and ratiocinative ability is incremental rather than sudden. Furthermore, decisions differ in their complexity and in the demands that they make on experience and intellectual sophistication.

What is true of decisions in general is also true of medical procedures in particular. Some are highly complex or require a broadly based experience not likely to be available to young children, others have clear-cut alternatives, the nature and consequences of which are likely to be understood even by a fairly young child. Clearly some allowance needs to be made for this. Allowance could be made in two ways. One is to nominate different ages for different kinds of treatment, where there is a rebuttable presumption that those above/below that age are competent/not competent to give or withhold consent. The other is to nominate a single age, where it is recognized that exceptions are more likely to be made where some kinds of decisions are involved than where others are. In each case a lower age might be nominated below which there is a conclusive presumption of noncompetence. The difficulty of classifying "kinds of treatment" favors the second alternative. Classifications like "surgical," "medical," and "psychiatric" are too varied in what they encompass to function usefully here.

Where a child is presumed noncompetent to consent to a particular therapeutic procedure, responsiblity for the decision will normally fall to the parents, though it should not fall to them in a way that discounts the child's wishes in the matter. There may, however, be exceptions to this. Because of their dependence, emotional and material, children are extremely vulnerable to parental power. This vulnerability may remain even after they become competent to make decisions of their own. There are certain kinds of medical procedures that children may wish to explore or have, but that they might (but ought not to) be deterred from pursuing if they require parental consent (or notification). Treatment for sexually transmitted diseases, the prescription of contraceptives, treatment for drug dependence, psychiatric help, and, where it is accepted, abortion, may not be sought if the parents have to be involved. Yet not to provide some means whereby the child may receive confidential help of an appropriate kind is to court tragedy and, in some cases, socially deleterious consequences. Parents may wish to complain that such provisions interfere with the integrity of the family and usurp a responsibility that is properly theirs, but the proper response to this is that in cases where the child is not willing to consult with the parents, there has already been a breakdown in communciation and parental responsiveness. The point of providing an alternative in such sensitive areas is not to provide children with a legal capacity to consent in cases where they lack the moral capacity, but rather to provide an environment in which any medical decisions made either by or for them will be free of duress and sensitive to their present and future circumstances. This is a somewhat more qualified position than that frequently advocated. It is not enough that the doctor or counselor to whom the child goes be willing to comply with its wishes; compliance needs to be grounded in an assessment of the interests and circumstances of the child, and of the long-term effects that the available alternatives would have.

One factor that might affect the stringency with which the age criterion is applied is the risk-gain ratio (cf. Gaylin 1982, p. 40ff). The fact that a person is not competent to make a certain kind of decision is not always a reason for denying him or her that opportunity. Experience can be a good teacher; we can learn much from our mistakes, including those made prior to our becoming competent. Noncompetent choice may help to provide conditions for competent choice. Where, however, substantial risks are involved, a concession of this kind would tend to be self-defeating. The point here is not that noncompetence is more likely where high risks are involved (cf.

Freedman 1981, pp. 66–72), but that the consequences of a mistaken assessment may be more serious and there is therefore a correspondingly higher burden on those who invigilate the consenting process to assure themselves that responsible (versus nonresponsible) decisions are being made.

Adult Welfare and Paternalism

As we have noted, the adult-child distinction, used so frequently to justify differential treatment, is a somewhat artificial even if not altogether arbitrary one. I have suggested that in so far as we give it any normative value, it be simply to shift the presumptive burden.

In this I depart from Mill. He asks the question: "If protection against themselves is confessedly due to children and persons under age, is not society equally bound to afford it to persons of mature years who are equally incapable of self-government?" (1859, p. 280). My response is that we should afford protection to the latter, but that in their case competence is presumed until disproved. In the case of children, however, noncompetence is presumed until disproved. Mill, I suspect, fears that this will open the door to adult paternalism, and answers the question in the negative.

> Society has had absolute power over them during all the early portion of their existence: it has had the whole period of childhood and nonage in which to try whether it could make them capable of rational conduct in life. . . . If society lets any considerable number of its members grow up mere children, incapable of being acted upon by rational consideration of distant motives, society has itself to blame for the consequences (1859, p. 282).

Francis Schrag is of a similar mind. Relativizing the adult-child distinction would open "the door to the possibility of an extension of paternalism beyond childhood, a possibility which could provide a basis for the kind of hierarchical society we abhor" (1977, p. 177). It is not, he believes, a bare possibility. Noting that adults are prohibited from purchasing powerful drugs without a prescription, he continues:

> If one imagines a world of increasing complexity, a world of vastly enlarged technical knowledge of antecedent and consequent in such areas as health, interpersonal relations and vocational satisfaction, and a world in which the adult/child distinction is no longer taken as absolute, the crack in the door does not seem so trifling (1977, p. 177).

The concerns voiced by Mill and Schrag are real enough. There ought to be some stimulus to treating childhood, not as a kind of never-never land, but rather as a stage through which one is expected to pass on the way to a mature adulthood. However, such concerns can be accommodated other than by means of an absolute distinction. If, as I have suggested, the age boundary line functions simply to shift the *onus probandi*, so far as competence is concerned, that should provide an adequate safeguard against unwarranted paternalism. It will also eliminate the otherwise arbitrary denial of paternalistic aid to adults who are not yet capable of extended self-government.

Although the adult-child distinction, by virtue of its connection with competence, has an important bearing on the question of justifiable paternalism, it is not, without further argument, decisive in that regard. Weak paternalism is not always justified and strong paternalism may sometimes be. I propose now to consider certain impositions on adults, conducive to their long-term welfare, that are often said to be paternalistic: the nonrecognition of slavery contracts and compulsory superannuation. As well, I look at the justifiability of singling out the elderly for paternalistic treatment.

The Nonrecognition of Slavery Contracts. In what is often considered to be the acid test for antipaternalism—permitting someone to sell him- or herself into perpetual slavery—Mill is usually said to have failed or at least equivocated. On the one hand, he states that the individual ought to have sovereignty with respect to his or her self-regarding concerns. On the other hand, he opposes the recognition of a contract in which an individual places him- or herself completely and irrevocably at another's disposal. But the reasons he gives are less than transparent, and one is left with some uncertainty as to whether he has actually compromised his position.

We might of course challenge the view that an antipaternalist would advocate the recognition of slavery contracts. A refusal to enforce them might be defended on nonpaternalistic grounds. Several such grounds are suggested by Joel Feinberg (1971, pp. 118–20). (a) Nonrecognition may be intended to deter one person from exploiting or profiting from the weakness, foolishness, or recklessness of another. (b) It might serve to hold the fort against a (further) weakening of respect for human dignity (with all the social consequences that could bring in its trail). (c) In view of the possible consequences for those who thus dispose of themselves, it helps to secure the benevolent against unreasonable demands on their charitableness. (d) Because of the potential for coerced acquiescence, the voluntariness of assent would need to be assured. This would be so costly, and possible mistakes so unacceptable, that nonrecognition may be considered the better policy. There is something to be said for each of these claims, though it may be doubted whether individually or conjointly they count decisively against the enforcement of slavery contracts. The claim against Mill, however, is that he does not appeal to arguments of these kinds but bases his opposition on paternalistic reasons. Even though that may be considered an attractive complement or alternative to the positions just sketched, it sits ill with his apparent rejection of all paternalism.

In order to assess Mill's position and the charges laid against him, it is worth quoting his argument in full. He begins the relevant paragraph by recalling that where people combine for purposes that affect them alone, their liberty and that of others remains intact. So long as this continues, there is no reason or occasion for external regulation. But because people are liable to change their minds, and because such changes will affect the success of their joint activity and thus the investment of others, those entering these arrangements will want to get from each other some form of commitment to which they can, if necessary, be held. But there are, Mills claims, some legitimate exceptions to this. One obvious case is an agreement to violate the rights of some third party. In addition to this,

it is sometimes considered a sufficient reason for releasing people from an engagement, that it is injurious to themselves. In this and most other civilized countries, for example, an engagement by which a person should sell himself, or allow himself to be sold, as a slave, would be null and void; neither enforced by law nor by opinion. The ground for thus limiting his power of voluntarily disposing of his own lot in life, is apparent, and is very clearly seen in this extreme case. The reason for not interfering, unless for the sake of others, with a person's voluntary acts, is consideration for his liberty. His voluntary choice is evidence that what he so chooses is desirable, or at the least endurable, to him, and his good is on the whole best provided for by allowing him to take his own means of pursuing it. But by selling himself for a slave, he abdicates his liberty; he foregoes any future use of it beyond that single act. He therefore defeats, in his own case, the very purpose which is the justification of allowing him to dispose of himself. He is no longer free; but is thenceforth in a position which has no longer the presumption in its favour, that would be afforded by his voluntarily remaining in it. The principle of freedom cannot require that he should be free not to be free. It is not freedom, to be allowed to alienate his freedom (1859, pp. 299–300; cf. 1848, pp. 801–2, 953–54).

Not surprisingly, Mill's remarks have been variously interpreted. It is perhaps easiest to see them as favoring a degree of strong paternalism, though the question then arises as to whether this should be seen as an argumentative aberration or an attempt to spell out a genuine exception to his general thesis. But as well as the variants on this interpretation, there is also the suggestion that Mill is attempting to provide reasons of only a weak paternalistic kind, or even that he has the harm principle at the back of his mind. It will be easiest if we start off with what seems to be the most natural interpretation.

There is strong textual evidence for thinking that in advocating the nonenforceability of slavery contracts Mill is making a concession to strong paternalism. He claims explicitly that nonenforceability would have the effect of "limiting [a person's] power of voluntarily disposing of his own lot in life," and that it has as its "sufficient reason . . . that [such an agreement] would be injurious to [himself]." Few writers actually deny that these phrases make a verbal concession to strong paternalism. But some, like John Hodson, argue that it was an unnecessary and mistaken one, since "there is no need to justify the refusal to enforce slavery contracts" (1981, p. 60). It is unnecessary, because the failure to provide for the enforcement of a slavery contract does not infringe anyone's liberty. It "does not prevent anyone from living in *de facto* slavery" (Hodson 1981, p. 60; cf. Ten 1980, p. 119). Mill is not advocating interference with self-enslavement as such, but only opposing the contractualization of such arrangements. If Marvin wishes to enslave himself to Marcia, submitting himself irrevocably and in all respects to her will, Mill is not going to stop it. All he wishes to do is to withhold legal standing from such an agreement. But this, Hodson, says does not restrict "his 'power to dispose of *his own* lot in life', for there is nothing which is his which is thus denied him" (1981, p. 61).

I believe that Hodson is mistaken about this. Though it is possible that Marcia will be willing to accept Marvin's offer, there is also a strong likelihood that without some guarantees she will be extremely cautious about doing so. Why would Marvin offer to become Marcia's slave? The most likely reason is some cause or goal of Marvin's that Marcia has the means of furthering. Perhaps Marvin wants nothing more than to see some political or religious cause furthered, and Marcia is a very wealthy woman. Marvin figures that he can do most for his cause by offering himself as a slave in return for a very large donation. Marcia is willing, but she is no fool. She wants some assurance that Marvin will keep to his commitment. It's no good if she gives the money, and then has Marvin renege on the agreement, without any means of either enforcing it or exacting some compensation. So, if Marvin and Marcia are unable to get some legal backing for the proposal, Marvin may find the option closed to him. Another, though less likely, reason that Marvin may have for his offer is that he finds enslavement to Marcia intrinsically appealing. Perhaps it is the admiration he has for her, perhaps the desire to escape responsibility, perhaps a need for self-abnegation. On Marcia's part, no consideration is involved: nothing of what she has is risked. In this circumstance, the need for legal recognition seems almost unnecessary. But not quite. If Marcia wants to enter into the agreement and to avail herself of Marvin's services, she will need to rely on him to perform them. Should Marvin change his mind (and it is hard to guarantee that he won't), Marcia may find herself seriously disadvantaged through misplaced reliance. To cover such possibilities, she may insist on formalization before she takes advantage of Marvin's offer. For this reason I want to argue, with Mill and against Hodson, that lack of enforceability may limit a person's "power of voluntarily disposing of his own lot in life."

Consider now the reasons that Mill gives for withholding legal recognition from slavery agreements. He argues that it "is consideration for [the potential slave's] liberty." There is more than one way of taking this. Donald Regan reads it as consideration for the person's *future* liberty (1974, p. 193; cf. Dworkin 1971, p. 118). By not recognizing slavery contracts we help to keep open people's future options. This, in essence, is the Argument from Freedom Protection (see above, pp. 53–55), and it is susceptible to the objections leveled at that argument. It would not of course necessarily be the case that enslavement would diminish a person's options. A suitably benevolent slave owner might even increase them, albeit revocably. However, the unlikelihood of that being generally true might lend some plausibility to a refusal to grant such agreements *legal* recognition. More worrisome are the expansionist possibilities permitted by an argument of this kind. There are many activities we engage in and agreements we make that diminish our future options. Why stop at slavery agreements? Not getting sufficient sleep and exercise, bad dietary habits, and so on are also likely to diminish our future options. May we interfere also with these?

This "slippery slope" or "wedge" objection carries some weight but is not decisive. Mill does not say that consideration for the person's liberty is the only factor standing in the paternalist's way. Indeed, immediately following the quoted passage, he observes that slavery agreements are simply the extreme in a range of cases in which people might want to bind their future selves. In these other cases, however, the force of his argument is limited "by the necessities of life, which continually require, not indeed that we should resign our freedom, but that we should consent to this and the other limitation of it" (1859, p. 300).[3] In other words, there are certain "necessities of life" that have to be accommodated, along with the resignation of freedom, in determining the justifiability of paternalistic noncooperation. The complete and irrevocable resignation of liberty, though a weighty consideration, is not decisive. The point is well-illustrated by Mill's discussion of Mormon polygamy (sometimes believed to be out of tune with his discussion of slavery contracts):

"Far from being in any way countenanced by the principle of liberty, it is a direct infraction of that principle, being a mere rivetting of the chains of one-half of the community, and an emancipation of the other from reciprocity of obligation towards them" (1859, p. 290). Although slightly less comprehensive than a voluntary slavery contact, it is clear that Mill sees Mormon marriage in much the same light. Yet he opposes interference with it. His basic reason parallels that for not wanting to extend the case for nonenforcement of slavery contracts to other contexts in which future options are voluntarily diminished. Because "this relation is as much voluntary on the part of the women concerned in it, and who may be deemed the sufferers by it, as is the case with any other form of marriage institution," nonrecognition would result in considerable social disruption—more than can be reasonably countenanced. At bottom, the springs of Mormon marriage are not different to the springs of marriage generally. It "has its explanation in the·common ideas and customs of the world, which teaching women to think marriage the one thing needful, make it intelligible that many a woman should prefer being one of several wives, to not being a wife at all" (1859, p. 290).[4] If polygamy is to be outlawed or refused recognition out of concern for women who are parties to it, so in consistency ought monogamy. The point is not that Mill finds the existing practice of marriage acceptable, but that its decontractualization would be socially disruptive and would probably leave women worse off than they already are.

The foregoing remarks go some way toward easing the "slippery slope" problem. But they do not dispel it altogether. It is difficult to see why it is only in the case of voluntary slavery contracts that nonrecognition will be attended by an acceptable level of social disruption. It may be the clearest case, but that is no reason to think that it is the only case. Perhaps the situation here is intensified by the fact that a complete resignation of future liberty is involved. But if that is so, why does Mill stop at nonrecognition and not advocate the prevention of even *de facto* slavery agreements? The question is not meant to discredit the "future options" interpretation. But it may stimulate us to look for other ways of understanding Mill's reasoning.

As I have already foreshadowed, interpreting Mill's reference to "consideration for [the individual's] liberty" as a concern for future liberty is not the only possibility. It may be a regard for *existing* "liberty" that he has in mind, and which weighs against interference. That this is a better way to read him is suggested by the sentence that follows. He writes that where what a person chooses is voluntarily chosen, we have "evidence" that—in relation to that person's goals, wants, and values—what is chosen comports with that person's good. Although it is only evidence, it is just about the best evidence we can have, and therefore his or her good, "on the whole," will be best served if that choice is allowed to prevail. Here Mill draws on what I have called the Argument from Paternalistic Distance. The point of this antipaternalistic argument is not that people will always choose what is in their best interests, but that they are more likely to do so than others on their behalf. They have a greater commitment to their own good and are better acquainted with their own feelings, values, etc. than others are likely to be. Now, Mill says, this presumption would be undermined were it possible to negotiate an enforceable slavery contract, for the person who enters into such an agreement "abdicates" his or her liberty. He or she alienates the right to make voluntary choices. The point is not that the capacity for making such choices is lost (though this could be a consequence), but rather that its exercise is abandoned and, given the agreement's enforceability, attended with penalties should there be an attempt to reactivate it (or at least to reactivate it as a matter of right or unilateral choice).

What, precisely, does Mill mean when he says that the person who "sells himself for a slave . . . defeats, in his own case, the very purpose which is the justification of allowing him to dispose of himself"? We must not lose sight of Mill's emphasis on *selling*. What he has in mind is not self-enslavement as such, but an enforceable slavery contract. The reason for not paternalistically overriding people's voluntary choices is that those choices represent our most reliable guide to their good, or to what is "desirable, or at the least endurable" to them. That continues to be the case where the self-enslavement is not enforced. But where there is an enforceable slavery agreement, we are no longer constrained from paternalistic interference by the presumption in favor of voluntary choice. There is no reason to regard the choices made subsequent to an enforceable slavery agreement as voluntary. It is for this reason that the argument in favor of liberty is defeated in the case of those who would sell themselves into slavery. And it is for the same reason that Mill goes on to remark that the principle of liberty cannot require that a person be "free not to be free." To require it would be to destroy its rationale—to remove the presumption that is in its favor. Thus, as Mill concludes, "it is not freedom, to be allowed to alienate [one's] freedom."

There is, as Gerald Dworkin notices, "some fudging on the meaning of freedom" in this last statement (1971, p. 118). From the way Mill puts his point, it looks as though he is saying that entry into a slavery contract would not be a free act, whereas all his previous argument has entitled him to say is that no one who enters into such an agreement can have security of tenure. Once having entered into it, the person disqualifies himself from the provisions of the principle of liberty. But why should this be so? Why can't we presume that since the agreement was voluntarily made, what occurs subsequently is to be respected as the outcome of a responsible choice? It then becomes irrelevant that subsequent choices do not have the usual presumption in their favor. The choice that matters did—the choice to enter into the agreement in the first place.

One attractive but compressed response to this difficulty is suggested by C. L. Ten (1980, pp. 118–19), who argues that what distinguishes an enforceable slavery contract from other contracts is the fact that freedom is given up "completely and permanently." He asks us to imagine a situation in which a person has sold himself into slavery but, after a time, comes to regret his decision: "his health suffers from the demanding work required of him, and he now refuses to obey the slaveholder any longer." Here, enforcement of the contract would make the law a party to "the slaveholder's harming of the slave." He continues:

> This example seems to fall between cases of self-harming conduct and cases of conduct harmful to others. The example is not a clear case of the harm done by one person to another with his full consent. For in these cases when *A* harms *B*, *B* consents to the harm and does not withdraw his consent at the time the harm is inflicted. But perpetual slavery is also not a clear case of conduct which harms others in the sense which allows the state to interfere. In the clear cases, one person harms another who has at no time consented to be harmed (1980, p. 119).

Ten conjectures that Mill might have seen such cases as falling within the scope of the harm principle and their nonenforcement therefore as nonpaternalistic. Of course, the harmfulness of enforcement would not itself justify nonenforcement, since that would have costs for the slaveholder. However, since, "in the case of perpetual slavery, the harm done to a subsequently unwilling person is very grave, . . . there will be sufficient reason for not recognizing the slavery contract." It would be different, Ten thinks, were the contract not perpetual but periodically renewable, with clearly defined conditions, for then it would "not be radically different from other freedom-limiting contracts."

I am not convinced that Ten has said enough to make out his case. If *B* purchases a house from *A*, to be paid for over a period of forty years, the hardship *B* may later suffer as a result of trying to meet the repayments is not in itself a reason for releasing *B* from its requirements. Of course, we may not be able to make *B* keep up his or her repayments. Perhaps *B* will have to sell the house and return the outstanding money to *A*, or maybe *A* will repossess the house, giving some consideration to payments already made. The point is that the law will tend to back *A*, even if this adds to *B*'s burdens. Any change of mind that *B* undergoes is not seen as justification for releasing *B* from the contract or for not recognizing contracts of that kind. How does this differ significantly from the slavery contract case? And do the differences justify nonrecognition in the latter context?

A slavery contract would of course be for the purchase of services, and as contract law now stands specific performance would most likely not be required for breaches of it (since to do so would constitute enslavement!). But the legal recognition and enforcement of slavery contracts would not demand specific performance (unless, perhaps, it was built into the initial terms of the contract?). The slave would not be made to continue in the owner's service or be returned should he or she abscond. All that would be necessary is that the owner be compensated for the loss of services and for any consideration given. What the parties to a contract need is assurance that there is some incentive to fulfill contractual requirements and recompense in the event of nonfulfillment. Mill, of course, does not make it clear whether the contractual situation he is envisaging does demand specific performance—though there is reason why it should. If it does, Ten's suggestion is made more plausible.

But suppose that slavery contracts are treated like other service contracts, requiring no specific performance, only penalties and compensation in the event of a breach. It is still possible to argue that there are distinctive features to voluntary slavery contracts that not only set them apart, but also make them problematic. For example, it might be very difficult to determine damages in such cases. Normally, in service contracts, the nature of the required services is spelled out in detail, and any losses arising from their nonfulfilment can be estimated, not with exactness, but at least with some sense of their reasonableness. A slavery contract of the kind Mill envisages, however, would be indeterminate so far as the nature of the services were concerned, for it would simply require that the slave do whatever (however much or little) was demanded by the slaveholder. Furthermore, it is possible that claims could be very large—large enough, perhaps, to leave a person's opportunities subsequent to the breach almost as restricted as they were before. Is it fair to have a contractual situation in which the costs of withdrawal cannot be known and may be almost as oppressive as those involved in staying in?

I am not sure how much weight should be given to questions of these kinds. Presumably they could be dealt with statutorily. Compensation could be based on a combination of the consideration given by the slaveholder and determinable losses up to a certain maximum. This would be sufficient to let the parties know what they would lose in the event of some breach, and enable it to be dealt with at law. Would this deter potential slaveholders from entering into agreements with those who want to become slaves? Only if the costs of opting out were too small. Ten fails to differentiate slavery contracts from others with sufficient clarity to justify their blanket nonenforceability.

However, there is another feature of such contracts that may work in favor of nonenforcement. Normally, when a person consents to some proposal, he or she has a reasonably clear idea of what it will involve. If B purchases a house from A, then, as part of the agreement B will know that he or she will have to pay A \$200 per month for the next forty years. As well, B will probably need to be told what this amounts to in terms of interest rate and what the consequences will be in case of default. If B is not made aware of these things, then the question may later arise as to whether B's consent was genuine, adequate, informed, or valid, and therefore whether B should be held to the terms of the agreement. But the voluntary slavery contract envisaged by Mill does not allow of this determinateness. What is asked for and supposedly given is a *carte blanche* consent. The intending slave consents to do whatever the prospective slaveholder asks and, in the situation under consideration, the details of that cannot be known in advance. If, for some reason, the slave finds the arrangement too burdensome, how are we to tell whether, and to what extent, he or she should be penalized for this? Unless the terms of the contract are fairly determinate, which *ex hypothesi* they cannot be, courts will be faced with an almost impossible task of adjudication. In such circumstances, they may well become, as Ten fears, instruments of oppression. Should it be countered that the slave consented to whatever would be asked of him or her, and therefore the right lies on the side of the slaveholder, then the validity or even the intelligibility of a *carte blanche* consent might be questioned.

In everyday discourse we sometimes use the language of *carte blanche* consent. I give my daughter some money for her birthday and she asks me what she should do with it. I reply: "Whatever you like." She uses it to buy heroin. Have I consented to her buying heroin? I think not. When I say to her, "Do what you like," I may not have any specific activities in mind. Nevertheless, a framework of understanding is presupposed that makes my response not that of an irresponsible fool or someone who doesn't know what he's talking about, but intelligible and reasonable. But what is being asked for in the slavery contract case is a *carte blanche* consent in which no holds are barred. Can the intending slave really mean to consent to *that*? Or, rather, and much more reasonably, does the intending slave signify consent, with certain expectations about what that will involve? They may not be very specific, but they are not likely to encompass every possibility. And so, when the slave wishes to pull out, how are we to determine who should bear the cost? Is it reasonable to hold someone responsible for a consent in which what is "consented" to could not have been detailed in advance?

The obvious response to this is to ask the person. Suppose we see the enslaved person being beaten. We ask: "Did you envisage this when you consented to becoming a slave?" But what is the point of asking? If slavery contracts are enforceable, if, as a result of enslavement the person has given him- or herself over to the will of another, why should we count what he or she has to say as "evidence" of the beating's "desirability" or "endurability" to him or her? And because this is so, we do not know what is the status of his or her continued involvement. For consent is not to be seen as a once-off commitment, but as a continuing activity, an ongoing process of acceptance. Enforceable slavery contracts, however, truncate it or at least treat it as a single act, since they deny us the means whereby its continued affirmation can be ascertained. Perhaps we could, from time to time, suspend the slaveholder's powers in order to review the commitment of the slave, to determine whether the slaveholder has exceeded his or her authorization, whether the slave's consent is continuing, and, if not, what compensatory action would be appropriate. But this sort of procedure would take away from the attractiveness of such an agreement, in much the same way as nonenforceability. In addition, it could expose the slaveholder to criminal charges.

I'm not sure that I wish to claim that the various complications that would attach to an enforceable slavery contract (the status of the apparent consent and the administrative difficulties in monitoring it) are themselves sufficient to show that it could never be justified. But I do think they count some way toward the nonprovision of facilities for concluding and recognizing such agreements. We can add to this one further consideration that Mill advances in another context. It is Mill's constantly iterated belief that those whose lives are not characterized by "choice" are degraded. If it is their choice to live in that way—as parasites—they are objects deserving of our contempt and we are justified in shunning them. We have no responsibility to aid them in their degradation. This applies to the case of the person who wishes to become another's slave. It is not for us to prevent such a person from doing so by paternalistically abducting him or her. But society has no obligation to create the facilities for enforcing such arrangements (cf. Haksar 1979, p. 255). This of course is not a paternalistic argument, and it is not one that Mill uses in the passage in question, but it coheres nicely with the fact that he goes no further than opposing enforceability.

To conclude, let me return to the initial problem. In opposing the recognition of voluntary slavery contracts, does Mill make a concession to strong paternalism? I think he does and believe that he does so because he bases his opposition on the probabilistic Argument from Paternalistic Distance, not the Argument from Oppression of Individuality. It is the fact that subsequent to such a choice being made, we have no longer the same reason for considering the individual's liberty, that the presumption in favor of it is defeated. Paternalism in such cases does not deny anything that a nonpaternalistic stance would allow. Provision for enforceable slavery contracts would be self-defeating, since those who availed themselves of such a provision would immediately lose their immunity to interference. I suspect it is for this reason that Mill does not see his concession as the thin edge of the wedge.

Even so, there is good reason for those who are worried by Mill's concession and skeptical about its compatibility with his overall position to feel that way. For Mill's arguments against paternalism are not restricted to the probabilistic one he draws upon here. If instead he had availed himself of his strongest argument—in which the claims of individuality are asserted against interference with self-regarding voluntary choices—then it is difficult to see how he could have acquiesced in the paternalistic language he employs. For then "consideration for [the individual's] liberty" would have required a willingness to recognize a choice for self-enslavement and to see that choice as overriding skeptical doubts about who is best placed to decide for the individual once the choice has been made.

That much said, however, Mill's argument still retains some bite. Even though he is committed to the sovereignty of voluntary choice, he is also deeply committed to the notion of "man as a progressive being." It is an important element in Mill's conception of individuality that individuals can learn from experience and amend their decisions (even though costs may sometimes be associated with this because of others' damaged expectations). They have a capacity for self-correction and self-improvement. But the person who sells him- or herself into slavery renounces the use of that capacity, and therefore the fact that he or she remains enslaved cannot be taken as evidence of *continuing* consent. When we ascribe sovereignty to a person's voluntary choices, we cannot assume that they will never change or that the consent once given will not be withdrawn. We cannot dispense with opportunities for the continued reaffirmation or withdrawal of those choices. The problem with voluntary slavery contracts is that the conditions for assuring oneself that there is a continuing affirmation do not exist.

Compulsory Superannuation. The downward pressure on retirement ages and tendency for people to live longer has extended the period during which people will not receive a regular income. Yet retirement is a time of considerable opportunity. This, however, requires preparation and resources, and people are notorious for focusing so exclusively on the present that they underestimate the claims of the future. It's not that they dispute its importance, but they rationalize it in a way that leads them to fail to connect its requisites to their present behavior. The need for present gratification presents itself more seductively than the need for delayed gratification demanded by preparation for retirement.

Considerations such as the foregoing might seem to provide a reason for requiring people to set aside a portion of their income during their more affluent, earning years so that their later years are not spent in poverty, degradation, and unduly limited options. Such a requirement would be paternalistic. In its favor it could be argued that those involved were not being made an instrument of others' conception of their good, but simply made to act in accord with what they could recognize as being in their own interests. C. Edwin Harris, Jr. sees this as a piece of weak paternalism, since he views lack of sufficient forethought and discipline as evidence of diminished voluntariness (1977, p. 88). I have already expressed my disagreement with this characterization (see above, p. 85). Even if there is a falling short of "full voluntariness" on the part of those who neglect to provide for their future, it is not substantial enough to take them below the threshold of responsibility. If we want to accommodate Harris's concerns, they are handled better by the Argument from Personal Integrity than one from weak paternalism.

Although there is something to be said for basing a compulsory savings requirement on factors highlighted by the Argument from Personal Integrity, the specific form that such requirements take strongly suggests that there are other factors involved as well. We might include the sorts of considerations that inform the Public Charge Argument, discussed in Chapter 4 (see above, pp. 92–94). Those who fail to provide for their future now will most probably become a charge on the rest of us at a later date. Theoretically, of course, we could leave them lie in the beds that they have made for themselves, but in practice it is unlikely that we could stand aside and watch them suffer. To turn our backs on them would be out of keeping with the spirit of a humane and civilized community. For that reason, then, it is fair to require that they set aside a portion of their present bounty, either in social security payments or in some annuities scheme.

There is, however, another way of approaching this issue, which gives a more plausible justification for many of the schemes now operating. It possesses features belonging to the Argument from Prior Consent, but also contains a "collective good" component. It can be developed as follows.

Individuals who wish to set aside a portion of their income for the anticipated years of retirement will need to dig fairly deeply into their present resources if they are to be adequately provided for later. Monies set aside will need to be invested in ways that will cover inflation and possibly a long retirement period. If a working life of, say, forty years, is followed by a retirement of, say, ten years, a fair proportion of the money earned during the earlier years will need to be set aside. Such a prospect can be pretty daunting, especially if there are (as is likely to be the case) heavy demands on one's resources even during the working years (children's education, mortgages, etc.). There are, however, ways of lightening this burden considerably, and these are features of most superannuation and retirement schemes. Under these arrangements, the earner's contribution is matched (or more than matched) by a contribution from the employer or government, and the monies are invested in ways that will (or should) ensure a reasonable income for the retired person.

The great attraction of superannuation schemes is that they enable people to do what they want to do, but would otherwise have found great difficulty in doing—preparing adequately for their retirement without an excessive present outlay. There is, of course, a risk involved. They may die prematurely and not taste the fruits of their enforced saving. But the probabilities lie sufficiently in favor of some need for savings to make participation a reasonable proposition.

Because the viability of many superannuation schemes is dependent on a high level of (continuing) participation, their stability is ensured by making them compulsory. This may seem puzzling. If such schemes are attractive, should compulsion be needed? Possibly not, if all we are thinking of is participation in *any* scheme. But there are many such schemes, and some ways of investing for the future will offer more attractive terms than those available in superannuation schemes. Some of those who are required to participate in a *particular* scheme may therefore feel improperly constrained. However, there are considerations of social justice in favor of such constraint. I think it would generally be true to say that the more profitable retirement arrangements are likely to be accessible only to those whose income enables them to make substantial contributions. The effect of a "free market" in retirement planning would leave schemes not requiring large contributions without needed support or with even more meager benefits. This would leave many low-income earners largely unprovided for, despite the desire they may have to do something about it. As a matter of fairness and in recognition of our social interdependence, there is reason to ensure that all who might wish to provide adequately for their retirement be enabled to do so. That may require the compelled participation in a particular scheme of those who would prefer to invest their monies in something more profitable. It will also compel those who would otherwise carelessly neglect their future requirements. But in this latter case the compulsion would not be paternalistically motivated. There is a "collective good" principle informing the compulsion: only if there is a high rate of participation can some benefit that many want to secure be obtained.

Paternalism and the Elderly. Who are the elderly? The question is not much easier to answer than: What is a child? We can, as we so often do with children, offer an age criterion, but this is as problematic here as it is there. What we are concerned about are certain kinds of vulnerabilities that create special duties of care in our treatment of them. These vulnerabilities are not created on reaching sixty-five. Looked at in one way, the very classification "elderly" is discriminatory and demeaning; but from another point of view, unless we do make some sort of distinction, we will be unresponsive to special needs that call for our understanding and specialized response.

For the most part, our culture has not been very tolerant or understanding of the elderly. It is not uncommon to characterize them as entering or passing through a "second childhood"—a description stripped, however, of some of the romantic and indulgent associations of childhood and used to express pity or even contempt. The elderly person is considered to have regressed to a state in which he or she is no longer in touch with reality, no longer possessed of a clear grasp of his or her interests, and thus stands in need of some form of guardianship. No doubt there are old people who fit such a description (as there are younger people), but the separation out of a special category of "aged" or "elderly" people has encouraged the formation of derogatory stereotypes. These are deeply ingrained in our literature and culture. Shakespeare's seven ages of man captures and gives definition to an image of age that has, if anything, been accentuated by the complexity, pace, and change that characterizes so much of modern Western culture.

To what extent are these stereotypes and the paternalism they encourage justified? It is probably true that as we get older our reflexes become slower and we become less inclined to adapt our ways to the world around us. The pace and change may also leave us somewhat puzzled and confused. To those who value the glitter of technological change and utilitarian values of an industrialized economy, the hesitations, confusions, and lack of flexibility of the elderly are seen as signs of their deterioration as persons and of the need for others to take control of their interests. But these conclusions would not be justified. Although the disorientation and vulnerability experienced by many elderly people constitutes a reason for making available to them resources that will protect their interests and enable them to deal creatively with their social world, this falls short of the paternalism that is so often prescribed. Such provisions will be premised on their requests, not thrust upon them as something of which they must avail themselves. The paternalism that is implicit in guardianship proceedings and the commitment of elderly persons to homes for the aged is premised on a much deeper incapacity—their inability to know any longer the direction in which their interests lie or to make use of the facilities that have been provided to secure those interests for them.

The various considerations that inform the Argument from Paternalistic Distance give us some reason to be skeptical of paternalism in relation to the elderly. At least we should be skeptical of any argument that relies mainly on the *age* of the person concerned. Although elderly people do not always perceive what is in their interests as well as they might (a failing to which we are all subject), they, unlike young children, nevertheless confront the world with a wealth of experience and a rich set of attitudes, understandings, and interests and, more often than not, are likely to be better positioned with respect to determining their good than those who would otherwise determine it for them. It is true that this is only a presumptive argument, but in the case of the elderly it is a very strong presumption. Whatever our *capacities* for perceiving the good of the elderly, our *interest* in securing that good is likely to distort their use. Powerful social attitudes that tend to see the elderly as dispensable, as having lost touch with reality, and, in Western industrialized societies at least, family patterns that are often unsympathetic toward the needs of older people, combine to undercut the sensitivity and compassion that might otherwise serve to set the presumption aside. It is no secret that most guardianship proceedings have been initiated by relatives desirous of protecting their own interest in an elderly relative's estate; concern for their good is secondary (cf. Kindred 1976, p. 64). Commitment proceedings, likewise, have frequently been motivated by considerations of manageability rather than sympathetic benevolence. Not that unalloyed benevolence is enough. Just because elderly people have a lifetime of experience behind them, developing their personalities in specific directions, it is easy to mis-interpret their needs and values, and paternalistic impositions are likely to overlook the subtle nuances in treatment they require.

It is common to think that because many elderly people are no longer employed or engaged in parenting, they are therefore "past it" or "out of touch with the world." So they are treated as spectators or passive recipients rather than initiators and agents, creative centers of activity. But this falsely assumes that the life of an elderly person is one of unremitting decline. It is true that certain of one's past skills may not be as effectively exercised, but there are also many capacities that we have probably not had the opportunity to develop during younger life, and these may provide scope for a great deal of creative activity. Packing the elderly in cotton wool, lest they come to harm, may frustrate this development, so that we fall foul of what I have dubbed the Argument from the Developmental Value of Choice. As Thomas Halper puts it, "By seeking to impose a risk-free, danger-free life on the aged, [we] may deny them the opportunity to mould a challenging existence for themselves from their penultimate years" (1978, p. 324). Although re-tirement frequently signals the end of a lifetime of "specialized" employment, it does not by that token signal the end of a person's productive and creative powers. Retirement ages are fixed as much by wider political and economic considerations as by judgments about capacity. What the retired person needs is not moth-balling but access to new fields and spheres of activity in which his or her experience and creative ability can be expressed and nurtured.

It is important to remember that the set of values in terms of which old age is conceived of as decline is neither sacrosanct nor exclusive. It may be a time of growth no less than a time of deterioration. In many cultures, status increases with age, for wisdom—practical understanding in human affairs—is seen as the special province of the elderly. Only they have sufficient experience in the ways of humankind to know best how life is to be conducted. We have tended to replace the sage by the expert, and it is not clear that this has led to an improvement in human life. This is not intended as an *apologia* for "ageism," but simply as a question mark against an oversimplified and fashionable model of the "stages" of life. The very pervasiveness of that model may be partly responsible for the truth that it conveys. People may become as they are seen and treated. If many older people display an obvious withering of their mental faculties, that may well be because they have been deprived of stimulation and opportunities for their exercise—a deprivation occasioned in part by myths about their incapacity.

But it is not simply the more utilitarian arguments that weigh against a too-ready paternalism in regard to the elderly. The Argument from Oppression of Individuality is equally apposite. Whatever doubts we may have about the very young—doubts grounded in their undeveloped capacities—we have little reason to have them in regard to the old. They do not differ qualitatively from those who are younger. They have much the same needs and problems, only sometimes somewhat accentuated, and though these may call for the creation of special facilities and opportunities, they do not justify their common confinement to the strait-jacket of a stereotype or a "home." But there is, as Halper brings out, something of a tension here. On the one hand, we want to acknowledge the increasing vulnerability of people as they get older, providing where possible for their safety and welfare, shielding them against exploitation. On the other hand, this reinforces their isolation as a group, perpetuating a characterization in terms of certain needs, vulnerabilities and deficiencies, and leads to an insulting and dehumanizing paternalism (Halper 1978, pp. 331–32). One area in which this tension is clearly shown is volunteering for research. Because elderly people have often been taken advantage of by researchers, there is a strong temptation to prohibit research on elderly subjects. This, however, prevents those who could and would consent to being research subjects from doing so (see Ratzan 1980).

It is because paternalism with regard to the elderly is so widespread and often so demeaning that I have tended to be very critical of it here. But I do not mean to rule it out altogether—whether as weak or strong paternalism. The considerations advanced in favor of paternalism in Chapter 3, in particular the Argument from Personal Integrity, are as appropriate in this context as elsewhere. Elderly people are as prone to foibles as the rest of us, but we should not accentuate them, and make them, as we so often do, an excuse for placing them under strict guardianship régimes or in homes for the aged. There is sometimes a place for such measures, but for the most part paternalistic impositions ought to be viewed in the same way as cortisone shots for back injuries—strategies for relieving a patient's pain long enough to enable the back muscles to be exercised into providing their own support. But this will need to go hand-in-hand with a reshaping of social attitudes toward the elderly lest the fragile independence regained is not then destroyed.

Political Paternalism

To this point my main concern has been with paternalism toward individuals rather than collectivities or groups. It is the latter that I have in mind when speaking of political paternalism. The occasion of such paternalism is a set of cultural or group traits that are believed to be an impediment to the self-advancement of its possessors. Somewhat unexpectedly, Mill shows himself to be sympathetic to it when he excludes "barbarians" from the protection of his principle of liberty. There are, he writes, "backward states of society in which the race itself may be considered as in its nonage" (1859, p. 224; cf. Mill 1861, ch. 18; Thompson 1976, ch. 2). These cultures do not possess greater sophistication or capacity for progression and development than one finds in the "society" of children. And, just as children require, not merely the stimulus but also the discipline of cultivated authority, so too do those who are yoked to benighted traditions.

This is a remarkable, if understandable concession. It is remarkable that it should come from the pen of someone so implacably opposed to strong paternalism. It is understandable as a reflection of nineteenth-century English attitudes—dominated as they were at the time by European ideas of "rationality" and "advancement." Not that Mill was merely a child of his time. Unlike many English people, he did not regard the inhabitants of colonized countries as inherently inferior. He believed that "despotism" ought to be aimed at its own demise. And he believed that local rulers were likely to be best suited to the purposes of advancement. Nevertheless, he seems to have been overconfident about the possibilities of colonial rule.

Mill's conjoining of political paternalism and paternalism toward children was no mere accident. Parental analogies are the stock-in-trade of colonizing ideology. Michael Wallace shows in some detail how heavily eighteenth-century politicians and political apologists relied on familial imagery in characterizing the British Empire and in rationalizing its impositions on subject peoples. The imagery is often self-serving rather than paternalistic. The colonies were seen as "Children of one common Mother, and embarked in one common cause, the Welfare of their Parent" (in Wallace 1974, p. 204). Sometimes it is patriarchal, in which the interests of the whole are seen as primary. But often it was overtly paternalistic. Thus, in the dispute between Britain and the American colonies, Charles Townsend, then chancellor of the Exchequer, reacted to colonist grumblings by asking:

> And now will these Americans, Children planted by our care, nourished by our Indulgence until they are grown to a degree of Strength and Opulence, and protected by our Arms, will they grudge to contribute their mite to relieve us from the heavy weight of that burden which we lie under? (Wallace 1974, pp. 204–5)

As relations became more strained, the rhetoric was used more insistently, but now, not as a justification for chastisement, but retribution:

> The law of God and of Nature is on the side of an Indulgent parent, against an undutiful Child; and should necessary correction render him incapable of future offence, he has only his obstinacy and folly to blame (Wallace 1974, p. 205).

Interestingly, the familial imagery, with its paternalistic overtones, was accepted by some of the colonists themselves. As one wrote: "The Colonies are yet but Babes that cannot subsist but on the Breasts, and thro' the Protection of their Mother Country" (Wallace 1974, p. 206). What was in dispute was the proper attitude of the parent toward the child. "But admitting we are children," John Adams conceded, "have not children a right to complain when their parents are attempting to break their limbs, to administer poison, or to sell them to enemies for slaves?" Or, as Thomas Paine was later to observe, since the children were now "just arriving at manhood, . . . to know whether it be the interest of the continent to be independent, we need only ask this easy, simple question: Is it the interest of a man to be a boy all his life?" (Wallace 1974, p. 206). The American colonists were not slow to use the same language in their dealings with the native Indian population:

It is idle to talk of treaties and national faith with such savages. The proper course to adopt with them is to treat them as wards or children, and make them do that which is to their benefit and our safety (Wallace 1974, p. 206; cf. Rogin, 1971).

When paternalistic control became impossible, the stronger measures taken were legitimized as the due of incorrigible children. Slavery, likewise, was rationalized in the same terms: "the Negro . . . in his true nature, is always a boy, let him be ever so old" (in Wallace 1974, p. 208).

What lies behind this assimilation of political to parental paternalism, Wallace suggests, is a technique for legitimizing control and violence. The family has traditionally been the context in which otherwise unacceptable force finds "justification." Parents have been seen as possessing virtually unlimited authority over children, an authority that has remained largely unquestioned because of the assumption that what it imposes will be tempered by love and a recognition of the use-value of children (Wallace 1974, p. 211). The need for violence is seen in the inner waywardness of the child, a waywardness that needs to be curbed if the child is to be brought to civilization. The use of familial imagery in political contexts, therefore, assimilates what is done by colonial powers to what goes on in the family, giving it a moral justification that it would otherwise have lacked. In view of this, it is remarkable that Mill, so sensitive in other areas, should have succumbed to the prevailing tradition. Although there is a more benevolent tradition of parent-child relations, he must have been aware that any likening of colonialism to parental paternalism would be unflattering. After all, the cultures in question were not dependent on others in the manner of young children. They had persisted and even flourished for many centuries.

Plamenatz offers a rationale for political paternalism that sheds some light on the Millian exception. First, we need to make a distinction between *taking* control of a country on the pretext that its people are not capable of self-government, and *retaining* control for the same reason. Of the various reasons that might be advanced for the former, the one most appropriate to the period in which Mill was writing, was "the ability to afford to modern trade and industry the security they need" (Plamenatz, 1960, p. 38).[5] The growth and expansion of European trade and its increasing importance to the economies of the European countries concerned made it essential that market relations be secure and predictable. This was interpreted in terms of the existence of a political and legal system comparable to that obtaining in the home countries. Where a country could not provide this, it was considered unfit for self-rule. The superimposition of European structures was called for.

There was nothing particularly paternalistic about the initial reasons for asserting colonial power. There was no missionary desire to civilize the uncivilized.[6] It was only after the European powers had established themselves in their new surroundings that they "acquired a sense of mission." What this amounted to was a desire to bring to such countries their own understanding of progress, culture, good government, judicial procedures, etc. This became the ground for a different assertion of unfitness for self-government, one that would justify retaining control where control was already a *fait accompli*. The criterion of fitness for self-rule became "the ability to work the institutions that make democracy and freedom effective" (Plamenatz 1960, p. 47).

I suspect that it is this latter notion of fitness for self-government that lies behind Mill's support for political paternalism. For the most part, the countries to which the Europeans had come were ruled despotically rather than democratically. A substantial proportion of the population was kept in subjection; in that respect European rule was not retrogressive. But having asserted their power, some reason for maintaining it was required. This was satisfied by the goal of establishing the social conditions necessary for democratic government. When Mill speaks of the incapacity of "barbarians" for improvement by free and equal discussion, what he has in mind is their unreadiness for a form of social organization within which they could and would function as free and equal individuals. For that to occur, there would need to be substantial change in educational level, traditions, etc; it would not come about "spontaneously," but only as a result of pressure from outside or above.

This sort of rationale for the continued exercise of colonial power is theoretically interesting rather than practically attractive. Political reality has little room for the serious pursuit of Millian ideals: power once assumed is not easily surrendered. Theoretically, however, it has something to be said for it. But this is partly because such paternalism also has an other-regarding dimension. Although, at one level, the colonized country is seen as incapable of managing its own affairs, at another level the external intervention promises the liberation of many from the oppression of a few. If we allow (as was sometimes but not always the case) that prior to colonial intervention the so-called barbarous countries were torn by internal dissension or administered by a brutal régime, then colonial administration might be seen in much the same way as intervention in a bully's terrorization. In practice, this was often not so, for the new administration tended to be as oppressive and debasing as the old.

The sort of political paternalism I have been discussing is sometimes internally initiated. Ethnic minorities have often been subjected to it. They may comprise the traditional or original inhabitants of the land (say, the native Indian populations of the United States and Canada, the Aborigines of Australia), those who for some reason have been brought into the country from an alien situation (indentured laborers, black slaves in the United States), or those who have migrated from cultural situations and traditions that are significantly different from those of the dominant culture into which they have come. Government policies in these situations have frequently been colored by paternalistic attitudes. The minority culture is seen as primitive or inferior, and efforts are made to eliminate it and replace it with the "progressive" dominant culture. Although the official rhetoric associated with such efforts has often been that of "national unity," paternalistic attitudes do not lie far below the surface. Elimination has taken the form of either "assimilation" or "separate development": both have presumed the inferiority of the culture to be assimilated or separately developed. Such presumptions, if not mistaken, are at least highly controversial. Aboriginal cultures, for example, are complex and better adapted to the environment than the European culture that has since been imposed on them. The resource and pollution problems that have begun to tax Europeanized society could not have occurred within their ecologically balanced life style; the threat of nuclear war and the problems of crime and unemployment that have become characteristic of our society would not have arisen. The point is not to turn a blind eye to the failings of Aboriginal society or to argue for the superiority of Aboriginal culture, but to indicate a certain tendentiousness about judgments of superiority/inferiority.

In many societies, past policies of "assimilation" and "separate development" have more recently been superseded by policies more appreciative of the integrity of alien cultures. Aid is given or recompense for past wrongs is made. Yet, although some kind of rectification is called for, even these new initiatives have frequently been suffused with paternalism—with what Paulo Freire calls "malefic generosity": help given in the spirit of cooperation, "provided you take it on our terms."

> Certain members of the oppressor class join the oppressed in their struggle for liberation. . . . However, they almost always bring with them the marks of their origin: their prejudices and their deformations, which include a lack of confidence in the people's ability to think, to want, and to know. Accordingly, these adherents to the people's cause constantly run the risk of falling into a type of generosity as malefic as that of the oppressors. . . . Our converts . . . truly desire to transform the unjust order; but because of their background they believe that they must be the executors of the transformation (Freire 1970, p. 46; cf. Benham 1978).

This is a form of paternalism that, though motivated by a desire to secure the good of others, is not motivated by a desire to secure their good *as they see it* or *as they believe it to be best ensured*, but only as it is seen or believed achievable by those who have power to help. There is a strong temptation toward this form of paternalism wherever there has been a history of oppression, and the erstwhile oppressors are not in the position of benefactors. Benefactors they must be, since the resources for self-improvement lie largely within their control, yet they find it difficult to provide aid without strings attached. To do that would be "wasteful," "irresponsible," or "unhelpful." This is a context in which the Argument from Paternalistic Distance carries a lot of weight.

One final candidate for political paternalism deserves mention. In Marxist-Leninist theory, societies in which the means of production are privately owned bifurcate into two antagonistic classes—the class of owners and the class of those whose access to the means of subsistence is effectively controlled by the class of owners. The relationship between these two classes is seen as one of exploitation. Just what makes the relationship exploitative is a matter of some dispute, and it is not necessary here that we take sides (cf. Cohen 1979; Roemer 1982; Buchanan 1982). What is relevant is that rectification can be achieved only through revolution—a radical reorganization of the prevailing basic economic and social relations. But how are these revolutionary aims to be achieved? Writers in the tradition have recognized that the laboring and dispossessed classes would have a central role, since for them emancipation was most pressing. But for Lenin in particular this was problematic. A truly revolutionary movement needed to be embedded in and guided by revolutionary theory, but revolutionary theory, though directed to the interests of the oppressed classes, was not accessible to their as-yet-unemancipated consciousness. They could feel their oppression but not understand it. As Lenin puts it, the strike action in which the oppressed had so far demonstrated their revolt,

> signified the wakening antagonism between workers and masters, but the workers did not have nor was it possible for them to have an awareness of the irreconcilable contradiction of their interests with the

whole modern political and social system, that is, they did not yet possess Social-Democratic consciousness. . . . This consciousness could only be brought to them from the outside (1902, p. 80).

By themselves, the workers were capable of developing only "trade-union consciousness"—the conviction that collective action was required in order to improve their bargaining power with employers. Such consciousness in no way questioned the basic relations in which they stood and thus offered no stable or permanent solution to their grievances. Instead, "the teaching of Socialism . . . has grown out of the philosophical, historical, and economic theories that were worked out by the educated representatives of the propertied classes—the intelligentsia" (Lenin 1902, p. 80). Lenin thus proposes a hierarchically ordered revolutionary party structure in which control resides with a small central group, informed by and acting in concert with a group of theoretical leaders. There is, however, to be a high level of participation by others, accomplished via the formation of a large number of territorial and functional groups, linked by a clear chain of command to the central committee. The whole exercise is conceived in military terms, and so there is a strong duty of obedience on the part of "inferiors" toward "superiors" (Utechin in Lenin 1902, p. 35).

There is, no doubt, a paternalistic streak within this Leninist position— one that continues to infuse Soviet thought and politics. The party is dedicated to the good of the people, yet the bulk of the people are ignorant of that wherein their true good lies. However, the party's central organ is positioned to determine that good and though it is assumed that what is decided will find acceptance by the members, it is nevertheless an acceptance born not of their individually sponsored reflections but of guided conscientization. But despite this paternalistic streak to the theory, the overall thrust is patriarchal, for the individual whose good is being secured has his identity only in terms of his location within the social whole. It is that whole that has primacy, and although individuals are formed and secured in their persons through it, their good is structured, not so much by their individual (yet diverse) natures and independently determined interests, as by requirements of the larger body. Such a view, as I have argued earlier (see above, pp. 39–40), embodies a welcome recognition of the interconnectedness of individuals, but tends to emphasize this to a degree that undermines its own moral basis. Only if there is some means whereby those whose good is being secured can give effect to *their own* albeit confused, yet corrigible conception of their good, can they escape from oppression.

Notes

1. *Wisconsin* v. *Yoder*, 406 U.S. 205 (1972).
2. *Bellotti* v. *Baird*, 443 U.S. 622, at 635 (1979).
3. It may be claimed that the "future liberty" interpretation leaves a problem so far as suicide and euthanasia are concerned. But Mill could reply (as Regan does) that there is a degradation involved in resigning one's liberty that does not attach to resigning one's life.
4. But he also adds a supplementary reason that, in the present context, is not irrelevant, viz., the *independence* of the Mormon community: "So long as the sufferers by the bad law do not invoke assistance from other communities, I cannot admit that

persons entirely unconnected with them ought to step in and require that a condition of things with which all who are directly interested appear to be satisfied, should be put an end to because it is a scandal to persons some thousands of miles distant, who have no part or concern with it" (1859, p. 291). Utah was not granted statehood until 1896, and at the time Mill wrote was administratively self-sufficient. The Mormons would have supervised their own marriage arrangements. Federal enforcement was neither sought nor required.

5. Two other notions of fitness for self-government that Plamenatz considers are "the ability to afford security of person and good government by the standards of Western Europe" (1960, p. 40), and the country's capacity to "produce native rulers strong enough and responsible enough to respect international law" (ibid.).

6. Plamenatz suggests that an exception might be found "towards the end of the nineteenth century, during the 'scramble for Africa' " (1960, p. 39).

7

Marketplace

Despite its Latin form, the maxim *caveat emptor* is not found prior to the sixteenth century and did not come into its own until the eighteenth and nineteenth centuries (Hamilton, 1931).[1] It had no place in mediaeval thought. In the early Middle Ages, trade for gain was seen as sinful and the merchant as unpleasing to God, but with the growth of craft guilds, the increase in foreign travel, the burgeoning of fairs, and the later development of market towns, a more complex position emerged. Central to it was a heavy onus on the seller of goods to ensure that they were as they appeared to be.

The voice of ecclesiastical polity is heard in Aquinas's discussion of commercial fraud (Aquinas 1975, pp. 213–31). Where a seller knows that the identity of what is sold is other than what is offered for sale, or differs in quantity or quality from what is claimed for it, "the sale is vitiated by fraud, and rendered illicit." Restitution must be made. No fraud is involved where the seller is unaware of the good's deficiencies, but this does not relieve him or her of the duty to make restitution. A seller is bound to make known to a potential buyer any unobvious defects that would occasion "danger or loss," though where a flaw is obvious and the price discounted, disclosure is not necessary, "since a buyer might be tempted to take off more from the price than is warranted by the flaw." The seller is "not always obliged to promote another's advantage by help or advice." Where expectations are damaged, restitution is demanded by commutative justice. This applies equally to the seller. Where a seller underestimates the value of the goods sold, the buyer likewise is bound to make restitution. If *caveat emptor* is alien to the medieval mind, so also is *caveat venditor*.

The temporal courts of the late Middle Ages and Reformation era reflect a position similar to Aquinas's. Their function is to ensure "to every good offered for sale a fair price, full measure, and good workmanship" (Hamilton 1931, p. 1150). Although their emphasis is on prevention and punishment rather than compensation, the latter is not altogether absent. All this is done in the name of the social solidarity. The fraudulent seller brings not only himself into disrepute, but also the town and church; his actions injure not only the buyer but also the community (Hamilton 1931, pp. 1152–53). The emerging civil order of the seventeenth century replaced spiritual with temporal goals, but even so did not, in its early stages at least, abandon the inherited traditions. There was still "no reputable place for a notion of *caveat emptor*," since business remained "the instrument of man's necessities" (Hamilton 1931, p. 1156). William Blackstone in the eighteenth century endeavored to perpetuate the traditional view (Blackstone 1783: 3. 165ff.), but by now the courts were beginning to move in favor of the seller. How this came about is not altogether clear, but it seems to have been prompted in some measure by the courts having to deal with cases in which innocent dealers became wedged between crooked suppliers/manufacturers and aggrieved buyers. The court's desire to protect the dealer was expressed in terms of *caveat emptor*.

With the fuller flowering of capitalism in the late eighteenth and nineteenth centuries, *caveat emptor* became a generalized expectation. The courts took the view that "the buyer who at the time of the sale has failed to exact positive assurances against future contingencies deserves to take the consequences of his slothfulness" (Hamilton 1931, p. 1178). In the United States this expectation reached its extreme in Chief Justice Gibson's dictum that "the naked averment of a fact is neither a warranty itself nor evidence of it."[2] Contributing to this change were a new understanding of the market and market relations. With the development of new technologies and the growth of industry, there was an increasing emphasis on production for the purpose of exchange. And with the emergence of an individualistic utilitarianism, market relations came to be seen as transactions between rational maximizers of self-interest. Unless slothful, buyers could be expected to take precautions against suboptimal purchases. The courts were needed only as a deterrence to force, fraud, breach of contract, and the exploitation of incapacity.

But at the same time as Chief Justice Gibson was requiring the most extreme skepticism of purchasers, others were recognizing that *laissez-faire* was not as well coordinated with "the invisible hand" as had been presaged, and that "transaction costs" in market interactions created a problem so far as the distribution of responsibility was concerned. The courts began to argue that, unless otherwise stated, it was implied that goods purchased would live up to certain minimum expectations (e.g., be merchantable and nonhazardous). With the multiplication of products and their increasing sophistication, legislatures have moved increasingly to shield the buyer (and in some cases the seller[3]) from some of the possible consequences of his or her purchases. The doctrine of *caveat emptor* has been eroded, and the complaint is now sometimes heard that it has been superseded by *caveat fabricator/venditor*. Some commentators have interpreted this as a move in the direction of paternalism and have criticized it on that ground. But there are other possible explanations as well, and it is my purpose in this chapter to explore the extent to which various market restrictions may be seen as paternalistic and whether, if they are, they can be justified. After looking at some of the difficulties involved in distinguishing rationales for limitations on the operation of the market, I then focus on some of the regulations relating to the purchase and financing of goods and services, sales practices, and labor contracts that might appear to be paternalistic in intent.

Detecting Paternalistic Rationales

I have already distinguished a paternalistic rationale as one in which the end sought in imposing a limitation on a person's freedom is that person's good.

That much is clear. What is not always clear is whether a particular piece of legislation manifests a paternalistic concern. The substantive requirements of the legislation may not give much assistance, though in some cases it might be difficult to see what else could account for the particular prescriptions involved. In the case of so-called consumer protection legislation, it is often quite difficult to tell what sort of reasons are at work. Is a regulation requiring a seller to volunteer certain information to a potential buyer intended to protect the buyer from fraud, from almost certain ignorance, or from carelessness in making a purchasing decision? Is a regulation requiring that manufactured goods of a certain kind be guaranteed against breakdown for a particular period intended to shield the buyer from cost-benefit gambling losses, sharp traders, or the consequences of his or her unequal bargaining power? It may be difficult to tell. The debate preceding a piece of legislation may reveal a mixture of reasons, as may also the subsequent judicial *dicta*. For our present purposes, perhaps the key question concerns whether legislation of a certain kind requires recourse to paternalistic considerations if it is to be justified. And then, if it does require this, is such an appeal legitimate? Of course, even if the legislation doesn't need paternalistic support, reasons of a paternalistic kind may favor it. And it would be worth knowing whether those reasons might be included among those that ought to count in its favor.

There is a further complication. Although rationales may be theoretically distinguished, and then illustrated by reference to certain paradigm cases, the real world of human interaction is not as simple as this. Rationales tend to shade into each other, or at least change their color, depending on a range of social conventions and expectations. If it can be assumed that people will ask certain questions if they want information of a particular kind, failure to offer that information may raise no moral eyebrows. But if the information is of a kind that is likely to be relevant to their concerns, but which it cannot be assumed they would inquire about or have, then the failure to offer it may constitute a form of deception (or negligence). At any time there may be disagreement about what can be assumed, and over time there may occur changes in what can be assumed. Within the capitalist marketplace, these problems tend to be accentuated. For here it can be presumed that sellers of goods and services will wish to maximize their "welfare," "satisfaction," or "advantage," and will therefore be strongly tempted to withhold, underplay, or otherwise obscure whatever information would (in the instant and/or in the long-run) detract from the attractiveness of their goods and services, and they will be strongly tempted to say or intimate whatever (in the instant and/or in the long-run) would enhance their attractiveness. In a situation like this, limits must be placed on what sellers may or may not say and on how they may say it, lest buyers become the victims of fraud. But what those limits should be constitutes a problem. It is hardly reasonable to require that buyers be told whatever will be optimally advantageous or minimally disadvantageous to them. Sellers can hardly be expected to jeopardize their sales or profits by showing their products in the worst possible light or by disclosing that comparable goods may be bought more cheaply elsewhere. Nor can they be expected to bear all the informational costs. On the other hand, they can be expected to refrain from knowingly misdescribing their goods and from neglecting to consider and make known the latent risks associated with their use. But this leaves a large gray area. Can we presume that potential buyers will see the blandishments of sellers for what they are, or should we place tighter restrictions on what may be said and how it may be said? Should those who were, to their cost, "taken in" by an advertisement, be able to recover, or should we attribute their loss to their own negligence, trusting that they will learn from their experience? How alert can we expect a buyer to be to the various ways in which a product or service will fall short of expectations? What expenditures of time, energy, and resources is it reasonable to assume that a buyer will undertake in assessing a possible purchase? Only when we have sorted out some of these messy and context-relative issues will we be able to determine with any confidence whether a particular restriction on sellers is to be viewed as paternalistic, as justified by the harm principle, as an attempt to equalize bargaining power, or whatever.

In a good deal of economic theory these issues are settled, or at least accommodated, by means of a model. Although it is usually acknowledged that the world of real economic relations does not correspond with any exactitude to this model, it is nevertheless represented as the only acceptable starting point. The core thesis is that the adult world is populated by rational maximizers of self-interest or utility (or value), individuals with *their own* needs, wants, and projects. These needs, wants, and projects, about which it is presumed that they have a clear apprehension, both with regard to their nature and what will satisfy them, they can set about satisfying by voluntarily entering into exchange relations with each other, giving in order to get, where the parties concerned come away satisfied that they have received "value for money." The basic scenario envisages no transaction costs, and no duress, fraud, or breach of contract. In such an arrangement, it is argued, two fundamental liberal requirements are met—justice and utility. Because the exchanges are voluntary no one is unjustly treated, and because the participants are rational maximizers of self-interest, aggregate wealth is increased. There is neither occasion nor justification for external interference with market processes.

But, as noted, the real world does not exactly instantiate this model. There is fraud, duress, and incapacity, and consequently, there are exchanges that do not conform to the voluntariness requirement. And there are transaction costs, creating difficulties for utility-maximization. How are these imperfections to be handled? According to the model's firmest adherents, regulation of the market is justifiable to the extent that exchanges fall short of the voluntariness requirement. As to the allocation of transaction costs, it is argued that the presumption of self-interested rational maximizers will lead to the most efficient apportionment between buyer and seller. Strong advocates of the model believe, therefore, that only a small amount of regulation can be justified.[4]

It is not claimed that the foregoing will always result in parties to market transactions making good buys. It is claimed only that exchanges transacted under the conditions of a free market are more likely to increase aggregate wealth and be less violative of autarchy/individuality than alternative arrangements. A purchaser may make a mistake in calculations or fail to bear certain transaction costs before buying, and so finish up with a product that fails to satisfy. But since the transaction was voluntary, no rights have been violated and the purchaser will have an incentive to undertake the necessary transaction costs next time. In cases where the transaction costs would have been allocated more efficiently had they been borne by the seller, the purchaser will have a reason for withdrawing his or her custom, thus giving the seller an incentive to bear them. Over time buyers and sellers will be mutually and optimally responsive. Proponents of the model presume that in a free market the demands of justice and utility will tend to coincide. External regulation of the market, beyond that required to ensure the voluntariness of transactions, is thus condemned as paternalistic and inefficient. It is paternalistic, because it treats participants in the market, usually buyers, as less than competent maximizers of self-interest. Others take upon themselves to determine and secure what is good for purchasers, thus treating them as children to be watched over. It is inefficient because the costs associated with external regulation are likely to be greater than those involved in market-based rectification. Individual buyers are both more knowledgeable about, and more interested in satisfying, their own interests than are regulatory agencies.

My point so far has been to indicate the extent to which the judgment that particular regulations are paternalistic is bound up with the sort of model of market relations one has, and the expectations it creates about actual market relations. To see how well it stands up, I turn now to some of the regulations at issue.

Regulations Relating to the Purchase of Goods and Services

So far as the sale/purchase of *goods* is concerned, regulations that set minimum quality and safety standards are most often charged with being paternalistic. Where we are dealing with the sale/purchase of *services*, it is licensing laws that attract the same charge. In each case it is argued that the purchaser's choice is being downgraded, that others are not merely presuming to know what is best for him or her, but are acting to impose it. It is claimed, furthermore, that these represent inefficient ways of dealing with market imperfections, at least less efficient than those implicit in the market itself.

To get a clearer grasp of these claims, a more detailed account of the sale/purchase transaction may be helpful. According to the model I outlined in the previous section, a purchaser (that is, a rational maximizer of self-interest/utility) will want to do the best that he or she can. In practice, this will mean securing the best balance between the suitability of some product for his or her purposes and the costs associated with that purchase. In order to determine that balance, certain information will be required. First, he or she will need to have a clear conception of his or her purposes—otherwise the task of rationally maximizing utility will be very hard, if not impossible. Second, he or she will need to know the extent to which particular candidates for purchase will serve his or her purposes. Third, he or she will need to know the various costs involved in the purchase. These will include not merely the purchase price but also subsequent expenditures (e.g., running, maintenance and/or replacement costs) and potentially deleterious side-effects and costs associated therewith (Reich 1979, pp. 20–21). To get clear about these three things, certain transaction costs may need to be borne. A rational maximizer will determine their extent by balancing the costs involved in obtaining that information against the cost savings that the information could be expected to yield. The end of this gathering process should be the "best buy." We can expect a potential seller of goods (who is also a rational maximizer of self-interest/utility) to go through a similar gathering-balancing process in order to obtain the "best sell"—the best balance between income gained from sales and the costs involved in producing and/or supplying the product. First, he or she will need to have a clear conception of the market—of the demand that there is likely to be for a certain kind of item. Second, he or she will need to know how well a particular product will satisfy the demand for that item. This may require comparison with other products directed to the same end. Third, he or she will need to know the costs involved in providing products that, to varying degrees, will satisfy the demand they are intended to meet. To find out these things, there will be certain transaction costs, and here again the costs of obtaining the requisite information will need to be weighed against the gains that that information can be expected to yield.

It is one of the implications of the model in question that sellers will have an interest in providing data relevant to the informational needs of buyers, and that buyers will have an interest in providing data relevant to the informational requirements of sellers. It is assumed that in a freely competitive market environment the optimal proportioning of informational costs will take place.

However, as we have already briefly noted, the market situation diverges substantially from what the model envisages. The transactional advantages are weighted heavily in favor of sellers. Various reasons for this are proposed and accordingly various responses recommended. For some writers, the basic problem is one of consumer education. Consumers need to be taught how to use to the best advantage the information that is made available to them. For other writers, the basic problem is one of the accessibility (including cost) of information. What is proposed is that strategies be evolved whereby "goodwill" considerations will be made sufficiently important to sellers to motivate them to minimize the consumer's informational costs. Some, though not onerous, legislation may be required to ensure this (see Reich 1979). Yet other writers see the problems as somewhat deeper than these analyses suggest and accordingly propose stronger solutions. Included is the requirement that products meet certain minimum quality and safety standards before they enter the market. On this approach, the government acts as a "purchasing agent"— interposing itself between the producer/seller and buyer, limiting the range of choice that might otherwise be available. Determining such minimum standards is probably some notional "average purchaser," with a limited range of purposes and expectations. Certain standard uses of a product-type are postulated, and the assumption is made that the "average purchaser" would wish to tolerate only such-and-such a degree of risk (of failure or damage) in using it. Buyers are thus protected against purchasing products in which the risk of failure is deemed to be unacceptably high. In some cases, goods are not prevented from coming onto the market unless they conform to some minimum quality standard, but are required to be covered by a guarantee in case of fault.[5]

The patterns of argument found in the sale/purchase of goods are also found in relation to the sale/purchase of services. There are some writers who believe that market forces are themselves sufficiently strong and efficient to ensure the optimal mix of benefit and cost (cf. Lee and McKnown 1975, ch. 7). Only blatant violations of market presumptions (the use of force and fraud) and incapacity to participate as a rational chooser justify external involvement in its operation. Others are less convinced that the actual market's imperfections can be so easily removed and minimized. Three progressively intrusive strategies for improvement have been put forward: occupational registration, certification, and licensing. Registration simply requires that those who sell a nominated service should (on pain of penalty for failure) have the fact recorded on some central register. This requirement does not place any substantial restriction on the offering of services or on people's access to them, but because it ensures traceability in the event of some dispute, it may serve to deter shysters and charlatans. Certification likewise constitutes no serious constraint on access to the marketplace, for it simply constitutes a formal recognition of competence. Theoretically, it offers valuable information to seekers of a "best buy" in services. Occupational registration and certification operate in much the same way as mandatory disclosure requirements in relation to manufactured goods.

Only occupational licensing has a substantial effect on access to the market in services, for it excludes from the marketplace those who are deemed unfit to provide a particular service. Here, some agency interposes itself between the seeker of services and potential suppliers of those services, determining the degree of risk that the former may be permitted to take.

Do product quality and safety standards and occupational licensing constitute paternalism, and if so, do they constitute paternalism of a justifiable kind? Strong proponents of the initial model are generally agreed that these constraints *are* paternalistic—in the worst sense of the word (cf. Reich, 1979, p. 4; Friedman 1962, p. 148). They are seen as a vote of no confidence in consumers, a judgment by government or other agencies that consumers are not capable of engaging in "best buy" decisions, but must be told what is good for them and how they must get it. But this is only one of a number of possible arguments for such regulations and in what follows I propose to canvass several of these arguments, both paternalistic and nonpaternalistic. I commence with two paternalistic arguments before passing on to a brief discussion of four nonpaternalistic alternatives.

PATERNALISTIC ARGUMENTS FOR MINIMUM QUALITY AND SAFETY STANDARDS AND OCCUPATIONAL LICENSING

The two arguments to be considered divide along the strong-weak paternalism axis.

The Argument from Purchaser Frailty. The model of market behavior with which I commenced presupposes that adult participants in the market are "rational maximizers of self-interest." It assumes that purchasers, no less than vendors, are motivated by self-interest and capable of maximizing it. Interpreted liberally, this is hard to dispute. Yet it is also clear that purchasers frequently come away not merely with suboptimal but "bad buys"—buys in which their losses are substantial or serious harm comes to them. Various reasons for this can be nominated: fraud, gullibility, miscalculation, preoccupation, carelessness, ignorance, and so on. Some of these reasons provide strong grounds for intervention in the market on the purchaser's behalf. Where fraud or ignorance is involved, the purchase cannot be said to have been voluntarily entered into. But in other cases the voluntariness of the purchase may not be in question; nevertheless, considerations of benevolence may prompt us to save the purchaser from the worst consequences of his or her weakness. This is the Argument from Purchaser Frailty. It does not deny that purchasers are often motivated by "best buy" considerations, but it recognizes that sometimes they are not, and that even when they are, they manifest an imperfect rationality. Concern for the purchaser calls for some intervention on his or her behalf.

An expected response to this might be that if purchasers lack the presence of mind, commitment, and discipline to "pull their weight" in exchanges, the fault lies with them. It is not for manufacturers/vendors to carry the cost of their mistakes. Given, further, that it is government that is acting as protector, the door is opened to an unlimited paternalism. As Reich expresses it:

> A consumer protection policy based on a bureaucratic calculus of risks and benefits has no principled limits. Once it is accepted that the government can intercede between consumers and sellers whenever intervention can produce "better" purchasing decisions, no obvious stopping-place can be found. . . . At bottom, the risk-benefit rationale for intervention approximates the kind of calculation that consumers traditionally make when they choose a product, choose to do without it, or decide to consult first with friends or *Consumer Reports* before purchasing. But, because bureaucrats rather than consumers undertake the calculation, the risk-benefit rationale becomes a veritable slippery slope (1979, pp. 13–14).

To some extent these points are well taken. It would obviously be wrong to lay every purchaser's mistake at the door of the manufacturer/vendor. It would equally be wrong were bureaucrats to take over the task of making purchasing decisions. But it is not the purpose—or inevitable consequence—of minimum quality and safety legislation (and occupational licensing) to bring these things about. The purpose is not to eliminate mistakes or "suboptimal buys" but to eliminate or at least minimize "bad buys" where these involve a high risk of failure or injury. The purpose is to secure a certain minimum, not maximum, so far as quality and safety are concerned, and then only where the losses or harms are likely to be substantial. The end is not to eliminate choice (or the lessons that may be learned from misguided choices), but to remove from the market choices that will more than likely be made only by those who are susceptible to nonmaximizing considerations.

Defenders of an unregulated market are unlikely to be impressed by this response. Even if the effect of regulation is to remove products (or services) that would most often be chosen by bad, incompetent, or imprudent judges, and that might not survive in the marketplace were it not for the "custom" provided by such choosers, their removal by means of regulation would be unjustified. The terms of the Argument from Oppression of Individuality would be violated. Making the choice not to buy *for* consumers would imply the latters' inability to take care of themselves. To quote Reich again:

> Substitution of the choices of bureaucrats for those of consumers carries with it a not so subtle implication that consumers are powerless, if not incompetent, when faced by the combined force of corporate greed and Madison Avenue hype. . . . The charge of "big brotherism" in this context may come less as a total rejection of consumer protection than as an affirmation of a preferred self-image of competence (1979, p. 13).

What is at issue is not the corrigibility of bureaucrats, but their presumptuousness. The implied insult in their taking it upon themselves to make others' choices for them is seen as a cause for just resentment.

The argument would stand up better were the "bureaucrats" to substitute their judgment in all the individual's purchasing decisions. But that it not the point of minimum quality and safety regulations (and occupational licensing). For the most part the consumer is still left with a fairly wide range of products (and services) from which to choose. Nevertheless, it must be granted that there is a suggestion that so far as "the combined force of corporate greed and Madison Avenue hype" is concerned, the consumer *is* vulnerable *and* well served by regulation. But is this so unreasonable? While it may be true that the fault is on us if we "fall for" the blandishments of advertisers and salespeople, it is also true that their desire to sell often induces them to exploit our vulnerabilities. Every effort is made to throw us off our guard, to channel our thoughts, to appeal to irrelevant but powerful motivations, so that we will come to see what is presented to us not against the wider background of our priorities, immediate and long-term interests, etc., but in terms of a limited, temporary, and possibly distorted assemblage of interests and values. If we succumb and later have reason for deep regret, then we have ourselves to blame. We *could* have been less hasty, more guarded, tougher-minded. And maybe we will be in future purchases.

There is, however, a personal and social cost in this—the abandonment of a posture toward others whereby we can assume that they are sincere and responsive to our intentions in their dealings with us. Instead we must adopt a fundamentally skeptical posture whereby it is assumed that the interest in making a sale exceeds the interest in providing the kind of information we need for a "best buy." What I come to confront in the marketplace is not a fellow human being, bound to me by sympathetic considerations, but a role-player whose job it is to interest me in some product (or service) and whom I must hold at arm's length lest I lose perspective. What in ordinary human relations is trust becomes gullibility in the marketplace. Consumer protection legislation serves not to save us from skepticism but to limit it; it enables us to exercise a degree of trust toward those with whom we deal commercially that is not too radically at variance with the trust that we must have as a part of our ongoing social existence.

Advocacy of a limited "purchasing agent" role for government, then, is not intended to insult purchasers, either by denying them adequate scope for choice or by implying an ineradicable incompetence. Nor does it, for the most part. Instead, it represents a recognition that market imperfections are not easily removed where maximization of profit is a central concern for sellers. It is not just that there is a concern to maximize profit, but it is a concern to maximize profit where communal bonds of trust count for very little. Given this, given the comparative advantage that sellers have with respect to knowledge about their products, and given the weaknesses and vulnerabilities of potential customers, minimum quality and safety standards (and occupational licensing) represent an attempt to overcome the worst effects of exploitation.

But even though the considerations presented here count in favor of some regulation of sellers of goods (and services), they may not be sufficient to justify minimum quality and safety standards. They may provide stronger support for ensuring that potential purchasers are provided with better quality and less biased information than they are accustomed to getting. If the Argument from Purchaser Frailty is to figure in a case for minimum quality and safety regulation (and occupational licensing), it will need to be supplemented by other considerations.

The Argument from Weak Paternalism. Opponents of minimum quality and safety standards and occupational licensing presume that parties to exchanges, in particular buyers of goods and services, are acting voluntarily. Where this is not so, there exists a case for intervention. But it is only where the transactions are marked by force, fraud, and incapacity that the voluntariness assumption is overturned, and the question of interference properly arises. It is commonly argued by supporters of regulation that the concern for voluntariness in exchange justifies far greater intervention in the marketplace than its opponents suggest. Several considerations are advanced in favor of this contention:

(a) It is sometimes argued that a reason for many "bad buys" is to be found in consumer ignorance rather than a lack of consumer motivation. The purchaser has not had available to him or her essential information or, if available, has not been able to understand it. The purchase, therefore, has been made in ignorance and it is not fair to saddle the purchaser with responsibility for it. Because this is not an isolated problem, it might be thought desirable to protect consumers from what would most likely be for them "bad buys"—where the products would not perform sufficiently well to make them attractive purchasing propositions or where the risks attached to their use would deter purchase. Of course, it is possible that even if all the facts were known, some of these substandard goods would still be attractive to some purchasers, but it might be argued that in view of the number who would be likely to purchase them in ignorance and for whom they would be "bad buys," it is better that they be excluded from the marketplace.

The obvious response to this sort of argument for minimum quality and safety legislation (and occupational licensing) is that it goes too far. If it is quantity and quality of information that is the problem, then improvements should be sought at the level of dissemination, intelligibility, etc. and not through the exclusion of products (and services) from the marketplace. But this is easier said than done. There are several impediments to an adequately informed purchasing community. Ironically, one of the impediments is a surfeit of information. We are assailed on every side by information, and find that in order to handle it in the time at our disposal, we have to be selective in our sources and in the kinds of information that we attend to. In the mass of material that is presented to us, it may be difficult to "retrieve" the kind of information we need, or, more likely, the information we need may be overlooked. Even where we have plenty of data, it may not be in a form that we need. This may be either because *our* questions are not addressed in the data to hand or because the language in which they are dealt with is too technical or too vague. Sometimes the information is available but may be inaccessible for cost reasons. Consumer associations tend to address themselves to many of the questions that consumers want to know, but subscriptions to their publications may be costly. There is a further consideration, too. Much product information is supplied by manufacturers/sellers—understandably so, because they are best suited to providing it. But they are also interested in sales, and information tends to be presented "persuasively." It needs to be discounted or approached *cum grano salis.* What is said may be true, but it is frequently presented in a way likely to mislead, either through the creation of irrelevant associations, through omission, or through ambiguity. A good example can be found in the practice of describing a product as "virtually" trouble-free, unbreakable, etc., which is not really a good guide to consumers (who may want to know how durable the product is), but is intended to secure a manufacturer against charges of misleading advertising in case of breakdown, breakage, etc. After all, the advertisements did not say the product *was* trouble-free. How a consumer understands "virtually" and what a manufacturer intends in using it may be quite different.

These points do not constitute insuperable objections so far as an informed purchasing community is concerned. Nevertheless, they point to practical problems of a sufficient magnitude to raise a serious question about the most efficient way of minimizing "bad buys" arising out of nonculpable ignorance. As well as seeking to improve both the quality and availability of information, we may remove from the marketplace buys that are likely to appeal only to the nonculpably ignorant (or "pressured")—those products (and services) that are very unreliable or place users at a significantly higher risk than they might have reason to suspect.

(b) It is common for those who work with the original model to accept the desires or wants of consumers as "given," and to believe that so long as the exchange process is not attended with force, fraud, or the incapacity of one of the parties, responsibility for a purchase lies with the purchaser. All the manufacturer is doing is giving the consumer what he or she wants. But, as a number of writers have noticed, it is not quite as simple as this, for the wants that are being satisfied in the exchange process may have been created in the consumer by the manufacturer *and* created in a manner that by-passed or otherwise subverted the consumer's deliberative processes. Subliminal advertising, while it was legal, was a good example of that (cf. Benn 1967; De George 1982, pp. 192–93), but there are many other techniques used by advertisers that are questionable on the same grounds. Advertising aimed at children, for example, designed to form and establish wants before they are able to reflect on them in relation to a worked-out and stable conception of their good, comes under suspicion. Some advertising aimed at adults may also come under suspicion for the way in which powerful wants are exploited in order to create an association between their satisfaction and the purchase of some particular product. The point in these cases is not simply that the product is attractively presented (to which there can be no objection), but that it is presented in a manner intended to exploit the consumer's vulner-abilities—inserting into the reflective process irrelevant considerations that have a strong emotional value for the consumer. It is not that the consumer is incapable of developing the kind of skepticism that will enable him or her to guard against this kind of exploitation. But it amounts to requiring that consumers relate to sellers less trustingly than they relate to others, an adjustment made problematic by the fact that sellers are usually interested in establishing a relationship in which ordinary levels of trust are observed.

It is difficult to know how far the weak paternalistic argument from want-creation can be taken. This is because it is very difficult to determine whether the advertising that subverts consumers' deliberative processes does so because of some failure on their part or because it would have been unreasonable to expect them to resist its influence. One of the issues we have to face here is the kind of society we want to belong to. In many respects, our flourishing is closely bound up with the quality of relationship that we have with others (see above, pp. 41–44). Where relationships are too depersonalized or com-petitive, it becomes difficult to realize life styles characterized by sensitivity and concern. Like doctors who cope by seeing their patients as bodies rather than persons, consumers must cope with the marketplace as depersonalized role-fillers. What might otherwise be seen as transactions in which our personal needs are more clearly defined and responded to becomes instead a (frequently unfair) game in which one party tries to take advantage of another. People who wish to retain or restore communitarian values may well consider that, although we could come to resist the techniques of advertisers, it would impoverish us were we to become the sort of persons for whom that was easy. We should not be expected to resist them. Minimum quality and safety standards may be seen as something of a compromise. They do not do away with the need to exercise care in purchasing but, by removing from the market products that are very unreliable or have an unacceptably high risk factor, they save us from having to become the kind of persons for whom trust is a scarce commodity, belonging almost exclusively to the world of private relations. However, it is just because this somewhat communitarian expectation is contentious that its use in an argument designed to limit the activities of manufacturers/sellers is problematic. If the defenders of a free market fail because they limit the grounds for intervention in the market too stringently, those who wish to add to them or to interpret them more broadly run the risk of allowing excessive interference with people's voluntary behavior.

(c) Although the language of unequal bargaining power and unconscionability can be found in nineteenth-century liberals such as Green, it is only in recent legal decision-making that it has become common to use "unconscionability" as a ground for setting aside or redrawing contractual agreements. One of the merits of "unconscionability" as a ground for intervening in contractual relationships has been that it allows a flexibility not possessed by "coercion," "duress," and "force." It is problematic, however, because it may open the door to too much intervention in contractual arrangements. But this possibility is not itself a sufficient reason for rejecting "unconscionability," provided that there is some principled way of defending appeals to it. What seems to be central to the idea is a certain "inequality" between the contracting parties that is taken advantage of by the stronger party and used to impose on the weaker party terms that the latter could have been expected to avoid had he or she had more bargaining power. The weaker party is not coerced or forced into the agreement, but neither is he or she free to negotiate it on equal terms with the other party (thus departing from one of the assumptions on the original model). The choice is not: 'Your money or your life," but only: "These are the terms: take it or leave it." But they are not terms that could have been expected to appeal had the weaker party more room to move.

What makes for inequality of bargaining power? No single factor. Obviously there must be an absence of known alternatives to the arrangement that expresses it. But this might be brought about in a number of ways. Often there is a certain urgency for the good (or service); there may be a large difference in knowledge and intellectual power; the weaker party may have meager resources. Inequalities of wealth tend to be associated with inequalities of power and place the poor at a serious disadvantage in the negotiation of agreements. As one way of attempting to keep stronger parties from taking improper advantage of their position, we may rule out certain contractual possibilities—e.g., goods and services that are unreliable or unsafe. It is not the only way of tackling the issue (redistribution through taxation may also contribute), but there is no strong reason why it should not be included (cf. Kronman 1980).

The Argument from Weak Paternalism is in principle unobjectionable. The difficulty is in applying it fairly and economically. I have attempted to indicate some of the factors that would count in favor of its appropriateness in defense of minimum quality and safety standards (and occupational licensing). To apply it to particular cases would, I believe, require considerably more argument than I have provided here.

NON-PATERNALISTIC ARGUMENTS FOR MINIMUM QUALITY AND SAFETY STANDARDS AND OCCUPATIONAL LICENSING

Each of the following arguments has something to be said in its favor. On their own they may not provide a strong enough case for interventions as intrusive as minimum quality and safety standards, etc. Taken together and conjoined with the paternalistic arguments just considered, I believe they weigh firmly in favor of some legislation of the kinds under consideration.

The Argument from Fraud-Protection. Where one party to a transaction obtains something from another party by means of deliberate misstatement, in which there is an intention to deceive, the former acts fraudulently. But it is not always easy to determine whether fraud is involved. Intentions are difficult to read, and it may have been carelessness or ignorance on the purchaser's part that led to the seller being taken one way rather than another. The difficulties involved in distinguishing fraudulent from nonfraudulent conduct in the marketplace are considerable, given, on the one hand, the competitiveness of sellers and their strong desire to persuade potential purchasers to deal with them, and, on the other hand, the varied backgrounds, expectations, and relative ignorance of purchasers. Minimum quality and safety standards (and occupational licensing) may be seen as one way of dealing efficiently with cases that would present great difficulties so far as adjudication is concerned.

But although defenders of a free market are unanimous in their opposition to fraud and their willingness to allow its penalization, they are strongly opposed to dealing with the problems of adjudication by means of minimum quality and safety standards, etc. The reason is that it is inappropriate. Fraud is a corruption of the exchange process; minimum quality, etc. standards are directed to the content of the exchange. The point is well taken but not decisive. Though distinct in theory, process and content tend to be related in practice. There are some goods (e.g., submerged building lots) that we have reason to believe would be chosen only by people who were being deceived (or otherwise taken advantage of); there are other goods (e.g., soft-metal tools) whose purchase makes it very likely that deception of some kind is involved. Minimum quality and safety standards may be understood as an attempt to deal with probable fraud by removing from the marketplace goods that consumers would not knowingly and voluntarily purchase. Given the diversity of consumers' requirements, this is bound to exclude goods and services that some would have considered "acceptable buys," but this might be a reasonable price to pay if there is reason to think that most purchasers would not have done so had they been aware of their characteristics.

The Argument from Externalities. It is one thing if a product is likely to fail or endanger its purchaser. That may be a risk the purchaser is prepared to take. It is quite another if some third party is likely to be the loser. The two possibilities are frequently connected. Our lives intersect in many ways and at many points; what we bring on ourselves may also spill over onto others.

An unsafe motor vehicle is likely to be unsafe not only for the purchaser but also for those who may innocently travel in it. Where significant externalities are predictable, there is a case for imposing standards that will minimize or diminish their likelihood (see J. Buchanan 1970, pp. 71–72; Duggan 1982, pp. 15–16, 57–58).

Much here will depend on the interpretation we give to "significant." There may also be questions of cost involved. A manufacturer can sometimes improve the quality or safety of a product considerably, with little addition to the cost. But where a small improvement is costly, some potential purchasers may be driven out of the market. This needs to be borne in mind and will be relevant to decisions about the standards to be required.

The Argument from Efficiency. As even its advocates recognize, the model of market relations that I initially described is not exemplified in the actual marketplace. The latter manifests various "imperfections." There are numerous reasons for this. Participants in market transactions do not always conform to their characterization as rational maximizers of advantage; the market is not perfectly competitive; there are various transaction costs that need to be borne; and there are externalities that the model leaves out of account (cf. Duggan 1982, pp. 12–17). It might be argued that consumer protection legislation of the sort we have been discussing represents an effective means of accommodating these imperfections, or at least a more effective means than market forces can be expected to provide (see Kronman 1980; Duggan 1982).

In some respects this is a surprising argument, for it is one of the most regularly heard and assiduously supported contentions of defenders of the free market that, barring the disruption caused by force, fraud, and incapacity, market forces are the most efficient antidote to market imperfections. A number of reasons for this are given:

(a) One of the effects of minimum quality and safety regulations (and occupational licensing) is to exclude some options from the marketplace—options that, given the great diversity of consumer purposes, would be "best buys" for some purchasers. By frustrating such purchases, regulation operates inefficiently. This is a variant on The Argument from Paternalistic Distance. The purchaser is assumed to be better placed and better motivated to choose a maximizing buy than some governmental agency.

The general point holds but only so far. Although the excluded products and services may be "best buys" for some, it is arguable that they would most often be purchased as a result of ignorance, mistake, or weakness of bargaining power. It might also be suggested that it is only because the producers/sellers can rely on such sales that the goods and services in question remain economically viable. If that is so, there is no real loss to the few for whom the excluded goods and services would have been "best buys." To this, a reply along the lines of the Argument from the Developmental Value of Choice might be made—viz., we learn from our mistakes. Fair enough. But we do not learn from all our mistakes, or not without excessive costs being exacted. Minimum standards regulations are not intended to rule out the possibility of mistake, but only to diminish the likelihood of mistake where those who choose badly would probably suffer disproportionately. With many items, particularly those that are more expensive, repeat buying is unlikely and the "lesson" will come too late.

(b) Not only do minimum standards exclude some goods and services from the marketplace, but they exclude some purchasers, for the regulations push goods and services that qualify out of their price range. This is often claimed to be unfair and inefficient with respect to the poor. As Buchanan puts it, provided there are no significant externalities, "poor users should be allowed to purchase unsafe automobiles. . . . By their own expressions of preference, they are better off with unsafe automobiles than with no automobiles at all" (J. Buchanan 1970, p. 71). It is true that poor users may be excluded from certain markets by minimum quality and safety regulations. But it is not clear that this is inefficient. The fact of their weak bargaining position must be taken into account. Their preparedness to shoulder the risks associated with an inferior product may signify not a "best buy" so much as an "only buy." Is it fair that the only option available is a fairly unreliable or unsafe product? We do not usually think so, so far as certain important services are concerned, such as medical care. Where people are too poor to purchase treatment from qualified doctors, it is not considered acceptable (or efficient) to leave them without treatment or to have them purchase cheaper treatment from unqualified practitioners. Rather, we seek to provide proper treatment via publicly supported services. Why not also for the goods that figure in the expectations of "average" members of a community—at least where failure would be attended by serious loss? For such goods, where minimum standards regulations have made them too expensive, low interest loans or subsidies could be made available. If a progressive taxation system performs an important redistributional function by increasing the bargaining power of the poorer members of the community, it may be coordinated with minimum standards regulations to enable the marketplace to be a site for transactions of greater voluntariness and, according to the model, greater efficiency.

(c) But is such legislation consistent with the doctrine of the least restrictive alternative? This commonly disputed. It is argued that the emphasis should be on improving the quality and/or quantity of information available to purchasers. This can be achieved by making goodwill more important to sellers.

Leaving aside the issues raised by unequal bargaining power, etc., it can be granted that the desire to maintain goodwill may be an important incentive to sellers so far as "best" or at least "good buys" are concerned. But as we have already had occasion to note, this solution is not as efficient as it promises. "Goodwill" can often be maintained relatively independently of quality by means of advertising and other publicity strategies (sponsorships, etc.). Further, where the deleterious effects of a product are temporally remote from its use, or the causal relationships are difficult to establish, and where the media rely on advertising for the bulk of their revenue, the effects on goodwill from failed or even hazardous products may not be very great. Add to this the unimportance of goodwill in certain cases (where repeat buys are unlikely or the seller is very mobile), and the argument for improving the information available to buyers via the goodwill requirements of sellers loses much of its force as a *substitute for* minimum standards regulations. "Brand name" buying is some help, but even that may be no safeguard against exploitation.

(d) There is, finally, the objection that where governments act as purchasing agents for consumers, the door has been opened to unlimited intervention. This, as we have seen (above, p. 183), is Reich's contention. But it relies on a caricature of the government's "purchasing agent" role. If it is scope for a "better" decision that justifies government intrusion into the marketplace, then there will indeed always be a reason for it. But consumer protection legislation isn't intended to ensure that consumers make the "best buy" possible. What it attempts to secure is a certain minimum, not maximum, so far as quality and safety are concerned. The point is to protect buyers from certain kinds of damage or loss, not to secure for them positive benefits.

But this may not be enough to stop the slide. For it will be claimed that an argument that allows the government to act as purchasing agent in the matter of refrigerators has no way of stopping it from acting as purchasing agent for pins. Pins, no less than refrigerators, may fall short of normal expectations. Given the large resources of government and the aggrandizing tendencies of bureaucrats, excessive involvement in the marketplace is all too likely. In a sense the concern is well founded. Governments constantly involve themselves too much in people's lives, in the wrong places, and for the wrong reasons. But they also fail to involve themselves enough, in the right places, and for the right reasons. Clearly, this is a matter where a number of considerations have to be taken into account and traded off or balanced: seriousness of the losses and dangers involved; the probability of those losses or harms occurring; the various demands that the government has to respond to; the degree of responsibility that it is reasonable to expect people to take for their purchasing decisions; whether *caveat emptor* will produce its own sizeable public costs (injury, loss of productivity, etc.); and other "externalities," such as inability to fulfill obligations to others, and so on. The slippery slope looks slippery only because we consider one factor in isolation from others that are also important if governmental interference is to be justified.

Once again, the foregoing arguments must be taken as suggestive rather than decisive. The calculation of utilities is extraordinarily difficult (perhaps impossible), there being so many variables and ripple effects involved. Nor should the argument be taken as favoring the *status quo*. Friedman and others have shown convincingly that much occupational licensing has worked against consumers, not for them. In the medical profession, for example, it has been used not so much to keep those in need of medical services out of the hands of charlatans and quacks, but to protect the status and income of doctors. The licensing system has enabled a group to gain a monopoly on a socially desired expertise. By controlling the numbers admitted to their ranks, the price of the service is driven up. Not that the members put it that way. It is said to be a way of keeping the profession from getting into a position where, "if 'too' many people are let in, this will lower their income so that they will be driven to resort to unethical practices in order to earn a 'proper' income" (Friedman 1962, p. 152; cf. Gellhorn 1976). However, the answer to these problems lies not in rejection of licensing (as Friedman suggests) but in some regular (and public) review of licensing criteria, procedures, and practices. If, as it is often asserted, the purpose of licensing is to protect the public, this should provide the basis for determining the fairness of actual licensing procedures.

The "Collective Good" Argument. Many of the previous arguments have operated on the assumption that the consumer protection legislation under review constitutes an imposition on consumers. This may not be the most profitable way of looking at it. Given the origins of much (though admittedly not all) consumer protection legislation in pressure brought to bear by the buying public, it is plausible to suggest that it functions not to restrict but facilitate consumer will. Most consumers wish for reasonably durable and safe goods but do not want to be saddled with high costs in time and effort in ensuring that the goods they are considering pass an acceptable threshold in that regard. After all, there are enough other matters to be looked at before making a purchasing decision. Minimum quality and safety standards may be seen as a convenient way of economizing in time and effort without constricting choice unduly. Of course, some will be frustrated by such regulations. But, unless the consequences of such restrictions are very serious and unremediable (which is unlikely), consideration for the "collective good" will take precedence.

Again, it needs to be emphasized that this is not intended as a defense of the *status quo*. Just because the goods secured by an argument of this kind are intended to reflect the desire of a substantial majority of people, it is important that the standards they embody remain accessible and responsive to criticism. As in the case of the present system of medical licensing, there are many examples of restrictions that reflect the lobbying power of greed rather than a collective concern about harm or serious loss.

Regulations Relating to the Financing of Purchases

There was a time when, except for certain basic items, if you lacked the wherewithal to purchase some desired object, you went without it. Naturally this tended to limit the market for goods (and services). It is clearly advantageous to manufacturers/vendors if they are able to expand their market by making their goods (or services) available to those who, at the time of purchase, do not have the full purchase price. This has been achieved by instituting some form of delayed- or time-payment system. The buyer repays the seller by means of regular installments or enters into an agreement with some intermediate finance institution that pays the seller in full and then collects from the buyer by means of regular installments. For the benefits of such a scheme, the buyer pays an additional charge.

The business community works hard to encourage the purchase of goods (or services), and since the financing of purchases by means of extended repayment agreements is instrumental to that end, it is given strong support. One of the problems engendered by this form of financing is overcommitment. The repayments required for some particular product or service may not be onerous, but sometimes this tempts people into many such agreements, which collectively leave them with little by way of cushioning should there be an unexpected call on their financial resources. Another problem, also concealed from obvious view, is the possibility of entering into an agreement for which the interest rates chargeable are excessive. It is possible to make a "bad buy" so far as finance is concerned. Partly in response to these sorts of situations, regulations have sometimes been drawn up that limit the extent to which or ways in which buyers can commit themselves and sellers can profit from credit agreements. Such limitations are frequently considered to be paternalistic. Four warrant attention in this context. They are, first, the exclusion of minors from finance agreements; second, restrictions on the amount of credit available to purchasers of goods and services; third, ceilings on the interest rates chargeable on credit; and finally, regulations requiring a minimum deposit or a short-term repayment period for goods or services purchased.

Since most of the arguments considered in the last section can be applied with equal appropriateness in the present context, I will not repeat them and will concentrate instead on some of the specifics of such regulations.

(a) Refusing to permit minors to enter into finance agreements is usually seen as a piece of weak paternalism. Except where goods or services are considered inherently risky, minors are not usually prevented from purchasing them for cash. However, they may not be able to obtain the same goods on credit or via a hire purchase agreement. This is because purchasing on credit requires a (relatively) long-term commitment, and minors cannot be assumed to be capable of responsibly making such commitments. For their own good, they ought to be prevented from entering into them.

Though the structure of the argument is clear enough, the details may be contentious. Some minors will be capable of entering hire-purchase agreements "with their eyes wide open"; some adults will not. As I suggested in the previous chapter, the fairest procedure might be to set a presumptive age of consent to such agreements, allowing for variations depending on the circumstances of the case. Given the strong pressures that there are to consume on credit, unless there is some barrier or onus, minors are likely to find their vulnerabilities exploited even more than they are at present.

(b) Limitations placed on the amount of credit available to purchasers—often determined as a percentage of income—may be seen as designed to deter them from committing so much of that income to the repayment of goods and services bought on credit that their life style becomes destabilized, vulnerable to serious disruption should some common contingency arise (illness, short-term unemployment, etc.). This has a paternalistic ring about it.

(c) A similar sort of rationale is commonly advanced where ceilings are placed on the amount of interest chargeable on loans. As William Warren puts it, their "principal function appears simply to be the protection of credit consumers against excessive gougings by those dealers and financers who, taking advantage of the public's notorious indifference to financial rates, exact exorbitant charges" (1959, p. 854).

(d) Efforts to justify minimum deposit or short-term repayment requirements evidence similar concerns. Minimum deposit regulations generally take the form of a requirement that those who purchase on credit make an initial down payment of, say 10 percent on the ticket price of the goods (or services) to be purchased. The rationale for this, John Peden suggests, is paternalistic: "The *principal* purpose of minimum deposit provisions in hire-purchase legislation is to protect hirers against themselves" (1967, p. 40). Short-term repayment periods may be seen as an alternative to the minimum deposit requirement —the higher repayments required constituting a deterrent to those whose financial position is insecure.

In so far as the foregoing limitations on access to finance are seen as paternalistic, they possess the strengths and weaknesses of the paternalistic arguments discussed in the last section. However, the Argument from Weak Paternalism is probably more appropriate to this context than the Argument from Purchaser Frailty. Financial matters are often confusing to purchasers and it is easy to be persuaded into agreements one does not fully understand. The purchaser of finance, moreover, does not usually possess much bargaining power. Unless a person is adept at calculations, it is often difficult to compare the terms offered by different lenders. Some of these difficulties might be met by a requirement that standarized information be placed before purchasers. But this would not make provision for cases in which the inequality of bargaining power had other bases. Some limitations—say, on maximum interest rates chargeable—might be thought justified simply because the people most likely to agree to them would be those without any bargaining power. While this may sometimes lead to money not being made available for loan (though not very often, given that the ceiling is usually set fairly high), alternative sources of public finance would be an option in cases of serious need.

But there are undoubtedly other factors at work too, and it would be improper (as is often done) to dismiss the various limitations we have been considering as "paternalistic," without further discussion. Minimum deposit requirements, for example, are sometimes supported by hire-purchase companies as an efficient way of financing purchases. Their claim that access to hire-purchase "should not be made so easy that it encourages people to undertake commitments they cannot really afford" (in Peden 1967, p. 40) is not paternalistic, but a reflection of their conviction that repossession/reselling is not their most efficient mode of operation. Their own interests are better served if those who enter into agreements meet their financial obligations. The same sort of argument has been used to defend short-term repayment requirements and restrictions on the amount of credit purchasers may obtain. These claims, though plausible, are not uncontroversial. Although some hire-purchase companies have supported minimum deposit regulations, many have not. This has led to the development of strategies for getting round them—a fairly easy task, since the purchaser him- or herself is party to them. The reason for the lack of support is a belief that there are better ways of gauging a purchaser's creditworthiness—for example, whether his or her financial position is sufficiently strong and secure to support a "commitment to pay the residual amount plus charges and insurance." Regulations fixing a maximum hiring period may show up better in this regard, since they will be cast in terms more relevant to people's purchasing behavior—some indication of the size of weekly or monthly repayments/installments (Peden 1967, p. 41).

Another reason for minimum deposit regulations might be that they help to control the money supply (Peden 1967, p. 40). But this could probably be no more than a side benefit since it would not be the most efficient means of controlling it, were that a major purpose. The fixing of interest rate levels is sometimes justified by reference to the Argument from Fraud-Protection. There are various ways of expressing interest rates and charges, and sellers may deliberately mislead buyers by concealing what is actually very expensive credit behind figures that appear much more reasonable. An interest rate maximum might protect people from some of the most serious cases of deceptive presentation. But there may be more economical ways of protecting purchasers of finance from fraud—by requiring a standarized form expressing all charges in credit agreements. This would have the added virtue of covering cases of fraud not captured by a maximum interest rate standard. The latter may, in fact, count against the buyer, encouraging a movement of interest rates in the direction of the maximum. Whereas they should "represent the outer limits of what the retail instalments consumer should have to bear," they come to be taken as "a legislative directive of what is a fair profit for the financer" (Warren 1959, p. 865).

The various restrictions that I have considered in this section represent, not so much the application of some single principle, but the expression of an assemblage of considerations pointing in the direction of some sort of intervention in the marketplace. Whether they are adequate to that task will be determined by taking into account not only their efficiency, but also their fairness and compatibility with the integrity of purchasers.

Regulations Relating to Sales Practices

Of the various regulations that circumscribe permissible sales practices, two in particular have been characterized (and sometimes criticized) as paternalistic: the incorporation of a "cooling-off" period into some sales contracts, and the banning of certain sales arrangements, such as pyramid selling.

It has become increasingly common for legislatures to require that sales contracts permit a limited period within which purchasers may withdraw from an agreement without penalty. Provisions of this kind originated in 1962, following the English Molony Report, but can now be found in parts of Australia, in Canada, and the United States. The "decompression" period involved is only two or three days, but it gives purchasers an opportunity to consider at leisure and in more detail whether the agreement they signed really conformed to their ongoing purposes and interests, or was instead the result of sales pressure, weakness of will, unconsidered impulse, or something of that sort. Generally such regulations have been restricted to door-to-door agreements, the assumption being that soon-to-be-regretted commitments are more likely to occur in that context than in a salesroom. The door-to-door salesperson calls unexpectedly, the purchaser is often alone, preoccupied, and may feel under pressure to sign just to get rid of the other person. There is, moreover, no opportunity for comparisons of price and quality.

It is possible to see "cooling-off" periods as a way of dealing with sales behavior that verges on the fraudulent, but that could not clearly be shown to be so in court. They might also be seen as a "collective good"—providing a breathing space sought by purchasers, but able to be guaranteed for them only if written into all door-to-door agreements. But it is quite likely that paternalistic considerations also enter in. Some will be weak—arising out of the unequal bargaining power of the parties, the purchaser's unpreparedness, etc. Others will be strong—taking into account the gullibility of purchasers, their tendency to make hasty and ill-considered decisions, etc.

But "cooling-off" periods are not without their critics. Some argue that they unfairly taint door-to-door sales transactions (but is this really undeserved?). It is true that showroom techniques are often not much better, though we probably need to draw a line somewhere. Others claim that "cooling-off" provisions have deleterious market consequences. By providing an "invitation to cancel," they leave what should have been seen as the conclusion of a process in a disruptive limbo:

> If the decision to buy is not final and conclusive, the purchaser may be exposed to all sorts of pressures, and the easiest way to resolve the matter may be to cancel out, if the opportunity to do so is available. This result is undesirable both for the consumer, whose decision is undermined, and for the seller, whose investment in this buyer and in this transaction will be lost (Sher 1968, p. 727).

This, surely, overrates a possibility. The point—and usual effect—of a "cooling-off" period is not to increase pressure on purchasers, but to diminish it. If the sales process has been fair to the buyer, the seller should have little to fear. Those who complain about "cooling-off" provisions are not buyers fearful that their decision will be undermined, but sellers fearful that what has been extracted through virtuosity may be less captivating the following day. Yet "cooling-off" periods do represent an imposition on buyers who are able to pay the total purchase price or would like to make immediate use of the goods or services, because sellers usually protect themselves by not delivering the goods or providing the services until after the "cooling-off" period has elapsed. However, we may be pretty confident that the inconvenience in these cases will be slight, for had they been wanted immediately, the buyer could have gone out and purchased them. The door-to-door saleperson usually arrives unannounced, with a product or service that is not (if at all) urgently required. The situation would change somewhat (though not necessarily decisively) were a "cooling-off" period to be included in most contracts for goods and services.

Pyramid selling, according to Justice Mehler, is an

> arrangement whereby one is induced to buy upon the representation that he cannot only regain his purchase price, but also earn profit by selling the same program to the public. It thus involves the purchase of the right to sell the same right to sell. A pyramid type practice is similar to a chain letter operation. Such a program is inherently deceptive, for the seemingly endless chain must come to a halt inasmuch as growth, cannot be perpetual and the market becomes saturated by the number of participants. Thus many participants are mathematically barred from ever recouping their original investments, let alone making profits.[6]

The claim here is that pyramid selling is "inherently deceptive." If that is so, then paternalistic reasons would not need to feature in its outlawing. All the work can be done by the harm principle. But the matter is not quite so simple. Even though the pyramid selling enterprise is doomed in that the market will eventually become saturated, that is something that can be known by those who participate in it. It may be a risk that they are prepared to take for the sake of the profit that might be obtained. Why should *caveat emptor* not apply? How does investment in a pyramid scheme differ from participating in a lottery? Not all can win, yet the possibility of winning (something) may be thought to justify the risk.

However, although there are similarities with a lottery, in that 'it is mathematically inherent . . . that many investors are going to lose their money" (Head 1974, p. 171), there are also some important differences. For most people, the investment required by a purchase of lottery tickets is small. It is also clearer in the case of lotteries that not all can be winners (though most ticket-buyers seem to have an inflated idea of the odds in favor of their winning a prize). Pyramid selling, however, presents itself as a form of more or less regular employment—a source of continuing income, rather than a once-off win-or-lose venture. It requires, moreover, a much larger investment by participants—the sort of investment that, if lost, would be financially disastrous for many. This is not to claim that pyramid selling is "inherently deceptive," though it is clearly an arrangement in which the temptation to deceive will be strong. It comes fairly close to being a condition of relieving many of the substantial sums involved that the prospects of their succeeding be painted in brighter-than-life colors. The Argument from Fraud-Protection, though not decisive, has a fairly good grip.

Even so, some defenders of *laissez-faire* policies are reluctant to see bans on pyramid selling as anything but paternalistic. As a former Victorian attorney-general put it: "You can't legislate to save a person from himself. If fools did not go to the market, bad goods would not be sold" (in Head 1974, p. 177). This presumes, and has its plausibility from presuming, that the "fools" who enter into pyramid selling schemes are the fools of the proverb, who are soon (and deservedly) parted from their money. But the victims of pyramid schemes are not usually fools of that kind, but people who are vulnerable in special ways. As Michael Head notes:

> This [*laissez-faire*] attitude fails to appreciate the intense sophistication of the pyramid selling schemes and the methods used to draw people into them. . . . Individuals, particularly migrants, the young person and the elderly find it impossible to appreciate the nature of the scheme, and commit their money before they have an opportunity to do so (1974, p. 177).

In other words, if there is paternalism involved here, it is most likely weak paternalism, in which the ignorance, dependence, and vulnerability of potential participants is exploited.

Labor Laws

In the controversial 1905 case *Lochner* v. *New York*, a statute limiting the maximum working week of bakers of sixty hours was appealed. In upholding the appeal, the court stated that

> the law must be upheld, if at all, as a law pertaining to the health of the individual engaged in the occupation of a baker. It does not affect any other portion of the public than those who are engaged in that occupation. . . . The limitation of the hours of labour does not come within the police power on that ground.[7]

In other words, it was argued that the statute was paternalistically motivated, making the prohibited behavior an inappropriate object of public concern. Similar judgments have been made about minimum wage and child labor laws, and measures used to exclude women and children from certain forms of employment, particularly those involving heavy physical labor.

The *Lochner* decision has proved controversial, not because it has been thought appropriate for the law to uphold this form of paternalism, but because it is doubted whether the intention of the law was paternalistic. It is probably best seen, not as an imposition on workers for the sake of a health that they are prone to neglect, but as a means of securing a health they desire but cannot otherwise ensure. In other words, its major support comes from the "Collective Good" Argument. Let us suppose that most workers are desirous of working a thirty-five-hour week. If as individuals they seek to negotiate an agreement to that effect with their employers, they are unlikely to succeed so long as there are some who would be willing to work a forty-hour week (perhaps for the same pay). The employer will be inclined to favor the latter, and the effect could be a lowering of conditions of employment and unnecessary and unjustifiable hardship for many. (A person without dependents will be at a bargaining advantage in such transactions.) The only way in which employees are likely to succeed in realizing their desire is through its legal enactment (cf. Mill 1848, pp. 956–58; Dworkin 1971, p. 112). Even though this will prevent some people from doing what they would have been willing to do, the reason will not be to ensure their good, but to prevent them from frustrating the desires of most workers. Not that they will suffer greatly thereby, for the thirty-five-hour week will benefit them as well as other workers.

But maybe the choice for the worker who is willing to work a forty-hour week is not a choice between that and a thirty-five-hour week, but between that and unemployment. However, a deregulation of work hours will provide at best a temporary benefit. For if, as we have to assume here, there are more people than jobs, and there are no limits on the hours that may be worked, those who are willing to work forty hours will find their position jeopardized by others who will (now) be willing to work forty-five hours. And so on, leading to what we can all recognize as a degrading situation. Only through collective activity in which all are required to participate, will the desire for a humane arrangement be satisfied.

The same sorts of arguments can be advanced in relation to safety standards in the workplace and minimum wage laws. Although some people may be willing to work in unsafe conditions or for less pay, if they are permitted to do so they will jeopardize the conditions and pay of others. Of course, I am not saying that there should *never* be a relaxation of safety measures or lowering of pay. In some cases it is arguable that workers are so interested in feathering their own nests that they are unreasonably diminishing job opportunities for others. But if there is movement one way or the other, it should apply across the board.

Policies to exclude women (and sometimes children) from certain kinds and conditions of employment have more frequently been represented as paternalistic. In *Muller* v. *Oregon*, for example, it was claimed that if women were required to work the same hours as men, their health would suffer disproportionately. To limit the hours a woman could work was said to be "necessary to secure her real equality of right."[8] Children, too, might be seen as physically more vulnerable than adult men. Added to that, they are susceptible to exploitation (by parents as well as employers). There is an appearance of paternalism here, but probably not too much reality. The latter would almost certainly dictate less restrictive measures. What is more likely to be operative are economic factors. Working men have believed that their own employment opportunities would be threatened were women and (in some circumstances) children given the same access to the workplace as they enjoy. But to say that would be overtly and selfishly discriminatory. In a world that has traditionally accorded women (and children) a diminished status, paternalistic arguments are likely to look better. In the case of children, there is the additional fact of their dependence/vulnerability. Were their ability to earn money unconstrained, parents might be tempted to exploit them. Some controls would seem to be necessary.

Notes

1. The epigraph to Hamilton's fascinating and helpful article reads: "A doctrine is like a family that is coming up in the world; it fits itself out with an ancient lineage." More generally, see Atiyah 1979.

2. *McFarland* v. *Newman*, 9 Watts 55 (Pa., 1839), quoted in Hamilton 1931, p. 1181.

3. An incompetent seller may be protected by means of a guardianship order (cf. Guttmacher and Weihofen 1952, p. 188). An ignorant seller may also be protected against mistake, as in *Sherwood* v. *Walker*, 66 Mich., 568, 33 N.W., 919 (1887), where the sale of a cow was cancelled when it was found, contrary to the belief of both parties, that the cow was not barren. Competent sellers may also be protected. Bernard Rudden cites a case in which doubt was expressed whether, in selling part of his property, an owner could agree to leave himself landlocked (*Nickerson* v. *Barraclough*, 2 All E.R. 312 [1979]). There are also laws that will not allow property owners or tenants to contract out of or forgo rights that have been established for their benefit (cf. *Johnson* v. *Moreton*, 3 All E.R. 37 [1978], discussed in Rudden 1980, pp. 87–88). In some cases, these restrictions may reflect the unequal bargaining power of those involved.

4. This, of course, represents something of a simplification. For a more detailed working out of the model, see Friedman 1962, and Posner 1977.

5. An alternative, at least so far as quality is concerned, is to associate variations in price with variations in warranty. In this way, buyers can choose the amount of risk they wish to take.

6. *Kugler* v. *Koscot Interplanetary*, 293 A. 2d. 682 (1972).

7. *Lochner* v. *New York*, 198 U.S. 45, at 57 (1905).

8. *Muller* v. *Oregon*, 208 U.S. 412 (1908).

8
Character

In speaking of people's welfare or good, we usually have in mind their bodily and psychological health, their social and economic stability, their level of education, and the extent of their liberty. Overlapping with some of these, but capturing an aspect that we have largely neglected, is the state or condition of a person's character or—as the ancients would have put it—soul. This was, in their view, the preeminent consideration. Harm, for Socrates, was paradigmatically a condition of character, a blight of the soul (Plato, *Gorgias*: 470 et seq.; *Apology*: 42a; cf. Winch 1965–66; Irwin 1977, pp. 179–80). A similar thought is present in Jesus's advice not to "fear those who kill the body, but cannot kill the soul. Fear him rather who is able to destroy both soul and body in hell" (Matt. 10:28). These thinkers would have found odd our almost exclusive preoccupation with other aspects of welfare.

"Character" can be understood broadly to refer to that cluster of established dispositions, attitudes, habits of mind, etc. that constitute someone as the particular person he or she is. It may have moral, aesthetic, intellectual, political, religious, and other dimensions to it, though in this chapter I shall be concerned with it in its moral and, to a lesser extent, religious dimensions. This is not wholly arbitrary, for, whatever we may ultimately want to say about the status of moral (and religious) considerations, it is these that tend to predominate in our descriptions of character. They are primary expressions of human life's distinctively relational and self-reflective nature.

To the extent that the state of a person's character may be included in our assessment of his or her good, it may become an object of paternalistic concern. Individuals may be imposed on in order to promote in them a particular kind of character or to preserve an already formed character from what are seen as degenerative changes. Parents, educational, and religious institutions often see the former as falling within their brief, and various legal provisions, particularly some concerned with expressions of human sexuality, seem to have reasons of a paternalistic kind among their supporting considerations.

Although the ancients saw damage to character or the soul as the most serious of evils, a paternalistic concern with character nevertheless strikes us as the most problematic of all paternalistic concerns. Isn't there something odd about this? From one point of view there is. The more important an interest, the more central it is to a person's good, the stronger we might expect the case for paternalistic intervention to be. But there is a particularly intimate connection between character and individuality, and what poses as beneficial to the former may seriously threaten the latter. Antipaternalists will insist that any attempt to ensure a person's good, whether physical, psychological, or economic, runs a strong risk of threatening individuality; in character paternalism, that risk is greatly magnified. We can make rough-and-ready generalizations about the ingredients of people's physical, psychological, and economic good; but judgments about the ingredients of their character's welfare are more tendentiously bound up with particular and partisan sets of values, and its "promotion" or "protection" will appear to violate the individuality in terms of which it might in other contexts be justified. Despite this, some character paternalism would seem unavoidable, since characters do not just evolve but are acquired through social interaction, and to some extent they are formed before we are able to take responsibility for them. Is there some way between the Scylla of neglect and the Charybdis of moralism?

We can approach this issue by seeing whether it is possible to articulate a notion of "harm to character" that is reasonably free of unwelcome partisan associations. If that can be done, some space for character paternalism may be found. But because character is multidimensional, I shall focus more specifically on moral harm and, later, religious harm. I shall also relate these discussions to a number of practices for which the rationales are (often) partially paternalistic and the end is moral or religious welfare.

Moral Harm

Bodily harms are relatively uncontroversial. What is viewed by one person as a bodily harm is most likely to be considered so by others. Where differences are likely to occur are in judgments about the importance of such harms in view of their varied projects, goals, life-plans, etc. Where paternalists frequently misfire is in thinking that their ordering of priorities is identical to that of those on whom they impose. Matters become more problematic when we start talking about psychological and economic harm, not just because interpersonal judgments of priority become more difficult to make, but also because the actual harmfulness of particular conditions is often moot. The difficulties are intensified when we start talking about "moral harm." Indeed, whether there is such a thing, or "harm" is simply being used honorifically—a cloak of respectability for authoritarian prejudice—is far from settled.

No doubt "moral harm" is often used persuasively, a ploy by moral conservatives to create space for the enforcement of their values. But this is not itself reason to shy off from the attempt to provide a more defensible account. The notion of moral harm predates its cannibalization by the contemporary moral conservative.

There is more than one way in which we might attempt to articulate an acceptable notion of moral harm. One is to extrapolate from the account in which bodily harm tends to be paradigmatic. Bodily invasions might be seen as harmful to the extent that there is some impairment of a person's welfare interests—those foundational interests that function as prerequisites to our engagement in activities representative and constitutive of our individuality (cf. Kleinig 1978, pp. 30–33). Where character traits are developed/eroded that place at risk the formation/realization of individual projects and purposes, harm to character can be said to have been perpetrated. Where the traits diminish the quality of relationships that a person is able to have with others, the harm will have a more specifically moral dimension. What classical writers spoke of as vices have been traditionally seen as character traits likely to be out of keeping with a person's own life-plans or, in some cases, antagonistic to the life-plans of others (see above, p. 36). Imprudence, lack of self-control or perseverence, and laziness affect the formation and execution of our life-plans and may also detract from our dealings with others and their ability to pursue life-plans of their own. The so-called other-regarding vices jeopardize others' projects more directly, but, because they alienate, they are also likely to make it more difficult for us to pursue the many projects for which we are in various ways dependent on others (see above, pp. 40–44). Of course there will be some dispute as to which character traits are likely to be important if our varied and variable plans and projects are to be pursued and realized, but the general shape of the argument is clear enough. It sees as requisite to the pursuit of our individual interests not only factors like bodily integrity, material security, and so forth, but also certain character traits, and it recognizes that these, like the former, are vulnerable.

A somewhat different account is suggested by Joel Feinberg (1977, pp. 287–90), who construes harm more broadly than I do, as encompassing the invasion of any of a person's interests (cf. Feinberg 1973, ch. 2). Taking over Brian Barry's distinction between "want-regarding" and "ideal-regarding" concepts (1965, pp. 38–41), he argues that *interest* is a want-regarding concept, and therefore, that any interest we have in a good character is dependent on our wants. Moral corruption and degradation are harms only to the person with an interest in moral excellence. Moral excellence is not something that is in a person's interest independently of his or her "relatively deep-rooted and stable wants" (Feinberg 1977, p. 286). Although many of the ancients claim that only the virtuous person can be happy (and, therefore, that moral excellence will necessarily be among one's interests), Feinberg disagrees. The morally inferior person may be happy as he or she is, and may not, therefore, have moral virtue among his or her wants (interests). Should we be reluctant to accept this, it shows only that *we* have an interest in moral excellence. If the moral defective, Feinberg says,

> is clever enough to make "a good thing" in material terms out of dishonesty and unscrupulousness, even while he is cold-hearted, mean, vulgar, greedy and vain, then it can hardly be in his interest to become warm, sensitive, cultivated and generous; much less witty, perceptive, tactful, disinterested and wise. We would not trade places with him to be sure, for it would not be in our interests to do so in so far as we have a stake, through the investment of our wants, in excellent character. We think, and rightly so in most cases, that we could only lose by becoming worse persons, and that the change itself would constitute a loss, whatever further losses or gains it caused to our other interests (1977, pp. 288–89).

There are two respects in which this account differs from the previous one. The first is in its underlying notion of interest, which, as I have noted, is broader and essentially want-regarding. The second is the way in which it makes the appropriateness of ascribing moral harmfulness to conduct dependent on a person's prior possession of an interest in moral excellence. Thus it does not suppose that whatever interests a person has, certain virtues will be necessary, making every individual vulnerable to moral harm. The two accounts need not be totally opposed, since the second focuses on what might be considered a "minimal" or "necessary" morality, and the interest in "moral excellence" is very likely to involve more than that. Nevertheless, it is difficult to see how Feinberg's moral defective could lack an interest in all virtues and yet have and be able to realize a lifeful of plans, projects and goals.

The classical view to which I earlier referred is rooted in a tradition that is ideal-regarding rather than want-regarding (if we can allow, what I suspect is not the case, that they can be clearly differentiated). For Socrates and the Stoics, the essential self was to be identified with the soul, and disorders of the soul constituted the greatest evils. No disorder was more shameful than vice, and thus no harm greater. To cause a person to do wrong was to harm both that person and oneself. The harmfulness of wrongdoing was constituted solely by its shamefulness and not by a connection with the inability to satisfy one's interests, though on this point Aristotle seems to differ, since his notion of *eudaimonia*, to which the virtues are constitutive means, has an essentially want-regarding dimension. What is problematic about the classical view is its tendency to conflate the immoral with the harmful, resulting in the paradoxical Socratic view that a good person cannot be harmed. On the other hand, it usefully draws attention to the fact that what a person becomes, in his or her character, can constitute a harm, because *human* welfare interests include not merely "material" conditions such as bodily health and economic security but also conditions of character.

The three views that I have briefly sketched take us some way toward a defensible notion of moral harm. Although there is considerable disagreement about what character traits it would be harmful to have, this should not lead us to conclude too readily that there is a special kind of relativity about judgments of moral harm. Though they are usually less divisive, disagreements about the ingredients of bodily and psychological harm are also possible. The discussion of welfare interests or primary goods does not go on in a normative vacuum. It would, moreover, be misleading to see the notion of moral harm as linked to wants in some way that distinguishes it from other kinds of harm. It may be that a desire for moral excellence is essential to certain character traits *being experienced as* harmful, but the same might be said for bodily harms. Should a person have no commitment to his or her bodily integrity, then "invasions" of it will not be viewed by that person as harmful. Can we do without an interest in moral wholeness any more than we can do without an interest in physical wholeness? I doubt it. As we have observed on a number of occasions, human lives do not develop and flourish in isolation but in a social environment. If that social environment is to provide a suitable atmosphere for the formation and prosecution of life-plans and goals, for the exercise of our distinctive talents and capacities, then it is very likely that we, along with others, will need to have dispositions and attitudes of a reasonably determinate kind. Of course there may be some disagreement as to their precise specification. And, just because the dispositions in question will constitute part of our self-identity, those disagreements will have a special significance for us. But this should not tempt us into giving moral harm as such a more questionable status than other kinds of harm. The likelihood of ideological manipulation is not in itself a reason for relegating it to a fringe status. We should question not the notion of moral harm but what are sometimes presented as particular moral harms.

Moral Harm and the Formation of Character

There are certain contexts in which character—and in particular moral— paternalism is readily accepted. The education of children includes the formation of character, and though parents and others are often justly criticized for their tendency to indoctrinate, this does not usually amount to a rejection of character paternalism as such. Not all inculcation of dispositions, attitudes, values, and habits is indoctrinatory, but only that which results in "fixing" them so that they are no longer accessible to critical reflection (see Kleinig 1982a, ch. 5).

The interest that parents might be legitimately expected to have in the development of their children's character arises not merely from a concern for the interests of others who may later be affected by their actions, but also out of a concern and regard for the children themselves, as the developing persons they are. There is a genuinely paternalistic aspect to their nurturing activity. One reason why no pressing problem is posed is the assumption that such character paternalism is only weakly paternalistic. The development of autarchy, the process of becoming the sort of person who is capable of moving in the direction of individuality through choices of his or her own, imposes its own character requirements, and parents who sensitively seek to realize in their children those qualities of personality do not thereby exceed what they are duty-bound to do. There is, of course, a question as to which character traits might be imparted, and in view of the absence of any clear and relatively uncontroversial social understanding of procedures for justification in this regard, there is a strong case for the inclusion of open-mindedness (cf. W. Hare 1979; Kilcullen 1981). The virtue of open-mindedness is not inconsistent with the possession of most—if not all—of the values for which critics of paternalism wish to reserve a place. It does not violate or jeopardize individuality; indeed, it enables it to be socially sustained. It allows for the imparting of specific values without indoctrination. It allows for those values to be held, even firmly held, while yet remaining open to scrutiny.

Character paternalism in the case of those who can be considered competent to make their own choices is much more problematic. Just because a person's identity is bound up with his or her having a character judged harmful to have, impositions designed to change it will almost certainly be very intrusive. But our resistance may be partly due to the sorts of examples we have in mind—e.g., interferences with people's sexual activity, to keep them from corruption or to morally improve them. Other examples are trickier. What if someone's drug-taking is bringing about degenerative personality changes? Or if a person's work environment begins to assert the sort of hold over him or her that has as its end the alienation of valued relationships and possibly a breakdown (cf. Shem 1979, ch. 22). Apart from the likely counterproductivity of paternalism in such cases, there is a strong likelihood that interventions will be moralistic—they will reflect a conception of good alien to that of the individual him- or herself. Nevertheless, at an individual level, particularly in the context of close relationships, there does seem to be some space for a character paternalism that keeps a person from enslaving him- or herself to dispositions and habits that will be self-destructive.

Paternalistic Punishment

Herbert Morris suggests that strong character paternalism might be justified in the context of punishment (1981). The point is not to recommend punishment for breaches of paternalistically motivated requirements, but to see the moral good of the person punished as its *telos*. The occasion for punishment may be any offense, and not necessarily (or even at all) some self-regarding one.

A crucial feature of punishment, Morris argues, is that punished persons be *made aware* that the deprivation is being imposed because of their wrongdoing. A partial justification for this can be found in its contribution to the wrongdoer's moral good, in the sense of his or her identity as "an autonomous individual freely attached to that which is good, those relationships with others that sustain and give meaning to a life" (1981, p. 265). This has four components. First, there is an appreciation of "the nature of the evil involved for others and for oneself in one's doing wrong." The wrongdoer comes to feel remorse or contrition for what he or she has done. Second, there is a feeling of guilt about what has been done. This is explicated to include not only a feeling of pain at having done wrong, but also distress with oneself, a disposition to repair the damage, and an acceptance of "the appropriateness of some deprivation, and the making of amends." Third, the disposition toward wrongdoing is rejected and the wrongdoer pledges him- or herself to abstain from it in future. This involves repentance and self-forgiveness. And finally, there is reinforcement of "a conception of oneself as a responsible person." By evoking these responses, a person's standing as a moral agent, committed to good, is restored and affirmed, and the punishment partially justified. But not only does this paternalistic end have justificatory value, it also constrains punishment in ways not adequately accounted for on other theories. Because the good concerned must be achieved "entirely through the mediation of the wrongdoer's efforts to understand the full significance of the wrongful conduct," etc., there is no place for punishments that bypass (as in aversive conditioning) or destroy (as in capital punishment) "the human capacity for reflection, understanding, and revision of attitude" (Morris 1981, p. 265).

When it comes to justifying the inclusion of this paternalistic aim in the practice of punishment, Morris takes parental punishment as his point of departure. There, the parent attempts to help the child learn

> what as a moral person it must know, that some things are not permitted, that some wrongs are more serious than others, that it is sometimes responsible for doing wrong and sometimes not, and that its degree of blameworthiness is not always the same (1981, p. 267).

It can do this because there is an internal connection between wrongdoing and punishment. Without punishment, wrongdoing would lose the significance it has as a breach of limits on conduct. So if, as a result of punishment, the child feels guilt and is accepting of the deprivation, and commits itself to acting differently in the future, this contributes to the restoration of its relationships with others and itself and its development as a moral person.

The fact that adults are, unlike children, already responsible beings does not, Morris believes, make his theory irrelevant. Societal laws, like the moral precepts enjoined and enforced by parents, mark out the boundaries of acceptable social conduct. Not to punish transgressions of those boundaries would "baffle our moral understanding" and deprive us of means whereby guilt can be purged and relations restored. No violation of individuality is involved, since the responsibility of the wrongdoer is acknowledged. Punishment provides not only for wiping the slate with respect to others, but also for removing the stains from one's own soul. Such a theory, Morris argues, has certain advantages over its rivals, particularly in regard to the kinds of punishments that it acknowledges to be morally acceptable. Not only does it allow for excuses and mitigating circumstances to be taken into account, which places it on a par with retributivism, but it also "implies that there is a nonwaivable, nonforfeitable, nonrelinquishable right—the right to one's status as a moral being, a right that is implied in one's being a possessor of any rights at all" (1981, p. 270). This represents an advance on the retributive theory, since the latter might countenance punishments that would destroy a person's status as an autonomous being.

So much for the general theory. How does it stand up? One possible objection is that it fails to account "for the accepted disposition to punish those who are already, as it were, awakened and repentant" (1981, p. 269). But this, Morris believes, presents no problem. Penitents may be punished, indeed, will be disposed to accept its appropriateness. Not only will this provide evidence—to themselves and others—of the genuineness of their feelings, but "punishment rights the wrong, brings about closure and restores relationships that have been damaged" (1981, p. 269). Repentance as such does not heal the breach.

A second objection might be that "it cannot account for the disposition to punish those who know what the values of society are but who are indifferent to or opposed to them" (1981, p. 269). The situation here is a bit more complicated. Morris agrees that his theory "presupposes that there is a general commitment among persons to whom the norms apply to the values underlying them." So, to the extent that there is no shared commitment, the punishment will lack moral justification. A burden is thus placed on society to mend its ways, either by adjusting its punishment practices or by working toward greater moral homogeneity. This is not altogether satisfactory. While it is true that there is (or ought to be) a double onus where two moral traditions come into conflict (since there is no reason to assume that the morality of those in power is to be preferred), nevertheless, it does not follow that where agreement cannot be obtained punishment would not be justified. Though right would not necessarily belong with the party having power to punish, it might, even though no agreement could be reached. Otherwise, what is to stop the intransigent racist from continuing on his or her discriminatory way? To forgo punishment as unjustified whenever moral agreement fails is to grant to moral autonomy a status that is fundamentally illiberal. The harm principle places a limit on the exercise of autonomy that is not removed by the appeal to one's status as an autonomous being.

A third problem is generated by Morris's disclaimer that the paternalistic arguments he advances constitute the sole justification for punishment. There are retributive factors at work too. But what happens where the two kinds of considerations come into conflict? Morris's allusions to the issue of capital punishment make it clear that he wishes to give priority to the paternalistic motif. However the only reason he gives is that it "matches our moral intuitions more closely." But does it? If capital punishment is objectionable even though permitted by retributivism, that may not have anything to do with paternalism. It may be what Charles Black speaks of as "the inevitability of caprice and mistake" (1974). Or it may be the form usually taken by such punishment, though it is no part of retributivism to allow for or to prescribe a particular form of capital punishment. Our moral intuitions do not necessarily favor paternalistic over retributive punishment. Like the paternalistic theory, the retributive theory is sensitive to the claims of autarchy, and the respect and dignity which that demands, but it would be incongruous were it to ignore in penalization what it upholds in conviction. This is not to deny a place to paternalistic considerations, especially where penalties are concerned, but Morris needs to show why they should take precedence in cases where retributive justice appears to demand capital punishment (cf. Berns 1979). Although he has drawn attention to a dimension of punishment that is easily overlooked, he has tended to overstate its importance.

I indicated earlier that where there is a difference between the punishing agent and alleged offender over the wrongfulness of conduct for which punishment is proposed, there is an onus on each party to make good his or her claim. The fact that one party has proscribed conduct that the other has engaged in does not show the proscribed conduct to be wrong, or, if wrong, appropriately punished by the party that proscribed it. In some areas of criminal law this is of critical importance. Proscribed conduct is partly justified as character paternalism; yet the values that some attempt is made to secure are highly contentious. Here I wish to provide a brief discussion of three areas in which character-paternalistic reasons are commonly found: prostitution, homosexual conduct, and the circulation of pornography. Regulations have frequently been promulgated that limit these activities, and among the reasons given for such limitations has been a concern for the moral welfare of those who would be or are involved.

It is not surprising or without significance that they are all concerned with sexual activity. On the one hand, each society regulates the expression of sexual desire as such in some way or other, even if there are very marked differences in the form and content of such regulation. On the other hand, people in industrialized societies presently display considerable confusion about what, if any, kinds of regulation would be acceptable. One of the reasons for regulation and now for the confusion has been the importance of sexual activity to the "replenishing" of social resources. This is not simply a matter of procreation but also of nurture, and most societies have associated some continuing responsibility for the products of sexual activity with that activity. Given the need for a relatively stable, personalized environment if children are to contribute usefully to social perpetuation, the desirability of confining sexual activity to contexts in which there are strong and continuing relational bonds can be explained. There is considerable oversimplification here, of course, but the sketch offers a clue to our present confusion. In societies with large populations, low infant mortality rates, and increased longevity, childbearing is no longer such a pressing and important task (and certainly not so important that mothering ought to exhaust a woman's identity). Furthermore, and probably more importantly, the development of reasonably efficient contraceptive techniques has brought the nexus between sexual activity and procreation under control. As a result, the social significance of sexuality has been called into question, as has been the association of sex and love.

But sexual desire has not diminished. If anything, capitalist society has cultivated and exploited it.

PROSTITUTION

Criminalization of "the world's oldest profession" is by no means universal, and even when proscribed it is largely for nonpaternalistic reasons. It is claimed to undermine socially valued institutions and conventions, to contribute to the spread of sexually transmitted diseases, or to provide a cover or avenue for criminal activity. Whatever truth there may be in these claims, it is not at all obvious that they are strong enough to justify the proscription, as distinct from regulation through licensing, of prostitution. Additional mileage has therefore been sought in a variety of paternalistic considerations. With regard to the prostitute (him- or) herself, it has been argued that the dangers of disease, assault, exploitation, psychological impairment, and later sexual problems are sufficiently great to warrant legal concern. Patrons, too, it is argued, may suffer through their association: they may contract a disease, deteriorate psychologically, or intensify the sexual problems that prompted their resort to a prostitute. Most of these claims have been considered at length in the literature, and I shall not rehearse that discussion (see, e.g., Ericsson 1980; Richards 1980). Of more relevance at this point are certain harms to character that are said to be involved.

The harms I have in mind are said to be a consequence of "objectification." The person (usually, though not necessarily, woman) who sells sexual services indiscriminately, allows herself to engage in a form of activity in which she becomes to her client not an "other" but an "it"—merely an instrument of his desires. This might not matter so much were her body not so closely identified with her person, but since it is, the effect of her dissociation must be to undermine, in her own eyes as well as in the eyes of others (something that itself will bear on her self-perception), her standing as a person. Although it would be an exaggeration to see the transaction as strictly analogous to voluntary slavery, the effect, nevertheless, is said to be similar. What ought to be an engagement in which two parties confront each other as full persons entitled to respect is transformed into one in which one of the parties becomes merely a sexual object for the other.

We need not deny that prostitutes are frequently seen, by clients as well as nonclients, merely as loci for dissociated sexual pleasure, as bodies without minds, possessed only of an animal nature, and that this perception does not leave the prostitutes themselves untouched. A prostitute may feel ashamed of her profession. But this need not be the case, often is not the case, and where it is, may be contingent on the particular circumstances in which it is practiced. The literature on prostitution indicates that many prostitutes perform services beyond the merely sexual, addressing needs in their clients of which the sexual are but symptomatic. To some extent they function as lay therapists, and, for this to be successfully carried out, there must exist a degree of sympathetic identification between prostitute and client. The point of this is not to glamorize the life of a prostitute or even to suggest that prostitution provides an indispensable social service. Nevertheless, the popular image of a prostitute's life as one that is both degraded and degrading is largely an extrapolation from one form of it (streetwalking), its social and economic determinants, and the legal sanctions that often accompany it, rather than a concomitant of commercial sex as such.

But as well as this, the idea that prostitution is degrading depends on the acceptance and acceptability of certain views about human sexuality. This is what casts a moralistic shadow over paternalistic reasons that focus on harm to character. Prostitution is seen as self-denigrating because of an ethic that limits sexual activity to certain intimate relationships. Where sexual activity is understood paradigmatically as a statement of enduring commitment, then the indiscriminate sale of sexual services will seem an appalling practice, to which the person who engages in it might be expected to react with feelings of self-disgust and self-loathing. However, sexual activity need not be seen in this way, and whether it ought to be is a question both complex and controversial. Compare it with the practice of table-sharing. I am happy to repast more or less indiscriminately with others. But there are many who see in a shared table the expression of a deep kinship, and would consider my practice and attitudes shameful. Is sexual activity like this—or might it be— in a society where procreation is not so urgent and sexual activity may be detached from conception? The question is not rhetorical. Although I personally doubt whether sexual desire can be amoralized in the way I have conjectured, the contentiousness of the issue functions as a warning against supporting the proscription of prostitution with character-paternalistic reasons.

We might try another tack. What is shameful about prostitution, it might be said, is its *mercenary* character. Donating blood is one thing, selling it is another (cf. Singer 1973). Sexual favors are not commodities to be sold but expressions of regard that are devalued by commercialization. But once again, the argument depends on a controversial premise about the interpersonal significance of sexual activity. Does the pianist who gains her income from performing at other people's functions necessarily degrade her skills? It surely depends. And just because it depends on taking up a particular and contested viewpoint on the "meaning" of sexual activity, character-paternalistic arguments against prostitution are liable to violate the claims of individuality.

One further source for the view that prostitution is shameful can be found in the claim that prostitutes are required to perform humiliating, degrading, or "unnatural" acts. The prostitute's situation might be compared to that of a person who, in order to gain an income, allows himself to be rolled in the mud, spat at, and abused in other ways. Undoubtedly there is a side to the prostitution industry for which this claim holds true. Our culture is one in which sexual pleasure and domination are frequently linked, and the erotic power that some sexual acts possess is often dependent on the humiliation they achieve or degradation they symbolize. But such abasement and self-demeaning is not special to prostitution and may not be more prevalent in that context than in others. It does not serve to single prostitution out. There is probably something else at work in the argument—a general belief that sexual activity is dirty and disgusting, sanctified only by childbearing, and certainly not the sort of thing one would sell oneself to. This view has deep roots in our cultural tradition, going back at least as far as Augustine and Jerome, and it has continued to find influential advocates. Whatever might be said for it, it depends on claims about which there is substantial disagreement, and appeals to it in order to proscribe it will almost certainly represent an unwarranted invasion of the individual's own domain. A strict Jew or Moslem may find it difficult to appreciate how someone could enjoy the abominable practice of eating pork and not feel any shame or embarrassment about it, but to enforce that perspective on others, out of concern for their dignity, would constitute intrusive paternalism of the worst kind.

My point in this discussion has not been to defend prostitution or even to support its decriminalization, but to argue for the inappropriateness of character-paternalistic reasons. Not only are the moral perspectives on which those reasons are based contentious, but even if correct they are most probably beside the point. For to enforce them on others will deny them the respect or regard that is their due as self-reflective agents, capable of initiating their own moral inquiries and of coming to their own conclusions. So far as the effects of prostitution on character are concerned, belief in its harmfulness calls at most for argument and remonstration.

HOMOSEXUAL BEHAVIOR

Although Gerald Dworkin sees antihomosexual legislation as paternalistic, support for it has generally reflected other concerns. Some of these have been unambiguously moralistic—e.g., the belief that its alleged immorality warrants legal attention. Others have focused on offensiveness, exploitation of the vulnerable, and various social detriments that are thought to follow from toleration (see Kleinig 1977; Richards 1982, ch. 2). But it is to be doubted whether these reasons carry sufficient weight to justify the conclusions they are intended to support, and so they are frequently supplemented by arguments of a paternalistic kind.

In his Preface to *The Enforcement of Morals*, Lord Devlin writes that he agrees "with everyone who has written or spoken on the subject that homosexuality is usually a miserable way of life and that it is the duty of society, if it can, to save any youth from being led into it" (1965, p. v). He is prepared to allow that some homosexually oriented persons may find their mode of sexual activity enjoyable, but believes that the large majority "would like to get free of it if only they could." One reason, therefore, for favoring legal restrictions on homosexual behavior can be found in its effects on vulnerable and unsuspecting youths who are not in a position to appreciate what they would be letting themselves in for: destruction of character, loss of moral fibre, unhappiness, insecurity, and so on. It would also provide a motive for those who are already ensnared to moderate the expression of their proclivities or to seek help for them. Such character paternalism would, Devlin thinks, be weak rather than strong (1965, p. 136). It would be designed to counter the subtle but powerful pressures to which some find themselves subject.

To a significant extent, Devlin's argument turns on the assumption that the male homosexual (he does not consider the situation of lesbians) is a sad individual, filled with self-pity and self-loathing, beset by inclinations that he is unable to overcome and that alienate him from the most important and enriching of interpersonal transactions—marriage and family. But this picture is at best a partial and misleading one (like that often associated with spinsterhood). While it is true that there have been and are homosexual males who have felt isolated and frustrated by their postion, having been raised with values and expectations that are incompatible with their sexual dispositions, it would be wrong to see such feelings as inevitable. Whatever one might want to say about the *telos* of sexual activity or the morality of homosexual conduct, it is clear that where self-deprecation and shame are associated with with homosexuality, much of this is due to the influence of alterable social attitudes. Were there less social opprobrium, there would be significant changes in the homosexual psyche.

Perhaps it could be argued that there is a complementarity about heterosexual relationships, a potential for mutuality that enriches and develops the character, that is absent from homosexual relationships. Or that there are possibilities in heterosexual relationships (marriage and family) that provide an important framework for growth as a person, possibilities unlikely to be realized in homosexual relationships. But the factual assumptions underlying these arguments, and their conclusions, are highly contentious. Even if they were not, paternalistically motivated proscription would not be indicated, any more than it would be for celibacy. More importantly, it would deter or prevent those concerned from giving expression to some of their most powerful and valued feelings, something that would be considered destructive of personality were it demanded of heterosexually inclined people. Whatever might be said about other reasons for proscribing homosexual conduct, there is little to be said for those of a character-paternalistic kind.

Quite apart from the contentiousness of supporting the proscription of homosexual conduct by reference to paternalistic considerations, it is fairly clear from the kinds of legal response that it has commonly evoked, that the minds of legislators have not been occupied with paternalistic benevolence. Penalties authorized for the "abominable" or "nameless" crime have expressed a moralistic rather than paternalistic concern.

CENSORSHIP OF PORNOGRAPHY

Just what constitutes "pornography" is itself vigorously debated (see Feinberg 1979). On one common account, pornography is distinguished from other sexually explicit writing/depiction in virtue of its end—sexual arousal or titillation. But sometimes a further distinction has been made between erotica and pornography; the end in both cases is arousal, but the latter is said to be sexist in a way that the former is not. An even finer distinction has been drawn between soft- and hard-core pornography. The objectification involved in the former becomes associated with domination and aggression in the latter. In practice these distinctions are not always easy to make, though they have some importance so far as censorship is concerned. Few have wished to censor all sexually explicit materials; on the other hand, where efforts are made to isolate proscribable categories of materials, it is difficult to draw the line in an acceptable way.

The reasons advanced for censoring pornography (or some suitably defined subclass of pornographic materials) are manifold. Most commonly it is argued to be offensive or significantly associated with other-regarding harms. Sometimes the harms alleged to be brought about (e.g., sexual assault) are legally proscribed; sometimes a more general kind of harmfulness is alleged (e.g., the reinforcement and perpetuation of a social milieu in which women are degraded and discriminated against). But another possible reason is that pornographic materials tend to corrupt their "users." We can suggest four ways in which this might happen:

(a) Pornography gives rise to psychically deleterious masturbational fantasies. Pornography is intended to be titillating. Although this may function as a prelude to sexual intercourse, it very frequently substitutes for it by stimulating masturbational fantasies. There are two ways in which these have been considered destructive of character. (i) There is a long tradition, prominently associated with Augustine, within which masturbation is seen as a moral wrong and, if persisted in, morally degenerative. Its wrongness is said to be a function of its unnaturalness: on the one hand, it diverts sexual desire from its *telos*, sexual intercourse; on the other hand, because it frequently involves fantasized sexual activity with a person to whom one is not bound, it dissociates sexual desire from marital love. (ii) In the eighteenth and nineteenth centuries, it was commonly held that the aetiology of various physical and mental disturbances was to be found in masturbation. They ranged, in the latter case, from listlessness to insanity. Habitual masturbation was considered a disease, destructive of a person's moral and mental fiber (see E. Hare 1962; MacDonald 1967; Engelhardt 1974).

There is much here that has gone amiss. For one thing it cannot be assumed that those to whom the argument is directed, and who would be affected by any legal contraint, share the ethic in terms of which the particular harm to character is said to brought about. It is only by virtue of a particular, partisan moral tradition that masturbational fantasies, by not conforming to a "marital intercourse" model, constitute a moral harm. There may be merit in the model, but the attempt to legislate it is more likely to display a moralistic than paternalistic concern. Another difficulty with the argument relates to some of the factual claims involved. Although a great quantity of "case-study" material was produced by nineteenth-century authors, the inferences drawn from it were suspect. From an "association" between some disorder and masturbation it was illegitimately concluded that the activity of masturbation was a precipitating factor. The causal issue was begged. Since it was assumed that masturbation constituted an "unnatural" act, it was only "natural" that it should have harmful side-effects. The connection was a bit better documented in the cases of some personality/character disorders, but here it was mediated by an ethic that condemned it. It was because of feelings of guilt and anxiety, and not the practice as such, that there were serious repercussions on character and personality.

(b) Pornographic materials tend to be grossly unrealistic, creating expectations in and for sexual relations that will most probably be disappointed, leading to frustration and demoralization. Beautiful bodies, insatiable sexual appetites, life styles uncluttered by the mundane, sexual combinations generally uncomplicated by personality differences: everything, or almost everything, is directed to the intensification of sexual feeling and offered as a model for the user of pornographic materials. But the user's world is likely to be very different: bodies there are not so comely, sexual appetite is often jaded or complicated by hang-ups or reservations of various kinds, the mundane constantly obtrudes itself, and it is not usually possible to isolate sexual activity from the wider dimensions of personality and the demands they make. Pornography may seem to provide an escape, a vision of something better, but its abstracted and idealized depictions only intensify frustration. It encourages a preoccupation with sex and with a "standard of performance" in sexual relations that, because of its detachment from the larger patterns of life in which we are all embedded, will be self-destructive so far as the capacity to engage in satisfactory relations with others is concerned.

There is, I suspect, something to be said for this scenario, but it is not the only one. An opposite effect is also well documented: pornographic materials can sometimes help to "free" ailing sexual relations. In addition, there is a cathartic value that cannot be wholly discounted: pornography may provide an outlet for those with sexual preoccupations that cannot be satisfied in the context of their existing relationships. The point, once again, is not to offer an *apologia* for pornography, but to indicate the incompleteness of the argument against it. Pornography may not be the genesis of a problem so much as a response to it. And even where it contributes, it is not obvious that censorship would be an appropriate response (at least so far as the interests of character are concerned).

(c) Pornography projects an objectified and overly sexualized image of women (usually), a projection whose power to exploit our vulnerabilities makes it difficult to attain or sustain mutually enriching relationships between the sexes. This has been a frequent complaint of feminist writers. Their focus has been on the consequences for women, but it can be argued that the users are also its victims, since they become incapable of entering into and developing what would otherwise be valued and valuable relationships.

There is something to be said for this concern. The effects of labelling on relationships are well known. If a person is labelled a homosexual or insane, this tends to predominate in subsequent relationships, distorting them and detracting from their capacity to contribute to personal growth. In a society that is inclined to see women as sex objects, it is difficult to move beyond the label to the person who has been made to wear it. And even if one can move beyond, the label constantly obtrudes. But it is not obvious that this provides a ground for paternalism, much less the censorship of pornography. If men are poorer for their preoccupation with a distorted image, that may be a ground for remonstrating with them. It does not provide a reason for trying to enforce their improvement.

(d) Both conservatives and liberals have argued that Gresham's Law tends to operate in the cultural sphere: the bad drives out the good. If freely available, pornography, because of its exploitation of a powerful human drive, will be an exceedingly attractive investment proposition, and funding will tend to be diverted from more ennobling cultural enterprises. Following the success of some of the "free speech" cases in the 1950s, many erstwhile liberals complained that the constraints these decisions placed on the censor's axe did not, as was hoped, result in a profusion of literary blooms, but only in invasion by pornographic weeds (Porter 1960, pp. 69–70). Market forces, responding to and cultivating a taste for sexually arousing though aesthetically and literarily bankrupt materials, have encouraged a cultural decline, and with it a debasement of human character (Kristol 1973).

But the argument overreaches itself. Even if our present cultural excrescences show something of an obsession with detached sexuality, there is still much of literary worth available, requiring no help from the censor. And even if the level of market support for culturally elevating materials should drop dramatically, the Millian response might be preferable: subsidization of culturally significant works rather than censorship of those thought unworthy. Quite apart from the need to leave somewhat open the issue of what is and what is not worthwile, censorship here would violate the claims of individuality on a matter that is likely to be significant to the individual, and for an end that, important though it may be, it will not advance greatly.

Religious Paternalism

The legal right of parents to bring up their children in a religious tradition of their own choosing may be viewed under the rubric of either a right to the free exercise of religion or a duty to attend to the welfare of their children. If it is the former, it will almost certainly be limited by the latter.

The free exercise of religion cannot encompass child sacrifice. Nor can it extend to acts incompatible with the public interest—the religious refusal to permit a child to be vaccinated against an infectious disease. Of course, from the fact that parents have a particular legal right, it does not follow that they are right to do as they do in regard to their children's religious understanding. This is due partly to the problematic status of religious *Weltanschauungen* and partly to their questionable compatibility with the goal of autarchy. A parent who shields its child from physical danger is almost certainly acting in the child's interests; the parent who inculcates in its child a particular religious understanding is less obviously doing so. Yet despite this, a parent may view the imparting of a particular *Weltanschauung* as a matter of preeminent importance. The reason for this becomes clear if religion is understood functionally rather than ontologically—as the concern with "ultimate" and synoptic questions rather than belief in God or gods. Our approach to such questions is generally crucial to our self-understanding, to our pattern of values, and consequently to the ordering of our life-plans and goals. Parents may therefore see it both as a central concern of their own and as of crucial importance to their children that the latter are nurtured within a particular religious tradition.

So far as young children are concerned, religious paternalism is likely to be weak rather than strong. As such it will not be violative of their individuality. Lacking autarchy, they are not able to make rational choices of their own, and it must fall to others to guide them in paths thought to be beneficial. However, just because religious education is usually considered so important by those who provide or require it, there is a serious risk associated with it. This is the likelihood of indoctrination. Weak paternalistic constraints are justified to the extent that they are aimed at growth in autarchy or at least do not impede it. But indoctrination in a religious tradition is not compatible with the requirements of autarchy and ultimately of individuality, for it removes from scrutiny a significant and substantial portion of belief and experience. Where religious beliefs have been indoctrinated, self-initiated remedies are unlikely, since the criteria in terms of which any self-scrutiny is likely to be undertaken will be suffused with values derived from and hence congruent with the religious tradition. It is important, therefore, that where religious traditions are consciously inculcated, intellectual and emotional space is left for genuine review.

The issue of religious paternalism has recently been given a critical focus by the activities of certain religious organizations and the methods used to counteract their influence. Young adults, frequently from middle-class backgrounds and engaged in preparation for a career, have suddenly given up their ambitions and rejected their families in order to associate with highly demanding religious groups with which they have previously had little association and for which they would have previously had little attraction. Parents and others have charged that their new-found allegiance has been produced by a combination of deception and "brainwashing," "mind-control," or "programming," and that there is justification for their forcible or legally coerced detention and "deprogramming" (see Enroth 1977; Delgado 1977). Some civil libertarians, however, have claimed that parental concern represents little more than an unwillingness by parents "to admit to themselves that the kid they devoted 15 or 20 years to has rejected them and their values" (Szasz, quoted in Delgado 1977, p. 81; cf. Kelley 1977).

Several issues are embedded in this debate. First, has commitment to the groups concerned been brought about by means subversive of autonomy? Second, if it has, do the consequences for those involved call for a weakly paternalistic response? Third, are there social consequences that warrant some form of social response? And fourth, does "deprogramming" constitute an acceptable counteraction? For present purposes, we can leave aside the third question.

(i) Although it is not always the case, we can assume that we are dealing with people who, up to the time of their involvement, would have been considered capable of making their own choices *vis-à-vis* religious matters. Why should their sudden change of orientation not be consistent with this? Appeals to the suddenness of the change and the unrelatedness of their new views to those previously held do not show the commitment to be nonvoluntarily arrived at. At most they serve to raise the question. What is of greater concern are the process and techniques used to bring about the reorientation. Here it is argued that despite an appearance of voluntary participation in the joining process, it is often permeated by responsibility-diminishing strategies. Deception is frequently charged. In the initial stages, information that might alienate the contact is withheld; it is made known only at a later stage of the induction process, when the initiate has a diminished capacity to assess it with any independence. There are two aspects to this: first, there is a segmentation of the joining process into a series of steps, "whereby the convert's assent is obtained before proceeding to the next step, but the final stage or end result is concealed from view" (Delgado 1977, p. 55); and second, there is a "conscious manipulation of knowledge and capacity in such a way that the convert's knowledge of the cult and his future role in it is increased only as his capacity to act intelligently and independently on that knowledge diminishes" (Delgado 1977, p. 8; cf. pp. 54–55).

In addition to deception, it is claimed that various forms of duress are frequently involved. For example, the induction program is conducted at at remote and isolated location, so that withdrawal and "reality-testing" are difficult; activities are arranged in such a way that exhaustion is likely and there is little time for serious reflection on the new perspectives that are being projected. As well, there is an exploitation of the initiate's vulnerabilities—usually his or her idealism and sense of guilt.

It is argued that these responsibility-diminishing factors, though sometimes present in other and unobstructed social transactions, are here concatenated and intensified, thus differentiating them with sufficient clarity to avoid most line-drawing problems. Of course, a mere recitation of such claims is not sufficient to establish them, and, even if sometimes correct, they ought not to become the cloak for a generalized attack on the groups concerned. In addition, it needs to be recognized that some of those who join may do so without any need for deception or manipulation. What may seem to some to be simplistic views may not appear that way to all.

(ii) Even if a person has come to hold opinions as a result of manipulation by others, that may not warrant our intervention. There could be two reasons for this. One, which we will take up later, is that the harms of intervention would outweigh any detriment resulting from the "programmed" ideas. The other is that the perspectives, life style, and identity acquired through manipulation is not harmful to the convert. Those who favor intervention dispute this latter claim.

However, we need to exercise a good deal of care in arguing for the harmfulness of a life style that the convert now enthusiastically espouses. Such claims are likely to betray moralistic concerns. As Dean Kelley writes,

> visions are conjured up of adolescents enslaved to an alien Moloch, bound to an endless round of mindless and abject servitude, obliterating from their lives the bright promise of upwardly-mobile business and professional careers (1977, pp. 27–28).

But there are other harms alleged, which if substantiated, would provide a less tendentious basis for paternalistic concern. These would include a tendency to disintegrate psychologically—the loss of a capacity to think for oneself, an inability to cope with the world and noncult relationships, maturational arrest, and physical degeneration (see Delgado 1977, pp. 10–25). Even here, however, there is a potential for exaggeration and bias, and the need for a case-by-case assessment, should interference with a cult member be contemplated, is strong.

(iii) The doctrine of the least restrictive alternative requires that where an end is justifiably sought, then, *ceteris paribus*, it ought to be effected by the least intrusive means. Given that a major aspect of concern is the techniques used to induce commitment, one strategy would be to require that the induction process be conducted in a manner that enables potential members to retain control over any decisions they make. Provisions found elsewhere in the legal system might be utilized here: identification of the group and a truthful statement of its purposes in making contact; a "cooling-off" provision; limitations on permissible techniques, etc. The point would not be to outlaw the group's doctrines or to deny its right to exist, but to ensure that in its operation it respected the requisites for individuality.

With regard to those who are already committed to the group, the least restrictive course would simply be to anticipate eventual disenchantment, which might not seem so fanciful, given the simplistic understandings that such groups espouse. But it is frequently maintained that group pressures and the maturational arrest induced by membership make this very unlikely. Stronger measures are justified. The belief that this is so has led, on the one hand, to informal nonvoluntary detainment of group members and their subjection to techniques that are designed to enable them to stand back from the web of belief and feeling within which they have become enmeshed. Alternatively, it has led to the securing of limited conservatorship orders so that supervised deprogramming can take place. Although the former method appears to have been the more usual and is probably the more streamlined, its informality has undoubtedly been responsible for considerable abuse. In some cases, this has involved the use of violence and humiliation; in other cases, the occasion for "deprogramming" has simply been a young adult's defection from parental values. There is a need to ensure that the claims of individuality are respected and that the deprogramming process be designed, not to erase commitment, but to restore a capacity for self-determination. Continued commitment to the group should be seen as an option, but as one freely chosen.

Nevertheless, it has to be recognized that process and content cannot be separated as easily as it is sometimes assumed. For an important ingredient of deprogramming technique has often been to confront the cult member with inconsistencies in the group's beliefs, and facts about its leader(s) and the group, which are designed to undermine certitude. But there may be an obligation to develop and use deprogramming strategies that leave maximal room for the option of voluntary recommitment.

It is the concern with ensuring restoration of autarchy that both illuminates and calls into question the legitimacy of religious paternalism. For what deprogramming is all about is not an ensuring of beneficial religious commitment or a securing from harmful religious commitment as such, but with reestablishing the capacity for choice over a large area of life. While that is not itself a reason for seeking to withdraw from all forms of genuinely religious paternalism, it emphasizes the importance of taking care that autarchy is not subverted in the process.

There is one final aspect of religious paternalism to which we might briefly advert, though it does not strictly fall under the rubric of character paternalism. Religion is not simply a matter of character, in the sense of beliefs, dispositions, attitudes, and so forth, but it also has a public aspect. Beliefs are embodied in practices. In some cases these practices may involve significant risk to those who engage in them, and the question arises as to whether paternalistically motivated interference might be justified. Participants in snake-handling cults, for example, run a significant risk of being injured or even killed; Jehovah's Witnessess who refuse blood transfusions greatly increase their chances of death during surgery; members of sects that eschew all medical treatment frequently come to grief as a result; and self-mutilation might be practiced in response to some "divine directive." Paternalistic reasons have sometimes been cited as justifications for interfering with such practices.[1]

Even though interference in these cases has bodily integrity as its immediate or direct concern, it is not unreasonable to see it as evidencing a measure of religious paternalism. For it is in virtue of their religious commitments that those involved run the risks they do, and the significance of what they do can be understood only in the light of their religious commitments. Just because this is so, paternalistically motivated interventions, except where there is good reason to think that the religious commitment is delusional, will almost certainly violate the requirements of individuality, and will do this in a particularly intrusive way.

Notes

1. For snake-handling cases, see *Lawson* v. *Commonwealth*, 291 Ky. 437, 164 S.W. 2d 972 (1942); *Harden* v. *State*, 188 Tenn. 17, 216 S.W. 2d 179 (1949), appeal dismissed *sub nom. Bunn* v. *North Carolina*, 336 U.S. 942 (1949); *Hill* v. *State*, 38 Ala. App. 623, 88 So. 2d 880 (Ct. App. 1956), cert. denied, 38 Ala. 697, 88 So. 2d 887 (1956). Discussions of transfusion cases can be found in How 1960, Milhollin 1965, Ford 1964, Anon. 1967, Anon. 1972a, Cantor 1973. The espousal of faith healing as against medical treatment is treated in Antieu 1949 and Cawley 1954, as well as some of the above. Self-mutilation is discussed in D.B.H. 1968 and Rubinow 1969.

Less risky practices have also been interfered with—e.g., the use of peyote by members of the Native American Church. However, in *People* v. *Woody*, 61 Cal. 2d 716, 394 P. 2d 813, 40 Cal. Rptr. 69 (1964) this prohibition was held to be unconstitutional, so far as members of the Native American Church were concerned. A similar point was made in *Shapiro* v. *Lyle*, 30 F. 2d 971 (W.D. Wash., 1929), where it was argued that the prohibition law did not apply to the use of sacramental wine.

References and Bibliography

Abernethy, Virginia, and Lundin, Keith. 1980. Competency and the Right to Refuse Medical Treatment. In *Frontiers in Medical Ethics: Applications in a Medical Setting*, ed. Virginia Abernethy, pp. 79–98. Cambridge, Mass.: Ballinger.

Abromovsky, Abraham, and McCarthy, Francis Barry. 1977. Civil Commitment of Non-Criminal Narcotic Addicts: Parens Patriae; A Valid Exercise of a State's Police Power; Or an Unconscionable Disregard of Individual Liberty? *University of Pittsburgh Law Review* 38 (Spring): 477–503.

Ackerman, Terrence F. 1982. Why Doctors Should Intervene. *Hastings Center Report* 12 (August): 14–17.

Alanen, Arnold R., and Peltin, Thomas J. 1978. Kohler, Wisconsin: Planning and Paternalism in a Model Industrial Village. *American Institute of Planners Journal* 44 (April): 145–59.

Alstyne, W.W. Van. 1968. The Demise of the Right-Privilege Distinction in Constitutional Law. *Harvard Law Review* 81 (May): 1439–64.

American Medical Association. 1848. *Code of Ethics*. New York: H. Ludwig & Co.

————. 1982. *Current Opinions of the Judicial Council of the American Medical Association—1982*. Chicago: AMA.

Annas, George, J. 1982. Prison Hunger Strikes: Why the Motive Matters. *Hastings Center Report* 12 (December): 21–22.

Anon. 1964. Note: The Disguised Oppression of Involuntary Guardianship: Have the Elderly Freedom to Spend?. *Yale Law Journal* 73 (March): 676–92.

Anon. 1966. Note: Compulsory Medical Treatment: The State's Interest Re-evaluated. *Minnesota Law Review* 51: 293–305.

Anon. 1967. Compulsory Medical Treatment and the Free Exercise of Religion. *Indiana Law Journal* 42: 386–404.

Anon. 1967a. Note: Civil Commitment of Narcotic Addicts. *Yale Law Journal* 76 (May): 1160–89.

Anon. 1968. Note: Seat Belt Legislation and Judicial Reaction. *St. John's Law Review* 42 (January): 371–93.

Anon. 1968a. Note: Constitutional Law—Police Power—Michigan Statute Requiring Motorcyclists to Wear Protective Helmets Held Unconstitutional. *Michigan Law Review* 67 (December): 360–73.

Anon. 1969. Note: Constitutional Law—Police Power—Motorcycle Crash Helmet Laws' Relation to Public Welfare—American Motorcycle Association v. Davids,—Mich. App.—, 158 N.W. 2d 72 (1968). *Wisconsin Law Review* 1: 320–27.

Anon. 1972. Laws Requiring Use of Seat Belts. *Traffic Laws Commentary* (U.S. Department of Transportation) 1 (October): 15–22.

Anon. 1972. An Adult's Right to Resist Blood Transfusions: A View Through John F. Kennedy Memorial Hospital v. Heston. *Notre Dame Lawyer* 47 (February): 571–87.

Anon. 1975. News item, *Status Report (Insurance Institute for Highway Safety)* 10 (15 September): 4.

Anon. 1977. *Jehovah's Witnesses and the Question of Blood*. Brooklyn, N.Y.: Watchtower Bible and Tract Society of New York, Inc. & International Bible Students Association.

Anon. 1977a. Helmet Law Repeals Bring More Deaths: NHTSA. *Status Report (Insurance Institute for Highway Safety)* 12 (2 March): 11–12.

Anon. 1981. Fasten Your Safety Belts. *The Guardian Weekly* (9 August): 10.

Antieu, Chester J. 1949. The Limitation of Religious Liberty. *Fordham Law Review* 18 (November): 221–41.

Aquinas, St. Thomas. 1975. *Summa Theologiae*, vol. 38, trans. Marcus Lefébure, London: Blackfriars, in conjunction with Eyre & Spottiswoode; New York: McGraw-Hill. Esp. 2a2ae, qu.77.

Arneson, Richard J. 1980. Mill versus Paternalism. *Ethics* 90 (July): 470–80. An earlier version appears in *Philosophy Research Archives* 5 (1979): 89–119.

—————. 1982. Democracy and Liberty in Mill's Theory of Government. *Journal of the History of Philosophy* 20 (January): 43–64.

Atiyah, P.S. 1979. *The Rise and Fall of Freedom of Contract*. Oxford: Clarendon Press.

Azumi, Koya. 1977. Japan's Changing World of Work. *Wilson Quarterly* 1 (Summer): 72–80.

Baker, Susan P., and Toret, Stephen P. 1981. Freedom and Protection: A Balancing of Interests. *American Journal of Public Health* 71 (March): 295–97.

Baron, Charles H. (1978). Assuring "Detached but Passionate Investigation and Decision": The Role of Guardians Ad Litem in *Saikewicz*-type Cases. *American Journal of Law & Medicine* 4 (Summer): 111–30.

—————. 1979. Medical Paternalism and the Rule of Law: A Reply to Dr. Relman. *American Journal of Law & Medicine* 4 (Winter): 337–65.

Barry, Brian. 1965. *Political Argument*. London: Routledge & Kegan Paul.

Barry, Vincent. 1982. *Moral Aspects of Health Care*. Belmont, Calif.: Wadsworth.

Bartholome, William G., and Gaylin, Willard. 1982. Correspondence: In Defense of a Child's Right to Assent. *Hastings Center Report* 12 (October): 44–45.

Battin, M. Pabst. 1982. *Ethical Issues in Suicide* ch.5. Englewood Cliffs, N.J.: Prentice-Hall.

Baumgarten, Elias. 1980. The Concept of "Competence" in Medical Ethics. *Journal of Medical Ethics* 6 (December): 180–84.

Baumgartner, Leona, and Ramsey, Elizabeth Mapelsden. 1933. Johann Peter Frank and his "System einer vollständigen medizinischen Polizei". *Annals of Medical History* 5: 525–32; 6: 69–90.

Bayer, Ronald; Dworkin, Gerald; Leichter, Howard; Field, Mark G.; and Powell, David E. 1981. Voluntary Health Rules and Public Policy. *Hastings Center Report* 11 (October): 26–44.

Bayles, Michael D. 1973. Comments: Offensive Conduct and the Law. In *Issues in Law and Morality*, eds. Norman S. Care, and Thomas K. Trelogan, pp. 111–26. Cleveland: Case Western Reserve University Press.

—————. 1974. Criminal Paternalism. In *Nomos XV: Limits of Law*, eds. J. Roland Pennock & John W. Chapman, pp. 174–88. New York: Lieber Atherton.

—————. 1978. *Principles of Legislation: The Uses of Political Authority*. Detroit: Wayne State University Press.

—————. 1979. Catch-22 Paternalism and Mandatory Genetic Screening. In *Medical Responsibility: Paternalism, Informed Consent, and Euthanasia*, eds. Wade L. Robison, and Michael S. Pritchard, pp. 29–42. Clifton, N.J.: Humana Press.

Beardsley, Elizabeth L. 1981. Legislators and the Morality of their Constituents. In *Ethical Issues in Government*, ed. Norman E. Bowie, pp. 83–89. Philadelphia: Temple University Press.

Beauchamp, Dan E. 1976. Public Health as Social Justice. *Inquiry* 13: 3–14.

—————. 1980. Public Health and Individual Liberty. *Annual Review of Public Health*. 1: 121–36.

Beauchamp, Tom L. 1976. An Analysis of Hume's Essay "On Suicide". *Review of Metaphysics* 30 (September): 73–95.

————. 1976. On Justifications for Coercive Genetic Control. In *Biomedical Ethics and the Law*, eds. Robert F. Almeder, and James M. Humber, pp. 361–73. New York: Plenum Press.

————.1977a. Paternalism and Biobehavioral Control. *Monist* 60 (January): 62–80.

————. 1977b. s.v. Paternalism. In *Encyclopedia of Bioethics*, ed. William T. Reich, vol. 3, pp. 1194–1201. New York: The Free Press.

————. 1978. The Regulation of Hazards and Hazardous Behaviors. In *Ethical Issues in Public Health Policy: Health Education and Lifestyle Interventions*, eds. Ruth A. Fadden, and Alan Faden. *Health Education Monographs* 6 (Summer): 242–57.

————. 1981. Paternalism and Refusals to Sterilize. In *Rights and Responsibilities in Medicine*, ed. Marc D. Basson, pp. 137–43. New York: Alan R. Liss.

————. 1983. Medical Paternalism, Voluntariness, and Comprehension. In *Ethical Principles for Social Policy*, ed. John Howie, pp. 123–43. Carbondale & Edwardsville: Southern Illinois University Press.

Beauchamp, Tom L., and Childress, James F. 1979. *Principles of Biomedical Ethics*. New York: Oxford University Press.

Beaver, James E. 1968. The "Mentally Ill" and the Law: Sisyphus and Zeus. *Utah Law Review* (March): 1–71.

Bedau, Hugo Adam. 1975. Physical Interventions to Alter Behavior: Some Reflections on New Technology. *American Behavioral Scientist* 18 (May/June): 657–77.

Benham, B.J. 1978. None so Holy as the Recently Converted—Malefic Generosity and Multicultural Education. *Educational Studies* 9 (Summer): 125–31.

Benjamin, Martin, and Curtis, Joy. 1981. *Ethics in Nursing*. New York: Oxford University Press.

Benn, S.I. 1967. Freedom and Persuasion. *Australasian Journal of Philosophy* 45 (July): 259–75.

————. 1975–76. Freedom, Autonomy and the Concept of a Person. *Proceedings of the Aristotelian Society*, N.S. 76: 109–30.

————. 1981. Benevolent Interference and Respect for Persons: Comments on Papers by John Kleinig, Cathy Lowy, and Robert Young. *Bulletin of the Australian Society of Legal Philosophy* 21 (December): 99–112.

————. 1982. Individuality, Autonomy, and Community. In *Community as a Social Ideal*, ed. E. Kamenka, pp. 43–62. London: Edward Arnold.

Bentham, Jeremy. 1789. *Introduction to the Principles of Morals and Legislation*. ed. Wilfrid Harrison. Oxford: Blackwell, 1948.

Berlin, Isaiah. 1969. *Four Essays on Liberty*. London: Oxford University Press.

Berns, Walter. 1979. *For Capital Punishment: Crime and the Morality of the Death Penalty*. New York: Basic Books.

Birenbaum, Rhonda. 1983. Seatbelts Save Heads, Bruise Chests. *The Medical Post* (Toronto) 19 (25 January): 24.

Bishop, Ronald C. 1980. The Legalization of Laetrile. In *Ethics, Humanism, and Medicine*, ed, Marc D. Basson, pp. 173–77. New York: Alan R. Liss.

Black, Charles L., Jr. 1974. *Capital Punishment: the Inevitability of Caprice and Mistake*. New York: W.W. Norton.

Blackstone, William. 1783. *Commentaries on the Laws of England*. London: reissued by Garland Publishing Co. (N.Y.), 1978. 4 vols.

Blustein, Jeffrey. 1982. *Parents and Children: The Ethics of the Family*. New York: Oxford University Press.

Bok, Sissela. 1974. The Ethics of Giving Placebos. *Scientific American* 231 (November): 17–23.

————. 1975. Paternalistic Deception in Medicine. In *Problems of Choice and Decision*, ed. Max Black, pp. 73–107. Ithaca, N.Y.: Cornell University Programs on Science, Technology and Society.

————. 1978a. Lying to Children: The Risks of Paternalism. *Hastings Center Report* 8 (June): 10–13.

————. 1978b. *Lying*. New York: Pantheon.

Bonnie, Richard J. 1978. Discouraging Unhealthy Personal Choices: Reflections on New Directions in Substance Abuse Policy. *Journal of Drug Issues* 8 (Spring): 199–219.

Bosanquet, Bernard. 1899. *The Philosophical Theory of the State*. London: Macmillan.

Brandon, E.P. 1979. The Key of the Door. *Educational Philosophy and Theory* 11 (March): 23–34.

Brock, Dan W. 1979. Moral Rights and Permissible Killing. In *Ethical Issues Relating to Life and Death*, ed. John Ladd, pp. 94–117. New York: Oxford University Press.

————. 1983. Paternalism and Promoting the Good. In Sartorius (1983).

Brooks, Alexander D. 1974. *Law, Psychiatry and the Mental Health System*. Boston: Little, Brown & Co.

Bruce, Andrew A. 1926. The Private Stock of Liquor and the Inherent Right of Self-Destruction. *Illinois Law Review* 20 (April): 757–76.

Brumbaugh, Robert S. 1968. Protection from One's Self: A Socratic Dialogue on Maycock [sic] v. Martin. *Connecticut Bar Journal* 42: 465–9

Buchanan, Allen. 1978. Medical Paternalism. *Philosophy & Public Affairs* 7 (Summer): 370–90.

————. 1979. Medical Paternalism or Legal Imperialism: Not the Only Alternatives for Handling *Saikewicz*-type Cases. *American Journal of Law & Medicine* 5 (Summer): 97–117.

————. 1981. The Limits of Proxy Decisionmaking for Incompetents. *UCLA Law Review* 29 (December): 386–408. Another version appears in Sartorius (ed.) (1983).

————. 1982. *Marx & Justice: The Radical Critique of Liberalism*. Totowa, N.J.: Rowman & Littlefield.

Buchanan, James M. 1970. In Defence of *Caveat Emptor*. *University of Chicago Law Review*. 38 (January): 64–73.

Burt, Robert A. 1971. Forcing Protection on Children and their Parents: the Impact of *Wyman v. James*. *Michigan Law Review* 69 (June): 1259–1310.

Byrn, Robert M. 1975. Compulsory Livesaving Treatment for the Competent Adult. *Fordham Law Review* 44: 1–36.

Calabresi, Guido. 1970. *The Costs of Accidents: A Legal and Economic Analysis*. New Haven: Yale University Press.

Callahan, Daniel. 1981. Minimalist Ethics. *Hastings Center Report* 11 (October): 19–25.

Cantor, Norman. 1973. A Patient's Decision to Decline Life-Saving Medical Treatment: Bodily Integrity Versus the Preservation of Life. *Rutgers Law Review* 26: 228–64.

Carlton, Wendy. 1978. *"In Our Professional Opinion . . . ": The Primacy of Clinical Judgment over Moral Choice*. Notre Dame: University of Notre Dame Press.

Carroll, Mary Ann, and Humphrey, Richard A. 1979. *Moral Problems in Nursing: Case Studies*. Washington, D.C.: University Press of America, ch. 7.

Carter, Rosemary. 1977. Justifying Paternalism. *Canadian Journal of Philosophy* 7 (March): 133–45.

Cassell, Eric J. 1976. *The Healer's Art: A New Approach to the Doctor-Patient Relationship*. Philadelphia: J.B. Lippincott.

————. 1981a. Do Justice, Love Mercy: The Inappropriateness of the Concept of Justice Applied to Bedside Decisions. In *Justice and Health Care*, ed. Earl E. Shelp, pp. 75–82. Dordrecht: D. Reidel.

————. 1981b. The Refusal to Sterilize Elizabeth Stanley is not Paternalism. In *Rights and Responsibilities in Modern Medicine*, ed. Marc D. Basson, pp. 145–52. New York: Alan R. Liss.

Cawley, C.C. 1954. Criminal Liability in Faith Healing. *Minnesota Law Review* 39 (December): 48–74.

Chambers, David. 1976. The Principle of the Least Restrictive Alternative: The Constitutional Issues. In *The Mentally Retarded Citizen and the Law*, eds. Michael Kindred et al., pp. 486–99. New York: Plenum Press.

Charrette, Edmond E., et al. 1976. Letters to Editor: Life Styles: Controlled or Libertarian. *New England Journal of Medicine* 294 (March): 732–33.

Chesney-Lind, Meda. 1977. Judicial Paternalism and the Female Status Offender: Training Women to know their Place. *Crime & Delinquency* 23 (April): 121–30.
Chesterton, G. K. 1909. *Orthodoxy: The Flag of the World.* London: John Lane.
Childress, James F. 1979a. The Burn Victim and Medical Paternalism. *The New Physician* 28 (September): 37–38.
————. 1979b. Paternalism and Health Care. In *Medical Responsibility: Paternalism, Informed Consent, and Euthanasia,* eds. Wade L. Robison, and Michael S. Pritchard, pp. 15–27. Clifton, N.J.: Humana Press.
————. 1980. Paternalism and Autonomy in Medical Decisionmaking. In *Frontiers in Medical Ethics: Applications in a Medical Setting,* ed. Virginia Abernethy, pp. 27–41. Cambridge, Mass.: Ballinger. A revised version appears as Paternalism and the Patient's Right to Decide, in James F. Childress. *Priorities in Biomedical Ethics.* Philadelphia: Westminster Press, 1981, ch. 1.
————. 1982. Beneficence and Health Policy: Reduction of Risk-Taking. In *Beneficence and Health Care,* ed. Earl E. Shelp, pp. 223–38. Dordrecht: D. Reidel.
Chodoff, Paul. 1976. The Case for Involuntary Hospitalization of the Mentally Ill. *American Journal of Psychiatry* 133 (May): 496–501.
Christy, Nicholas P. 1980. Who's in Charge Here? *Man and Medicine* 5: 203–6.
Clark, Brian. 1978. *Whose Life Is It Anyway? A Play.* London: Samuel French.
Clarke, John R.; Sorenson, John H.; and Hare, John E. 1980. The Limits of Paternalism in Health Care. *Hastings Center Report* 10 (December): 20–22. [seperate entry]
Clarke, P.H. 1975. Unequal Bargaining Power in the Law of Contract. *Australian Law Journal* 49 (May): 229–33.
Cobey, Christopher. 1974. Note: The Resurgence and Validity of Anti-Smoking Legislation. *University of California Davis Law Review* 7: 167–95.
Cohen, Carl. 1978. Medical Experimentation on Prisoners. *Perspectives in Biology and Medicine* 21 (Spring): 357–72.
————. 1980. On the Right of the Patient to Know. In *Ethics, Humanism, and Medicine,* ed. Marc D. Basson, pp. 23–30. New York: Alan R. Liss.
Cohen, G.A. 1979. The Labor Theory of Value and the Concept of Exploitation. *Philosophy & Public Affairs* 8 (Summer): 338–60.
Countermeasures Development, Road and Motor Vehicle Traffic Safety, Ministry of Transport. 1974. *The Seat Belt Argument.* Ottawa: Transport Canada.
Cranston, Ross. 1978. *Consumers and the Law.* London: Weidenfeld and Nicolson.
Crawford, Robert. 1978. Sickness as Sin. *Health/Pac Bulletin* 80: 10–16.
Crimm, Allan, and Greenberg, Raymond. 1981. Reflections on the Doctor-Patient Relationship. In *Ethical Dimensions of Clinical Medicine,* ed. Dennis A. Robbins, pp. 104–10. Springfield: C.C. Thomas.
Crocker, Lawrence. 1980. *Positive Liberty: An Essay in Normative Political Philosophy.* The Hague: Martinus Nijhoff.
Cryer, Philip E., and Kissane, John M. 1978. Primary Amenorrhea in an Elderly Woman. *American Journal of Medicine* 65 (September): 514–20.
Culver, Charles M.; Ferrell, Richard B.; and Green, Ronald M. 1980. ECT and Special Problems of Informed Consent. *American Journal of Psychiatry* 137 (May): 586–91.
Culver, Charles M., and Gert, Bernard. 1981. The Morality of Involuntary Hospitalization. In *The Law-Medicine Relation: A Philosophical Exploration,* eds. Stuart F. Spicker, Joseph M. Healy, and H. Tristram Englehardt, Jr., pp. 159–75. Dordrecht: Reidel.
————. 1982. *Philosophy in Medicine: Conceptual and Ethical Issues in Medicine and Psychiatry.* New York: Oxford University Press.
D'Agostino, Fred. 1982. Mill, Paternalism and Psychiatry. *Australasian Journal of Philosophy* 60 (December): 319–30.
Davis, Anne J., and Aroskar, Mila A. 1978. *Ethical Dilemmas and Nursing Practice.* New York: Appleton-Century-Crofts.
Day, J.P. 1970. On Liberty and the Real Will. *Philosophy* 45 (July): 177–92.
De George, Richard T. 1982. *Business Ethics.* New York: Macmillan, ch. 11.
Delgado, Richard. 1977. Religious Totalism: Gentle and Ungentle Persuasion under the First Amendment. *Southern California Law Review* 51 (November): 1–98.

Department of Health, Education, and Welfare (U.S.). 1972. *The Health Consequences of Smoking: A Report of the Surgeon General.* DHEW Publication No. (HSM) 72–7516. Washington, D.C.: U.S. Government Printing Office.

_____. 1979. *Healthy People: The Surgeon General's Report On Health Promotion and Disease Prevention. Background Papers.* DHEW Publication No. (PHS) 79–55071A. Washington, D.C. U.S. Government Printing Office.

Dershowitz, Alan M. 1968. Psychiatry in the Legal Process: "A Knife that Cuts Both Ways". *Judicature* 51 (May): 370–77.

Devlin, Patrick. 1965. *The Enforcement of Morals.* London: Oxford University Press.

Dooley-Clarke, Dolores. 1981. Medical Ethics and Political Protest. *Hastings Center Report* 11, (December): 5–8

Downie, R.S. 1971. *Roles and Values: An Introduction to Social Ethics.* London: Methuen.

Dresser, Rebecca S. 1982. Ulysses and the Psychiatrists: A Legal and Policy Analysis of the Voluntary Commitment Contract. *Harvard Civil Rights—Civil Liberties Law Review* 16 (Winter): 777–854.

Duggan, A.J. 1982. *The Economics of Consumer Protection: A Critique of The Chicago School Case Against Intervention.* University of Adelaide: Adelaide Law Review Association.

Dworkin, Gerald. 1971. Paternalism. In *Morality and the Law*, ed. Richard A. Wasserstrom, pp. 107–26. Belmont, Calif.: Wadsworth.

_____. 1982. Is More Choice Better Than Less? In *Midwest Studies in Philosophy*, ed. Peter A. French, vol. 7. Minneapolis: University of Minnesota Press.

_____. 1983. Paternalism: Some Second Thoughts. In Sartorius (1983).

Ellin, Joseph. 1978. Comments on "Paternalism and Health Care". In *Contemporary Issues in Biomedical Ethics*, eds. John W. Davis; Barry Hoffmaster; and Sarah Shorten, pp. 245–54. Clifton, N.J.: Humana Press.

_____. 1981. The Solution to a Dilemma in Medical Ethics. *Westminster Institute Review* (May): 3–6.

Elliott, Rogers, and Tighe, Thomas. 1968. Breaking the Cigarette Habit: Effects of a Technique Involving a Threatened Loss of Money. *Psychological Record* 18 (October): 503–13.

Elster, Jon. 1977. Ulysses and the Sirens: A Theory of Imperfect Rationality. *Social Science Information* 16: 469–526.

_____. 1979. *Ulysses and the Sirens: Studies in Rationality and Irrationality.* Cambridge: Cambridge University Press.

Engelhardt, H. Tristram, Jr. 1974. The Disease of Masturbation: Values and the Concept of Disease. *Bulletin of the History of Medicine* 48 (Summer): 234–48.

_____. 1978. Rights and Responsibilities of Patients and Physicians. In *Medical Treatment of the Dying: Moral Issues*, eds. Michael D. Bayles, and Dallas M. High, pp. 9–29. Cambridge, Mass.: Schenkman.

Enroth, Ronald M. 1977. *Youth, Brainwashing, and the Extremist Cults.* Grand Rapids: Zondervan.

Ericsson, Lars O. 1980. Charges against Prostitution: An Attempt at a Philosophical Assessment. *Ethics* 90 (April): 335–66.

Ewin, R.E. 1981. *Co-operation and Human Values.* New York: St. Martin's Press.

Faden, Ruth R., and Beauchamp, Tom L. 1980. Decision-Making and Informed Consent: A Study of the Impact of Disclosed Information. *Social Indicators Research* 7: 313–36.

Faden, Ruth A., and Faden, Alan. 1977. False Belief and the Refusal of Medical Treatment. *Journal of Medical Ethics* 3: 133.

Fedden, Henry Romilly. 1938. *Suicide: A Social and Historical Study.* London: Peter Davies.

Feinberg, Joel. 1971. Legal Paternalism. *Canadian Journal of Philosophy* 1 (September): 105–24.

_____. 1973. *Social Philosophy.* Englewood Cliffs, N.J.: Prentice-Hall.

_____. 1977. Harm and Self-Interest. In *Law, Morality, and Society: Essays in Honour of H.L.A. Hart*, eds., P.M.S. Hacker and J. Raz, pp. 285–308. Oxford: Clarendon Press, 1977.

————— . 1979. Pornography and the Criminal Law. *University of Pittsburgh Law Review* 40: 567–604.

————— . 1980a. *Rights, Justice, and the Bounds of Liberty.* Princeton: Princeton University Press.

————— . 1980b. The Child's Right to an Open Future. In *Whose Child? Children's Rights, Parental Authority, and State Power*, eds. William Aiken, and Hugh LaFollette, pp. 124–53. Totowa, N.J.: Littlefield, Adams & Co.

————— . 1981. Protecting a Way of Life. In *Absolute Values and the Search for the Peace of Mankind.* vol. I, pp. 185–201. New York: The International Cultural Foundation Press.

————— . Forthcoming. *The Moral Limits of the Criminal Law.* New York: Oxford University Press.

Foot, Philippa. 1958–59. Moral Beliefs. *Proceedings of the Aristotelian Society* 59: 83–104.

Ford, John C. 1964. Refusal of Blood Transfusions by Jehovah's Witnesses. *Catholic Lawyer* 10 (Summer): 212–26.

Fotion, Nicholas. 1979. Paternalism. *Ethics* 89 (January): 191–98.

Frank, Johann Peter. 1777–1817. *A System of Complete Medical Police.* Selections, ed. Erna Lesky. Baltimore, Md.: Johns Hopkins University Press, 1976.

Franklin, Benjamin. 1759. *An Historical Review of the Constitution and Government of Pennsylvania.* London: R. Griffiths; reissued by Arno Press (N.Y.), 1972.

Freedman, Benjamin. 1981. Competence, Marginal and Otherwise: Concepts and Ethics. *International Journal of Law and Psychiatry* 4: 53–72.

Freire, Paulo. 1971. *Pedagogy of the Oppressed*, New York: Herder & Herder.

Friedman, Milton. 1962. *Capitalism and Freedom.* Chicago: University of Chicago Press.

Gaus, Gerald F. 1983. *The Modern Liberal Theory of Man.* London: Croom Helm; New York: St. Martin's Press.

Gaylin, Willard (ed.). 1978. Sterilization of the Retarded: In Whose Interest? *Hastings Center Report* 8 (June): 28–41.

Gaylin, Willard; Glasser, Ira; Marcus, Stephen; and Rothman, David J. 1978. *Doing Good: The Limits of Benevolence.* New York: Pantheon.

Gaylin, Willard, and Macklin, Ruth (eds.). 1982. *Who Speaks for the Child: The Problems of Proxy Consent.* New York: Plenum Press.

Gellhorn, Walter. 1976. The Abuse of Occupational Licensing. *University of Chicago Law Review* 44 (Fall): 6–27.

Gert, Bernard, and Culver, Charles M. 1976. Paternalistic Behavior. *Philosophy & Public Affairs*, 6, 1 (Fall), 45–57.

————— . 1979. The Justification of Paternalism. *Ethics* 89 (January): 199–210.

Gibson, Mary. 1977. Rationality. *Philosophy & Public Affairs* 6 (Spring): 193–225.

Gilbert, Richard M. 1980. Ethical Considerations in the Prevention of Smoking in Adults and Children. *Medico-legal News* 8 (June): 4–7, 18.

Gill, Peter. 1976. Free Schools: The New Paternalism. *Problems in Education: a philosophical approach*, ed. Don Cave. Victoria: Cassell Australia, ch. 8.

Gintis, Herbert, and Bowles, Samuel. 1975. The Contradictions of Liberal Educational Reform. In *Work, Technology and Education: Dissenting Essays in the Intellectual Foundations of American Education*, eds. Walter Feinberg and Henry Rosemont, pp. 92–141. Urbana: University of Illinois Press.

Glover, Jonathan. 1977. *Causing Death and Saving Lives.* Harmondsworth: Penguin.

Golding, Martin P. 1971. Private Right and the Limits of Law. *Philosophy East & West.* 21 (October): 375–88.

————— . 1975. *Philosophy of Law.* Englewood Cliffs, N.J.: Prentice-Hall.

Goldman, Alan H. 1980. *The Moral Foundations of Professional Ethics.* Totowa, N.J.: Rowman & Littlefield.

Goodin, Robert E. 1979. Retrospective Rationality: Saving People from Their Former Selves. *Social Science Information* 18: 967–90. A slightly revised version appears in Goodin (1982), as ch. 3: Anticipating Evaluations: Saving People from their Former Selves.

————. 1982. *Political Theory and Public Policy.* Chicago and London: University of Chicago Press.

Goodman, Lenn Evan. 1971. Commentary on Martin P. Golding's "Private Right and the Limits of Law," *Philosophy East & West* 21 (October): 389–93.

Gorovitz, Samuel, et al. (eds.). 1976. *Moral Problems in Medicine.* Englewood Cliffs, N.J.: Prentice-Hall.

Gorovitz, Samuel. 1982. *Doctor's Dilemmas: Moral Conflict and Medical Care.* New York: Macmillan, ch. 3.

Graber, Glenn C. 1978. On Paternalism and Health Care. In *Contemporary Issues in Biomedical Ethics,* eds. John W. Davis; Barry Hoffmaster; Sarah Shorten, pp. 233–44. Clifton, N.J.: Humana Press.

Graham, Clay P. 1980. Helmetless Motorcyclists—Easy Riders Facing Hard Facts: The Rise of the "Motorcycle Helmet Defense". *Ohio State Law Journal* 41: 233–69.

Gray, Jan Charles. 1972. Compulsory Sterilization in a Free Society: Choices and Dilemmas. *University of Cincinnati Law Review* 41: 529–87.

Green, T.H. 1881. Liberal Legislation and Freedom of Contract. In *The Political Theory of T.H. Green: Selected Writings,* ed. John R. Rodman, pp. 43–73. New York: Appleton-Century-Crofts, 1964.

Greenawalt, Kent. 1971. Criminal Law and Population Control. *Vanderbilt Law Review* 24 (April): 465–94.

Greenberg, David F. 1974. Involuntary Psychiatric Commitments to Prevent Suicide. *New York Unversity Law Review* 49 (May-June): 227–69.

Guggenheim, Martin. 1977. Paternalism, Prevention, and Punishment: Pretrial Detention of Juveniles. *New York University Law Review* 52 (November): 1064–92.

Guiora, Alexander Z. 1980. Freedom of Information vs. Freedom from Information. In *Ethics, Humanism and Medicine,* ed. Marc D. Basson, pp. 31–34. New York: Alan R. Liss.

Gutman, Amy. 1980. Children, Paternalism and Education. *Philosophy & Public Affairs* 9 (Summer): 338–58.

Guttmacher, Manfred S., and Weihofen, Henry. 1952. Mental Incompetency. *Minnesota Law Review* 36 (February): 179–212.

H., D.B. 1968. Comment: Freedom of Religion—Public Safety—Mentally Ill Person and Possibility of Future Dismemberment: *Mayock v. Martin. Connecticut Law Review* 1: 419–23.

Hafen, Bruce C. 1976. Children's Liberation and the New Egalitarianism: Some Reservations about Abandoning Youth to their Rights. *Brigham Young University Law Review* 2: 605–68.

Haksar, Vinit. 1979. *Equality, Liberty, and Perfectionism.* London: Oxford University Press.

Halper, Thomas. 1978. Paternalism and the Elderly. In *Aging and the Elderly: Humanistic Perspectives in Gerontology,* eds. Stuart F. Spicker, Kathleen M. Woodward, and David D. Van Tassel, pp. 321–39. Atlantic Highlands, N.J.: Humanities Press. A later version is published as The Double-Edged Sword: Paternalism as a Policy in the Problems of Aging. Milbank Memorial Fund Quarterly/*Health and Society* 58 (1980).

Hamilton, Walton H. 1931. The Ancient Maxim Caveat Emptor. *Yale Law Journal* 40 (June): 1137–87.

Hare, E.H. 1962. Masturbatory Insanity: the History of an Idea. *Journal of Mental Science* 108 (January): 1–25.

Hare, William. 1979. *Open-Mindedness and Education.* McGill: Queens Unversity Press.

Harman, John D. 1981. Harm, Consent and Distress. *Journal of Value Inquiry* 15: 293–309.

Harris, C. Edwin, Jr. 1977. Paternalism and the Enforcement of Morality. *Southwestern Journal of Philosophy* 8 (Summer): 85–93.

Harris, John. 1981. Bad Samaritans Cause Harm. *Philosophical Quarterly* 32 (January): 60–69.

Harris, Robert N., Jr. 1967. Private Consensual Adult Behavior: The Requirement of Harm to Others in the Enforcement of Morality. *UCLA Law Review* 14 (January): 581–603.

Hart, H.L.A. 1961. *the Concept of Law*. Oxford: Clarendon Press.
————. 1963. *Law, Liberty, and Morality*. London: Oxford University Press.
————. 1967. Social Solidarity and the Enforcement of Morality. *University of Chicago Law Review* 35: 1–13.
Head, Michael. 1974. Pyramid Selling Legislation—Effective? *Australian Business Law Review* 2 (September): 167–79.
Hegland, Kenney F. 1965. Note: Unauthorized Rendition of Lifesaving Medical Treatment. *California Law Review* 53 (August): 860–77.
Henderson, Michael, and Freedman, Kathleen. 1974. The Effect of Mandatory Seat Belt Use in New South Wales, Australia. *Report 3/74*. Traffic Accident Research Unit, Department of Motor Transport, New South Wales.
Henley, Kenneth. 1978. Children and the Individualism of Mill and Nozick. *The Personalist* 59 (October): 415–19.
Hill, Evan. 1969 It's *My* Life, Isn't It? *Reader's Digest* 94 (January): 49–51.
Hill, Irvin B. 1950. Sterilization in Oregon. *American Journal of Mental Deficiency* 54: 399–403.
Hisert, George A. 1970. Limiting the State's Police Power: Judicial Reaction to John Stuart Mill. *Unversity of Chicago Law Review* 37: 605–27.
Hobhouse, L.T. 1911. *Liberalism*. Oxford: Oxford University Press.
Hodson, John Darrel. 1976. Philosophical Problems of Therapeutic Rehabilitation. Unpublished Ph.D. thesis, University of Arizona.
————. 1977. The Principle of Paternalism. *American Philosophical Quarterly* 14 (January): 61–69.
————. 1981. Mill, Paternalism, and Slavery. *Analysis* 41 (January): 60–62.
Hoffmaster, Barry. 1978. Comments on "Legalism and Medical Ethics. In *Contemporary Issues in Biomedical Ethics*, eds. John W. Davis, Barry Hoffmaster, and Sarah Shorten, pp. 37–42. Clifton, N.J.: Humana Press.
————. 1980. Physicians, Patients, and Paternalism. *Man and Medicine* 5: 189–202.
Hoglund, John A., and Parsons, A. Peter. 1974. Caveat Viator: the Duty to Wear Seat Belts under Comparative Negligence Law. *Washington Law Review* 50: 1–27.
Holland, R.F. 1969. Suicide. In *Talk of God*, ed. G.N.A. Vesey, vol. 2, pp. 72–85. Royal Institute of Philosophy Lectures. London: Macmillan.
Höpfl, H.M. 1983. "Isms". *British Journal of Political Science* 13 (January): 1–17.
Hospers, John. 1980. Libertarianism and Legal Paternalism. *Journal of Libertarian Studies* 4 (Summer): 255–65.
Houlgate, Laurence D. 1979. Children, Paternalism and Rights to Liberty. In *Having Children: Philosophical & Logical Reflections on Parenthood*, eds. Onora O'Neill and William Ruddick, pp. 265–78. New York: Oxford University Press.
How, W. Glen. 1960. Religion, Medicine and Law. *Canadian Bar Journal* 3 (October): 365–421, 430–32.
Howell, Timothy; Diamond, Ronald J; and Wikler, Daniel. 1982. Is There a Case for Voluntary Commitment? In *Contemporary Issues in Bioethics*, eds. Tom Beauchamp and Leroy Walters, pp. 163–67. Encino, Calif.: Dickenson.
Husak, Douglas Neil. 1976. Paternalistic Legislation. Unpublished Ph.D. dissertation, Ohio University.
————. 1981. Paternalism and Autonomy. *Philosophy & Public Affairs* 10 (Winter): 27–46.
Ilfeld, Frederic W., Jr., and Lindemann, Erich. 1971. "Professional and Community: Pathways Toward Trust". *American Journal of Psychiatry* 128 (November): 75–81.
Illich, Ivan. 1976. *Medical Nemesis: The Expropriation of Health*, New York: Random House.
Ingelfinger, Franz J. 1980. Arrogance. *New England Journal of Medicine* 303 (25 December): 1508–10.
Irwin, Terence. 1977. *Plato's Moral Theory: The Early and Middle Dialogues*. Oxford: Clarendon Press.
Jellinek, Michael; Brandt, Richard B.; and Litman, Robert E. 1979. A Suicide Attempt and Emergency Room Ethics. *Hastings Center Report* 9 (August): 12–13.

Jones, Gary E. 1982. The Doctor-Patient Relationship and Euthanasia. *Journal of Medical Ethics* 8 (December): 195–98.

Kao, Charles C.L. 1976. Maturity and Paternalism in Health Care. *Ethics in Science and Medicine* 3 (1976): 179–86.

Kaplan, John. 1971. The Role of the Law in Drug Control. *Duke Law Journal*, pp. 1065–1104.

Katz, Jay; with assistance of Capron, Alexander Morgan, and Glass, Eleanor Swift. 1972. *Experimentation with Human Beings: The Authority of the Investigator, Subject, Professions, and State in the Human Experimentation Process.* New York: Russell Sage Foundation, ch. 10.

Katz, Jay; Goldstein, Joseph; and Dershowitz, Alan (eds.) 1967. *Psychoanalysis, Psychiatry and Law.* New York: Free Press.

Katz, Michael. 1980. Commentary on Hoffmaster, "Physicians, Patients, and Paternalism". *Man and Medicine* 5: 207–8.

Katzner, Louis I. 1975. *Man in Conflict: Traditions in Social and Political Thought.* Encino, Calif.: Dickenson.

Kelley, Dean M. 1977. Deprogramming and Religious Liberty. *The Civil Liberties Review* 4 (July/August): 23–33.

Kennedy, Ian. 1982. *The Unmasking of Medicine.* London: Allen & Unwin.

Kidd, Alexander M. 1953. Limits of the Right of a Person to Consent to Experimentation Upon Himself. *Science* 117 (27 February): 211–12.

Kilcullen, John. 1981. Keeping an Open Mind. *Philosophy Research Archives* 7, No. 1440.

Kilduff, Marshall, and Javers, Ron. 1978. *Suicide Cult: Inside Story of the People's Temple Sect and the Massacre in Guyana.* New York: Bantam Books.

Kindred, Michael; Cohen, Julius; Penrod, David; and Shaffer, Thomas (eds.). 1976. *The Mentally Retarded Citizen and the Law.* New York: The Free Press.

Kleinig, John. 1976. Good Samaritanism. *Philosophy & Public Affairs* 5 (Summer): 382–407.

————. 1976. Mill, Children, and Rights. *Educational Philosophy and Theory* 8 (October): 1–16.

————. 1977. Reflections on Homosexuality. *Journal of Christian Education* 57 (September): 32–57.

————. 1979. Consent as a Defence in Criminal Law. *Archiv für Rechts- und Sozialphilosophie* 65: 329–46.

————. 1981. Compulsory Schooling. *Journal of Philosophy of Education* 15 (December): 191–203.

————. 1982. The Ethics of Consent. In *New Essays in Ethics and Public Policy*, eds. Kai Nielsen and Steven C. Patten, Canadian Journal of Philosophy, Supplementary vol. 8, pp. 91–118. Guelph, Ont.: Canadian Association for Publishing in Philosophy.

————. 1982a. *Philosophical Issues in Education.* London & Canberra: Croom Helm; New York: St. Martins Press.

Knerr, M.E. 1979. *Suicide in Guyana.* New York: Tower Books.

Knowles, John H. 1977. The Responsibility of the Individual. In *Doing Better and Feeling Worse: Health in the United States*, ed. John H. Knowles, pp. 57–80. New York: W.W. Norton.

Kogan, B.I. 1969. Constitutionality of Mandatory Motorcyle Helmet Legislation. *Dickenson Law Review* 73: 100–14.

Kogan, Terry S. 1976. Note: The Limits of State Intervention: Personal Identity and Ultra-Risky Actions. *Yale Law Journal* 85 (May): 826–46.

Kottow, Michael H. 1978. When Consent is Unbearable—a Case Report. *Journal of Medical Ethics* 4 (June): 78–80.

Kraus, Jess F.; Riggins, Richard S.; and Franti, Charles E. 1975. Some Epidemiologic Features of Motorcycle Collision Injuries. *American Journal of Epidemiology* 102: 74–109.

Krimerman, Leonard. 1978. Compulsory Education: a Moral Critique. In *Ethics and Educational Policy*, eds. Kenneth A. Strike and Kieran Egan, pp. 79–102. London: Routledge & Kegan Paul.

Kristol, Irving. 1973. Pornography, Obscenity, and the Case for Censorship. *Quadrant* 17 (September-December): 48–50, 53–57.

Kronman, Anthony T., and Posner, Richard A. 1979. *The Economics of Contract Law.* Boston: Little, Brown & Co., ch. 7.

Kronman, Anthony T. 1980. Contract Law and Distributive Justice. *Yale Law Journal* 89 (January): 472–511.

Kuhn, James. 1972. Business and Its Publics. *Christianity and Crisis* 32 (7 February): 9–13.

Ladd, John. 1978. Legalism in Medical Ethics. In *Contemporary Issues in Biomedical Ethics,* eds. John W. Davis, Barry Hoffmaster, and Sarah Shorten, pp. 1–35. Clifton, N.J.: Humana Press.

Lee, Steven. 1981. On the Justification of Paternalism. *Social Theory & Practice* 7 (Summer): 193–204.

Livermore, Joseph M.; Malmquist, Carl P.; and Meehl, Paul E. 1968. On the Justifications for Civil Commitment. *University of Pennsylvania Law Review* 117 (November): 75–96.

Locke, John. 1690. *Second Treatise of Civil Government.* In *Two Treatises of Civil Government,* intro. W.S. Carpenter. London: J.M. Dent, 1924.

Lomasky, Loren E., and Detlefsen, Michael. 1981. Medical Paternalism Reconsidered. *Pacific Philosophical Quarterly* 62 (January): 95–98.

Long, Douglas G. 1977. *Bentham on Liberty: Jeremy Bentham's Idea of Liberty in Relation to his Utilitarianism.* Toronto: University of Toronto Press.

Lowy, Cathy. 1981. The Doctrine of Substituted Judgment: Deciding for the Incompetent. *Bulletin of the Australian Society of Legal Philosophy* 21 (December): 55–71.

————. 1982. Consent and Paternalism in Medical Practice. *New Doctor* 24 (June): 14, 27.

Luban, David. 1981. Paternalism and the Legal Profession. *Wisconsin Law Review* 3: 454–93.

Lyons, David. 1975. On Justifying Enforced Requirements: A Reply to Baier. *Journal of Value Inquiry* 9 (Spring): 42–47.

Mack, Eric. 1980. Bad Samaritanism and the Causation of Harm. *Philosophy & Public Affairs* 9 (Spring) 230–59.

McCarthy, Colman. 1973. Why Not Make Seat Belt Use Mandatory? *Washington Post* (22 January), A20.

McDermott, Walsh. 1978. Medicine: The Public Good and One's Own. *Perspectives in Biology and Medicine* 21 (Winter): 167–87.

MacDonald, Robert, H. 1967. The Frightful Consequences of Onanism: Notes on the History of a Delusion. *Journal of the History of Ideas* 28: 423–31.

Macklin, Ruth, and Gaylin, Willard (eds.). 1981. *Mental Retardation and Sterilization: A Problem of Competency and Paternalism.* New York: Plenum Press.

Macklin, Ruth. 1982. *Man, Mind, and Morality: the ethics of behavior control.* Englewood Cliffs, N.J.; Prentice-Hall, ch. 3.

McLatchie, G.R., et al. 1981. Injuries in Karate—A Case for Medical Control. *Physicians & Sportsmedicine* 9 (October): 8.

McPherson, Thomas. 1967. *Political Obligation.* London: Routledge & Kegan Paul, ch. 4.

Mahowald, Mary B. 1980. Against Paternalism: A Developmental View. *Philosophy Research Archives* 6, No. 1386.

Mann, Ronald A. 1972. The Behavior—Therapeutic Use of Contingency Contracting to Control an Adult Behavior Problem: Weight Control. *Journal of Applied Behavior Analysis,* 5 (Summer): 99–109.

Margolis, Joseph. 1981. Democracy and the Responsibility to Inform the Public. In *Ethical Issues in Government,* ed. Norman E. Bowie, pp. 237–48. Philadelphia: Temple University Press.

Marsh, Frank H. 1977. An Ethical Approach to Paternalism in the Physician-Patient Relationship. *Ethics in Science and Medicine* 4: 135–38.

Marsh, Robert M., and Mannari, Hiroshi. 1972. A New Look at "Lifetime Commitment" in Japanese Industry. *Economic Development and Cultural Change* 20 (July): 611–30.

Masters, Roger D. 1975. Is Contract an Adequate Basis for Medical Ethics? *Hastings Center Report* 5 (December): 24–28.

May, Larry. 1980. Paternalism and Self-Interest. *Journal of Value Inquiry* 14 (Fall and Winter): 195–216.

Meenan, Robert F. 1976. Improving the Public's Health—Some Further Reflections. *New England Journal of Medicine* 294, (1 January): 45–46.

Milhollin, Gary L. 1965. The Refused Blood Transfusion: An Ultimate Challenge for Law and Morals. *Natural Law Forum* 10: 202ff.

Mill, John Stuart. 1848, 1871. *Principles of Political Economy.* In *Collected Works of John Stuart Mill* ed. John M. Robson, vols. 2 & 3. Toronto: University of Toronto Press, 1965.

———. 1859, 1869. *On Liberty.* In *Collected Works of John Stuart Mill,* ed. John M. Robson, vol. 18: *Essays on Politics and Society* pp. 215–310. Toronto: University of Toronto Press, 1977.

Miller, Bruce L. 1981. Autonomy & the Refusal of Lifesaving Treatment. *Hastings Center Report* 11 (August): 22–28.

Moertel, C. G., et al. 1982. A Clinical Trial of Amygdalin (Laetrile) in the Treatment of Human Cancer. *New England Journal of Medicine* 306 (28 January): 201–6

Mooney, Gavin H. 1977. *The Valuation of Human Life.* London: Macmillan.

Moore, M.S. 1975. Some Myths about "Mental Illness". *Archives of General Psychiatry* 32 (December): 1483–97.

Morris, Herbert. 1971. Review of Thomas S. Szasz. *U.C.L.A. Law Review* 18: 1164–72.

———. 1981. A Paternalistic Theory of Punishment. *American Philosophical Quarterly* 18 (October): 263–71.

Moskowitz, Joel S. 1975. Parental Rights and State Education. *Washington Law Review* 50 (June): 623–51.

Munson, Ronald. 1979. *Intervention and Reflection: Basic Issues in Medical Ethics.* Belmont, Calif.: Wadsworth, ch. 4.

Murcko, Thomas C. 1968. The Validity of Motorcycle Helmet Legislation. *University of Pittsburgh Law Review* 30: 421–27.

Murdock, Charles W. 1972. Civil Rights of the Mentally Retarded: Some Critical Issues. *Notre Dame Lawyer* 48 (October): 133–88.

Murphy, Jeffrie G. 1974. Incompetence and Paternalism. *Archiv für Rechts- und Sozialphilosophie* 60: 465–86. Reprinted in *Retribution, Justice and Therapy.* Dordrecht: D. Reidel, 1979, pp. 165–82.

———. 1981. Consent, Coercion, and Hard Choices. *Virginia Law Review* 67 (February): 79–95.

Muyskens, James L. 1982. *Moral Problems in Nursing: A Philosophical Investigation.* Totowa, N.J.: Rowman & Littlefield.

Neuwirth, Gloria S.; Heisler, Phyllis A.; and Goldrich, Kenneth S. 1974–75. Capacity, Competence, Consent: Voluntary Sterilization of the Mentally Retarded. *Columbia Human Rights Law Review* 6: 447–72.

Newton, Lisa H. 1981. Liberty and Laetrile: Implications of Right of Access. *Journal of Value Inquiry* 15: 55–67.

Nozick, Robert. 1969. Coercion. In *Philosophy, Science, and Method: Essays in Honor of Ernest Nagel.* eds. Sidney Morgenbesser et al., pp. 440–72. New York: St. Martin's Press.

———. 1974. *Anarchy, State and Utopia.* London: Blackwell.

O'Connell, John D. 1964. The Right to Die—A Comment on the *Application of the President and Directors of Georgetown College. Utah Law Review* 9 (Summer): 161–71.

Parfit, Derek. 1971. Personal Identity. *Philosophical Review* 80 (January): 3–27.

———. 1973. Later Selves and Moral Principles. In *Philosophy and Personal Relations: An Anglo-French Study,* ed. Alan Montefiore, pp. 137–69. London: Routledge & Kegan Paul.

———. 1976. Lewis, Perry, and What Matters. In *The Identities of Persons,* ed. Amélie Oksenberg Rorty, pp. 91–107. Berkeley: University of California Press.

Paris, John J. 1975. Compulsory Medical Treatment and Religious Freedom: Whose Law Shall Prevail? *University of San Francisco Law Review* 10 (Summer): 1–35.

Paulson, Jerome A., and Thomas, Laurence. 1981. Should States Require Child Passenger Protection? *Hastings Center Report* 11 (June): 21–22.

Peden, John R. 1967. Minimum Deposits in Hire-Purchase Transactions. *Australian Law Journal* 41 (30 June): 40–46.

Peele, Roger; Chodoff, Paul; and Taub, Norman. 1974. Involuntary Hospitalization & Treatability: Observations from the District of Columbia Experience. *Catholic University Law Review* 23: 744–53.

Peltzman, Sam. 1975. *Regulation of Automobile Safety*. Washington, D.C.: American Enterprise Institute for Public Policy Research.

Pence, Gregory E. 1980. *Ethical Options in Medicine*. Oradell, N.J.: Medical Economics Co., ch. 6.

Pennock, J. Roland, and Chapman, John W. (eds.). 1972. *Nomos XIV: Coercion*. New York: Atherton Press.

Pierce, Christine. 1975. Hart on Paternalism. *Analysis* 35 (June): 205–7.

Plamenatz, John. 1960. *On Alien Rule and Self-Government*. London: Longmans.

Pollard, Michael R., and Brennan, John T., Jr. 1978. Disease Prevention and Health Promotion Initiatives. In R. & A. Faden (eds.). Ethical Issues in Public Health Policy: Health Education and Lifestyle Interventions. *Health Education Monographs* 6 (Summer): 211–22.

Popham, Robert E.; Schmidt, Wolfgang; and de Lint, Jan. 1976. The Effects of Legal Restraint on Drinking. In *Social Aspects of Alcoholism; The Biology of Alcoholism*, vol. 4, eds. Benjamin Kissin and Henri Begleiter, pp. 579–625. New York: Plenum Press.

Porter, Katherine Anne. 1960. A Wreath for the Gamekeeper. *Encounter* 14 (February): 69–77.

Posner, Richard A. 1977. *Economic Analysis of Law*. Boston: Little, Brown & Co.

Powers, William C. 1975. Autonomy and the Legal Control of Self-Regarding Conduct. *Washington Law Review* 51: 33–59.

Provis, C. 1975. Coordination and Individuals. Unpublished Ph.D. dissertation. University of Sydney.

Purver, Jonathan M. 1970. Validity of Traffic Regulations Requiring Motorcyclists to Wear Protective Headgear. *American Law Reports, 3d. Cases and Annotations* 32: 1270–85.

Rachlin, Stephen; Pam, Alvin; and Milton, Janet. 1975. Civil Liberties Versus Involuntary Hospitalization. *American Journal of Psychiatry* 132 (February): 189–92.

Ratzan, R.M. 1980. "Being Old Makes You Different": The Ethics of Research with Elderly Subjects. *Hastings Center Report* 10 (October): 32–42.

Rawls, John. 1971. *A Theory of Justice*. Cambridge, Mass.: Harvard University Press.

Reed, T. M., and Johnston, Patricia. 1980. Children's Liberation. *Philosophy* 55 (April): 263–66.

Regan, Donald H. 1974. Justifications for Paternalism. In *Nomos XV: Limits of Law*, eds. J. Roland Pennock and John W. Chapman, pp. 189–210. New York: Lieber-Atherton.

―――――――. 1983. Paternalism, Freedom, Identity, and Commitment. In Sartorius (1983).

Reich, Charles A. 1964. The New Property. *Yale Law Journal* 73 (April): 733–87.

Reich, Robert B. 1979. Toward a New Consumer Protection. *University of Pennsylvania Law Review* 128 (November): 1–40.

Reich, Warren T. (ed.). 1978. *Encyclopedia of Bioethics*. New York: Free Press, 4 vols.

Relman, Arnold S. 1978. The *Saikewicz* Decision: A Medical Viewpoint. *American Journal of Law & Medicine* 4 (Fall): 233–42.

Relman, Arnold S. 1979. Correspondence: A Response to Allen Buchanan's Views on Decision Making for Terminally Ill Incompetents. *American Journal of Law & Medicine* 5 (Summer): 119–23.

―――――――. 1982. Closing the Books on Laetrile. *New England Journal of Medicine* 306 (28 January): 236.

Rescher, Nicholas. 1972. *Welfare: The Social Issues in Philosophical Perspective*. Pittsburgh: University of Pittsburgh Press.

Richards, David A. J. 1980. Commercial Sex and the Rights of the Person: A Moral Argument for the Decriminalization of Prostitution. *University of Pennsylvania Law Review* 127.(May): 1195–287.

————. 1982. *Sex, Drugs, Death, and the Law: An Essay on Human Rights and Overcriminalization.* Totowa, N.J.: Rowman and Littlefield.

Rieger, Dean. 1980. Medicine and the Recalcitrant Prisoner. In *Ethics, Humanism, and Medicine,* ed. Marc. D. Basson, pp. 201–4. New York: Alan R. Liss.

Ritchie, D. G. 1894. *Natural Rights,* London: Allen & Unwin.

Roemer, John E. 1982. Property Relations vs. Surplus Value in Marxian Exploitation. *Philosophy & Public Affairs* 11 (Fall): 281–313.

Roethe, John W. 1967. Seat Belt Negligence in Automobile Accidents. *Wisconsin Law Review* 1 (Winter): 288–300.

Rogin, Michael Paul. 1971. Liberal Society and the Indian Question. *Politics and Society* 1 (May): 269–312.

Rosenak, Julia. 1982. Should Children be Subject to Paternalistic Restrictions on their Liberties? *Journal of Philosophy of Education* 16 (July): 89–96.

Rosenthal, Douglas E. 1974. *Lawyer and Client: Who's in Charge?* New York: Russell Sage Foundation.

Roth, Loren H.; Meisel, Alan; and Lidz, Charles W. 1977. Tests of Competency to Consent to Treatment. *American Journal of Psychiatry* 134 (March): 279–84.

Royalty, Kenneth M. 1969. Motorcycle Helmets and the Constitutionality of Self-Protective Legislation. *Ohio State Law Journal* 30 (Spring): 355–81.

Rubinow, Laurence P. 1969. Society's Right to Protect an Individual from Himself. *Connecticut Law Review* 2: 150–62.

Rudden, Bernard. 1980. Ius Cogens, Ius Dispositivum. *Cambrian Law Review* 11: 87–100.

Sartorius, Rolf E. 1975. *Individual Conduct and Social Norms: A Utilitarian Account of Social Union and the Rule of Law.* Encino, Calif.: Dickenson.

————. 1980. Paternalistic Grounds for Involuntary Civil Commitment: A Utilitarian Perspective. In *Mental Illness: Law and Public Policy.* eds. Baruch A. Brody and H. Tristram Engelhardt, Jr., pp. 137–45. Dordrecht: Reidel.

————. ed. 1983. *Paternalism.* Minneapolis: University of Minnesota Press.

Scarre, Geoffrey. 1980. Children and Paternalism. *Philosophy* 55 (January): 117–24.

Schelling, Thomas C. 1973. Hockey Helmets, Concealed Weapons, and Daylight Saving. *Journal of Conflict Resolution* 17 (September): 381–428.

Schrag, Francis. 1977. The Child and the Moral Order. *Philosophy* 52 (April): 167–77.

Schulman, R. E. 1968. Suicide and Suicide Prevention: A Legal Analysis. *American Bar Association Journal* 54 (September): 855–62.

Schuman, Samuel I. 1979. Informed Consent and the "Victims" of Colonialism. In *Medical Responsibility: Paternalism, Informed Consent, and Euthanasia,* eds. Wade L. Robison and Michael S. Pritchard, pp. 75–99. Clifton, N.J.: Humana Press.

Schwartz, Adina. 1973. Moral Neutrality and Primary Goods. *Ethics* 83 (July): 294–307.

Shem, Samuel. 1979. *The House of God,* New York: Dell Publishing Co.

Sher, Byron D. 1968. The "Cooling-Off" Period in Door-to-Door Sales. *UCLA Law Review* 15: 717–86.

Sherlock, Richard K.; Haykal, Radwan F.; and Dresseer, Rebecca. 1982. Saying "No" to Electroshock. *Hastings Center Report* 12 (December): 18–20.

Sidgwick, Henry. 1891. *The Elements of Politics.* London: Macmillan.

Singer, Peter. 1973. Altruism and Commerce: A Defense of Titmuss against Arrow. *Philosophy & Public Affairs* 2 (Spring): 312–20.

Skegg, P.D.G. 1974. A Justification for Medical Procedures Performed Without Consent. *Law Quarterly Review* 90 (October): 512–30.

Soble, Alan G. 1976. Legal Paternalism. Unpublished Ph.D. dissertation. State University of New York at Buffalo.

————. 1978. Deception in Social Science Research: Is Informed Consent Possible? *Hastings Center Report* 8 (October): 40–46.

————. 1982. Paternalism, Liberal Theory, and Suicide. *Canadian Journal of Philosophy* 12 (June): 335–52.

Spahr, Margaret. 1962. Mill on Paternalism in its Place. In *Nomos IV: Liberty*, ed. C.J. Friedrich, pp. 162–75. New York: Atherton Press.

Spicker, Stuart F., and Gadow, Sally (eds.). 1980. *Nursing: Images and Ideals. Opening Dialogue with the Humanities.* New York: Springer Publishing Company.

Stallsmith, William P., Jr. 1955. Note: Legal Aspects of the Fluoridation of Public Drinking Water. *George Washington Law Review* 23: 343–57.

Stell, Lance K. 1979. Dueling and the Right to Life. *Ethics* 90 (October): 7–26.

Stephen, James Fitzjames. 1874. *Liberty, Equality, Fraternity.* Ed. R.J. White. Cambridge: Cambridge University Press, 1967.

Stich, Stephen P. Forthcoming. Could Man Be an Irrational Animal?

Stocker, M.A.G. 1976. The Schizophrenia of Modern Ethical Theories. *Journal of Philosophy* 73 (12 August): 453–66.

Stone, Alan A. 1971. Psychiatry and the Law. *Psychiatric Annals* 1 (October): 18–19, 23–25, 28–29, 33–39, 43.

Stone, Clarence N. 1977. Paternalism Among Social Agency Employees. *Journal of Politics* 39 (August): 794–804.

Storch, Janet. 1982. *Patients' Rights: Ethical and Legal Issues in Health Care and Nursing.* Toronto: McGraw-Hill Ryerson.

Straker, M. 1975. Current Medico-Legal Issues—A Psychiatrist's View. *Diseases of the Nervous System (Journal of Clinical Psychiatry)* 36 (June): 331–35.

Strike, Kenneth A. 1974. Philosophical Reflections on Tinker vs. Des Moines. In *Philosophy of Education 1974*, Proceedings of the Thirtieth Annual Meeting of the Philosophy of Education Society, ed. M.J. Parsons, pp. 397–410. Edwardswille, Ill.: Philosophy of Education Society.

Stroll, Avrum. 1967. Censorship, Models and Self-Government. *Journal of Value Inquiry* 1 (Fall): 81–95.

Struhl, Paula Rothenburg. 1976. Mill's Notion of Social Responsibility. *Journal of the History of Ideas* 37 (January-March): 155–62.

Struve, Guy Miller. 1967. The Less-Restrictive-Alternative Principle and Economic Due Process. *Harvard Law Review* 80 (May): 1463–88.

Swanton, Christine. 1979. The Concept of Overall Freedom. *Australasian Journal of Philosophy* 57 (December): 337–49.

Szasz, Thomas S. 1957. Commitment of the Mentally Ill: "Treatment" or Social Restraint. *Journal of Nervous & Mental Disease* 75: 293–307.

————. 1961. *The Myth of Mental Illness.* New York: Harper & Row.

————. 1963. *Law, Liberty and Psychiatry: an Inquiry into the Social Uses of Mental Health Practices.* London: Routledge & Kegan Paul, 1974.

————. 1970. *Ideology and Insanity.* Garden City, N.Y.: Doubleday Anchor.

————. 1970a. *The Manufacture of Madness.* New York: Harper & Row.

Tamerin, John S., and Scavetta, Joseph F. 1972. Iatrogenic Depression: A Case of Misguided Paternalism. *Journal of the American Medical Association* 219 (17 January): 375–76.

Tantlinger, W.A. 1969. Note: Constitutional Law—Validity of Safety Helmet Requirements. *West Virginia Law Review* 71: 191–95.

Taylor, Gabriele, and Wolfram, Sybil. 1968. Mill, Punishment and the Self-Regarding Failings. *Analysis* 28 (April): 168–72.

————. 1968a. The Self-Regarding and the Other-Regarding Virtues. *Philosophical Quarterly* 18: 238–48.

Teitelman, Michael. 1972. The Limits of Individualism. *Journal of Philosophy* 69 (5 October): 545–56.

Ten, C. L. 1969. Crime and Immorality. *Modern Law Review* 22 (November): 648–63.

————. 1971. Paternalism and Morality. *Ratio* 13 (June): 56–66.

————. 1980. *Mill on Liberty* Oxford: Clarendon Press.

Thomas, Michael. 1981. Should the Public Decide? *Journal of Medical Ethics* 7 (December): 182–83.

Thompson, Dennis F. 1976. *John Stuart Mill on Representative Government* Princeton: Princeton University Press.

_____ . 1980. Paternalism in Medicine, Law, and Public Policy. In *Ethics Teaching in Higher Education* eds. Daniel Callahan and Sissela Bok, pp. 245–72. New York: Plenum Press.

Thompson, James B. 1952. Comment: Fluoridation of Public Water Supplies. *Hastings Law Journal* 3: 123–35.

Thurow, Lester C. 1976. Government Expenditures: Cash or In-Kind Aid? *Philosophy & Public Affairs* 5 (Summer): 361–81.

Tibbles, Lance. 1978. Medical and Legal Aspects of Competency as Affected by Old Age. In *Aging and the Elderly: Humanistic Perspectives in Gerontology*, eds. Stuart F. Spicker, Kathleen M. Woodward, and David D. Van Tassel, pp. 127–52. Atlantic Highlands, N.J.: Humanities Press, Inc.

Tipton, Carol. 1974. Interpreting Ethics. *Journal of Rehabilitation of the Deaf* 7 (January): 10–16.

Tönnies, Ferdinand. 1887. *Gemeinschaft und Gesellschaft*. 1935. *Community and Society*. Trans. Charles P. Loomis. London: Routledge, 1955.

Treffert, Darold A. 1975. The Practical Limits of Patients' Rights. *Psychiatric Annals* 5 (April): 91–96.

Tribe, Laurence H. 1978. *American Constitutional Law*. Mineola, N.Y.: Foundation Press.

Tuker, Lt.-General Sir Francis. 1961. *The Yellow Scarf: the Story of the Life of Thuggee Sleeman*. London: J.M. Dent; White Lion edn., 1977.

Turnbull, Colin M. 1973. *The Mountain People*. London: Jonathan Cape.

VanDeVeer, Donald. 1976. Intrusions on Moral Autonomy. *The Personalist* 57 (Summer): 251–65.

_____ . 1979. Paternalism and Subsequent Consent. *Canadian Journal of Philosophy* 9 (December): 631–42.

_____ . 1979a. Coercive Restraint of Offensive Actions. *Philosophy & Public Affairs* 8 (Winter): 175–93.

_____ . 1980a. The Contractual Argument for Withholding Medical Information. *Philosophy & Public Affairs* 9 (Winter): 198–205.

_____ . 1980b. Autonomy Respecting Paternalism. *Social Theory & Practice* 6 (Summer): 187–207.

_____ . 1982. Paternalism and Restrictions on Liberty. In *And Justice for All: New Introductory Essays in Ethics and Public Policy*. eds. Tom Regan and Donald VanDeVeer, pp. 17–41. Totowa, N.J.: Rowman & Littlefield.

Vaughan, R.G.; Wood, R.; and Croft, P.G. 1974. Some Aspects of Compulsory Seat Belt Wearing. *Proceedings*, 7th Conference, Australian Road Research Board (Adelaide, 1974) 7: 103–24.

Veatch, R.M., and Steinfels, Peter. 1974. Who Should Pay for Smokers' Medical Care? *Hastings Center Report* 4 (November): 8–10.

Veatch, Robert M. 1978. The Hippocratic Ethic: Consequentialism, Individualism, and Paternalism. In *No Rush to Judgment: Essays on Medical Ethics*, eds. David H. Smith and Linda M. Berstein, pp. 258–64. Bloomington, Ind.: Poynter Center.

_____ . 1980. Voluntary Risks to Health. *Journal of the American Medical Association* 243 (4 January): 50–5.

_____ . 1981. *A Theory of Medical Ethics*. New York: Basic Books.

Vidal, Gore. 1954. *Messiah*. New York: E.P. Dutton.

Vollmer, H.M., and Mills, D.L. (eds.). 1966. *Professionalization*. Englewood Cliffs, N.J.: Prentice-Hall.

Von Humboldt, Wilhelm. 1854. *The Sphere and Duties of Government*. Trans. Joseph Coulthard. London: Chapman.

Wakeling, T.W. 1977. Legislative Notes: Seat Belt Legislation: An End to Cruel and Unusual Punishment. *Saskatchewan Law Review* 42: 105–15.

Wallace, Michael. 1974. Paternalism and Violence. In *Violence and Aggression in the History of Ideas*, eds. Philip P. Wiener and J. Fisher, pp. 203–20. New Brunswick: Rutgers University Press.

Warren, William D. 1959. Regulation of Finance Charges in Retail and Instalment Sales. *Yale Law Journal* 68 (April): 839–68.

Wasserstrom, Richard. 1975. ·Lawyers as Professionals: Some Moral Issues. *Human Rights* 5: 1–24.

Watson, Geoffrey S., Zador, Paul L.; and Wilks, Alan. 1980. The Repeal of Helmet Use Laws and Increased Motorcyclist Mortality in the United States, 1975–1978. *American Journal of Public Health* 70 (June): 579–85.

————. 1981. Helmet Use, Helmet Use Laws and Motorcyclist Fatalities. *American Journal of Public Health* 71 (March): 297–300.

Weale, Albert. 1978. Paternalism and Social Policy. *Journal of Social Policy* 7 (April): 157–72.

Webb, Edwin C. 1977. Report: *Australian Government Committee of Inquiry into Chiropractic, Osteopathy, Homeopathy and Naturopathy.* Canberra: AGPS.

Wegman, Myron E. 1980. Should Laetrile be Legalized? In *Ethics, Humanism, and Medicine,* ed. Marc D. Basson, pp. 179–84. New York: Alan R. Liss.

Weinrib, Ernest J. 1980. The Case for a Duty to Rescue. *Yale Law Journal* 90 (December): 247–93.

Weinstein, W.L. 1965. The Concept of Liberty in Nineteenth Century English Political Thought. *Political Studies* 13: 145–62.

Westen, Peter. 1980. Letting Prisoners Die. In *Ethics, Humanism, and Medicine,* ed. Marc D. Basson, pp. 191–99. New York: Alan R. Liss.

Wexler, David B. 1972. Therapeutic Justice. *Minnesota Law Review* 57: 289–338.

White, A. A. 1972. The Intentional Exploitation of Man's Known Weaknesses. *Houston Law Review* 9 (May): 889–927.

White, Arthur A. 1974. Paternalism. Unpublished Ph.D. dissertation. University of Virginia.

White, Leon S. 1975. How to Improve the Public's Health. *New England Journal of Medicine.* 293 (9 October): 773–74.

Whitlock, F.A. 1975. *Drugs, Morality, and the Law.* Brisbane: University of Queensland Press, ch. 4.

Wikler, Daniel I. 1978a. Persuasion and Coercion for Health: Ethical Issues in Government Efforts to Change Life-Styles. *Health and Society* 56: 303–38.

————. 1978b. Coercive Measures in Health Promotion: Can They be Justified? In Ruth A. Faden and Alan Faden (eds.), Ethical Issues in Public Health Policy: Health Education and Lifestyle Interventions, *Health Education Monographs* 6 (Summer): 223–41.

————. 1979. Paternalism and the Mildly Retarded. *Philosophy and Public Affairs* 8 (Summer): 377–92.

Williams, Bernard. 1976. Persons, Character and Morality. In *The Identities of Persons,* ed. Amélie Oksenberg Rorty, pp. 197–216. Berkeley: University of California Press.

Winch, Peter. 1965–66. Can a Good Man be Harmed? *Proceedings of the Aristotelian Society* 66: 55–70.

Winnett, Richard A. 1973. Parameters of Deposit Contracts in the Modificaion of Smoking. *Psychological Record* 23 (Winter): 49–60.

Winston, Morton E.; Winston, Sally M.; Appelbaum, Paul S.; and Rhoden, Nancy K. 1982. Can a Subject Consent to a "Ulysses Contract"? *Hastings Center Report* 12 (August): 26–28.

Wollheim, Richard. 1973. John Stuart Mill and the Limits of State Action. *Social Research* 40 (Spring): 1–30.

Wood, Ellen Meiksins. 1972. *Mind and Politics: An approach to the meaning of liberal and socialist individualism.* Berkeley: University of California Press.

Woodward, James. 1982. Paternalism and Justification. In *New Essays in Ethics and Public Policy.* Canadian Journal of Philosophy, Supplementary vol. 8, eds. Kai Nielsen and Steven C. Patten, pp. 67–90. Guelph, Ont.: Canadian Association for Publishing in Philosophy.

World Health Organization. 1975. *Smoking and its Effects on Health.* WHO Technical Report Series, No. 568, Geneva.

Wormuth, Francis D., and Mirkin Harris G. 1964. The Doctrine of the Reasonable Alternative. *Utah Law Review* 9: 254–307.

Young, Robert. 1982. Autonomy and Paternalism. In *New Essays in Ethics and Public Policy*, Canadian Journal of Philosophy, Supplementary Vol. 8, eds. Steven C. Patten and Kai Nielsen, pp. 47–66. Guelph, Ont.: Canadian Association for Publishing in Philosophy.

Younger, Stuart J.; Jackson, David L.; and Ruddick, William. 1980. Family Wishes and Patient Autonomy. *Hastings Center Report* 10 (October): 21–22.

Zellick, Graham. 1976. The Forcible Feeding of Prisoners: An Examination of the Legality of Enforced Therapy. *Public Law* (Summer): 153–87.

Zembaty, Jane S. 1981. A Limited Defense of Paternalism in Medicine. Reprinted in *Biomedical Ethics*, eds. Thomas A. Mappes & Jane S. Zembaty, pp. 55–61. New York: McGraw Hill.

Index

Abortion, 154
Active paternalism, 14
Adams, John, 170
Adults, paternalism and welfare of, 156–69
Advertising, 108, 115, 179, 184, 186
Age: and competence, 148–50, 155, 167; of consent, 154; of decision, 149; of discretion, 28
American Hospital Association, *Patient's Bill of Rights*, 125–26
American Medical Association, *Code of Ethics*, 117, 125
American Motorcycle Association v. *Davids*, 92, 94
Amish, and compulsory schooling, 153
Animals, and paternalism, 7
Anticipated Consent Argument, 59–61, 65, 66
Aquinas, Thomas, 97, 176
Aristotle, 203
Augustine, 97, 209, 211
Autarchy, 20, 21, 25, 31; development of in children, 147–56, 204; identification of, 52–53; and religion, 217. *See also* Autonomy; Choice; Liberty
Authority, limits to, 145–47
Autonomy, 19, 20, 21, 25, 31, 32, 55, 214. *See also* Autarchy; Individuality; Liberty

Bargaining power inequalities, 187, 190
Barry, Brian, on wants and character, 202
Beauchamp, Tom, on weak paternalism, 8
Bellotti v. *Baird*, 154
Benevolence, 4, 5, 72
Benn, Stanley, 20, 42, 77n; on identifying autarchy, 52–53
Bentham, Jeremy, 32, 33, 37n
Bisenius v. *Karns*, 84
Blackstone, William, 177

Bosanquet, Bernard, 42, 58, 71, 78n
Brainwashing, 62
Brave New World (Huxley), 50

Capacities, individual, 25, 43–44, 67
Capital punishment, 206
Capron, Alexander, and doctor-patient relationship, 123
Carter, Rosemary, and subsequent consent, 61–63
Caveat emptor, 177, 178, 196
Censorship, 127, 211–13
Character, 30, 200–217; and moral harm, 201–4
Character paternalism, 204, 205–7
Child abuse, 146
Children and paternalism, 144–56, 204, 214. *See also* Parental paternalism
Choice, 9, 164, 165; developmental value of, 30–32; freedom of, 50, 54–55; and individuality, 30; rational, 19, 20, 21, 25, 28. *See also* Autarchy; Voluntariness
Civil liberties, 23
Clark, Brian, 122
Coercion, 5–6, 13; and education, 152, 153
Collective good argument, 85, 166, 167; in marketplace, 191–92, 195, 197
Colonialism and political paternalism, 169–72, 175n
Community, and individual, 39–45
Competence and incompetence, 7–8; in children, 148–50, 155; and civil commitment, 138–41
Compulsory life-saving treatment: contingencies argument for, 132–33; marginal-because-false beliefs argument for, 133–34; weak paternalistic arguments for, 131–32
Compulsory savings, 165, 166

Compulsory schooling, 13, 150–54
Compulsory superannuation, 165–67. *See also* Elderly
Conduct. *See* Other-regarding conduct; Self-regarding conduct
Consent: arguments for paternalism, 55–67, 129; informed, 123; to medical treatment, 154–56
Consequentialism, and arguments for paternalism, 48–55
Consumer education, 181
Consumer protection, 177, 178, 183, 184, 189, 191
Contingencies Argument and life-saving treatment, 132–33
Contracts: marketplace, 187, 195–96; marriage, 159–60; slavery, 157–65
"Cooling-off" period in sales agreements, 195–96
Credit. *See* Financing of purchases
Culture, tax support for, 29–30, 42, 213
Culver, Charles, 6

Danger to Others Argument, and seat belt-safety helmet legislation, 91
Day, J.P., 58
Death: and individuality, 100; as only option, 102
Decision-making: and age, 149; and autarchy, 52; encumbered, 86; and medical patients, 120
Degrees: of freedom, 21–23; of psychological continuity, 45–46; of voluntariness, 9–10
Deprogramming, 215–17
Desires, and freedom, 19, 23. *See also* Wants
"Desperate Play" Argument, and suicide intervention, 102–4
Developmental Value of Choice Argument, 30–32, 54; and elderly, 168; and marketplace, 189
Devlin, Lord Patrick, on moralism and paternalism, 14, 16, 94, 210
Diet, and health regulations, 108, 109
Direct paternalism, 11, 14
Disrespect for Persons Argument, 28, 31, 54, 73, 87. *See also* Oppression of Individuality Argument
Distributive Justice Argument, and health regulations, 113–15
Doctor-patient relationship models: authority model, 117–18; contractual model, 123–25; fiduciary model, 120–23; free market model, 118–20
Doctrine of Best Interests, 61, 65, 66, 132
Doctrine of Informed Consent, 123
Doctrine of Substituted Judgment, 60, 132

Drunkenness, and paternalism, 42, 45
Duty, to others, 35, 41
Dworkin, Gerald, 161, 210; on choice, 72; defining paternalism, 5, 7; justifying paternalism, 10, 12, 13; on limiting paternalism to securing goods, 63; on parental paternalism, 61

Education: as alternative to paternalism, 30, 95, 110, 115; of children, 150–52, 204; and consumers, 181. *See also* Compulsory schooling; Free schools
Educative Argument, and compulsory schooling, 150–54
Efficiency Argument, in marketplace, 189–91
Elderly, paternalism and, 167–69. *See also* Compulsory superannuation
Enforcement of morals, 210
Erotica, 211
Euthanasia, 174*n*
Externalities Argument, in marketplace, 188–89

Feinberg, Joel: on freedoms, choice, and liberty, 22, 50, 54–55; and full voluntariness, 69, 85; on interest in good character, 202–3; on slavery contracts, 157
Financing of purchases regulations, 192–94
Flourishing, human, and community, 41–45
Forfeiture Act of 1870, 97
Fraud-Protection Argument, in marketplace, 188, 194
Freedom, 5, 6, 14; enhancement of, 51–55; instrumentality of, 48–51; justification of, 24–27; nature of, 19–24; and paternalism, 27–36; protection of, 53–55; relative value of, 86–91. *See also* Liberty
Freedom Enhancement Arguments, 51–55
Freedom maximization, 53, 77*n*
Freedom Promotion Argument, 52–53, 65, 66, 141
Freedom Protection Argument, 53–55, 77*n*, 159
Free schools, 17*n*
Future Selves Argument, 45–48, 77*n*

Gert, Bernard, 6
Good: concept of, 29; and paternalism, 75, 173
Goods, regulations on purchase of, 180–92
Government. *See* Legal paternalism; Political paternalism; State
Green, T.H., xiii, 42, 45
Guiora, Alexander, on information as medicine, 127

Hales v. *Petit*, 98
Halper, Thomas, on the elderly, 168, 169
Harm Prevention Argument, and suicide, 99–100
Harm principle, xii, 38, 41, 100, 179; and moralism, 16; and personal identity, 45; and slavery, 158, 162; and weak paternalism, 8–9
Harris, C. Edwin, Jr., 85, 165
Hart, H.L.A., on moralism and paternalism, 14–16, 37*n*
Hazardousness Argument, and health regulations, 111–12
Health regulations, 106–8; paternalistic arguments for, 108–11; public interest arguments for, 111–15
Hodson, John: on encumbered decisions, 86; on slavery, 158
Homosexuality, 210–11
Human beings: covered by paternalism, 7–8; liberals' conception of, 24–27, 32, 67, 165; sexuality, 208–13; social nature of, 39–45. *See also* Individuality
Hypothetical Rational Consent Argument, 61, 63–67

Identity, Simple and Complex Views of, 45–48
Illnesses, terminal, and suicide, 103
Impositions, paternalistic, 7–8, 12, 13, 18; more effective preferred, 76–77
Incest, 146
Incompetence. *See* Competence and incompetence
Indirect paternalism, 11, 14
Individuality: and community, 39–40; concept of, xii, 20, 25–27, 32, 34, 52, 67; and death, 100; and flourishing, 41–45; and information, 126, 128; oppression of, 28; and personal integrity, 72–73; and survival, 40–41. *See also* Autarchy; Autonomy; Human beings
"Infectious Disease" Argument, and suicide intervention, 98
Information: and consumerism, 178, 181, 185; and liberty of action, 6; and medical patient decision-making, 123, 125–30
Ingelfinger, Franz, 119
Injury, 33
Instrumentality of Freedom Argument, 48–51, 53, 54
Integrity. *See* Personal integrity
Interconnectedness Argument, 39–45; and suicide, 98
Interest rates, 192, 193
Interests, 33; accumulative, 50–51; good character, 202–3; public, 91–96, 97–99,

111–15; security, 50–51; welfare. *See also* Welfare interests
Involuntary civil commitment, arguments for, 138–42
Involuntary sterilization, 134–37; enhanced autonomy argument for, 135–36; inability to cope argument for, 136–37; protection from exploitation argument for, 136

Jehovah's Witnesses, and medical care, 132, 146, 217
Jerome, 209
Justification: of freedoms, 24–27; of paternalism, xii, 10–14, 38–78

Kant, Immanuel, 24, 25–26, 28
Katz, Jay, 127
Kelley, Dean, 215–16
Kogan, Terry, 77*n*

Labor laws, 197–98
Legal paternalism, xi, 31, 49; and marketplace (*see* Consumer protection; Labor laws); and physical protection, 81; and prior consent, 57; and seat belt-safety helmet legislation, 82–96; and suicide, 97. *See also* Doctrine of Best Interests; Doctrine of Informed Consent; Doctrine of Substituted Judgment
Lenin, Vladimir, 173, 174
Liberalism: concept of humanity, 24–27, 32, 67, 165; critique of paternalism, xi, xii, 3, 18, 24–36, 38; and freedom, 19, 21, 23, 24–27; and liberty, 20, 21
Liberty: of action, 5, 6–14; arguments for, 24–27; as interest, 50–51; principle of, 20, 21, 86–87, 160–61, 169; types of, 23–24; as a value, 87. *See also* Autarchy; Autonomy; Freedom
Life plans, 63; and truth-telling in medicine, 126
Life-style decisions, 13, 32, 33; and health, 106–115
Lochner v. *New York*, 197
Locke, John, 145
Long-term paternalism. *See* Welfare interests, long-term
Loss of Productivity Argument: and seat belt-safety helmet legislation, 91–92, 112; and suicide, 98

Marginal-because-False Beliefs Argument, and compulsory life-saving treatment, 133–34
Marketplace paternalism. *See* Consumer protection

Marriage contract, 159–60
Marxist-Leninist theory, 173
Medical care: compulsory, 130–34; cost of, 113
Medical deception, 125–30; harm prevention arguments for, 126–29
Medical paternalism, 115–42
Mental illness and involuntary civil commitment, 138–42
Mill, John Stuart: on adults and paternalism, 156; on children, 146, 150–54; on choice, 164, 165; and critique of paternalism, 28–36, 73, 78n; on education, 150–51; and flourishing of individual, 42; on harm principle, 8, 12, 158, 162; on liberty, 20, 21, 23, 24–27, 52, 53, 160, 161, 169; and moralism, 14, 15; on Mormon marriage, 159–60; and other-regarding acts, 32–36, 37n, 91; and paternalistic legislation, 49; on political paternalism, 169–70; and "real will," 58; on self-regarding acts, 32–36, 37n; on voluntary slavery, 53, 157–65
Minimum deposit on purchases, 193, 194
Minimum quality regulations: nonpaternalistic arguments for, 188–92; paternalistic arguments for, 182–88
Minimum wage laws, 197, 198
Moore, M.S., on mental illness, 140
Moral harm, and character, 201–4
Moralism, and paternalism, 4, 7, 9, 14–16, 72. *See also* Religious paternalism
Mormons, 159–60, 174n
Morris, Herbert, 140; and punishment, 205–7
Motives for paternalism, 10–11, 36
Muller v. *Oregon*, 198

Native American Church, 217
Native Americans, paternalism toward, 170–71
Negative paternalism, 13, 14, 30

Occupational licensing, 181; nonpaternalistic arguments for, 188–92; paternalistic arguments for, 182–88
On Liberty (Mill), 24, 30, 32, 34, 150
Oppression of Individuality Argument: and consumer protection, 183; as critique of paternalism, 28; and elderly, 169; and harm prevention, 128; and relative value of freedom, 87, 90; and slavery, 164; and strong paternalism, 96; and weak paternalism, 183
Options: and death, 102; and freedom, 19, 22, 23

Other-regarding conduct, xii, 18, 32–36, 37n; and risk-taking, 91; vices, 202
Other: as alter egos, 43; as completion, 43–44; as inspiration, 42; as instruments, 43; obligations to, 98; as partners, 42–43; necessary for flourishing, 41–45; necessary for survival, 40–41; self as, 39–40

Paine, Thomas, 170
Parental paternalism, 4, 74, 143, 144–56; and compulsory schooling, 150–54; and consent to medical treatment, 154–56; and development of child autarchy, 147–56, 204; and hypothetical rational consent, 65; limits to authority in, 145–47; and punishment, 205; and religion, 213, 214; and subsequent consent, 61
Parfit, Derek, 77n; on Simple and Complex Views of identity, 45–48
Passive paternalism, 14
Paternalism: arguments against, 28–36; justification for, xii, 10–14, 38–78; limits to, 74–77; terminology of, xii–xiii, 3–5. *See also* Character paternalism; Consumer protection; Legal paternalism; Medical paternalism; Parental paternalism; Political paternalism; Religious paternalism
Paternalistic Distance Argument, 28–30, 31, 48, 160, 189; and elderly, 167; and political paternalism, 173; and slavery, 164
Paternalistic Precedent Argument, and seat belt-safety helmet legislation, 84
Patriarchalism, 3, 38
Peden, John, on minimum deposits in sales, 193
Personal integrity, 60, 141; argument from, 67–73; and compulsory savings, 165; and elderly, 169; and health regulations, 110; and medical deception, 128, 134; and seat belt-safety helmet regulations, 90–91, 96; and suicide, 103
Petchesky, Rosalind, on sexual activity among retarded, 135, 137
Physical protection and paternalism. *See* Safety helmet regulations; Seat belt regulations; Suicide
Plamenatz, John, on political paternalism, 171, 175n
Political paternalism, 144, 169–74; in marketplace, 190–91
Polygamy, 159–60
Pornography, censorship of, 211–13
Positive paternalism, 13, 14
Presumptive age of decision, 149
Principles of Political Economy (Mill), 29, 37n

Prior Consent Argument, 56–58, 66, 166; and health regulations, 110–11; and suicide, 103

Privilege Argument, and seat belt-safety helmet legislation, 83–84

Prostitution, 208–10

Protectionist Argument, and compulsory schooling, 150

Public Charge Argument: and elderly, 165; and seat belt-safety helmet legislation, 92–94

Public Disaster Argument, and seat belt-safety helmet legislation, 92, 94–96, 112; and suicide, 98

Public Interests Argument: regulating healthy lifestyles, 111–15; and seat belt-safety helmet legislation, 91–96; and suicide, 97–99

Public Welfare Argument, and health regulations, 112–13

Punishment, paternalistic, 205–13; and homosexuality, 210–11; and pornography censorship, 211–13; and prostitution, 208–10

Purchaser Frailty Argument, and marketplace, 182–84, 193

Pyramid selling, 195, 196

Rationale: for moralism, 15; for paternalism, 10–14, 15, 18, 177–80

Rawls, John, 25; and hypothetical rational consent, 64–66; on others as completion, 43–44; on primary goods, 119

Real Will Argument, 58–59, 63, 78*n*; and suicide, 102, 103

Regan, Donald, 46, 47, 77*n*; on Mill and freedoms, 53–54, 159

Reich, Robert, on consumer protection, 183, 190

Relative Value of Freedom Argument, and seat belt-safety helmet legislation, 86–91, 96

Religious paternalism, 213–17. *See also* Moralism

Rescher, Nicholas, 119

Respect for persons, 25, 28

Restrictions, paternalistic, least preferred, 74–75

Retarded persons, and sterilization, 135–37

Retirement. *See* Compulsory superannuation

Risk, and paternalism, 76, 88, 91

Safety helmet regulations, 57, 104*n*, 107, 109; and Future Selves Argument, 47, 77*n*; paternalistic arguments for, 83–91; public interest arguments for, 91–96

Safety standards regulations, 198; non-paternalistic arguments for, 188–92; paternalistic arguments for, 182–88

Sales practices regulations, 195–97

Sartorius, Rolf, on paternalistic legislation, 49

Savings, compulsory, 164, 165

Schooling. *See* Compulsory schooling; Free schools

Schrag, Francis, 156

Seat belt regulations, 48–49, 57, 75, 104*n*, 107, 109; paternalistic arguments for, 83–91; public interests arguments for, 91–96

Self-determination. *See* Voluntariness

Self-realization, and community, 39–40

Self-regarding conduct, xii, 18, 29, 32–33, 37*n*; in children, 145; and law, 90

Services, regulations on purchase of, 180–92

Sexism, 4, 208, 213

Sexual behavior, and paternalism, 207, 208–11

Sikhs, and safety helmet legislation, 89, 104*n*

Slavery, 53, 171; nonrecognition of contracts for, 157–65

Smoking: and freedom protection, 53, 54; and health regulations, 108, 109, 111, 114

Snake-handling, 217

Soble, Alan, xiii; on competency and paternalism, 8

Social conduct. *See* Other-regarding conduct

Social spin-offs, from paternalism, 77

Social Subversiveness Argument, and suicide, 98–99

Socio-Economic Argument, and compulsory schooling, 150

Socialism, 173, 174

Socrates, 200, 203

Sovereignty, 72

State, ideology of, and compulsory schooling, 151

Sterilization. *See* Involuntary sterilization

Stoics, 203

Strong paternalism, 8, 9, 10, 14, 81; and freedom protection, 53–55; and interconnectedness, 44; and moralism, 16; and personal integrity, 71; and slavery, 158, 164

Subsequent Consent Argument, 61–63, 65

Suicide, 96–104, 174*n*

Suicide intervention: paternalistic arguments for, 99–104; public interest arguments for, 97–99

Survival, others necessary for, 40–41
Szasz, Thomas S., on mental illness, 139–40

Taxation, and health regulations, 108, 114; and marketplace, 190
Ten, C.L.: on moralism and paternalism, 15; on risk, 88, 89; on slavery contracts, 161–63
A Theory of Justice (Rawls), 64
Townsend, Charles, 170
Transcendent collective enterprises, 42
Truth-telling in medicine, 125–30

"Unconscionability" and contractual agreements, 187
Utilitarianism, 48, 49. *See also* Liberalism

Value, freedom as a, 86–87
VanDeVeer, Donald, and prior consent paternalism, 56
Violated Obligations Argument, and suicide, 98
Voluntariness, xii; full, 69–70; threshold of, 9–10. *See also* Choice
Von Humboldt, Baron Wilhelm, 24

Wallace, Mike: on parental and political paternalism, 170, 171
Wants, settled and episodic, 56, 78n
Warren, William, on loan interest, 193, 194
Weak paternalism, 8, 9, 10, 14; and autarchy, 31; and autonomy, 21, 31; and compulsory life-saving treatment, 131–32; and freedom promotion, 52–53; and health regulations, 108–10; justified, 75; and marketplace regulations, 185–88, 193; and medical deception, 129–30; and moralism, 15; and personal integrity, 71; and seat belt-safety helmet legislation, 85–86; and slavery, 158; and suicide intervention, 100–102
Welfare interests, 50, 75, 76; of adults, 156–69; and character, 200–203; of children, 144–56; of groups, 169–74; long-term, 143–75; and medical care, 119
Whose Life Is It Anyway? (Clark), 122, 133
Wikler, Daniel, on health, 113, 114
Will. *See* Real Will Argument
Williams, Bernard, 46
Women: and labor laws, 197, 198; and prostitution, 208
Work week laws, 198